Baudelaire in China

Baudelaire in China

A Study in Literary Reception

Gloria Bien

UNIVERSITY OF DELAWARE PRESS
Newark

Published by University of Delaware Press
Co-published with The Rowman & Littlefield Publishing Group, Inc.
4501 Forbes Boulevard, Suite 200, Lanham, Maryland 20706
www.rowman.com

10 Thornbury Road, Plymouth PL6 7PP, United Kingdom

British Library Cataloguing in Publication Information Available

Library of Congress Cataloging-in-Publication Data
Bien, Gloria.
Baudelaire in China : a study in literary reception / Gloria Bien.
p. cm.
Includes bibliographical references and index.
ISBN 978-1-61149-389-4 (cloth : alk. paper) -- ISBN 978-1-61149-390-0 (electronic)
1. Baudelaire, Charles, 1821-1867--Influence. 2. Baudelaire, Charles, 1821-1867--Appreciation--
China. 3. French literature--19th century--History and criticism. 4. Chinese literature--History and
criticism. 5. Chinese literature--French influences. I. Title.
PQ2191.Z5B44 2013
841'.8
[23]
2012032432

ISBN 978-1-61149-564-5 (pbk : alk. paper)

Printed in the United States of America

Contents

Acknowledgments

This book has been too many years in the making, and owes debts too many to enumerate. I deeply regret not completing it while all my mentors were still alive.

My first debt naturally is to my parents, who brought me to the United States as a child and gave unfailing support to my studies. At the University of California, Berkeley, where I learned close reading of French poetry, Professor Basil Guy introduced me to the field of Sino-French literary relations and continued to support my projects long after I had graduated. I first became acquainted with modern Chinese poetry through K. Y. Hsu's translations while studying Chinese at a summer NDEA program for teachers that he founded at San Francisco State University. Some years later at the University of Washington, as a student of Comparative Literature, I learned to read the poems in Chinese by auditing a course by Ching-hsien Wang; a course on French poetry by Richard Vernier enhanced my enthusiasm for Baudelaire. An NEH Summer Seminar with James J. Y. Liu deepened my knowledge of reader's response theory and helped in my study of Baudelaire and traditional Chinese poetry; another NEH Summer Seminar with Albert Sonnenfeld broadened my acquaintance with European Symbolist poetry. I am especially grateful to the late Professor Liu for inviting me to his home to meet Bian Zhilin, for arranging my visiting scholar status for a year at Stanford University, and for the helpful suggestions he gave to some of my early chapters. A Chinese scholar whom I have yet to meet, Guo Yangsheng, bolstered my interest in Sino-French literary relations by publishing his translations of my journal articles into Chinese. He also sent me books from China that I otherwise would not have known about or been able to obtain. I am also indebted to those who commented on various early drafts and conference presentations, and gave suggestions of poets to read. They include Ching-hsien Wang, Tien-yi Li, Angela Jung Palandri, Freeman G. Henry, Irving Lo, Leo Ou-fan Lee, Julia Lin, and Edward Gunn. Anonymous readers of this and earlier drafts gave invaluable suggestions. Friends, colleagues, and family members gave encouragement and support. Brooke Bascietto at Rowman and Littlefield was unfailingly patient and helpful in preparing the final manuscript. The faults and omissions that remain are of course entirely my own.

For financial support, early research was funded by the Mary Laura Bean AAUW Fellowship. Later research was supported by grants from the Colgate University Humanities Division and the Colgate Research Council. Colgate's support for my efforts to build the Chinese language program over these thirty years also gave me the opportunity to continue my research.

Finally, I dedicate this book to my late husband, Frank W. Jones, who gave unfailing intellectual, emotional, and moral support, and helped with many early translations and drafts until he became too ill to do so. I hope he would have liked the final result.

A NOTE ON ROMANIZATION

The Pinyin romanization system is used throughout the book, with some exceptions. Quoted material and the names of Chinese authors writing in English follow the romanization system of the original, usually Wade-Giles system. For authors who write in both English and Chinese, Pinyin is used for their works in Chinese, and given in parentheses after their original spelling in English. For place names, *Taipei* is used in lieu of the Pinyin *Taibei*.

PERMISSIONS

Chapter 1 is revised from an earlier version, "Baudelaire in China" published in the journal *Comparative Literature Studies* 21, no. 1, used courtesy of the Pennsylvania State University Press.

"Grievance on the Marble Steps" from *The Interlingual Critic : Interpreting Chinese Poetry* , translated by James J. Y. Liu, copyright 1982 by James J. Y. Liu. Used by permission of Indiana University Press.

Excerpt from "Gallery" from *A Splintered Mirror: Chinese Poetry from the Democracy Movement* translated by Donald Finkel. Translation copyright © 1991 by Donald Finkel. Reprinted by permission of North Point Press, a division of Farrar, Straus and Giroux, LLC.

Excerpt from "Insects at the Lamp," from *Pien Chih-lin: A Study in Modern Chinese Poetry* translated by Lloyd Haft. Copyright by Lloyd Haft. Used by courtesy of Lloyd Haft.

Poems from *Twentieth-Century Chinese Poetry* by Kai-yu Hsu, translated by Kai-yu Hsu, translation copyright © 1963 by Kai-yu Hsu. Used by permission of Doubleday, a division of Random House, Inc.

"Vespers" translated by Harry S. Kaplan. Used by courtesy of Harry S. Kaplan.

Excerpt from "Night," from *Statements: The New Chinese Poetry of Duoduo,* translated by Gregory Lee. Used by courtesy of Gregory B. Lee and John Cayley.

Excerpt from "Without title," from *The Poetry of Li Shang-yin: Ninth-Century Baroque Chinese Poet,* translated by James J. Y. Liu, copyright by James J. Y. Liu. Used by permission from the University of Chicago Press.

Excerpt from "Suffering from the Shortness of Days" from *Li Ho* by Kuo-ch'ing Tu. Copyright by G.K. Hall. Used by courtesy of Kuo-ch'ing Tu.

Introduction

Charles Baudelaire (1821–1867) never traveled or lived in China. He was never a Sinophile à la Voltaire; he did not write about China or set his works in a Chinese locale in the manner of Pierre Loti or Paul Claudel; nor did he make quaint references to things Chinese in the manner of his friend Théophile Gautier.[1] Yet of all the French poets, he has been compared most often, by critics both Chinese and Western, with Chinese poets; poets as diverse as Li Bo and Du Fu, Li Ho and Li Shangyin of the Tang dynasty, and Yu Dafu, Li Jinfa, and Dai Wangshu of the twentieth century. Major writers of the twentieth century, including Lu Xun, Xu Zhimo, Bian Zhilin, and He Qifang, all directly responded to his work.

Baudelaire is known primarily by a single volume of verse, *Les Fleurs du mal* [*The Flowers of Evil*], first published in 1857. It was highly praised by some discriminating readers, but did not realize popular success. Six of the poems were condemned by the courts as being harmful to morals; they were omitted from the second edition in 1861, which added a number of poems, and a section "*Tableaux parisiens*." Not until after his death did the work gradually gain in reputation to become a classic.[2] His prose poems were gathered after his death into a volume, *Petits Poèmes en prose*, alternatively entitled *Le Spleen de Paris*, and published by friends in 1869. Baudelaire also published art criticism, essays, and translations that have become increasingly admired. The Pléiade edition of his complete works appeared in 1975–1976.[3]

Baudelaire was the first French poet whose work transcended national boundaries, according to his compatriot Paul Valéry.[4] His work became an important source for Symbolism and Modernism in Western literature. By the 1960s, *Les Fleurs du mal* had become one of the most often edited and translated books in world literature.[5] New editions and translations have continued to appear into the present century. In 2004 a website solely dedicated to his poetry was launched. In 2008 another website was launched for videos inspired by his work. He has become an icon of popular culture.[6] The English title "Flowers of Evil" has been applied to everything from drugs to leukemia cells under an electronic microscope;[7] "the downtown Baudelaire" was named a "timeless New York species" in 2009.[8] In 1980 Mo Yu declared Baudelaire to be the French poet best received in China;[9] that claim still holds true today.[10]

The current study began with one of literary influence before moving on to broader considerations. The influence study seemed relatively

1

straightforward: find evidence that the later poet had read the earlier poet, and look for common elements in their works. This allowed for the pleasures of close reading and interpretation of the poems themselves. Further, in the case of modern Chinese poetry, many poets happily pointed out Baudelaire's influence on their own work. Hunting out evidences of such influence afforded joyous hours of literary detective work. Often the evidence would yield up instances of misreading. Such "gotcha!" moments of discovery were soon complicated by Harold Bloom's theory of deliberate misreading, resulting from the "anxiety of influence."[11] And then there were the numerous instances of Chinese critics finding in the works of their contemporaries influence from Baudelaire that would not yield to positive evidence. Yet echoes of Baudelaire must have sounded during the critics' act of reading. Inevitably, the influence study evolved into a study of literary reception.

To explore the reception of Baudelaire in China, the theoretical and methodological framework that has proven most useful is Hans Robert Jauss's "Aesthetic of Reception" (*Rezeptionsaesthetik*). Jauss points out that a reader receives a new work of literature not as an empty receptacle, but as a "consciousness" informed by previous experiences and milieux both of reading and of life; those previous experiences and milieux form a "horizon of expectations." The receiving "consciousness" "recognizes" a "tensional relationship between the text and the present," in an understanding and interpretation that are "not merely a reproductive but a productive attitude as well." Moreover, since the newly received work then becomes part of the horizon of expectations, that horizon is constantly changing. Jauss demonstrates how this works with the specific example of Baudelaire's "Spleen II" in successive readings. In the first reading, moving through the poem phrase by phrase and line by line from beginning to end, he is neither a "super-reader" nor a "naïve reader," but one with "the educational horizon of our contemporary present." In a second reading he proceeds "retrospectively" to reexamine the poem as a whole. He then examines previous interpretations of the poem from its original appearance through to his own time, both within the changing historical horizons of the previous readings and the resulting changes in his own horizons. Finally he places his own aesthetic experience of the poem into the changing horizons.[12] The notion of "horizons" with its inclusion of historical as well as aesthetic experience creates a space for examining the reception of literary works from different cultures.

In the context of Chinese poetry, James J. Y. Liu proposes a "tetradic circle" where (1) the world affects (2) the artist, who responds to it, and creates (3) a work of art with an "imaginary world," which in turn affects (4) the reader.[13] The reader (4) in the process of reading the work (3) "comes into contact with the artist's mind (2) and recaptures the latter's interaction with the world (1)." Thus the four points form a circle where the relationships go in both directions. Taking as point of departure

Wolfgang Iser's theory of reading, Liu stresses that the experience of reading is not "a passive experience of receiving a message or being affected by the work, but an active experience of re-creation." In this process, the reader does not "come to the work with a blank mind, but with all his previous experiences of the world and of art." Like Jauss, Liu emphasizes that the reader's own mind is not a static whole, unchanging entity: after experiencing the work of art, "his interaction with the world will be modified." Liu's description of "worlds" experienced and created by author and reader comes close to Jauss's "horizon of expectation."

For both Jauss and Liu, not all readings of a poem are equally valid. Jauss warns against the "the theory of the 'plural text' with its notion of 'intertextuality' as a limitless and arbitrary production of possibilities of meaning and of no less arbitrary interpretations."[14] Liu puts it in more concrete terms: a reader's act of re-creating the poem should not result in "as many 'poems' as there are readings." Liu's quest for "a common core among all the readings" leads him to state that instead of asking what a poem means, the reader should first ask "What does the author mean by this poem?" Evading the ontological problem, Liu then suggest that the reader ask "What would I mean by this poem if I were writing it?" Liu's comments are directed at translators, whom he divides into two types: the poet-translator and the critic-translator. The poet-translator's "primary aim is to write a good poem . . . based on his understanding or misunderstanding of a Chinese poem, however he might have arrived at this." Castigating such a translator as "a poet manqué whose native Muse is temporarily or permanently absent," Liu clearly prefers the critic-translator, whose "aim is to show what the original poem is like, as part of his interpretation."[15] Both types can be found among Baudelaire's Chinese translators, who include scholars, critics, and poets, many of whom wrote both poetry and criticism.

While Jauss's theory provides a broad framework and focuses on aesthetic appreciation, and Liu's theory is useful in analyzing how some Chinese readers might have read and interpreted Baudelaire, neither theory engages the question of why the Chinese chose Baudelaire from the vast number of "Western" poets available. Here, Henri Peyre offers a persuasive approach. In his "Baudelaire and English Poets," Peyre observes that the "predilection of English-speaking readers for Baudelaire is to a large extent made easier, more sensually and imaginatively felt, thanks to affinities between his work and that of earlier poets in English."[16] In other words, the English-speaking readers could recognize something from previous experience, something from their "horizon of expectations," to help create that productive tension between the text and the present.

Was there something in the Chinese readers' horizon of expectations that made them more receptive to Baudelaire? Were there affinities between Baudelaire's work and that of earlier poets in Chinese? The comparisons of Baudelaire with Tang dynasty poets that both Western and Chinese critics have made would suggest as much. The poems are separated not only by time and distance, but by language and vastly different cultures. Yet from the short, concentrated lyric poems with multiple possibilities for meaning, readers have found specific lines, images, or attitudes that seem to echo each other and suggest affinities in the poetic worlds. These comparisons are explored in chapter 1. Of course affinities are not limited to particular responses to specific poems, but can encompass the entire range of instinct, emotion, thought, and experience. Baudelaire knew this. That is why he addressed his poems to *"Hypocrite lecteur, mon semblable, mon frère."* [17]

The constant change in horizons of expectation for literary reception involves not only reading, but external milieu, or "world." When Baudelaire's work was first published in France, the Chinese horizon seemed to be dominated by political events. French troops were deployed in China for the Anglo-French Expedition (1856–1860), also known as the Second Opium War, which resulted in another of a long series of defeats for the tottering Qing Dynasty. Chinese scholars, asking why the West was so strong while China was so weak, hoped to keep "Chinese learning for the fundamentals," while adopting Western science and technology purely for utilitarian purposes. They had little time or inclination for reading French poetry.

When the last imperial dynasty collapsed by 1911, with it collapsed the sociopolitical order as well as the cultural-moral order. [18] Rather than sink into despair, many Chinese saw a chance for renewal, and began a race toward modernity that included avidly studying models from the West. Political demonstrations on May 4, 1919 gave name to the May Fourth Movement to reform and renew Chinese culture; a "literary revolution" stood at its center. Not only were literary expectations changing, but the very language used for literature went through a fundamental change. Western models of literature were as passionately seized as political and economic models. A brief introduction to these changing horizons is offered in chapter 2.

In the movement to introduce Western writings into China, translation played a major role. Although translations from English far outnumbered those from other languages, as Wolfgang Bauer has shown, in the case of belles-lettres, translations from Russian and French represented the larger proportion. [19] And as Jerome Chen has pointed out, "French education and culture had been admired by the Chinese since the 1840s. As time went on, her art, literature, and philosophy were to win great esteem among Chinese scholars." [20] The length and continuity of the French literary tradition as compared with that of the English were particularly admired. (Thus the early thirteenth-century work *Aucassin et Nicolette* appeared in Chinese in the 1920s alongside works from nineteenth-century fiction, of which Dumas's *La Dame aux camélias* was particularly popular). As may be expected due to its relative difficulty, translation from poetry developed more slowly and sporadically.

Translations into Chinese from Baudelaire's poetry began appearing as early as 1922. The early choices of poems for translation are interesting in reflecting the comparisons introduced in chapter 1. Translations from Baudelaire made by major poets, including Xu Zhimo, Bian Zhilin, and Dai Wangshu, appeared in successive decades. Study of these translations is particularly rewarding in revealing both the poets' modes of reading and their experiments with form in developing a new Chinese poetry. At the same time, although "Classical Chinese" had been pronounced "dead" in 1917, the leading philologist Wang Li published Classical Chinese versions of *Les Fleurs du mal* in 1940, and again as recently as 1980. New translations into modern Chinese continue to appear in the present century. The choices of poems for translation, as well as the forms the translations took, are the subject of chapter 3.

Like translation, critical analysis is an important part of the cross-cultural reception of any literary work. Studying the critical reception of Baudelaire in China is both challenging and rewarding because the responses to his life and work cover an exceptionally wide range. Students, scholars, critics, and poets variously depicted Baudelaire as an odd eccentric and a romantic lover, a deplorable decadent and a laboring hero, a revolutionary and an escapist, a demonic genius and a saint; they describe his poetry as difficult and obscure, nihilistic and depressing, shocking and unimaginative, musical and inspired, transcendent and inspiring. Most of the published articles place Baudelaire in the context of a general "Western" literature that included English, French, and occasionally Spanish or Russian literature. Only a few, such as Tian Han, Liang Zongdai, and Hu Pinqing, put his work in the context of Chinese tradition. These various critical responses are examined in chapter 4.

Chinese critics who compared Baudelaire's work with that of their contemporaries soon found "The Chinese Baudelaire" in Yu Dafu and "The Baudelaire of the Orient" in Li Jinfa. Some based their comparisons more on Baudelaire's reputation than on their own readings of his work. Others drew parallels between poems, lines, and fragments, and readily presented them in terms of "influence." Although the word "influence" often implies imitation and derivative work in place of "pure inspiration" and originality, in general Chinese critics use it in a broader, more fluid sense, and Chinese poets accept it without "anxiety."[21]

In the aesthetics of reception and influence, according to Hans Robert Jauss, "a literary event can continue to have an effect . . . if there are readers who again appropriate the past work or authors who want to imitate, outdo, or refute it."[22] Here, Baudelaire's work as a "literary event" gains an effect in an entirely new literary field.[23] The Chinese authors "who want to imitate, outdo, or refute" it are the subject of part II in the present study.

The chapters in part II treat the writers individually in loose groupings according to their relation to Baudelaire. While many of the poets formed societies, coteries, or associations whose members have reminisced about discussions of Baudelaire, it would be going too far to say that the French poet singly played a major role in their programs, however short-lived. Many of the comparisons that Chinese critics have made are based on as little as a single poem. But Lu Xun, known as the "Father of Modern Chinese Literature," and Xu Zhimo, often considered the greatest poet of the May Fourth period, each responded directly to Baudelaire. The Chinese "Decadents" Yu Dafu and Yu Gengyu were compared with Baudelaire by critics, while Shao Xunmei made deliberate references to the French poet's work. The "Chinese Symbolists" were and are most often compared with Baudelaire, alluded to him in their writings, and appropriated his work along with other French sources for their poetry. Wang Duqing, Mu Mutian, and Feng Naichao evoked his work in their discussion of poetics; Li Jinfa translated from *Les Fleurs du mal* and named Baudelaire as his master. Liang Zongdai and two lesser-known poets, Qin Zihao and Xu Yunuo, are loosely associated with the Symbolists through their poetry. "Modernists" are represented by the major poets Dai Wangshu and Bian Zhilin, who were often identified as Symbolists in their earlier work, and He Qifang, who bade farewell to Baudelaire in a poem. Less known, Cao Baohua wrote a few lines that are reminiscent of Baudelaire, and Chen Jingrong makes a direct reference to Baudelaire, whose poems she translated. A final chapter is devoted to three major poets. Wen Yiduo, a leading member of the Crescent Moon Society along with Xu Zhimo and later Bian Zhilin, studied in America, and made no published references to the French poet. Ai Qing, like Li Jinfa, studied art in France, but unlike Li, was not drawn to Baudelaire. Yet poems by both Wen Yiduo and Ai Qing have led Chinese readers to draw parallels to Baudelaire. A final example, the contemporary poet Duoduo, overtly claims Baudelaire as his inspiration, and offers rich material for comparison. Some of what emerges in these comparisons are the attitudes toward tradition and authority, the search for new poetic forms, the tension between "pure poetry" and nation-building, and most prominently, the prestige that Western poetry, in particular that of Baudelaire, enjoyed in the Chinese literary scene.

Baudelaire's reception in England, Spain, Mexico, Japan, Russia, and Germany has been the subject of previous books and articles.[24] His reception in China mainly has been studied in the context of Chinese Symbolist poetry.[25] The present study examines that reception, but finds that just as Baudelaire's work goes beyond those elements identified with European Symbolism, so his reception in China goes beyond what has been identified with Chinese Symbolism. The subject is necessarily complex, not only because of differences in language and literary history, but because of differences in religious, philosophical, and cultural traditions as well as economic, social, and political conditions. When modern Chinese writers rebelled against tradition, their rebellion was not aimed at Judeo-Christian traditions. What was traditional in Baudelaire, including his practice of the alexandrine, the sonnet, and the prose poem, was for the Chinese new and foreign. What was new with Baudelaire was embraced by some, and deplored by others. These and other broad questions form the background for this study, which mainly focuses on particular authors and particular works.

NOTES

1. On Voltaire, see Basil Guy, *The French Image of China Before and After Voltaire* (Geneva: Droz, 1963), and Arnold Rowbotham, "Voltaire, Sinophile," *PMLA* 47 (Dec. 1932): 1050–65. On Pierre Loti and Théophile Gautier, see William L. Schwartz, *The Imaginative Interpretation of the Far East in Modern French Literature 1800–1925* (Paris: Honoré Champion, 1977), 17–46. On Paul Claudel, see Gilbert Gadoffre, *Claudel et l'univers chinois, Cahiers Paul Claudel*, 8 (Paris: Gallimard, 1968), and Schwartz, 136–43.

2. Walter Benjamin, "On Some Motifs in Baudelaire," in *Illuminations*, trans. Harry Zohn (New York: Schocken Books, 1968), 156.

3. Charles Pierre Baudelaire, *Oeuvres complètes*, ed. Claude Pichois (Paris: Gallimard, 1975–1976). Hereafter abbr. *OC*.

4. Paul Valéry, "*Situation de Baudelaire,*" *Variété II* (Paris: Gallimard, 1930), 144–45.

5. Wallace Fowlie, ed. and trans., *Flowers of Evil and Other Works* (1963; New York: Dover, 1992), 11: "Today *Les Fleurs du Mal* is one of the most frequently edited books in world literature (the claim is made that it is the most often edited book after the Bible). It is undoubtedly the book translated into the largest number of languages during the past fifty years."
A quick glance at WorldCat in 2006 shows translations into Czech, Danish, Dutch, English (England, USA, Australia), German, Hebrew, Hungarian, Italian, Japanese, Korean, Polish, Portuguese, Romanian, Russian, Serbian, Slovak, Spanish (Spain, Mexico), Swedish, Turkish, Ukrainian, Yiddish, and Chinese in several versions.

6. See http://fleursdumal.org, launched February 2004. For references in rock music, see "Trivia" in http://en.wikipedia.org/wiki/Baudelaire (accessed 6 July 2006). For YouTube videos, see http://ckuik.com/Charles_Baudelaire (accessed 12 June 2010).

7. *Newsweek* (19 November 1979): 151

8. Alan Feuer and Allen Salkin, "Terrible End for an Enfant Terrible," *New York Times* (26 July 2009): Metro section, 1.

9. Mo Yu 莫渝, "*Qiuge yu yixiang ren*" 秋歌與異鄉人 ["Chant d'automne et l'étranger"], *Yushi wenyi* 幼詩文藝 315 (March 1980): 140.

10. Guo Shaohua 郭紹華, "Bodelai'er zai Zhongguo" 波德萊爾在中國 (Master's thesis, Beijing Shifan Daxue Yanjiusheng Yuan, 2003), presents a large number of sources to support this claim.

11. Harold Bloom, *The Anxiety of Influence: A Theory of Poetry* (New York: Oxford University Press, 1973).

12. Hans Robert Jauss, *Toward an Aesthetic of Reception*, trans. Timothy Bahti (Minneapolis: University of Minnesota Press, 1982), 22–28, 31; and "The Poetic Text within the Change of Horizons of Reading: The Example of Baudelaire's 'Spleen II,'" 139–85.

13. James J. Y. Liu, *The Interlingual Critic: Interpreting Chinese Poetry* (Bloomington: Indiana University Press, 1982), 1–2, 12, 37. My understanding of Liu's theory is influenced by participation in his NEH Summer Seminar on this subject in 1980.

14. Jauss, 147.

15. Liu, *Interlingual*, 37.

16. Henri Peyre, "Baudelaire and English Poets," in *Du Romantisme au Surnaturalisme: Hommage à Claude Pichois*, ed. James S. Patty et al. (Neuchatel: La Baconniere, 1985), 186.

17. *OC*, 6. For *"mon semblable, mon frère,"* Richard Howard, *Les Fleurs du mal* (Boston: D. R. Godine, 1982), 6, uses "my alias,—my twin!" James McGowan, *66 Translations from Charles Baudelaire's Les Fleurs du mal* (Peoria, IL: Spoon River Poetry Press, 1985), 5, offers "my image, my twin!"

18. See Lin Yü-sheng, *The Crisis of Chinese Consciousness* (Madison: University of Wisconsin Press, 1979), 20.

19. Wolfgang Bauer, *Western Literature and Translation Work in Communist China* (Frankfurt/Main: A. Metzner Verlag, 1964), 3.

20. Jerome Chen, *China and the West: Society and Culture 1815–1937* (Bloomington: Indiana University Press, 1979), 84.

21. Stephen Owen, "The Anxiety of Global Influence: What Is World Poetry?" *New Republic* (19 Nov. 1990): 28–32, points out complexities of this question as it relates to contemporary Chinese poetry.

22. Jauss, 22.

23. Michel Hockx, ed., *The Literary Field of Twentieth-Century China* (Honolulu: University of Hawaii Press, 1999), 19. Having adopted the definition of "literary field" from Pierre Bourdieu's theory that focuses on modes of production and capital, authority and power, Hockx sees it as complementary to the study of authors and texts, and concedes that many scholars would consider it to be the "context" of literature. "Field" is used in the latter sense here.

24. See Gladys Rosaleen Turquet-Milnes, *The Influence of Baudelaire in France and England* (New York: E.P. Dutton, 1913); William F. Aggeler, *Baudelaire Judged by Spanish Critics 1857–1957* (Athens: University of Georgia Press, 1971); Hans George Ruprecht, "Aspects du Baudelairisme méxicain," *Comparative Literature Studies* 11, no. 2 (June 1974): 99–122; Sekigawa Sakio, *Bodereru, Bocho, Sakutaro no shiho heiretsu* (Tokyo: Showa Shuppan, 1982); Adrian Wanner, *Baudelaire in Russia* (Gainesville: University Press of Florida, 1996); Thomas Keck, *Der deutsche "Baudelaire:" Studien zur ubersetzerischen Reception der Fleurs du mal*; (Heidelberg: Winter, 1991) 2 vols.; Irène Kuhn and Claude Pichois, *Baudelaire et l'Allemagne, L'Allemagne et Baudelaire* (Paris: Honoré Champion Éditeur, 2004).

25. These include Michelle Loi, *Poètes chinois d'écoles françaises* (Paris: Maisonneuve, 1980); Harry Kaplan, "The Symbolist Movement in Modern Chinese Poetry," PhD diss. (Harvard University, 1983); Sun Yushi 孫玉石, *Zhongguo chuqi xiangzhengpai shige yanjiu* 中國初期象徵派詩歌研究 [*Study of Early Period Chinese Symbolist Poetry*], (Beijing: Beijing daxue chubanshe, 1983) (hereafter, *Chuqi*); and *Xiangzhengpai shi xuan* 象徵派詩選 [*Selected Symbolist Poems*] (Beijing: Renmin wenxue chubanshe, 1986) (hereafter, *Shixuan*); Jin Siyan 金絲燕, *Wenxue jieshou yu wenhua guolü: Zhongguo dui Faguo xiangzheng zhuyi shige de jieshou* 文學接受與文化過濾—中國對法國象徵主義詩歌的接受 [*literary Reception and Cultural Filters: Chinese Reception of French Symbolist Poetry*] (Beijing: Zhongguo Renmin daxue chubanshe, 1994) (hereafter *Wenxue jieshou*); Jin Siyan, *La métamorphose des images poétiques 1915–1932: Des symbolists français aux symbolists chinois [Metamorphosis of Poetic Images 1915–1932: From French Symbolists to Chinese Symbolists]* (Dortmund: Projekt Verlag, 1997) (hereafter, *Métamorphose*). Zhang Daming 張大明, *Zhongguo xiangzheng zhuyi bainian shi* 中國象徵主義百年史 (Kaifeng: Henan Daxue chubanshe, 2007) is encyclopedic in its coverage but too recent to be used in most of this study.

Part I

The Critical Reception

This study begins with an examination of the horizons of expectations for Baudelaire's reception in China. It seeks to discover whether references to China in Baudelaire's work played a role. It then examines the comparisons that critics have made between Baudelaire and traditional Chinese poetry to look for those points of affinity that may have prepared the horizon for his later reception. A second chapter describes both literary and extra-literary aspects of that horizon by giving a brief sketch of the "literary revolution" and the social and political changes that dominated China in the twentieth and into the twenty-first century.

Baudelaire's literary reception through Chinese translations and critical studies form the subject of the next two chapters. Although the translations are often embedded in critical studies or are accompanied by critical introductions so that the separation is artificial, the questions involved are so varied and complex that such separation was necessary to achieve clarity. The translations are presented in a roughly chronological framework, with exceptions due not only to political factors, but to the continued endurance of Classical Chinese. The fourth chapter begins with the critical studies that included Baudelaire as part of the general introduction of Western writers and movements into China. It then examines the biographical essays and their fascination with Baudelaire's life, loves, and death. Essays on his work associated sex, alcohol, drugs, and death with Decadence. The moral disapproval of Decadence expressed by many critics was countered by others who found redemption for Baudelaire through his finding "beauty in ugliness" and creating lasting works of art. While many critics associated Baudelaire with Symbolism and Modernism as European movements, a few brought him into the Chinese context through comparative criticism.

ONE

Baudelaire and Traditional Chinese Poetry

What drew Chinese readers to Baudelaire's work? Was there something familiar in the work that awakened answering echoes in their "horizon of expectations"? Were there "affinities between his work and that of earlier poets" in Chinese? Did Baudelaire write about China, or did he evoke that country in his poetry?

In Baudelaire's France, although the vogue of China had fallen from the heights reached in the eighteenth century, a more serious approach to Chinese studies had taken its place; there were Chinese scholars residing in Paris, and a chair for Chinese studies had been established in the Collège de France in 1814.[1] There were opportunities everywhere for contact with things Chinese, and Baudelaire is known to have kept some knickknacks of either Chinese or Japanese origin in his domicile. He alludes to Chinese art objects in an article on the 1855 Paris World's Fair.[2] He frequented Théophile Gautier's home, and could not have failed to know of Gautier's interest in China, although it is open to conjecture whether or not he met Ding Dunling, the sonorously named Chinese literatus who was tutor to the Gautier daughters and who collaborated with Judith on her translations of Chinese poetry for Le Livre de jade.[3] Although Baudelaire's own interest in China was limited—he mentions that country only twice in Les Fleurs du mal, and only twice more in the Petits Poèmes en prose—there is evidence he read at least one book on China. The prose poem "L'Horloge" ["The Clock"] begins: "The Chinese tell time by looking at the eyes of a cat," and continues with the following story:

> One day a missionary, wandering in the environs of Nanking, noticed that he had forgotten his watch, and asked a small boy what time it

11

was. The child of the Celestial Empire hesitated: after a moment he
replied, "I shall tell you." Almost immediately afterwards he returned,
holding in his arms a very fat cat, and, to use a colloquial expression,
gazing into the whites of its eyes, he affirmed without hesitation: "It is
not quite noon." Which was true.[4]

As has been pointed out by Gustave von Roosbroeck, Baudelaire did not
invent this missionary. The anecdote is found in the work of the well-
known missionary and explorer Father Evariste Régis Huc (1813–1860),
entitled *L'Empire chinois* [*The Chinese Empire*], published in 1854, three
years before the publication of Baudelaire's poem.[5] Many Chinese will
object that they do not in fact tell time by looking at a cat's eyes, yet this
very practice is described in a poem by the twentieth-century poet Bian
Zhilin, himself also from the Nanking (Nanjing) area.[6] Significantly,
Baudelaire does not use the account simply for its anecdotal or exotic
value; in his poem, it is absorbed to form part of the opposition between
time and eternity.

The second prose poem in which China is named is "*L'Invitation au
voyage*" ["Invitation to the Voyage"], which evokes a land where "everything is beautiful, rich, quiet, genuine, where order holds up the mirror to
luxury, happiness is wed to silence, and even cooking is poetic."[7] But
Baudelaire is well aware that this is a mythic Orient; the country he
names is an ideal one; this land of Cockaigne is an "Occidental Orient,"
the "China of Europe." This prose poem invites comparison with its forerunner by the same title in *Les Fleurs du mal* with its famous refrain

> *Là, tout n'est qu'ordre et beauté,*
> *Luxe, calme et volupté.*

[There, all is but order and beauty, / Luxury, calm, and sensual pleas-
ure].[8]

Hung Cheng-fu, in his 1934 thesis studying Chinese influence on French
literature 1815–1930, points to the refrain as "suggesting more intensely
the landscapes of China than the most precise lines of Gautier.[9] Baudelaire's interest, however, is not in China, mythic or otherwise; both the
verse and prose poems are essentially founded upon a correspondence
between the woman loved, who is simultaneously his chosen sister, and
the landscape described; and in the case of the verse poem, commentators
agree that the country evoked is not China, but Holland, "Oriental"
through its trade with the East Indies.[10] In fact, Baudelaire had no more
direct knowledge of Holland than of China.

When Baudelaire names China in *Les Fleurs du mal*, each time it is to
represent supreme distance. In "*Moesta et errabunda*" ["Sad and Wandering"], he evokes a faraway paradise, "innocent yet full of furtive pleasures," and asks whether it is more distant than India or China. In "*Le
Voyage*," the poet looks back to a time when a voyage to China would

have been new and exciting, but in this final poem of the entire collection, he suggests that only by going beyond death will one find something truly new.

China remains for Baudelaire the distant, the unknown, and the finite as opposed to the infinite. Yet there is something in his poetry that invites comparison with that of the Chinese. One such comparison was made by his older contemporary and friend, Théophile Gautier, to whom he had dedicated *Les Fleurs du mal*.

Gautier, in his biography of Baudelaire, cites the prose poem "*Les Bienfaits de la lune*" ["The Moon's Benefits"], and comments:

> We know of no other analogy to this perfect piece than in the poetry of Li Taï-pé, so well translated by Judith Walter, in which the empress of China draws, among the rays, on the stairway of jade made brilliant by the moon, the folds of her white satin robe. A *lunatique* only is able to understand the moon and her mysterious charm. [11]

Judith Walter, so fondly evoked, is the name Gautier's daughter used in the first edition of her *Livre de jade*. Li Taï-pé is the courtesy name of Li Bo (李白 also read Li Bai, also spelled Li Po, 701–762). The English translator of Gautier's biography has left *lunatique* in the original French, in which language "*la lune*" has kept its close association with the word "lunacy" lost by the English "moon," and this association is essential to the comparison. The poem in question is Li Bo's "*Yujieyuan*" 玉階怨 ["Jade Staircase Grievance"]:

玉階生白露 / 夜久侵羅襪 / 卻下水晶簾 / 玲瓏望秋月

Judith Gautier's version reads:

L'Escalier de jade

L'Escalier de jade est tout scintillant de rosée.
Lentement, par cette longue nuit, la souveraine le remonte; laissant la gaze de ses bas et la traîne du vêtement royal, se mouiller, aux gouttes brillantes.
Sur le seuil du pavillon, éblouie, elle s'arrête, puis baisse le store de cristal, qui tombe, comme une cascade, sous laquelle on voit le soleil.
Et, tandis que s'apaise le clair cliquetis, triste et longuement rêveuse, elle regarde, à travers les perles, briller la lune d'automne. [12]

A poetic English version of Gautier's version has been made by E. Powys Mathers, [13] but as it adds another layer of interpretation, I have rendered the French poem into English more literally:

The jade staircase is sparkling with dew.
Slowly, in the long night, the queen ascends it, letting the gauze of her stockings and the train of her royal garments be dampened with brilliant drops.
On the threshold of the pavilion, dazzled, she stops, then lowers the crystal blinds, which fall, like a cascade, beneath which one sees the sun.

And, while the clear tinkling dies away, sad and as if in a long dream,
she gazes, through the pearls, at the shining autumn moon.

In James J. Y. Liu's closely literal translation from the Chinese, Li Bo's
poem reads:

> On marble steps white dew grows.
> Deep in the night, it soaks silk stockings.
> Yet she lowers the crystal curtain—
> Glittering—to gaze at the autumn moon. [14]

Judith Gautier has added a few images, invented a dramatic situation,
identified the dramatis personae, and here, clothed her properly. (Her
father then goes on to specify even the material of the garments—white
satin). William Hung labeled her efforts "pseudo-translations," and
found many to "represent only the creative imagination of a talented
French lady at twenty-two." [15] Baudelaire's prose poem resembles Gautier's version in that it is dramatic, but it is the moon, personified, who
comes down her staircase of stars, through the window, to bewitch a
sleeping girl, to whom she says:

> You will love what I love, and what loves me: the water, clouds, si-
> lence, and night; the immense green sea, the formless and multiform
> water, wherever you will not be, the lover that you will not know,
> monstrous flowers, perfumes that bring on delirium, cats that swoon
> on pianos and moan like women with their hoarse and sweet voices! [16]

The association of images, whether or not they go back to some kind of
occult symbolism (as has been suggested by René Rousseau), [17] has a
compelling force whose parallels to the Chinese poem become, paradoxically, far clearer upon comparison with the Chinese original. In both
poems, the moon is associated with woman and with water. In the Chinese poem, even the crystal might be associated with moon and water,
since, according to Edward Shafer, both moon and crystal are "*shuijing*"
水晶, or "germ of water." [18] (Shafer's work has led one reviewer to note
that the men of Tang were really lunatics in the modern sense). [19] This
interpretation of "crystal" supports Professor Liu's view that "*linglong*"
玲瓏 (Gautier's "*clair cliquetis*" [clear tinkling]) in the last line goes beyond its onomatopoeic and etymological meaning to refer to the moon's
effect on the crystal curtain. For François Cheng, "*linglong*" describes the
moon, and the face of the woman gazing at the moon. [20] Thus both poems
are pervaded by the moon, and although in this post-Etiemble era of
comparative literature one need not be a lunatic to go from here to specu-
late on various theories of universal correspondences, [21] one might wonder what happy intuition led Théophile Gautier to compare the two
poems. The more so since in the traditional interpretations of the Chinese
poem, these correspondences would not have been at all evident. In
translations by Bynner, Giles, Pound, and others, the subject of the poem

is limited to the woman, perhaps a discarded palace favorite, who waits, not because she is moonstruck, but because she still hopes for her lord's visit. Pound adds, "The poem is especially prized because she utters no direct reproach."[22] The original poem comes far closer to Verlaine's ideal: "Pas la couleur, rien que la nuance" [No color; nothing but nuance].[23]

Gautier's comparison is taken up by Hung Cheng-fu in his study of Chinese influence in French literature. Hung then suggests another affinity between Baudelaire and Li Bo. Quoting the first few sentences of "*Enivrez-vous*" ["Get Drunk"],—"Il faut être toujours ivre. Tout est là. C'est l'unique question" [One must always be drunk. It's all there. It's the only question], Hung asks, "Could it not have been written by Li Tai-pe whom we call the immortal who loves to drink?"[24] The Chinese "immortal" might have sympathized even with Baudelaire's reason for wishing to remain drunk—that it is the only possible escape from the terrible burden of time—but one wonders what Li Bo would have thought of the French poet's statement that it does not matter whether one is drunk on wine, poetry, or virtue. Hung's suggestion of an unconscious influence from *Le Livre de jade* is the less convincing since Baudelaire's poem first appeared in February 1864, when Judith Gautier had only begun to learn Chinese, and *Le Livre de jade* was not published until 1867.[25]

Wine and the moon occupy a far larger place in Li Bo's poetry than in Baudelaire's and support the legend of his death, that he drowned while reaching into the river to embrace the moon. As a romantic Taoist poet of free and spontaneous inspiration, he contrasts sharply with his contemporary and friend, Du Fu (杜甫 712–770), the classic Confucian poet who sought technical perfection and social involvement. Yet Du Fu, too, has been compared with Baudelaire.

Robert Payne, in his anthology *The White Pony*, first published in 1947, writes:

> If one could compare Tu Fu (Du Fu) with anyone—though he is incomparable—it would be with Baudelaire, for his strange suggestive images derived from poverty and spiritual exhaustion. He has Baudelaire's power of evoking the real terrors, the long nights, the cruelties, the starvations, the miseries of the common people; and there are lines of Baudelaire that read like translations of Tu Fu:

> *Et les vagues terreurs de ces affreuses nuits*
> *Qui compriment le coeur comme un papier qu'on froisse . . .*

> *Mon coeur est un palais flétri par la cohue . . .*

> *Ainsi dans la forêt où mon esprit s'exile,*
> *Un vieux souvenir sonne à plein souffle du cor . . .*[26]

Payne continues:

> Like Baudelaire, he was untamable and spoke of himself as:

The seagull who plays on the white waves,
And flies to heaven superb and tameless . . .

And like Baudelaire, too, he was possessed of an extraordinary tenderness and sensitivity, especially toward suffering, while at the same
time and almost in the same breath he could evoke a sense of majesty
and dignity and regal splendor.[27]

Payne's purpose is to introduce Du Fu to an English-speaking public, and
comparisons with familiar poets often form an effective bridge. Although
one might question his fanciful attribution of lines from Baudelaire to Du
Fu, and although it is not clear what he means by "untamable," the other
two points on which the comparisons are made are persuasive; that is,
images that recall poverty and spiritual exhaustion, and tenderness and
sensitivity, especially toward suffering.

Julia Lin, in her *Modern Chinese Poetry: An Introduction*, quotes Payne's
statement, but raises some objections, pointing out:

In spite of their striking resemblances, there is a fundamental difference between these two geniuses. Tu Fu's sensitivity to "suffering, terror, and death" stems from an intense moral conviction. A Confucian
humanist, he accepted life's suffering with typical Confucian stoicism.
He did not regard society as hostile, nor did he consider himself an
exile as most of the French Symbolists did. Baudelaire, on the other
hand, rebelled against accepted standards. His poetry is a revolt
against tradition, an escape as well as a "sacred ritual," a kind of religion to which he dedicated his life and service.[28]

Though Lin attributes the last remark to Symons's *The Symbolist Movement*, there seems to be in her objections confusion among the poet, poetry, and poetics. Certainly, Baudelaire rebelled against the society of his
time, with its positivism, its belief in science and progress, and its com-
mercialism, but he was not a misanthrope; this rejection only intensified
his sensitivity toward, and sympathy for, "suffering, terror, and death."
This was expressed in such poems as *"Les Petites Vieilles"* ["The Little Old
Women"] in *Les Fleurs du mal*, where Baudelaire shows at least as close an
identification with the "terrors, the long nights and the miseries of the
common people" as does Du Fu in his famous "Stone Moat Village" (also
known as "The Recruiting Officer" or "The Recruiting Officer at Shih
Hao" and available in many anthologies);[29] in the prose poem *"Le Vieux
Saltimbanque"* ["The Old Circus Performer"] or *"Les Veuves"* ["Widows"],
this identification is made even more closely. But then the usefulness of
such a comparison is limited; Hugo, Bo Juyi (白居易 772–846, also read
Bai Juyi) and others in either tradition have demonstrated the same sympathy. Even the view that Baudelaire's poetry is a revolt against tradition
is only partly true. Like Du Fu, Baudelaire was familiar with his tradition,
and used it in his poetry. As Martin Turnell has pointed out, "he stands at
once for tradition and experiment, for discipline and revolt. His versifica-

tion and syntax are in the main traditional. They provide a discipline, but they are at the same time the vehicle of a new vision."[30]

That "new vision" originates in a simultaneous attraction toward good and evil, and a search for an absolute that at the same time he does not believe exists. This ambivalence accounts for the greatest differences between Du Fu and Baudelaire's poetic worlds, in the Liuvian sense of the term. Kenneth Rexroth takes up the same comparisons in his *Classics Revisited*, declaring that Du Fu "shares with Baudelaire and Sappho, his only competitors in the West, an exceptionally exacerbated sensibility, acute past belief," but that

> Tu Fu's faults are microscopic in comparison with the blemishes that cover Baudelaire like blankets. Behind Baudelaire's carapace is a sensibility always struggling for transcendence. In Tu Fu the vision of spiritual reality is immanent and suffuses every item presented to the senses. Behind the conventions, behind the faults which made him human and kin to all of us, are a wisdom and humaneness as profound as Homer's... For Tu Fu the realm of being and value is not bifurcated. The Good, the True, and the Beautiful are not an Absolute.[31]

Rexroth credits the Chinese with a "sense of unbreakable wholeness: the quality is the quantity; the value is the fact. The metaphor, the symbols are not conclusions drawn from images; they are the images themselves in concrete relationship." For Rexroth, it is this immediacy of utterance that has made Chinese poetry in translation so popular with modern Western poets.[32]

It should surprise no one that comparisons based on generalizations should point out differences as well as similarities between two poets. After all, Du Fu himself has also been compared with a large number of other Western poets, including Virgil, Horace, Ovid, Shakespeare, Milton, Burns, Wordsworth, Béranger, and Hugo.[33] And Li Bo has been read as "a combination of François Villon, Omar Khayyam, and Heine."[34]

The Tang dynasty poet with whom Baudelaire has been compared most frequently is Li Ho (Li He 李賀 790–816). While Li Bo and Du Fu stood at the pinnacle in the Golden Age of Chinese poetry, Li Ho lived during the decline and decadence of the dynasty. Thwarted from government office by a minor bureaucratic regulation, he lived—in the words of a modern critic who compares him with Keats—a life of poverty, illness, and frustration.[35] His death at twenty-six was caused by tuberculosis according to some, by sexual overindulgence according to others.[36] While Li Bo and Du Fu are regarded as China's greatest poets, Li Ho remained relatively unknown and unappreciated after the ninth century. As Zhou Chengzhen pointed out in 1971, the Chinese poet had received more notice from Western scholars than from his compatriots.[37] This fact alone makes him particularly interesting for comparative literature.

In his introduction to translations from Li Ho, A. C. Graham warns:

Li Ho reminds many readers of Baudelaire. The affinity is not altogether an illusion, but in one respect it can mislead. When we read that Li
Ho was called a *kueits'ai (guicai)*, a ghostly or demonic genius, and
notice his apparently familiar constellation of pessimism, voluptuousness, aestheticism, and an imagination haunted by dark forces, it is
tempting to read him as a nineteenth-century Satanist. But the Western
sense of evil of course assumes a Christian background, and the *kuei* of
Li Ho's poems are generally not devils but ghosts, sad rather than
malevolent beings. Nor are there any overtones of flesh and the devil in
Li Ho's sensuality, which may be disreputable for a strict Confucian,
but hardly sinful. His pessimism also has none of the ambivalence
which one expects in a Western artist obsessed by original sin, who is
at least half on the side of the destructive element because he finds it at
the bottom of his own heart.[38]

While it is true that these differences of philosophical and religious back-
grounds are too often ignored, there is also the temptation here to retort,
"Neither should one simply read Baudelaire as a nineteenth-century Satanist!"

J. D. Frodsham, for one, does not. In the introduction to his translations of Li Ho's complete poems, Frodsham quotes Baudelaire's lines *"Là,
tout n'est qu'ordre et beauté, Luxe, calme, et volupté"* to describe Li Ho's
concept of Heaven as "a place of exquisite beauty where immortals
dwelt," and that "recurs constantly in Li Ho's poems;" it even forms part
of a story about his deathbed, where he saw a man in purple, driving a
red dragon, who told him "life up in Heaven is delightful; there is no
hardship there."[39] Such voluptuousness, while "disreputable for a strict
Confucian," would presumably not be out of place in a Buddho-Taoist
Heaven. Frodsham goes on to state:

Ho's feeling for religion, whether for Zen or for Shamanism, his sense
of the ultimate identity . . . of the world-of-birth-and-death . . . and
Nirvana, is central not peripheral to his poetic art. He wrote verse
ultimately not for aesthetic pleasure but to express . . . the state of
intuitive awareness of inner truth. It is perhaps this which makes the
perceptive Western reader want to link him with that great occult tradition which includes Baudelaire and Blake, Rimbaud and Yeats.[40]

In the end, Frodsham brings his comparisons back to Keats, "in his sensuality and the despairing intensity with which he strives to hold the passing moment eternally in his art, like a frozen flame," and to Beddoes, in
his being "half in love at times with easeful death."[41]

Bringing the subject back to the poems themselves, Qian Zhongshu, to
whom Frodsham refers for the Beddoes comparison, points out a preference for hard, material images shared by Li Ho and Baudelaire.[42] Qian
alludes to J. M. Murry's *Countries of the Mind*, which offers a small collection of examples, including:

> *Je savourais dans mon tableau*
> *L'enivrante monotonie*
> *Du métal, du marbre et de l'eau.*

[I savored in my picture / The intoxicating monotony / Of metal, marble, and water.]

"Even at the outset only one-third of his universe—the water—has any chance of moving," observes Murry, for whom "his stately pleasure house needs the movement of water to make the contrast of his motionless marble more intense and oppressive," but "at the cost of an artistic blemish," Baudelaire "indulges his obsession," and "(literally) petrifies even that third:"

> *Et des cataractes pesantes*
> *Comme des rideaux de cristal*
> *Se suspendaient obéissantes*
> *A des murailles de métal.*

[And cataracts heavy / as crystal curtains / were hanging obedient / to metal walls].

Here again is the association of water with crystal! Murry explains: "Baudelaire makes solid everything he can. His very ideal of beauty is an absolute immobility; Beauty itself declares:

> *Je hais le mouvement qui déplace les lignes*
> *Et jamais je ne pleure et jamais je ne ris.*

[I hate movement which displaces lines / and never do I cry, and never do I laugh.]

This is the ideal of beauty shared by the Parnassians, and Murry gives a number of other examples from Baudelaire.[43] Qian Zhongshu offers numerous examples from Li Ho's poems, where the word "congeal" (*ning* 凝),which acts to solidify images, frequently occurs. Examples particularly reminiscent of Baudelaire include "shan pu wu sheng yu hong han" 山瀑無聲玉虹寒 [Cascades hang noiseless in the mountains, rainbows of jade][44] which, describing the frozen north, evokes the lines from "*Rêve parisien*" ["Parisian Dream"] quoted above, and "hei yun ya cheng cheng yu cui" 黑雲壓城城欲摧 [Black clouds press on the city wall, the wall about to be crushed], which recalls Baudelaire's "*Quand le ciel bas et lourd pèse comme un couvercle*" [When the low heavy sky weighs like a lid] from "*Spleen IV*."[45] Qian points out that this preference for *le bloc résistant* is also shared by Gautier, Hebbel, and Poe, thus making no claim that this aspect of Li Ho's poetry is particularly "Baudelairian."

In his study on Li Ho, Tu Kuo-ch'ing draws parallels between images and themes in Li Ho and Baudelaire.[46] He supports Qian's remarks on the *bloc resistant*, and adds Li Ho's use of synaesthetic images, as in "The flute sounds blowing sun color" or "Cold redness weeping dew; the color of delicate sobbing." These images occur in poems on the passage of time, toward which Tu finds Li Ho's stance to be "hostile, even defiant." For example, in the poem "The Sun Rising," Tu notes that "the poet faults the sun for not only melting rocks but for consuming men, who are not insensible. Time is no longer an impassive flow, but the active tool of the sun." In another poem, "Suffering from the Shortness of Days," Li Ho sees "the moon's cold and the sun's heat come to burn human lifetimes," and "rages against the legendary dragons that draw the chariot of the sun, the vehicle of on-rushing time." Tu translates Li Ho's lines:

> I will cut off the dragon's feet, chew the dragon's flesh,
> So that they can't turn back in the morning or lie down at night;
> Left to themselves the old won't die; the young won't cry[47]

and remarks: "Li Ho's hostility to time calls to mind the nineteenth-century French Symbolist poet Charles Baudelaire's lines:

> —O douleur! ô douleur! Le Temps mange la vie,
> Et l'obscur Ennemi qui nous ronge le coeur
> Du sang que nous perdons croît et se fortifie!" [48]

[Ah woe! ah woe! Time eats our lives, / and the obscure Enemy who gnaws our hearts / Grows and strengthens himself on the blood we lose!]

It might be pointed out that while there is hostility to time in these lines from "L'Ennemi" ["The Enemy"] where time devours human lives, Baudelaire does not hurl defiance at the leech-like enemy, swelling on our blood, and douleur is closer to "pain and sorrow" than to "rage," so that here, in a reversal of stereotypes, the Westerner is more passive than the Oriental.

Professor Tu quotes from a similar poem by Baudelaire in his explication of a poem entitled "Exhortation No. 5," which "depicts the sterile eremitic life of a disenchanted poet living alone at the foot of a wild mountain." In the autumn moonlight, "Chilled and dreary, the gardenia seeds fall, / A mountain rift weeps clear trickles." The season, the sound of seeds dropping from the gardenia, and the weeping of the water remind him of Baudelaire's lines from "Chant d'automne" ["Autumn Song"]:

> Il me semble, bercé par ce choc monotone,
> Qu'on cloue en grande hâte un cercueil quelque part.
> Pour qui? [49]

[It seems to me, lulled by this monotonous thud, / That somewhere a coffin is being nailed in a hurry / For whom?]

More than a season or theme, it was sound—suggesting but not naming either the clepsydra or the pendulum clock—which evoked the echo of one poet in the poem of another, so far removed in time and space.

In a sense, Professor Tu, who has published several volumes of his own poetry in Chinese, forms a bridge himself between the two poets. Besides his book on Li Ho, he has translated all of *Les Fleurs du mal* into Chinese.[50]

The comparison between Li Ho and Baudelaire is pursued at length by Frances A. LaFleur in her 1993 Princeton dissertation, "The Evolution of a Symbolist Aesthetic in Classical Chinese Verse: The Role of Li Ho Compared with That of Charles Baudelaire in Nineteenth-Century French Poetry." Finding that both poets led "short, illness plagued, and frustrated lives" in "sumptuous, circumscribed, and artificial" environments where they could feel that "Nature was no longer the most important shaper of landscape or of lives," she posits that both "turned defensively toward personal preoccupations" in their poetry, and expressed "rebellion against a complacent world around them" through "the macabre, the fantastic, and the grotesque," and "coped" with the "randomness" and "artificiality" of city life by adopting the "literary strategy" of "the constituitive symbol." LaFleur defines "the constituitive symbol" as the "catalytic and unifying agent around which other images and verbal patterns could arrange themselves, thereby imposing order on what might otherwise appear to be wholly unfocused or disparate elements," and as serving "intrinsic laws of poetry which operate independent of time, space, or culture." Her comparisons of specific poems are too intricate to summarize with justice here, but her suggestion that we can see Li Ho as a ninth-century "modern" in a "purely conceptual and normative" sense has interesting implications for the twentieth-century poets who turned to Baudelaire in their search for modernity.[51]

In addition to Baudelaire, Li Ho has also been compared systematically with Keats[52] and Georg Trakl.[53] He has been seen as an "unintended precursor" of "many Western literary 'isms,'" including Surrealism, Aestheticism, and Symbolism.[54]

Li Shangyin (李商隱 813–858) also lived in the Late-Tang dynasty, barely a generation later than Li Ho. There is no blood relation among Li Bo, Li Ho, and Li Shangyin, whose surname is one of the commonest in China. The last-named is the subject of a study subtitled "Ninth-Century Baroque Chinese Poet" by James J. Y. Liu. In his final chapter, "Li Shangyin and the Modern Western Reader," Professor Liu suggests that

> the worlds explored in some of his poems, with their languorous beauties, exotic perfumes, strange drugs, embroideries and precious stones, music and dance, are reminiscent of Baudelaire[55]

While it is difficult to select examples because Li Shangyin's poetry is so full of allusions, a few lines may suffice to illustrate Liu's point. The following lines are from an eight-line poem without title (*wuti* 無題):

> The east wind soughs and sighs as a fine drizzle falls;
> Beyond the lotus pond there is the noise of a light thunder.

The golden toad bites the lock through which the burnt incense enters;
The jade tiger pulls the silk rope while turning above the well. [56]

The specific images, lotuses, jade, silk, a golden toad which is a censer, evoke a Chinese world, but the atmosphere of the poem recalls Baudelaire's "*Harmonie du soir*" ["Evening Harmony"]:

> *Voici venir les temps où vibrant sur sa tige*
> *Chaque fleur s'évapore ainsi qu'un encensoir;*
> *Les sons et les parfums tournent dans l'air du soir;*
> *Valse mélancolique et langoureux vertige !* [57]

[Here the time has come when trembling on its stalk / Each flower fumes like a censer; / Sounds and scents circle in the evening air; / Melancholy waltz and languorous giddiness!]

Although the Chinese poem, allegorically interpreted by Professor Liu, seems to be one about thwarted passion while Baudelaire's is one of nostalgia for past time and past love, and although the identification of the natural with the artificial is presented differently, if we take these lines on a literal level, they express a similar mood of sensuous melancholy.

In another of Li Shangyin's untitled poems, the lines "The candle's light half encircles the golden kingfishers / The musk perfume subtly permeates the embroidered lotus flowers" [58] describe an interior scene, and again call to mind Baudelaire's praise of artifice as well as his attention to perfume.

While a similar atmosphere can be found in many poems from later generations, especially in the *ci* (詞) genre, Li Shangyin's poetry comes closer than the *ci* to Baudelaire's by virtue of its density of expression and complexity of feeling. In summarizing Li Shangyin's appeal to the modern Western reader, Liu also points to his "sophisticated attitude toward life and his no less sophisticated manner of expression," his "commitment to life" (as opposed to Buddho-Taoist detachment), his "ability to probe into experiences and see them in a dramatic or ironic light," and his "explorations of the mysterious and the fantastic." [59] The combination of commitment and irony would certainly invite more comparisons with modern poets were Li Shangyin's language not so difficult to read and nearly impossible to translate.

In these four comparisons we have seen facets of the Baudelaire of the *Petits Poèmes en prose* in Li Bo, of the *Tableaux parisiens* in Du Fu, of "*Spleen et Idéal*" in Li Ho, and in a general aesthetic with Li Shangyin. They show how the Chinese readers' "horizons of expectation" prepared them to receive poetry from the supreme opposite side of the world. They show points of affinity which would be as important as the Chinese poets' self-professed iconoclasm in the 1920s and 1930s, when in looking to Europe for models for their "new literature," they would give Baudelaire a prominent place in the translations and critical essays that appeared in numerous journals, and many modern Chinese poets variously labeled Decadents (*tuifeipai* 頹廢派), Symbolists (*xiangzhengpai* 象徵派) and Modernists (*xiandaipai* 現代派) would look upon the French poet as their forebear.

NOTES

1. Paul Demiéville, "Aperçu historique des études sinologiques en France," Extr. *Acta Asiatica*, 11 (Tokyo: Toho Gakkai, 1966): 76.

2. Claude Pichois, "Baudelaire et l'épouse chinoise," *Mélanges de littérature en homage à Albert Kies*, ed. Claudine Gothot-Merscht and Claude Pichois (Bruxelles: Publications des Facultés universitaires Saint-Louis, 1985), 87–89. Pichois also traces an allusion to a "Chinese wife" in Baudelaire's correspondence from 1863 that suggests his acquaintance with translations from Tang poetry by d'Hervey-Saint-Denys.

3. Schwartz, *The Imaginative Interpretation*, 36. Judith Gautier, *Le Livre de jade* (Paris: Plon, 1933), 93–94, includes a poem by Ding, spelled Tin Tun-Ling and accompanied by the characters 丁墩齡 in childish handwriting—probably Judith's. Some of the other calligraphy in the volume is quite accomplished.

4. Arthur Symons, trans., *Baudelaire: Prose and Poetry* (New York: Albert and Charles Boni, 1926), 25.

5. Gustave L. van Roosbroeck, "The Source of Baudelaire's Prose-poem 'L'Horloge,'" *The Romanic Review*, 20, no. 4 (Oct.–Dec. 1929): 357.

6. Bian's poem appears in English in Harold Acton and Ch'en Shih-hsiang, *Modern Chinese Poetry* (London: Duckworth, 1936), 119.

7. Symons, trans. *Baudelaire*, 27.

8. *OC*, 53. For rhymed translations, see McGowan, 61, and Richard Wilbur, in *Charles Baudelaire: The Flowers of Evil*, ed. Marthiel and Jackson Mathews (Norfolk, CT: New Directions, 1955), 67–69.

9. Hung Cheng-fu, *Un Siècle d'influence chinoise sur la littérature française 1815–1930* [*A Century of Chinese Influence upon French Literature 1815–1930*], Thèse pour le doctorat d'université, Université de Paris (Paris: Domat-Montchrétien, 1934), 114.

10. *OC*, 929.

11. Théophile Gautier, *Charles Baudelaire* (1868, Paris: L'Aventurine, 2001), 92; *Charles Baudelaire: His Life*, trans. Guy Thorne (New York: Brentano's, 1915), 90.

12. Gautier, *Le Livre de jade*, 107–8.

13. In Joseph Lewis French, ed., *Lotus and Chrysanthemum: An Anthology of Chinese and Japanese Poetry* (New York: Horace Liveright, 1928), 24.

14. James J. Y. Liu, *Interlingual Critic*, 36. Liu translates the title "Grievance on the Marble Steps." For more literal French translations, see Robert Ruhlmann, trans. "Complainte des degrés de jade," in *Anthologie de la poésie chinoise classique*, ed. Paul Demiéville (Paris: Gallimard, 1962), 238, and François Cheng, *L'Ecriture poétique chinoise* (Paris: Editions du Seuil, 1977), 98.

15. William Hung, *Notes for Tu Fu: China's Greatest Poet* (Cambridge, MA: Harvard University Press, 1952), 10.

16. *OC*, 341. All translations are my own unless otherwise noted.

17. René Rousseau, "Baudelaire adorateur de la lune," *Synthèses*, 19, no. 217–18 (June–July 1964): 281–94, and no. 219 (Aug. 1964): 87–98.

18. Edward Schafer, *Pacing the Void: T'ang Approaches to the Stars* (Berkeley: University of California Press, 1977), 174.

19. John Major, in the *Harvard Journal of Asiatic Studies*, 40, no. 1 (June 1980): 280.

20. Cheng, *L'Ecriture*, 98–99.

21. See especially René Etiemble, "Le Sonnet des Voyelles," *Revue de littérature comparée*, 19 (1939), 239.

22. Witter Bynner and Kiang Kang-hu, *The Jade Mountain* (New York: Knopf, 1929, repr. Garden City, NY: Anchor Books, 1964, Random House Vintage Books, 1972), 54; Herbert A. Giles, *Gems of Chinese Literature* (1884, New York, Paragon Books Reprint, 1965), 333; Ezra Pound, *Cathay* (London: Elkin Mathews, 1915), 13.

23. Paul Verlaine, *Oeuvres poétiques complètes*, ed. Y.-G. le Dantec (Paris: Gallimard, 1948), 207.

24. Hung Cheng-fu, *Un Siècle*, 114.

25. *OC*, 1341; Schwartz, *The Imaginative Interpretation*, 46–48.

26. The lines are from three poems in *Les Fleurs du mal*, "Réversibilité," *OC* 44, "Causerie," *OC* 56, and "Le Cygne," *OC* 85.

27. Robert Payne, *The White Pony: An Anthology of Chinese Poetry from the Earliest Times to the Present Day* (New York: The John Day Company, 1947), 225.

28. Julia Lin, *Modern Chinese Poetry: An Introduction* (Seattle: University of Washington Press, 1972), 156.

29. For translations, see Payne, *White Pony,* 197–98; Cyril Birch, ed., *Anthology of Chinese Literature* (New York: Grove Press, 1965), 1:239–40; Liu Wu-chi and Irving Lo, eds., *Sunflower Splendor: Three Thousand Years of Chinese Poetry* (Bloomington: Indiana University Press, 1975), 131; and in French, François Cheng, *L'Ecriture*, 226–27.

30. Martin Turnell, *Baudelaire: A Study of his Poetry* (Norfolk, CT: New Directions, 1954), 32.

31. Kenneth Rexroth, *Classics Revisited* (Chicago: Quadrangle Books, 1968), 129.

32. Ibid., 130.

33. William Hung, *Tu Fu: China's Greatest Poet* (Cambridge, MA: Harvard University Press, 1952), 1.

34. John Albert Macy, *The Story of the World's Literature* (New York: Boni and Liveright, 1925), 26

35. David Ying Chen, "Li Ho and Keats: Poverty, Illness, Frustration and a Poetic Career," *Tsing Hua Journal of Chinese Studies*, n.s. 5, no. 1 (1965): 67–84.

36. J. D. Frodsham, in *The Poems of Li Ho (791–817)* (Oxford: Clarendon Press, 1970), xxvii, asserts that "pulmonary tuberculosis notoriously exacerbates sexuality," thus linking the two possible causes of Li Ho's death. Tu Kuo-ch'ing, however, consulted a medical doctor to refute this in *Li Ho (790–816)* (Boston: Twayne, 1979), 136–37.

37. Zhou Chengzhen 周誠真, "Zixu"自序["Preface"], *Li He Lun* 李賀論: *Lee Ho Reevaluated* (Hong Kong: Wenyishuwu 文藝書屋, 1971), 1.

38. A. C. Graham, trans., *Poems of the Late T'ang* (London: Penguin, 1965), 91–92.

39. Frodsham, *The Poems of Li Ho*, xli.

40. Ibid., lxiii.

41. Ibid., lxiv.

42. Qian Zhongshu 錢鍾書, *Tan yilu* 談藝錄 (Hong Kong: Longmen, 1965, repr. of Shanghai: Kaiming, 1935), 57. Also in: *Zhongguo shi yu Zhongguo hua* 中國詩與中國畫 (Hong Kong: Longmen, 1969), 8.

43. J. M. Murry, *Countries of the Mind* (London: W. Collins Sons, 1922), 161–62. The lines quoted are from "Rêve parisien" ["Parisian Dream"] and "La Beauté" ["Beauty"]

44. Graham, trans., *Poems of the Late T'ang*, 98.

45. *OC*, 74.

46. Tu, *Li Ho* , 109.

47. Tu, *Li Ho*, 44.

48. *OC*, 16

49. *OC*, 119.

50. Tu Kuo-ch'ing (Du Guoqing) 杜國清, ed. and trans., *E zhi hua* 惡之華 [*Flowers of Evil*] (Taipei: Chunwenxue, 1977).

51. Frances A. LaFleur, "The Evolution of a Symbolist Aesthetic in Classical Chinese Verse: The Role of Li Ho Compared with That of Charles Baudelaire in Nineteenth-Century French Poetry," PhD diss. (Princeton University, 1993), 206, 328–29.

52. David Ying Chen, "Li Ho and Keats," 1; Naotaro Kudo, *The Life and Thoughts of Li Ho Part II* (Tokyo: Waseda University Press, 1972), 159–205.

53. Pauline Yu, "The Poetics of Discontinuity: East-West Correspondences in Lyric Poetry," *PMLA* 94, no. 2 (Mar. 1979): 261–74.

54. Tu, *Li Ho*, 131.

55. James J. Y. Liu, *The Poetry of Li Shang-yin: Ninth-Century Baroque Chinese Poet* (Chicago: University of Chicago Press, 1969), 251.

56. Liu, *Li Shangyin*, 64.

57. *OC*, 47.

58. Liu, *Li Shangyin*, 62

59. Ibid., 251.

TWO

Horizons of Reception

> If Baudelaire is one of our favorite poets . . . then we are likely to encounter Chinese poetry with tempered admiration. On the other hand, if we are attracted by the classical qualities of definiteness, harmony, and restraint, we are apt to value it more highly. . . .
>
> . . . [Chinese] poets express neither the sense of sin nor the sense of the infinite; neither the romantic revolt against society nor a romantic exultation in the terrors of nature; and they are ignorant, besides, of that search for the *new* which is the underlying motive of so great a part of poetry; I mean the desperate descent which Baudelaire describes: "Au fond de l'Inconnu pour trouver du *nouveau*." [1]

This view of Chinese poetry appears in Malcolm Cowley's review of a volume of Tang Dynasty poetry published in 1927. In attributing his remarks to Chinese poetry as a whole, Cowley had ignored the Chinese poets who were his contemporaries. The search for the *new* was precisely what engaged Chinese poets most passionately in the 1920s. The "classical qualities of definiteness, harmony, and restraint" were precisely what many rejected in their assertion of modernity. As they sought to plumb the depths of the unknown, they simultaneously reached across the oceans to find new experiences. In this sense, contact between Chinese poets and Baudelaire lies not only in the meeting of East and West, but in the meeting of Classic and modern.

The confrontation of classic and modern was crystallized a decade earlier by Hu Shi (胡適 1891–1962) in his "Modest Proposal for the Reform of Literature." Declaring the literary language (*wenyan* 文言) "the dead words of 3,000 years ago," Hu Shi likened it to Latin, and called for using plain speech (*baihua* 白話) to create a "Chinese Renaissance." In a practical sense, *wenyan*, often known as "Classical Chinese," had already lost its position as the avenue to wealth, status, and power in 1905 when the imperial examination system had been abolished. Succinct, suggestive, elegant, and representing a long, proud tradition, it required many years of concentrated study to learn, leaving little time for foreign languages, mathematics, science, and other modern subjects. By 1920 *baihua* had replaced *wenyan* in the elementary schools; soon the younger generation lacked the training to read the defense for *wenyan*, as they pronounced and hastened its demise.[2] Even though poems in "Classical Chinese" continue to be read and memorized and even newly composed to the present day, *baihua* moved into the mainstream in every sphere, including poetry.

Flexibility and acceptance of change in *baihua* made it easier to use in translation, and translations in turn fed the development of new conventions in the spoken language. Neologisms proliferated both from transliteration and from translation; words were "borrowed back" from Japanese, resulting in a growing number of disyllabic and multisyllabic words. Western languages also influenced Chinese grammar and usage.[3] Whereas in literary Chinese, one word might function as noun in one context and as verb in another; words in *baihua* now became more fixed in their grammatical categories. In prose, the growing use of relative clauses (which many still consider "non-Chinese") made sentences longer and longer. Punctuation, unknown in literary Chinese, was adopted to clarify the long sentences.

The changes in language brought about new possibilities in prosody. The increase in disyllabic words, which carried stressed and unstressed syllables in normal speech, led to experiments with rhyme and meter that resembled English prosody.[4] Syllabic stress is not a prosodic element of French verse, and paradoxically, Verlaine's "revolution" in French verse, promoting the use of *l'impair* (an odd number of syllables in the poetic line instead of the traditional eight, ten, and twelve), actually brought French poetry closer to the traditional *shi* 詩 line of five and seven syllables. But the new longer line in Chinese poetry did put it closer to the French verse, and was identified for a time with Chinese "Symbolist" poetry. Experiments with form were a central concern of the new poetry. Hu Shi provided the first model in 1921 with a slim volume in free verse, appropriately entitled *Experiments*.[5] In choosing free verse, Hu was trying to come as close as possible to everyday spoken language, in a style described as *wo shou xie wo kou* 我手寫我口 [my hand writes my mouth].[6] Other poets pursued metrical regularity, known as "formalist verse." Since each character represents a single syllable, each syllable occupies one space. Traditionally poetry was printed in running text. When printed line by line following Western typographical convention, lines with equal numbers of syllables in poems of equal numbered lines made a strong visual impact of rectangular regularity. They earned the nickname *doufugan shi* 豆腐干詩 [dried bean curd poetry] or *fangkuai doufu shi* 方塊豆腐詩 [squares of bean curd poetry]. Translations from *Les Fleurs du mal* often fell into this pattern. However, Baudelaire's influence was cited far more frequently in the development of the prose poem form, and poems with widely varying line length became identified with Chinese Symbolist poetry.

The change in forms was of course accompanied by a change in content, much of it appearing somewhat "Westernized." The theme of romantic love provides the most striking example. Western readers of Chinese poetry—Arthur Waley, Malcolm Cowley, and Soulié de Morant, for example—have remarked on the absence of romantic love in traditional poetry.[7] While more recent Chinese critics have argued that such work as Li Shangyin's "Untitled" (無題) poems were indeed love poems, the poetic expression is veiled and indirect. Passionate and daring love poems did exist, but with rare exceptions, they did not represent the mainstream of respectable and serious literature.[8] Nor could the large body of erotic literature have inspired such lines as these written by the well-known poet Wen Yiduo (聞一多 1899–1946):

> O, my soul's soul!
> My life's life!
> . . .
> Let me be drowned in the deep blue of your eyes.
> Let me be burnt in the furnace of your heart.[9]

The self-abasement, the exaltation of the woman, and the spiritualization of love reflect a chivalric tradition not shared by the Chinese. Blue eyes in China generally suggest those blinded by cataracts; yet Hsu's translation of *"yanjingde wangbo"* 眼睛底汪波 [eyes' watery waves] as "the deep blue of your eyes" seems particularly apt, not because "cataracts" in English refers both to the eye disease and the waterfall, but because the exaggeration and verve on the subject of love in the poem already seem so foreign. But is Wen's poem "derivative?" In Chinese society there were growing possibilities for free choice in marriage, changing the meaning of love and courtship. Experience was no longer limited to frustrated, spousal, or illicit love. New forms and expressions had to be developed for new experiences and feelings. Although some modern Chinese poets did resort to wholesale borrowing from and imitation of Western literature, for the best of them, Western literature provided only one source of inspiration. In order to express a new reality, they could not ignore Western influence as an integral part of that reality. With broad social change, a shift in sensibility was inevitable.

Critics of modern Chinese poetry have tended to compare it with "Western" poetry as opposed to "traditional" Chinese poetry. Many have pointed out the vast generalization that the word "Western" represents. Yet equal emphasis needs to be given to the tremendous diversity and development encompassed in the Chinese tradition. The influx of Buddhism, frequently cited as the only foreign influence comparable in scope to the "impact" of the West, brought about changes in literature that have long since been accepted as part of the tradition. Perhaps a broader view of what is "Chinese" would also temper indictments of modern Chinese poetry as "derivative" and "immature."[10]

The 1920s and early 1930s were an exciting time for the development of Chinese literature. Writers formed schools, societies, or coteries.[11] Three major groups were particularly involved in Baudelaire's reception.

The Association for Literary Studies (*wenxue yanjiu hui* 文學研究會) formed in 1920 advocated "Art for Life's Sake" and realism in literature. Their main organ was the *Xiaoshuo yuebao* 小說月報 [*Fiction Monthly*], which they changed from a "butterfly fiction" magazine to include works in all genres, though they gave it the subtitle *Short Story Monthly*. In its pages appeared the first translations of Baudelaire into Chinese. A thick supplement was entirely devoted to French literature in 1922. The Association promoted the idea of evolution in literature, taking as natural progress the development from Classicism to Romanticism to Realism and Naturalism to Symbolism, leading to Modern and Futurist literature. Their publishing program designed to reflect this development remained unrealized, but they published over seventy books, including several collections of new poetry, and a literary history that integrated the Chinese tradition into world literature. Zhou Zuoren (周作人 1885–1967), one of the founders, introduced Baudelaire's prose poems, and was among the first practitioners of the form in Chinese. Zhou played a major role in publishing poetry by Li Jinfa (李金髮 1900–1976), and in identifying him as a Symbolist.

A rival group established in 1921 by a group of Chinese students in Japan upheld the idea of "Art for Art's Sake." Claiming that the Association for Literary Studies had "monopolized" Chinese literature, they advocated Romanticism in opposition to the Realism supported by the Association. Naming themselves the Creation Society (*Chuangzao she* 創造社), they successively launched in 1922 and 1923 the *Creation Quarterly* (*Chuangzao jikan* 創造季刊); *Creation Monthly* (*Chuangzao yuekan* 創造月刊); *Creation Weekly* (*Chuangzao zhoubao* 創造週報), each short-lived; and *Creation Daily* (*Chuangzao ri* 創造日), which lasted for one hundred days.[12] As Bonnie McDougall has pointed out:

> The Literary Association and the Creation Society have been regarded as polarizing the literary world into sober, studious and socially-conscious realistic writers and extravagant, inspirational, and individualistic romantic writers, and there is no doubt that the latter did see themselves as rebelling against an aesthetically dull literary scene. But from the point of view of their enthusiastic interest in Western literature and literary theory, they did have much in common. . . . In their eagerness to discover the literary riches of the West, members of both groups frequently encroached on each other's reading.[13]

Their reading in "the literary riches of the West" of course included Baudelaire. Although the Society was founded in Japan, Cheng Ch'ing-mao has shown that its members evinced little interest in contemporary Japanese literature.[14] Among the founders, Tian Han (田漢 1898–1968) wrote on Baudelaire, and Yu Dafu (郁達夫 1896–1945) was called "China's Baudelaire" for reasons that will be analyzed later. Feng Naichao (馮乃超 1901–1983), Mu Mutian (穆木天 1900–1971), and Wang Duqing (王獨清 1898–1940) carried out discussions in the *Creation Monthly* that would include Baudelaire.

A third literary group, the Crescent Moon Society (*Xinyue she* 新月社 [New Moon Society]) started as a gathering of friends in Shanghai in 1923. They had no slogan and no program, and only began to publish their own journal, *Crescent Monthly* (*Xinyue yuebao* 新月月刊), in 1928. Xu Zhimo (徐志摩 1897–1931), Wen Yiduo(闻一多 1899–1946), and later Bian Zhilin (卞之琳 1910–2000) served as chief editors. All three had studied in America or England. *Crescent Monthly* quickly became the leading journal in introducing Western literature and new Chinese poetry. Wen Yiduo was also known for his research on Chinese language, prosody, and poetic theory. In advocating strict rules and forms, he brought modern Chinese poetry to its second stage of development; many of the Crescentists, under his influence, came to be identified with formalist poetry. Xu Zhimo and Bian Zhilin wrote on Baudelaire and translated his works, while their fellow Crescentist, Shao Xunmei (邵洵美 1906–1968), who had also studied at Cambridge, named his poetry collection *The Flowerlike Evil* (*Hua yibande zui'e* 花一般的罪惡) after *Les Fleurs du mal*.

Other literary societies formed in the 1920s include the "Threads of Talk" (*Yu si* 語絲), founded by Zhou Zuoren, also a founder of the Association for Literary Research in 1924, and the "Unnamed Society" (*Weiming she* 未名社), founded in 1925 by his brother Zhou Shuren (周樹人 1881–1936), better known as Lu Xun 魯迅. While in Japan, the brothers had translated works of Western literature, but the volume had not sold well.[15] Lu Xun, generally regarded as China's greatest modern writer, is best known for socially conscious fiction and essays. His one volume of prose poems, *Wild Grass* (*Yecao* 野草) has been compared by many readers with Baudelaire.

One important literary development in the 1920s, the appearance of "Symbolist" poetry, overlapped the literary groups. While most of the "pioneers" of the new poetry wrote free verse and belonged to the Association for Literary Studies, and while the "formalists" pursued metric regularity, the "Symbolists" were identified with irregular lines. The first "Symbolist" collection was so called by Zhou Zuoren, a member of the Association for Literary Studies and the "Threads of Talk." Entitled *Light Rain* (*Weiyu* 微雨), it was sent from France by Li Jinfa to Zhou Zuoren, who saw to its publication in 1925. Three members of the Creation Society, Feng Naichao, Mu Mutian, and Wang Duqing, were also known as

"Symbolists" for their poetry appearing between 1926 and 1928. They had met as students in Japan; Wang Duqing also studied for some time in France. This group expressed interest in Baudelaire, but drew their inspiration from the later French Symbolist poets such as Verlaine, Laforgue, and Valéry.

Meanwhile, a series of political crises continued. The death in 1925 of Sun Yatsen, the "Father of the Republic" who had tried to unify the country, left China divided among warlords. In the same year, the shooting of a Chinese trade union organizer by a Japanese overseer under British command led to a number of strikes, demonstrations, and boycott of British goods, known as the "May Thirtieth Movement." The incident raised the political consciousness of many writers, notably the members of the Creation Society. Sun's Nationalist Party (*Guomindang* 國民黨) joined with the Chinese Communist Party (*Gongchandang* 共產黨) in a "United Front" to unify the country against the warlords. But in 1927 the Nationalists turned on Communists, executing many leaders and gunning down protestors. In the terror that followed and lasted nearly a year, by one account, tens of thousands of people were killed.[16] Chinese writers became increasingly disillusioned with the government and its practice of severe censorship; by 1929 it had disbanded the Creation Society, which had become increasingly engaged in leftist politics.[17]

In the next decades, the literary scene could not escape politics and war. The 1930s became dominated by the League of Leftwing Writers (*Zuoyi lianmeng* 左翼聯盟), established in 1928, with the slogan "All art is propaganda." In calling for a socially conscious literature, and a literature for the masses, the leading Marxist critic Qu Qiubai (瞿秋白 1899–1935) even attacked the use of *baihua*; asserting (justifiably) that it had become so Europeanized in vocabulary and syntax that it no longer reflected the everyday speech of ordinary people, he called for developing *putonghua* 普通話 [ordinary speech], and returning to the native oral traditions. In 1931, five leftist writers, including Hu Yepin (胡也頻 1903–1931), a minor Symbolist poet, were captured and executed without public trial; in 1935 Qu Qiubai was executed. In this atmosphere of censorship and oppression, the leftists soon gained the moral high ground. Thus while their actual contribution to poetry was negligible, the leftists played an important role in changing the environment for the reception of poetry. At the same time, poets like Wen Yiduo, unable to resolve the conflict of artistic values and social consciousness, stopped writing poetry.

Those who wished to remain apolitical, and thought it possible to do so, argued from the ground of a "third type of people" (*disan zhong ren* 第三種人). They took the side of "human nature" against "class nature," denying the assertion that anyone not for the proletariat is against it (an assertion that would be repeated with increased insistence in the 1960s). In their review *Xiandai* 現代 [*Modern Times*], first published in 1932 with the French subtitle *Les Contemporains*, they continued the work of the

Association for Literary Studies and the Crescent Moon Society in introducing Western literature through articles and translations, and published original works by members of all the earlier societies except the
leftists, who had their own organs. Their manifesto was "to represent
modern life"; their leading poet was Dai Wangshu (戴望舒 1905–1950),
who had studied in France, would later translate Baudelaire, and bridge
the development in Chinese poetry from "Symbolist" to "Modernist."

One political fact became inescapable, even for the most determinedly
apolitical: that of Japanese aggression. By September 1931, the Japanese
had taken over Northeast China and set up a puppet government in what
they called "Manchukuo." In 1932 they extended their attack to Shanghai.
The Commercial Press in Shanghai, which published the *Short Story
Monthly*, was among the victims of their bombs. The Nationalist government adopted a policy of appeasement toward Japan, believing it more
important to rout the Communists first. After several expeditions, in
1934, the Communists were driven from their bases in the central prov-
inces to make the epic "Long March" north to Yan'an. Decimated during
the march, they had regained enough strength by 1937 to force the Nationalists to fight in a second "United Front," this time against Japan.

During the war from 1937 to 1945, conditions were desperate for development of further sophistication in poetry. Staff and students of entire
universities moved, sometimes on foot, away from the coastal cities to the
interior. Universities from Beijing joined together in Kunming to form the
Southwest Associated University (*Xinan lianda* 西南聯大); its faculty included famous poets and critics like Wen Yiduo, Zhu Ziqing (朱自清
1989–1948), Feng Zhi (馮至 1905–1993), Qian Zhongshu (錢鍾書
1910–1998), Bian Zhilin; and Wang Zuoliang (王佐良 1916–1995). The
English poet-critic William Empson taught a course on modern English
poetry. A new generation of poets and critics emerged.[18]

In the meantime, the Communist movement continued to grow. Many
poets were attracted to Yan'an, including Bian Zhilin, He Qifang (何其芳
1912–1977), and Ai Qing (艾青 1910–1966). In 1942 at a Forum on Literature and Art, Mao Zedong set forth the policies that would guide literature and art until his death. Denying the possibility of a human nature
that transcended class nature, he declared that literature was to be written for, by, and about workers, peasants, and soldiers. Although he
granted that "for the time being, the petit bourgeois may write," he insisted that they must learn from the workers, peasants, and soldiers.[19]
The attendant "agitation-propaganda" poetry produced only jingoes and
doggerel. With the end of the war against Japan in 1945, the clash between the two parties turned into a full-fledged civil war that ended with
the victory of the Communists in 1949.

When Mao Zedong stood at the top of the Gate of Heavenly Peace in
Peking and declared the establishment of the People's Republic of China
on 1 October 1949, the Nationalist army and leaders had already retreat-

ed to the island of Taiwan, at that time better known by its Portuguese name of Formosa. While the Communists were restructuring society on the Mainland based on the Soviet Russian model, the exiles on Taiwan, dreaming of a glorious return to the Mainland, regarded themselves as the true inheritors and continuators of Chinese civilization. Some pursued antiquarian studies and wrote essays in Classical Chinese; others continued the fledgling Westernized *baihua* tradition.

Interest in Baudelaire followed the Nationalist exiles to Taiwan, while on the Mainland Communists turned their attention to literature from the "small weak nations." Communications in every sphere—personal, political, economic—were broken for nearly three decades. Literary development diverged widely, as did language change and evolution.

In Taiwan, Chinese was reestablished as the official language after a half-century of Japanese rule (1895–1945), when the Japanese language had been taught in all the schools, and almost all publications had been made in Japanese. Refugees from the Mainland now dominated the literary scene. Exile was a constant theme: their memories were often filled with years of chaos and wandering. Their arrival in Taiwan meant broken ties, not only with the native soil, but often with wives and children left behind on the Mainland. The atmosphere of crisis still prevailed in 1970, when Wai-lim Yip (Ye Weilian 葉維廉 1937–) wrote in the preface to his English translations of poets from Taiwan that he was

> [d]riven by an almost superstitious fear that much of the poetry included in this anthology would be obliterated by the avalanche of world crises very much the way a few significant poets of the forties and fifties had been buried by untimely eventfulness.[20]

Once more poets formed groups and societies, each publishing its own journals and newspaper literary supplements. Two major figures were enamored of French literature and of Baudelaire in particular. Chi Hsien (Ji Xian 紀弦, 1913–) had published in *Xiandai* before the war under the penname Lu Yishi 路易士, and formed the Modernist school (*xiandaipai* 現代派) anew in Taiwan. Ch'in Tzu-hao (Qin Zihao 覃子豪 1911–1963), who had studied at l'Université franco-chinoise in Beiping (Beijing's name during the war), formed the Blue Stars Poetry Society (*Lanxing shi she* 藍星詩社) in Taiwan, and edited their journals.[21] The two poets did much to popularize French literature in Taiwan.

A generation later, the *Li* 笠 [bamboo hat] Poetry Society was founded by Chinese who had lived in Taiwan for generations. These "native Taiwanese" were inspired by modern Japanese poetry as well as Western works. Their members Tu Kuo-ch'ing (Du Guoqing 杜國清 1941–) would become first to translate all of *Les Fleurs du mal* into Chinese based on four English versions, and Mo Yu (莫渝, penname of Lin Liangya 林良雅 1948–), whose comments on Baudelaire's reception in China were published in the journal of the Young Lions, *Youshi wenyi* 幼獅文藝 [*Young*

Lions Literature and Art],[22] would publish in 1986 a fully annotated translation of *Les Fleurs du mal* made from the original French.

On the Mainland, Baudelaire found himself in unusual company as nearly all Western culture was condemned as "decadent." French poetry simply remained irrelevant, outside the sphere of possible discussion or translation for publication, except during the briefest periods of relaxation of controls. In the early 1950s during the Korean War, writers were directed to write anti-American pieces; translators worked mainly from the Russian. The government's invitation to writers to express themselves more freely during the "Hundred Flowers Movement" of 1957 was followed by an anti-Rightist "correction" a few months later, when many Westernized poets were criticized and sent to the countryside for reform. After the Sino-Soviet split in 1960, translations from the literatures of "small weak nations" predominated. Directed to look to their "native" tradition for models, the most sophisticated poets (e.g., Feng Zhi and Bian Zhilin) began writing doggerel on steel mills, electricity, and heroic peasants. The nadir came with the "Cultural Revolution" that began in 1966. Some of the most radical ideas advanced in the 1930s were made into policy: language was to be standardized; dialects were no longer to be spoken; mental work was to be regarded on the same level as manual work; all literature was to be written only by, for, and about peasants, workers, and soldiers, often working in teams; writers who had been trained abroad or who had studied Western literature were sent to "learn from peasants" and feed pigs, dig tunnels, clean latrines, or sweep floors. It was not until Mao's death in 1976, followed by the fall of the "Gang of Four," that interest in Western literature again dared to reassert itself. Writers reemerging after what they call the "ten bad years" were actually free for the first time since the early 1930s to elevate literary concerns above political ones. From 1979 on, literary journals sprang up on a scale not seen since the May Fourth Era. For more than one generation of readers, China's reception of Western literature was starting anew. The first issue of the journal *Foreign Literature* (*Waiguo wenxue* 外國文學) carried an article about Baudelaire.[23]

As mainland Chinese poets in the late 1970s and early 1980s expressed their disillusionment with socialist society, their poetry was described as *"menglong"* 朦朧, the very word that had been used to describe the Chinese Symbolists of the 1920s and 1930s. The new poetry again inspired comparison with Symbolist and Modernist poetry, and with Baudelaire. Although Chinese critics had used *"menglong"* to castigate the poetry as obscure or obscurantist, translations of the term were later revised and prettied to "misty," and the authors of "misty poems" became known as "the Misties" (*menlong shiren* 朦朧詩人) in efforts to establish a place for them in literary history.

The 1980s was a complex decade. A campaign against the "cultural pollution" (*wenhua wuran* 文化污染) and "spiritual pollution" (*jingshen wuran* 精神污染) in 1983–1984 attacked cultural influence from the West. Writers turned to "literature in search of roots" (*xungen wenxue*尋根文學), focusing on local culture prior to the influx of communism, especially in China's Far West, where communism had less influence. Before long a new campaign was waged, to open to the world (*zou xiang shijie* 走向世界 [go toward the world]). Again translations from and studies of Western literature proliferated. A collection of essays on Chinese and Western literary relations published in 1985 under the title *Zou xiang xijie wenxue* 走向世界文學 [*Go toward World Literature*] carried a subtitle in English and several articles on Baudelaire.[24] At the end of the decade, demonstrations in Tian'anmen Square led to government suppression on 4 June 1989, with tanks and live ammunition. Most of the "Misty" poets fled to exile in the West. But the effect of the Tian'anmen incident on the scholarly world seems to have been brief; journals on Western literature and articles on Baudelaire continued to appear.

Since the 1990s China has continued to engage with the Western world. The return of Hong Kong to Chinese sovereignty in 1997 did not result in the repression that many feared. By 2000 Gao Xingjian (高行健, 1940–) became the first Chinese writer to receive a Nobel Prize; that he was living in self-exile in Paris diminished the sense of pride for some Chinese, but is all the more interesting for comparative literature. In the same year China won the bid for the 2008 Olympic Games, emphasizing China's turn toward the West. The destruction and construction that ensued in Beijing surely dwarfed Baron Haussmann's in Paris that had so dismayed Baudelaire.

Contacts with Taiwan grew and shrank with political changes on both sides. Taiwan's "three no's" policy (*san bu zhengce* 三不政策: no contact, no compromise, no negotiation) is gradually giving way to the "three links" policy (*san tong zhengce* 三通政策: postal, transportation, and trade). In addition to ideology and physical constraints, intellectual contacts are partially hampered by political considerations and by the divergence in script: simplified characters prevail on the Mainland while Taiwan still uses the more complex traditional characters. Studies on Baudelaire from Taiwan reflect more sources from Europe and America than from the Mainland, and studies from the Mainland often neglect sources from Taiwan.

In the tumult of twentieth-century Chinese history, Baudelaire's fortunes rose and declined, but he was never totally neglected or forgotten. When the Chinese literary world first opened its arms to embrace works from all over the world and from all different times, how did they become acquainted with Baudelaire's work? What did they actually know of his work? What drew them to it? How did they interpret it? These questions will be approached in the next chapter through examining translations from the French poet's work.

NOTES

1. Malcolm Cowley, "The Golden House," *Dial* (Oct. 1927): 341.

2. For a full translation of Hu Shi's essay, see Kirk Denton, *Modern Chinese Literary Thought: Writings on Literature, 1983–1945* (Stanford, CA: Stanford University Press, 1996), 123–39. On the debate between defenders of *wenyan* and promoters of *baihua*, see Tse-tsung Chow, *The May Fourth Movement: Intellectual Revolution in Modern China* (Cambridge, MA: Harvard University Press, 1960). For a discussion of language change, see Y. R. Chao, *The Mandarin Primer* (Cambridge, MA: Harvard University Press, 1964), 3–18. Harold Acton, "Contemporary Chinese Poetry," *Poetry: A Magazine of Verse* 46 (Apr.–Sept. 1935): 39, notes that "In 1920 the Chinese ministry of education decreed that text-books for the first two grades in primary schools were to be written in the plain language of the people instead of the venerable language of the classics. This was the first triumph of the vernacular movement." Strictly speaking, "*baihua*" is not fully equivalent to "vernacular," as Chinese fiction had been written in the vernacular for several centuries before the *baihua* movement.

3. See Edward Gunn, *Rewriting Chinese: Style and Innovation in Twentieth-Century Chinese Prose* (Stanford, CA: Stanford University Press, 1991), and Lydia Liu, *Translingual Practice: Literature, National Culture, and Translated Modernity — China, 1900–1937* (Stanford, CA: Stanford University Press, 1995).

4. Cyril Birch, "English and Chinese Metres in Hsü Chih-mo," *Asia Major*, n.s. 8 (1961): 258–93, found a poem by Xu Zhimo to match the scansion, line for line, of Keats's "La Belle dame sans merci."

5. Hu Shi 胡適, *Chang Shi Ji* 嘗試集 [*Experiments*] (Shanghai: Yadong tushuguan, 1920, 1926). The volume also includes a number of translations, primarily from English poetry.

6. The phrase "*wo shou xie wo kou*" 我手寫我口 [my hand writes my mouth] was first used in a poem by Huang Zunxian (黃遵憲1848–1905). See Feng Shengli 馮勝利, "Hanyu Shumian yuti de xingzhi yu jiaoxue" 漢語書面語體的性質與教學 ["Chinese Written Language Style's Characteristics and Pedagogy"], 13. www.people.fas.harvard.edu/~sfeng/articles/Teaching_Chinese/teaching_Chinese.htm (accessed 20 May 2010).

7. Arthur Waley, *Translations from the Chinese* (New York: Knopf, 1919, 1941), preface, n.p.; Cowley, "The Golden House," 342; Georges Soulié de Morant, *Anthologie de l'amour chinois: Poèmes de lascivité parfumée* (Paris: Mercure de France, 1932), Introduction.

8. See Chung Ling and Kenneth Rexroth, *The Orchid Boat: Women Poets of China* (New York: McGraw-Hill, 1973). Soulié de Morant's anthology similarly takes poems from outside the mainstream.

9. Kai-yu Hsu, *Twentieth-Century Chinese Poetry: An Anthology* (New York: Doubleday, 1963; repr. Ithaca, NY: Cornell University Press, 1970), 51–52. The original lines read: "a! wode linghun de linghun! / wode shengming de shengming, / rang wo yansi zai ni yanjingde wangpo li! / rang wo shaosi zai ni xinfang de rongxiu li!" 啊！我的靈魂底靈魂！/ 我的生命底生命，/ 讓我淹死在你眼睛底汪波裏！/ 讓我燒死在你心房底熔銹裏! [Ah! My soul's soul! / My life's life, / Let me drown in your eyes' waves / Let me burn to death in your heart's furnace!]

10. See, for example, James R. Hightower, *Topics in Chinese Literature* (1950; Cambridge: Harvard University Press, repr.1966), 116, and Achilles Fang, "From Imagism to Whitmanism in Recent Chinese Poetry: A Search for Poetics That Failed," in Horst Frenz and G. L. Anderson, eds., *Indiana University Conference on Oriental-Western Literary Relations* (Chapel Hill: University of North Carolina Press, 1955), 177–92.

11. For a detailed introduction, see Amitendranath Tagore, *Literary Debates in Modern China* (Tokyo: The Centre for East Asian Cultural Studies, 1967). For detailed essays, see Kirk A. Denton and Michel Hockx, *Literary Societies of Republican China* (Lanham, MD: Lexington Books, 2008).

12. Tagore, *Literary Debates* 53.

13. Bonnie McDougall, *Western Literary Theories in Modern China* (Tokyo: The Centre for East Asian Cultural Studies, 1971), 40.

14. Cheng Ch'ing-mao, "The Impact of Japanese Literary Trends on Modern Chinese Writers" in Merle Goldman, *Modern Chinese Literature in the May Fourth Era* (Cambridge, MA: Harvard University Press, 1977), 72–73.

15. Zhou Zuoren 周作人, trans., *Ouzhou Dalu xiaoshuo ji* 歐洲大陸小說集 (1909, repr. Shanghai: Shangwu yinshuguan, 1924), Preface.

16. Witold Rodzinski, *The Walled Kingdom: A History of China from Antiquity to the Present* (New York: The Free Press, 1984), 317.

17. Tagore, *Literary Debates* 58.

18. See Ping-kwan Leung, "Literary Modernity in Chinese Poetry," in *Lyrics from Shelters: Modern Chinese Poetry 1930–1950*, ed. Wai-lim Yip (New York: Garland Publishing Inc., 1992), 43–68.

19. See Bonnie McDougall, ed. and trans., *Mao Zedong's Talks at the Yan'an Forum* (Ann Arbor: University of Michigan Center of Chinese Studies, 1980).

20. Wai-lim Yip, *Modern Chinese Poetry: Twenty Poets from the Republic of China, 1955–1965* (Iowa City: University of Iowa Press, 1970), ix.

21. See Angela Palandri, *Modern Verse from Taiwan* (Berkeley: University of California Press, 1972), 5–6.

22. "Faguo Wenxue zhuan hao" 法國文學專號 [Special issue on French Literature], *Yu shi wen yi* 幼獅文藝 315 (Mar. 1980).

23. See chapter 3.

24. Zeng Xiaoyi 曾小逸, ed., *Zouxiang shijie wenxue: Zhongguo xiandai zuojia yu waiguo wenxue* 走向世界文學：中國現代作家與外國文學 [*Going Toward World Literature: Modern Chinese Authors and Foreign Literature*], English subtitle: *To the World Literature: The Influence of Foreign Literature upon the Modern Chinese Writers* (Changsha: Hunan renmin chubanshe, 1985). Poets analyzed include Guo Moruo, Xu Zhimo, Wen Yiduo, Li Jinfa, Bing Xin, Jiang Guangci, Feng Zhi, Dai Wangshu, Ai Qing, Bian Zhilin, and He Qifang.

THREE

Baudelaire in Chinese Translation

Charles Baudelaire's name is most commonly rendered into Chinese as *Cha-li Bo-de-lai-er* 查理·波德萊爾 [Seek-reason Wave-virtue-goosefoot-thus]. Charles, *Cha-li* from the English pronunciation, also has been transliterated as *Xia-er* 夏爾 or 夏尒 [Summer-thus and Summer-you] and *Sha-er* 沙兒 [Sand-son] based on the French pronunciation. Baudelaire has variously been *Bao-te-lai-er* 鮑特來兒 [Abalone-especially-come-son], *Bo-tuo-lei-er* 波陀雷爾 [Wave-declivity-thunder-thus], *Bo-de-nai-er* 波得乃爾 [Wave-obtain-like-thus], *Pu-te-lei* 浦特雷 [Riverside-special-thunder], and so forth. The names do not result from pursuit of exotic, philosophical or quaint effects. Rather, transliteration of any foreign name into Chinese requires choosing among existing characters, which already bear other meanings. Unlike Japanese, the Chinese language does not possess a separate syllabary for transliteration. To signal the reader to read a set of characters as a name, translators choose from the less commonly used characters, and put them in combinations that would not make syntactical sense. Some translators were introduced to French writers through Japanese, English, or Russian sources, and were affected in their pronunciation of names by those sources. Regional variation in the pronunciation of Chinese characters also led to variations. Only in the last few decades has there been a successful move to standardization, with *Bo-de-lai-er* 波德莱尔 most commonly used in Mainland sources, while *Bo-te-lai-er* 波特萊爾 is more common in Taiwan. Forty versions of Baudelaire's name in Chinese which have appeared in print are listed in appendix 1.

EARLY SELECTIONS

When the Chinese began translating from Baudelaire's work, they made their selections from general anthologies. In that sense, it involved an "accident of the bookshelf." Yet the earliest selections reflect parallels to Chinese tradition strong enough to suggest that the translators found affinities with Baudelaire's poems. Their choices reflect those affinities as well as the Chinese literary scene of the times. They cast light on aspects of Baudelaire's work that crossed boundaries of the Western literary world.

The first translations into Chinese from Baudelaire's work were made from the *Petits Poèmes en prose*. Translators were drawn by themes and images as well as the form.

Petits Poèmes en prose

> —*J'aime les nuages . . . les nuages qui passent . . . là bas . . . là bas . . . les merveilleux nuages!*
> ["I love clouds . . . the passing clouds . . . there . . . there . . . the marvelous clouds!"]

Baudelaire's prose poem *"L'Etranger,"* according to Hung Cheng-fu, could have been written by any Tang dynasty poet, many of whom shared the love for clouds.[1] The brevity and suggestibility of the piece reflect classical Chinese poetic values. The moral and social values it questions reflect traditional Chinese modes of thought. The series of questions the unknown interlocutor asks *l'étranger*: "Whom do you love best: your father, mother, sister, brother, friends, or country?" are reminiscent of the Confucian emphasis on five relations: prince-subject, father-son, husband-wife, brother-brother, and friends (sisters do not count in the Chinese scheme). The stranger responds that he has no father, no mother, no sister, and no brother; that the meaning of the word "friend" is unknown to him; that he does not know where his country lies; he loves only the clouds. These responses suggest the classic Taoist retort to Confucians, rejecting human and social relations to embrace Nature, here represented by the clouds. *"L'Étranger,"* which can mean "the foreigner" as well as "the stranger," would seem foreign to the Chinese reader only in his love for "beauty as a goddess" and in his hatred for God. His questioning of personal and national identity especially would have struck a chord with early twentieth-century Chinese intellectuals, as they struggled to find a new identity and to build up a nation from a crumbled empire that was no longer the center of the known world, but only one nation among many.

"L'Étranger" first appeared in Chinese in 1922 in a translation by Zhou Zuoren 周作人, a founder of the Association for Literary Studies.[2] By 1980 Mo Yu could present eight versions, not including Zhou's, as one of two French poems most frequently translated into Chinese.[3] *"L'Etranger"* may have inspired Lu Xun's *"Guoke"* 魯迅:過客 ["The Passerby"], as Michelle Loi has suggested; He Qifang alludes to it in a poem of his own; it is associated with both Shang Qin (商禽 1930–) and Zheng Chouyu (鄭愁

予 1933–) in *Liushi Niandai* 六十年代 [*The Sixties*], a collection of poetry of the nineteen-sixties from Taiwan.[4]

The various renderings of the title alone indicate the range of interpretations. Zhou Zuoren's *"Youzi"* 游子 ["Wanderer"] puts the poem in a romantic framework reminiscent of the Rousseau of the *Rêveries*. For a reprint in *Tuoluo* 陀螺, he changed the title to *"Waifang ren"*外方人 [outside or remote place person]. Other translators use *"ren"* 人 [person], with different descriptors. The choice by Ji Xian 紀弦 and Jin Hengjie 金恆杰 of *"Yibang ren"* 異邦人 [foreign-country person], and by Ye Di 葉笛 of *"Yiguo ren"* 異國人 [foreign-nation person], both emphasize the question of nationality. Xiu Tao's 秀陶 *"Mosheng ren"* 陌生人 [unfamiliar-person] emphasizes social intercourse, whereas Li Liewen 黎烈文 chooses *"Qi-ren"* 奇人 [odd or strange-person] to highlight unconventionality. Hu Pinqing 胡品清 and Ya Ding 亞丁 offer the most suggestive and resonant alternative when they bring back traditional diction with *"Yixiang ren"* 異鄉人 [different native-place person].[5]

As is the case with *"L'Etranger,"* most of the early selections for translation from the *Petits Poèmes en prose* contain at least some elements that were already familiar to readers of Chinese poetry. The first translators seem not to have been guided by a quest for the exotic.

"Enivrez-vous" ["Get Drunk"], which Hung Cheng-fu suggested could well have been written by the Tang dynasty poet Li Bo, "the immortal who loves to drink," was translated in 1918 by Zhou Zuoren, and in 1923 by Yu Pingbo. Yu pairs the poem with "Any where out of the world" (Baudelaire's original title in English). Both can be read as poems of escape, one through intoxication, the other through travel, although mundane geographical change is seen as inadequate. If one is reminiscent of Li Bo's wine-drinking poems, the other recalls his "A Song of Lu Mountain" in which the poet magically visits all five holy mountains in one morning.[6]

"Les Bienfaits de la lune" ["The Moon's Benefits"], the poem compared by Théophile Gautier with Li Bo's "Jade Staircase Grievance," appeared in 1924–1926 in four versions by Zhou Zuoren 周作人, Zhang Dinghuang 張定璜, Su Zhaolong 蘇兆龍, and Xu Weinan 徐蔚南.[7] The moon is an age-old favorite theme in Chinese poetry, but the pun on *"lunatique"* with which Baudelaire ends his poem, and on which Gautier also played, is untranslatable into Chinese. Lunacy is not among the many associations the Chinese make with the moon, which is inhabited by a rabbit, a cassia tree, and the immortal Chang E 嫦娥 who had fled to the moon to escape her husband's wrath after she stole his elixir of immortality. There she lives forever. The Late-Tang poet Li Shangyin, for one, imagines her regret at this.[8] Baudelaire's verse poem *"Tristesses de la lune"* ["The Moon's Sorrows"] from *Les Fleurs du mal*, in which the moon is personified as a languid, sad woman, whose tear is to be hidden in the poet's heart, comes closer to the Chinese story.

"*Laquelle est la vraie?*" ["Which Is the Real One?"] is reminiscent of countless Chinese ghost stories as it tells the story of a woman who returns from the dead to visit her adorer. Zhang Dinghuang's 1925 version, "*Na yige shi zhende?*" 哪一個是真的 ["Which Is the Real One?"] avoids Baudelaire's irony: whereas in the original, the woman taunts the poet, declaring herself "*une fameuse canaille*" [a notorious slut] and condemning the poet to love her as such, in Zhang's version she is a mere "*huai dongxi*" 壞東西 [bad thing, or naughty thing], a term commonly used to chide a wayward child; gentle teasing replaces the bitter taunts. In the Chinese stories, women who return from the dead do so more often to help rather than taunt their beloved.

A few early selections do not find ready parallels in the Chinese tradition. "*Le Chien et le flacon*" ["The Dog and the Flask"], with its image of a dog sniffing at excrement, seems too extreme for Chinese taste. Still, it is not hard to imagine strugglers in the Chinese literary marketplace finding delight in a poem where the reading public is likened to the dog that chooses excrement over perfume. The poem inspired a poetic response by Zhou Zuoren's brother Lu Xun, which will be discussed in the next chapter. "*Le Miroir*" ["The Mirror"] presents an ugly man who insists on looking at himself in the mirror because "the immortal principles of 1789" had granted him equal rights. The 1789 Revolution, according to Jerome Chen, was the event in French history best known to the Chinese.[9] Did translator Zhang Dinghuang choose it for its local color? Or did he see certain similarities in China? Having adopted the slogans of "equality" and "liberty" if not "fraternity," the Chinese could be just as dogmatic and intolerant as the French radicals during the Terror. The question of legal rights was a timely one as China passed from empire to constitutional government. Finally, both Zhou Zuoren and Zhang Dinghuang translated "*Les Fenêtres*" ["Windows"], which affirms the power and reality of the imagination.[10]

"*L'Horloge*" ["The Clock"], the piece which begins "The Chinese tell time by looking at the eyes of a cat," did not appear until 1938, as one of eight selections by Li Liewen. Li also rendered "*Le Désespoir de la vieille*" ["The Old Woman's Despair"], which had also inspired a poetic response by Lu Xun. Li's remaining six selections repeat earlier selections, perhaps because as one of the first to translate directly from the French, Li wished to invite comparison with his predecessors. His versions are, if anything, overly faithful to the originals. Reproducing the original sentence structures including inversions and modifier clauses result overall in a heavy, overloaded effect.[11]

By the 1930s, complete versions of the *Petits Poèmes en prose* were advertised.[12] Selection of individual pieces ceased to be an interesting issue. While the prose poem form continued to be associated with Baudelaire's name, it was adopted by a growing number of Chinese poets, some of whom learned it from Turgenev rather than Baudelaire. Zhou

Zuoren's 1919 prose poem "Small River" was eclipsed in 1926 by Lu Xun's collection *Wild Grass*; the latter will be discussed in a later chapter.

Les Fleurs du mal

In contrast with the early selections from Baudelaire's prose poems which contained elements familiar to readers of Chinese poetry, those from his verse poems diverged widely from the Chinese tradition. One of the earliest selections from *Les Fleurs du mal* was also one of the most notorious: "*Une Charogne*" ["Carrion"] offered a prime example of ugliness as a subject for poetry.

"*Une Charogne*" first appeared in modern Chinese in 1924 by Xu Zhimo, the leading light of the Crescent Moon Society. The poem narrates in twelve four-line stanzas how the poet and his mistress, strolling on a sweet summer morning, come upon a suppurating corpse, crawling with flies, legs outstretched "like a wanton woman," open to the sun "like a flower," while a dog watches from behind some rocks, waiting for them to pass before devouring morsels from the skeleton. The tenth stanza reads:

> —*Et pourtant vous serez semblable à cette ordure,*
> *À cette horrible infection,*
> *Étoile de mes yeux, soleil de ma nature,*
> *Vous, mon ange et ma passion!*

[And yet you will resemble this filth, / this horrible putrefaction, / star of my eyes, sun of my being, / you, my angel and my passion!]

The eleventh stanza emphasizes the fact that the mistress would one day molder in the grave, and the poem concludes:

> *Alors, ô ma beauté! dites à la vermine*
> *Qui vous mangera de baisers,*
> *Que j'ai gardé la forme et l'essence divine*
> *De mes amours décomposés!* [13]

[Then, my beauty, tell the worms / who will devour you with kisses, / that I have kept the form and the divine essence / of my decomposed loves!]

The sense of irony is enhanced by the form: the "noble" alexandrine (twelve syllables) alternates with the eight-syllable line traditionally reserved for comic poems.

Xu's version successfully captures the horror and odor of decay, but misses the full savagery of Baudelaire's irony. The sarcasm of "*Vous crûtes vous évanouir*" [you thought you might faint], which concludes the first third of the poem, becomes "Fortunately you did not faint." In Baudelaire's poem, the woman's squeamishness makes more ironic the reminder that one day she, too, will become a stinking corpse. Xu's tone is gentler, almost tender in the tenth stanza with "Even [you], my love, cannot avoid the same decay." The interplay of spiritual and physical where the poet calls his mistress his "angel and passion" is lost when Xu transmutes the figure to "pure softness." Xu completes his sentimentalizing of Baudelaire's poem by rendering the last two lines as:

> *shuo wode xin yong baozhe nide miaoying*
> *jishi nide rou hua qun qu*
> 說我的心永葆著你的妙影
> 即使你的肉化群蛆

[Say my heart will forever preserve your wondrous shadow / Even if your flesh becomes a mass of maggots.]

Xu Zhimo's translation is accompanied by a brief introduction, in which he declares the poem to be "the most evil and most strangely beautiful immortal flower in *Les Fleurs du Mal*":

> Its sound and color are like shadows reflected in the last glow of the evening sun: distant, bleak, declining. It is not an owl or a skylark, but the last echo of a wounded cuckoo who has vomited out its last ounce of blood . . . It is like a tropical poisonous weed, its long leaf like an alligator tail, and its big flower like a wide-open brocade parasol; its smell is strangely poisonous, yet strangely fragrant. You could not forget its fragrance even if you died from its intoxication. In the second half of the nineteenth century, all literary Europe smelled its odd stench; many died from its poison, and many more were drunk on it. Now the dead have revived, and the drunken have sobered, but not only do they not resent it, they adore it.[14]

Xu also compares the poem with music: "to hear it is to understand it. Just as the call of insects, the speech of swallows, the sound of water and of breeze through the pines all have meaning, their meaning is like the perfume on the lips of your beloved—all in your imagination." He then goes on to declare that everything in the universe, and the universe itself, is music, but that translation, including the two or three English versions he had consulted, cannot capture the music, life, soul, fragrance, and poison of the original.

Three years before Xu Zhimo published his translation, the poet and dramatist Tian Han had presented several poems and excerpts from *Les Fleurs du mal* in a two-part article commemorating the centenary of Baudelaire's birth. The article quotes *"La Vie antérieure"* ["Previous Life"] in full (though with one line missing), without translation, to illustrate Baudelaire's life, and then to illustrate his death, it offers the first quatrain from *"Le Mort joyeux"* ["The Gladly Dead"] mistranslated *"si zhi huanxi"* 死之歡喜 [the joy of death]. Part two offers full translations, presenting the sonnet *"Correspondances"* to illustrate decadence, degeneration, and the influence of hashish; the three poems of *"La Révolte"* to illustrate Satanism; and *"Hymne à la Beauté"* to represent the "the artist's religion." By tracing the biblical references at length, and by subordinating the poems to his thesis, Tian Han effectively directed attention away from his translations.[15]

TRANSLATIONS INTO CLASSICAL CHINESE

Ten selections from *Les Fleurs du mal* appeared in Classical Chinese in 1925. They were part of an anthology entitled *Xianhe ji* 仙河集 [*Immortal River Anthology*]: "*xianhe*" 仙河 is an earlier transliteration than the current, less poetic "*sai-na*" 賽納 [border-accept] for the River Seine. The selection included writers from Charles d'Orléans (1391–1465) to Paul Bourget (1852–1935), and was translated from the original French by Li Sichun.[16]

In the case of "*Une Charogne*," Classical Chinese created a greater tension between form and content, with the effect of making Baudelaire's shocking images more so. For example, the lines

> *Les mouches bourdonnaient sur ce ventre putride,*
> *D'où sortaient de noirs bataillons*
> *De larves . . .*

[Flies buzzed on this putrid belly, / From which emerged black battalions / of larvae. . .]

become in Li's version:

> *cang-ying ji weng weng*
> *hei tuan chu xiong fu*
> 蒼蠅積嗡嗡。
> 黑團出胸腹。

[flies gather bzz bzz / black mass exit chest belly].

Li's use of the onomatopoeic "*weng weng*" 嗡嗡 for the swarming of the flies, and the word "*tuan*" 團, which not only means an army group, but suggests a glob of matter, fully captures the sight and sound of the original. Since the odor suggested by "putrid" had been fully exploited in the previous stanza, it would still be lingering in the reader's senses. Like Xu, Li abandons the pretended exaltation of the woman in the tenth stanza, rendering it as:

> *jia ren li ruo xian*
> *zhong dang ru ci wu*
> *wu hu huai zhong bao*
> *wu hu yan zhong zhu*
> 佳人麗若仙。
> 終當如比污。
> 嗚呼懷中寶。

嗚呼眼中珠。

[Beautiful woman lovely like fairy / finally must resemble this filth /
Alas treasure in my breast / Alas pearl in my eye.]

The last couplet is composed of clichés roughly equivalent to "heart of
my heart" and "apple of my eye." The addition of "alas" (pronounced
"ooh hoo") may have an unintended comical effect on some modern
readers. Like Xu, Li Sichun sentimentalizes the poem, stating its theme as
"mourning a dead loved one."

   The journal in which Li Sichun's anthology was published, *Xue heng:
The Critical Review* 學衡, was once called "a die-hard opponent to the
literary revolution."[17] Classical Chinese is indeed dying hard. Long after
the literary revolution had been accomplished, in 1980, another selection
of poems from *Les Fleurs du mal* was published in Classical Chinese. This
was the work of the preeminent philologist Wang Li (王力1900–1986).[18]

   Wang's Classical Chinese translation of *"Une Charogne"* concentrates
on the scene and the carcass.[19] He omits the direct address to the woman
in the first stanza, and the line *"Vous crûtes vous évanouir"* is rendered into
a more general statement with the carcass as subject: *"Ci bi yu hun pu"* 刺
鼻欲昏仆 [assail-nose-wish-faint-fall: so putrid one could faint]. As for
the tenth stanza, Wang follows Li Sichun by beginning with "Alas," and
then reverses the couplets from the original:

> *jie hu wu hun ling*
> *wu xin zhi ri xing*
> *ru jiang you yi ri*
> *yi ru ci shou xing*
> 嗟呼吾魂靈，
> 吾心之日星。
> 汝將有一日，
> 亦如此獸形。

[Alas, my soul spirit / my heart's sun star /you will have one day/ also
resemble this beast shape.]

The concrete image "beast shape" of the carrion replaces the *"ordure"* and
"infection" of the original. The poem ends with the poet's love outliving
both the woman and his own mortal body:

> *chong qu lai wen ru*
> *ru yi wu yong jing*
> *wu ti sui fen jie*
> *wu xin bao jing ying*
> 蟲蛆來吻汝，
> 汝亦毋庸驚。
> 吾體雖分解，
> 吾心保精英。

[worms maggots come kiss you / you also not need to be startled / my body although divide dissolve / my heart preserve essence beauty].

Although Wang does not avoid the disgusting image of worms and maggots kissing the body, by omitting the image of the worms devouring the body, he fails to capture the sense of violation and violence in the original. Wang achieves a less savage, but still ironic love poem.

Both Li Sichun and Wang Li emphasized the importance of translations going beyond words. In Li's case this meant summarizing a theme in a single phrase for each poem and placing it after the title. For example, *"Le revenant"* ["Revenant"] is "a symbol of evil;" *"Les hiboux"* ["Owls"] is a "symbol of evildoers;" while *"Le Vin de l'assassin"* ["Murderer's wine"] "dissects a murderer's psychology;" and *"Causerie"* ["Chat"] "meditates on love's falseness and viciousness." If these brief statements overly restrict the meaning of the poems, Li justifies them with the charge that contemporaries too often merely translate the words and leave the meanings unclear. Wang stated in his preface that he chose Classical Chinese as a kind of "inverse experiment," in which he aimed at translating the meaning and poetic flavor (*shiwei* 詩味) of the poems, rather than the words and prosody (*shilü* 詩律). As with Li Sichun, Wang sacrificed possibilities for conveying multiple meanings of the originals to support a single central meaning for each poem. Both omitted words and images to satisfy the demands of form. In spite of the rigidity of their chosen forms, however, their results are often surprisingly supple and suggestive.

Li Sichun's use of the traditional five or seven syllable lines gives most of his versions a ballad-like quality. This is sometimes quite effective, as when the lines from "Le Vin de l'assassin"

> *Ma femme est morte, je suis libre!*
> *Je puis donc boire tout mon soûl.*
> *Lorsque je rentrais sans un sou,*
> *Ses cris me déchiraient la fibre.*

[My wife is dead, I am free! / I can now drink my fill. / When I used to come home without a cent, / Her cries would tear up the fiber of my being.]

are rendered:

> *qi si wu zi-you*
> *jin-liang yin bu xu,*
> *dang wu zui gui wu yi qian,*
> *bi hu shi wo nao sui lie.*
> 妻死吾自由。
> 盡量飲不恤。
> 當吾醉歸無一錢。
> 彼呼使我腦髓裂。

[wife dead I am free / to-the-full drink no regard / when I drunken
return without one cent / that-one yelling cause my brain tissue crack.]

The translation works the more because "brain tissue crack" is an actual
expression for a splitting headache. Li went so far as to write in a note
that Baudelaire's poems could cause his readers "to feel benumbed, as if
driven insane."[20]

Wang Li chose the classical seven-syllable line for the famous refrain
from *"L'invitation au voyage"* which Hung Cheng-fu had identified with
traditional Chinese poetry:

> *Là, tout n'est qu'ordre et beauté,*
> *Luxe, calme et volupté.*

[there, all is but order and beauty, / luxury, calm and sensual pleasure.]

Wang expanded the couplet into a quatrain:

> *xianxiang wu di bu zhengjie,*
> *xianxiang wu wu bu keyue.*
> *xianxiang zhi li ru tiangong,*
> *xianxiang zhi jing ru mingyue.*
> 仙鄉無地不整潔，
> 仙鄉無物不可悅。
> 仙鄉之麗如天宮，
> 仙鄉之靜如明月。

> [immortal land there-is-no place not neat and clean,
> immortal land no-thing not cause delight.
> immortal land's beauty is like heavenly palace,
> immortal land's stillness is like the bright moon].

Typographical disposition as well as repetition aid the reader to identify
the lines as a refrain. *"Xianxiang"* 仙鄉 [land of immortals or fairies],
repeated at the start of each line, is more ethereal than Baudelaire's original *"pays"* [land, country, region], as Wang gives Baudelaire's entire
poem a spiritual reading.

Wang Li explains his project in classical style verse in the preface to
his 1980 work:

> *pin-nian ge-wu tan pian ku*
> *ou yi jia shi zhi zi yu*
> *bu zai wen ci zhi ke hua*
> *yao jiang shen tai huo miao mo*
> 頻年格物嘆偏枯
> 偶譯佳詩只自娛。
> 不在文辭只刻畫，
> 要將神態活描摹。

Wang Zuoliang translated these lines as:

> To relieve tedium of studious years,
> Rendering fine verse only to please (my)self,
> Aiming not at stiff word-for-word translation,
> I strive to catch the live expression.

However, Wang Zuoliang admonishes, "live expression" cannot be caught with the "over-familiar rhythm and worn-out phraseology of Classical Chinese poetry," and adds that "indeed, Baudelaire himself had dismissed all attempts at classical revival as *'pastiche inutile et dégoûtant.'"* [21] Although the declaration that Classical Chinese is "dead" has been made repeatedly from 1917 until today, many literate Chinese who do not regard themselves as Poets in the modern sense still use the traditional language, rhythms, and forms in composing poems for each other on special occasions. Wang Li's view of poetry as a game or polite pastime reflects a living part of the Chinese tradition. [22]

A NEW GENERATION

As the written vernacular came to occupy the mainstream of Chinese literature, a new generation of writers and translators became prominent in the 1930s. In contrast with their elders, who had been trained in traditional literary Chinese, the generation of the thirties had begun their education with modern Chinese, and no longer had to discover or invent new patterns for writing the vernacular. They set about refining the language as it emerged from an amalgam of classical texts, popular fiction, everyday speech, Japanese borrowings, and Europeanized vocabulary and syntax. At the same time, because writing in the vernacular was now generally accepted, they were also freer to experiment with reintroducing some classical vocabulary and structures into their work. As poets moved away from "my hand writes my mouth" poetry to formal experiments in translations as well as in their own poetry, the range of texts chosen for translation expanded apace. In their search for new forms many now focused on Baudelaire's verse poems, especially on his practice of the sonnet. A growing number acquired firsthand knowledge of French language and literature. In the 1930s and 1940s Baudelaire's verse drew attention from three major poets, Bian Zhilin, Liang Zongdai, and Dai Wangshu.

Bian Zhilin (卞之琳1910–2000) set a new standard for translation with ten poems from *Les Fleurs du mal* published in the March 1933 issue of the *Crescent Monthly.* [23] His elegant versions reproduced the twelve-syllable line (alexandrine) as well as the rhyme schemes of the originals, while preserving natural diction and supple syntax in Chinese. Bian chose from among poems that critics had indicated as representative of Baudelaire, including *"La Cloche fêlée"* ["The Cracked Bell"], *"Correspondances,"* and *"Spleen IV."* Eight of the ten selections are sonnets, reflecting Bian's well-known interest in form. Perhaps because his interest in form was as much musical as it was mathematical, Bian eschews the more common translation of "sonnet" as "*shisi hang*" 十四行 [fourteen lines], choosing instead "*shanglai*" 商籟 where "*shang*" is a note on the musical scale, and "*lai*" is an ancient musical pipe. Bian's mastery of form is evident from his translation of "*La Musique*," an irregular sonnet of alternating twelve and five syllables suggesting the movement of waves, to which the effect of music is likened. Baudelaire's poem begins:

> La musique souvent me prend comme une mer!
>> Vers ma pâle étoile,
> Sous un plafond de brume ou dans un vaste éther,
>> Je mets à la voile;

[Music often carries me off like the sea! / Toward my pale star, under a ceiling of mist or in a vast ether, / I set sail]

Bian renders the lines:

> Yinyue you shihou piao wo qu, xiang yipian dayang!
>> Xiang wo cangbai de xing-er,
> Mao yitian nong wu, huoshi dui wuji de qiongcang,
>> Wo changchang qile cheng-er
> 音樂有時候漂我去，像一片大洋！
>> 向我蒼白的星兒，
> 冒一天濃霧，或是對無極的穹蒼
>> 我常常起了程兒；

[Music sometimes floats me away, like a big ocean! / Toward my pale star / In a sky of thick fog, or toward the limitless firmament / I often set forth.]

Bian follows the syntax of the original throughout the poem, but pads the lines by substituting alternate lines of thirteen and six syllables for the original twelve and five, and adding "*you shihou*" 有時候 [sometimes] to the first line and shifting "*changchang*" 常常 [often] to the fourth. The "*-er*" 兒 ending is elided with the preceding syllable in northern speech, so that the alternation of odd and even-numbered syllables is preserved. Bian uses "*-er*" 兒 in the quatrains and "*-zhe*" 着 in the tercets; as grammatical particles, known in Chinese as "empty" rather than "full" words, they are pronounced as a shorter syllable, and represent the feminine rhymes, which alternate with masculine rhymes as they do in the original. This careful attention to prosody characterizes each of Bian's selections.

   Bian Zhilin is known in his own work for experimentation with form, and skillful interweaving of traditional Chinese poetic elements with new, sometimes Western-inspired techniques or subjects. Baudelaire's influence on that work, which Bian freely acknowledged, will be examined in a later chapter. His translations from Baudelaire occupy only a tiny part of his work; having studied only two years of college French, Bian translated far more from English.

Liang Zongdai (梁宗岱 1903–1983) had studied in France and helped Bian Zhilin with his Baudelaire translations, but published only four selections of his own. *"Bénédiction," "Le Balcon," "Chant d'automne,"* and *"Correspondances"* appeared in 1934 in a collection of translations from French and German, to which he gave the title *Yiqiede fengding*一切的峰頂 [all the peaks]—after Goethe's *"Über allen Gipfeln."*[24] To provide one example, here is the first quatrain from *"Chant d'automne"* ["Autumn Song"]:

> *Bientôt nous plongerons dans les froides ténèbres;*
> *Adieu, vive clarté de nos étés trop courts!*
> *J'entends déjà tomber avec des chocs funèbres*
> *Le bois retentissant sur le pavé des cours.*

[Soon we will plunge into the cold darkness / Goodbye, live clarity of our too-short summers! / I already hear falling with funereal shock / Wood echoing on the courtyard stones]

Liang's version reads:

> *Bujiu women jiang lunru sen leng de hei'an,*
> *Zaihui ba, tai duancu de xiatian de jiaoyang!*
> *Wo yijing tingjian, daizhe canchuang de zhenhan,*
> *Kumu qiqide luozai tingyuan de jie shang.*
> 不久我們將淪入森冷的黑暗，
> 再會罷，太短促的夏天的驕陽！
> 我已經聽見，帶著慘愴的震撼，
> 枯木槭槭地落在庭院的階上．

[Soon we will sink into cold darkness! / Goodbye, blazing sun of too-short summer! / I already hear, with anguished shock, / withered wood falling on the courtyard steps].

He thus reproduces the alexandrine, and the abab rhyme sonorously with *"an, yang, han, shang."* In the third line, he describes the sound as anguished or grieved rather than funereal, but brings in the image of death in the fourth line, with *"ku"* 枯, dried or withered wood. For the evocation of sound (*retentissant*), he substitutes the onomatopoeia *"qiqi"* 槭槭. By choosing characters usually meaning maples rather than the more common *"qiqi"* 凄凄, which mean cold and desolate, he was perhaps deliberately using the visual resource of the Chinese language: the first four characters in the line all have "wood" (*mu* 木). (The second character means "wood," and the first, third, and fourth characters bear the wood radical.)

Liang's attention to form is reflected in all four of his selections. The first three are in the alexandrine. His version of *"Correspondances,"* rendered into decasyllabic lines, is one of the best Chinese versions of the sonnet (see appendix 2).

Liang's appreciation of Baudelaire is evident from an article on Symbolism that will be introduced in the next chapter. His own volume of poetry, *Wandao* 晚禱 [*Vespers*], published more than a decade earlier, has invited comparison with Baudelaire.[25]

Dai Wangshu (戴望舒 1905–1950) stated his intention to carry forward the experiments with form that Bian Zhilin and Liang Zongdai had begun. Dai had graduated from the French Jesuit college l'Université l'Aurore in Shanghai, and had studied in France. His translations of twenty-four poems from *Les Fleurs du mal* along with Valéry's article on Baudelaire were published in 1947. In Wang Zuoliang's judgment, "Dai managed to capture [Baudelaire's] quintessence in passage after passage of a rare felicity," and "learned to deal with Baudelaire's abstractions and personifications, always a problem to translators."[26] Although Dai's avowed aim was to offer a wider selection for fuller appreciation of Baudelaire and his work, he duplicated two of Liang's four, and nine of Bian's ten choices.[27]

Dai Wangshu's choice of poems reflects a wide variety of forms and rhyme schemes, including eleven sonnets, five poems in rhymed couplets, and six with four-line stanzas. Among his most successful formal experiments is with "*L'Invitation au voyage*":

> *Mon enfant, ma soeur,*
> *Songe à la douceur,*
> *D'aller là-bas vivre ensemble!*
> *Aimer à loisir,*
> *Aimer et mourir*
> *Au pays qui te ressemble!*

[My child, my sister, / think of the sweetness, / of going there to live together! / to love at leisure, / to love and to die, / in the country that resembles you!]

Dai's version reads:

> *Haizi a, meimei*
> *Xiang xiang duo tianmei*
> *Dao neibian qu yiqi shenghuo*
> *Xiaoyaode xianglian*
> *Xianglian you chang mian*
> *Zai he ni xiangside jiaguo*
> 孩子啊，妹妹，
> 想想多甜美
> 到那邊去一起生活!
> 逍遙地相戀
> 相戀又長眠
> 在和你一樣的家國!

[Child, oh younger sister / think think how sweetly lovely / to go there to live together / freely to love one another / Love one another and die / in that country that resembles you].

The rhyme scheme in aabccb is preserved; the original line lengths of 5, 5, 7 are expanded to 5, 5, 8, emphasizing the rhythm and distancing them more from the traditional Chinese poetic lines. The diction is appropriately colloquial. *"Ma soeur"* [my sister] requires a choice in Chinese between *"jiejie"* 姐姐 for elder sister and *"meimei"* 妹妹 for younger sister. Whereas *"jiejie"* might command respect, *"meimei"* captures the affectionate tone, and *"meimei"* in its slang meaning of "girlfriend" offers the appropriate ambiguity. The reduplication of *"xiang"* 想 [think] in the next line gives an appropriately informal aspect.

As for the refrain in this poem that Hung Cheng-fu had found so reminiscent of Chinese landscapes:

> *Là, tout n'est qu'ordre et beauté,*
> *Luxe, calme et volupté.*

Dai's version expands the lines from seven syllables to ten:

> *nali, yiqie zhi shi zhengqi he mei,*
> *haochi, pingjing he na huanle mizui.*
> 那裡，一切衹是整齊和美，
> 豪侈，平靜和那歡樂迷醉。

[there, all is but neatness and beauty, / sumptuousness, quiet, and that happy intoxication].

In the second line, *"haochi"* 豪侈 carries an implication of wastefulness and extravagance not present in the original, and *"volupté"* is expanded into *"na huanle mizui"* 那歡樂迷醉 [that happiness and intoxication or fascination]. Thus the "Chinese landscape" proved paradoxically resistant to translation into Chinese.

The classical French line, the alexandrine with its twelve syllables, seems inordinately long in Classical Chinese, but Dai achieves great naturalness with it in his version of the untitled *"La Servante au grand coeur . . ."* ["The Great-Hearted Servant . . ."]. By only occasionally sacrificing a rhyme or the order of description, and by choosing such colloquial equivalents as *"zhen mei liangxin"* 真沒良心 [really has no conscience] for *"bien ingrats,"* rather than the usual *"wang'en"* 忘恩 [to be ungrateful; lit. to forget benevolence], and *"jian'ao"* 煎熬 [to put someone in hot water, make someone suffer] for *"dévoré"* [devoured] rather than the literal *"bei tunshi yu"* 被吞食於 [be swallowed by] which appear in other translations, Dai more fully captures the meaning and tone of the original.

Dai's attention to poetic tone and level of language is no doubt what he means by *"zhidi"* 質地 [texture, quality, grain]. He assigns primary importance to tone and register in the theory of translation, which appears as a postface to his translations from *Les Fleurs du mal*,[28] noting that capturing *"zhidi"* is both more important and more difficult than simply reproducing form. He adds that sometimes reproducing form can have "laughably awkward" results, and suggests substituting for meter a broadly defined *ping-ze* 平仄 [level and deflected] tone pattern. Unfortunately how this tone pattern works in his translations is not altogether clear. Dai had repudiated musicality in his own poetry more than a decade before these translations were published.

Dai was clearly more confident in the French language than many of his compatriots. His ready and frequent departures from literal equivalents may well come from that confidence, and tend to heighten, by contrast, the odor of the bilingual dictionary in other translations.

Dai Wangshu, Liang Zongdai, and Bian Zhilin made important contributions to the Chinese literary world through their translations. By introducing poems that were considered representative of Baudelaire's poetic practice rather than choosing those with familiar themes or shocking images, they contributed to a more serious knowledge of the French poet's work and helped to expand the range of subjects for Chinese poetry. By their attempts to reproduce syllable count and rhyme scheme in their translations, they contributed to formal developments in *baihua* poetry.

A translation into prose of a single poem from *Les Fleurs du mal* appeared in 1933 in a book introducing French literature. It is the work of Xu Zhongnian (徐仲年 1904–1971), whose knowledge of French was unassailable: he held a doctorate from France, and wrote on Chinese literature in French as well as French literature in Chinese. His volume, *Faguo wenxue ABC* 法國文學ABC [*The ABC's of French Literature*] formed part of a series intended for high school and college students. Xu's choice of poem is somewhat surprising for such a didactic work, even though he introduces it with the explanation that whereas conventional poets seek the good and the beautiful, Baudelaire sought the evil and ugly, and that like Flaubert's *Madame Bovary*, several of Baudelaire's poems were condemned as harmful to morals. The poem he presents, *"Les métamorphoses du vampire"* ["The Vampire's Metamorphoses"] is one of those that had been condemned.[29]

Other translations that appeared in newspapers and ephemeral journals during these decades could not have had wide influence. That may be fortunate, judging by one example: Bao Qianyuan's rendering of *"Don Juan aux Enfers"* [Don Juan in Hell] is remarkable mainly by its lack of any resemblance to the original.[30]

A NEW ERA

The establishment of the People's Republic of China in 1949 brought not only political changes, but profound changes in literary development. For the next three decades, literary trends in Taiwan and the Mainland would diverge.

The People's Republic 1949–

In the People's Republic of China, the break with the past included the May Fourth *baihua* tradition as well as the old *wenyan* tradition. In accordance with Mao Zedong's "Talks at the Yan'an Forum" in 1942, all literature was to be written by the people, for the people, and about the people, in order to serve the people. Government control of literature included work in translation, which was devoted almost solely to works from the Soviet Union and the "weak small nations." But by coincidence, the few months of the "Hundred Flowers Movement" coincided with the centennial of the publication of *Les Fleurs du mal*. Nine poems from that collection appeared in the July 1957 issue of the journal *Yiwen* 譯文 [*Translated Literature*]. Mao Zedong's justification for retightening of control proved strangely apt: instead of flowers, too many "poisonous weeds" had sprung up.

The nine selections and accompanying brief introduction published in 1957 reveal much about the intellectual climate in the People's Republic at the time. They were the work of Chen Jingrong (陳敬容 1917–1989), who had published her own poetry in Shanghai in the 1940s, when she was also translating from Baudelaire. Her translations often matched those of Bian, Liang, and Dai for diction, form, and tone.[31]

In explaining the title *Les Fleurs du mal*, Chen asserts that Baudelaire's original intention was to indicate *"bingtai zhi hua"* 病態之花 [morbid or sickly flowers], as in his introduction the poet had referred to the poems as *"fleurs maladifs"* [*sic*]. Translated into Chinese as *"E zhi hua"* 惡之花, where *"e"* 惡 had the double sense of *"chou'e"* 醜惡 [ugly] and *"zui'e"* 罪惡 [crime, evil], it became understood as *"zui'e"* 罪惡 [evil] in the sense of *"du'e"* 毒惡 [poisonous], so that the flowers were taken for poisonous weeds, and even poisonous drugs. Thus Chen seemed to be anticipating Mao's figurative language for the "correction" of "rightists" only a month later.

But it is neither as poisonous weeds nor as morbid or sickly flowers that Chen presents the poems. Chen puts at the forefront the poet's sympathy for the poor by offering first *"Crépuscule du matin"* ["Morning Twilight"], which begins with reveille in the barracks, moves through scenes of poverty and suffering, and ends with Paris as a *"vieillard laborieux"* [hardworking old man].This is followed by *"Crépuscule du soir"* ["Evening Twilight"], which contains these lines portraying the worker:

> *Dont les bras, sans mentir, peuvent dire: Aujourd'hui*
> *Nous avons travaillé! . . .*

[whose arms, without lying, can say: Today/ We have worked! . . .]

rendered as:

> *yinwei tamen ganyu shenchu shoubi, chengshi de*
> *shuo: "women you laodong le yitian!" . . .*
> 因為他們敢於伸出手臂，誠實地
> 說："我們又勞動了一天! . . ."

[Because they dare stretch out their arms and honestly / say: "we have labored another day! . . ."]

In addition to this image of the worker, Chen's selection also offers as symbol of the imprisoned and defeated *"La Mort des pauvres"* ["Death of the Poor"] and *"Le Cygne"* ["The Swan"], the latter chosen in spite of its many Classical references.

These images of the laborer, the poor, and the oppressed are supported by Chen's biographical note. While conceding that Baudelaire's life was "undisciplined" (*sanman* 散漫), Chen redeems him by declaring that "when he labored (*laodong* 勞動) he was very intense; the word 'labor' (*laodong* 勞動) often appears in his poetry." Accordingly, Chen uses "labor" (*laodong* 勞動) to translate both *"laborieux"* [hardworking] in *"Crépuscule du matin"* and *"le travail"* [work] in *"Le Cygne."*

Unlike her predecessors of a generation earlier, Chen does not attempt to reproduce line length and rhyme scheme, thus gaining more freedom in choice of diction and syntax. In *"Harmonie du soir"* ["Evening Harmony"], for example, the line "Chaque fleur s'évapore ainsi qu'un encensoir" [Each flower emits perfume like a censer] rendered in thirteen rather than twelve syllables, reads *"meiduo hua tuchu fenfang xiang luxiang yiyang"* 每朵花吐出芬芳像爐子香一樣 [each flower spits out perfume like a censer]. The assonance in *"-ang"* gives a pleasingly musical effect. In her translation of *"Spleen IV,"* Chen achieves a powerful, economical statement that makes both Bian and Dai's versions seem padded and contrived. This power in simplicity is evident in many of her translations.

The 1957 selections are drawn from larger number that Chen Jingrong had translated a decade earlier. Not until 1984 was she able to publish additional selections, together with translations from Rilke, to form a volume entitled *Tuxiang yu huaduo* 圖像與花朵 [*Pictures and Flowers*]. In the preface to that work, Chen writes that she had published other selections in 1946, now lost, and had been attacked in Shanghai's Chinese Communist Party organ *Wenhui bao* 文匯報, in its January 30, 1947 literary supplement (*Bihui* 筆會). Her translating and introducing Baudelaire's poetry, the writer had charged, showed an "unhealthy and harmful tendency," and Chen's own poetry was "one hundred percent walking Baudelaire's path." Chen should be "brought up for discussion" 提出

來討論, which she explains as code for being subject to attack (群起而攻 之).[32] It must have taken much courage in 1957 to include the gloomy "*Spleen IV*" (*Quand le ciel bas et lourd* [When the low heavy sky]) alongside the more "politically correct" selections.

Chen Jingrong's 1984 *Tuxiang yu huaduo* 圖像與花朵 adds some thirty poems to the nine poems previously published all arranged according to the order they appear in the French original. She includes all nine poems of the "*Fleurs du mal*" section of *Les Fleurs du mal* (the two titles differ only by the use of the definite article). In this section are found the poems on lesbians, corruption, debauchery, destruction, and death. Images include a man providing a fountain of blood for whores to drink from, and a corpse being picked at by birds. Chen includes a note that the poems had been condemned for being harmful to morals, and had been omitted from the 1861 edition, and then restored in the 1868 edition. The selections serve to underscore how circumspect she had been in 1957, and how much the world had changed in the People's Republic by 1984. The relation of Chen's own poetry to Baudelaire will be treated in Chapter 8.

Taiwan 1949–

In Taiwan, refugees from Communism dominated the literary scene and considered themselves to be the true inheritors of the Chinese tradition. While some pursued antiquarian studies, others continued the legacy of the May Fourth writers, believed in the value of literary influence, and looked to Western poetry for inspiration. Translations from Baudelaire appeared sporadically, usually accompanying critical introductions or essays. Major contributions were made in each decade.

Prominent among those who introduced French poetry in Taiwan, Qin Zihao (覃子豪 1912–1964) published translations of three of Baudelaire's sonnets as part of his introduction to Symbolist poetry: "*Correspondances*," "*Le Chat*" ["Cat"], and "*Les Chats*" ["Cats"].[33] As editor of the *Modern Poetry Quarterly* and of the poetry supplement to the *Taipei Evening Post*, and as teacher of correspondence courses on poetry, Qin had a wide audience. His translations were made from the French, with the aid of Japanese versions, though his command of both those languages has been questioned.[34]

Translations from Baudelaire by Hu Pinqing (胡品清 1921–2006) were part of a series of articles on French poetry published in 1962 in *Zhongguo yizhou* 中國一週 [*One Week in China*], a magazine known as "Taiwan's *Newsweek*." Hu had lived in France, and had published under the name Patricia Guillermaz two volumes of translations from Chinese into French, *La Poésie chinoise des origines à la révolution* and *La Poésie chinoise contemporaine*.[35] Here she offers twelve poems in a discussion on different facets of Baudelaire, including his contradictory attitudes toward love, religion, and authority. The translations keep to the original number of lines, but the great variations in line length and redistribution of ideas and images often result in strange shifts of emphasis. For example, the first tercet in the octosyllabic sonnet *"Les Hiboux"* ["Owls"] reads:

> *Leur attitude au sage enseigne*
> *Qu'il faut en ce monde qu'il craigne*
> *Le tumulte et le movement*

[Their attitude teaches the wise / that in this world he must fear / tumult and movement]

The lines become in Hu's version:

> *Tamende zitai*
> *yi chushi-zhi-dao shi yu zheren:*
> *xuyao weiju dongluan*
> 他們的姿態，
> 以處世之道示予哲人；
> 需要畏懼動亂。

[Their posture / by means of the way of the world shows sages, / one must fear movement and tumult]

The first line is impoverished by being reduced to a possessive and a single noun. In the second line, the meanings of *"ce monde"* are reduced to "the way to behave in society." In the third line, *dongluan* 動亂 as separate characters are "movement" and "tumult," but in modern Chinese they more commonly form a compound meaning "turmoil, upheaval, disturbance." Hu Pinqing's language is closer to Classical Chinese, as evidenced by her choice of *"chixiao"* 鴟鴞 for the title rather than the modern *"maotouying"* 貓頭鷹 for "owl."

Of Hu's twelve selections, two are incomplete: only the first part of *"Chant d'automne"* ["Autumn Song"] and the last part of *"Les Litanies de Satan"* ["Satan's Litanies"] are offered, suggesting that she dashed off these entries in some carelessness and haste. Hu's interest in Baudelaire is better developed in her criticism, which will be discussed in the next chapter.

Cheng Baoyi (程抱一 1929–) published his translations from Baudelaire in Taiwan in the 1960s and 1970s. An expatriate in France since 1949, he published in 1977 under the name François Cheng *L'Écriture poétique chinoise*, a semiotic analysis of Tang poetry accompanied by his own translations. His translations and essays on Baudelaire appearing in various journals from 1967 to 1968 are collected in a book called *He Ya Ding tan Faguo shi* [*Chatting about French Poetry with Ya Ding*], with the French subtitle *La Poésie française de Hugo à Reverdy*, published in 1970.[36]

Cheng's translations from *Les Fleurs du mal* preserve the forms and line lengths of the originals, but often rearrange images and ideas to follow the requirements of Chinese syntax. They do not strive to rhyme, and give an overall impression of naturalness. The seven selections are arranged in a framework to present Baudelaire as the poet of Paris, who "learned to see reality with fearless eyes," and who "rejected superficial enjoyment and empty ideals to experience life in the raw, as a far-sighted, serious artist." Cheng's framework sometimes seems forced, as when "*Les Petites Vieilles*" ["The Little Old Women"] is said to be "penetrated with an inner fire," which "fire" leads to "*Le Soleil*" ["The Sun"]. More convincing is the connection between "*Le Soleil*" where the poet is compared with the sun with "*Les Plaintes d'un Icare*" ["Complaints of an Icarus"]. "*Une Charogne*" is presented as affirming Baudelaire's faith in art's power to create the essence of life out of the corruption of death. Seeing in this the interplay of man and nature, Cheng accordingly concludes with the sonnet "*Correspondances.*"

A major moment in the reception of Baudelaire in China came in 1977 with the publication in Taiwan of the first full translation into Chinese of *Les Fleurs du mal*. Tu Kuo-ch'ing (Du Guoqing) followed the 126-poem 1861 edition, finally making available to Chinese readers the work in its original "architecture." His succinct introduction offers background material and a guide to the structure; the table of contents usefully places Chinese and French titles side by side, and a biographical outline is offered at the end.[37]

Tu sets forth as his basic principles for translation conveyance of the original meaning, accuracy in diction, and naturalness in form. His versions nevertheless reveal an ambitious program of reproducing line lengths and end rhymes, resorting to near-rhymes when necessary. In line length, whereas other translators shortened, Tu preferred to fill out, often replacing the alexandrine with a tridecasyllabic line, using the meaningless interjection "*yo* 喲" with distressing frequency. The heptasyllabic lines in "*L'Horloge*" become octosyllabic, thus changing a daring departure from traditional prosody into the stock comic line. These variations possibly resulted from misreading the *e caduc* (mute e), the unaccented letter "e" at the end of a word that is silent in conversational French but counts as a full syllable in poetry except when it precedes a vowel, occurs at the caesura, or occurs at the end of the line. The Chinese versions, printed in block characters and in blocks of lines, give an overwhelming sense of formal regularity and control quite surpassing the original. In an afterword Tu confides that, having studied only two years of college French, he relied on William Aggeler's English-French bilingual edition, Francis Scarfe's renditions into prose, and four Japanese versions. His diction is learned, often recherché. If some of the versions seem labored, Tu himself has confessed in the preface that he had transpired "a drop of sweat with each word." Whatever shortcomings may be found in individual versions, however, the collection as a whole made an invaluable contribution to Chinese knowledge of Baudelaire.

Convergences

By the 1980s readers, critics, and translators in Taiwan and on the Mainland began to converge. Tu Kuo-ch'ing's translations from Baudelaire were quoted by Mainland critics. Cheng Baoyi's translations were published on the Mainland. Political considerations no longer played a major role in translation and selections for translation. Indeed, even literary politics played a diminishing role. Of translations from the 1930s, Ma Yiu-Man has declared that Liang Zongdai's translations play a secondary role in his "hidden agenda" to promote "pure poetry" in China, and Paul Manfredi has argued that accuracy was beside the point in Xu Zhimo's translations, since Xu's real intent was to "bolster the power of poetry and the security of his own position in the literary circles of his day."[38] But the work of recent decades, more often by scholars and critics, seem to have more straightforward aims—at least until future sleuths uncover their "hidden agendas."

In 1985 Mo Yu published in Taiwan a full translation of *Les Fleurs du mal* made directly from the French. It includes all the poems that had been omitted from the 1861 edition. Mo Yu's diction is at great variance from Tu Kuo-ch'ing's. He does not strive for regular line lengths or rhymes; but does offer copious annotations and illustrations. A second edition published in 1998 includes an original poem that he had composed for Baudelaire.[39]

Translations from Baudelaire also began appearing in complete volumes on the Mainland in the 1980s. A new version of the *Petits Poèmes en prose* appeared in 1982 for which the translator, Ya Ding 亞丁, used the alternative title *Le Spleen de Paris* (*Bali de youyu* 巴黎的憂鬱 [*Paris's Melancholy*]). Ya Ding's language is natural and supple, and many of the poems were arranged in short lines in the manner of verse poetry.[40] Chen Jingrong's translations from Baudelaire and Rilke were published in a collection in 1984, as previously mentioned. Qian Chunqi (錢春綺 1921–2010) published a selection from *Les Fleurs du mal* in 1986. Qian's readings were informed by his knowledge of English, French, German, Japanese, and Russian; originally a medical doctor; he translated prolifically, especially from German, and eventually devoted full time to translation.[41] His combined volume containing both *Les Fleurs du mal* and the *Petits Poèmes en prose* appeared in 1991.[42]

Continuing in the 1990s, Guo Hong-an (郭宏安 1943–) published 100 selections from *Les Fleurs du mal* together with an introductory study comprised of ten articles most of which he had previously published in journals starting in 1984.[43] Guo had studied in Switzerland, and had proofread Ya Ding's translation of the prose poems. He would go on to translate other works by Baudelaire, including Baudelaire's art criticism, *Le Peintre de la vie moderne* [*The Painter of Modern Life*] and the *Salon de 1846* [*1846 Art Salon*].[44]

In the same decade, Su Fengzhe 蘇鳳哲 published a selection from *Les Fleurs du mal*.[45] In 1996 appeared *Bodelai'er shi quan ji* 波德萊爾詩全集 with the English subtitle *C. Baudelaire: The Complete Poems*; it was edited by Hu Xiaoyue 胡小躍, and contains his own translations and some by Zhang Qiuhong 張秋紅. The volume also includes the prose works *Mon Coeur mis à nu [My Heart Laid Bare]* and *Pauvre Belgique [Poor Belgium]*.[46]

Chinese translations from Baudelaire continue into the present century. Translations that had been published in simplified characters on the Mainland were republished in traditional characters in Taiwan. Such was the case with Qian Chunqi's translations, which appeared in Taiwan in 2001.[47] Guo Hong-an, whose translation of *Les Fleurs du mal* was originally published in Guilin (Guangxi Province), and already republished in Taiwan in 1997,[48] saw them republished in Beijing in 2005 and 2006.[49] Ya Ding's translation, originally published in Nanning (also Guangxi Province) was brought to the capital Beijing in 2004, and republished in Taiwan in 2006.[50] New translations have also appeared, of *Les Fleurs du mal* by Wen Aiyi,[51] and a revised version of the *Petit Poèmes en prose* by Hu Xiaoyue.[52] A selection of Qian Chunqi's translations appeared with a major publisher in 2008.[53] In December 2011 a new version of Tu Kuo-ch'ing's *E zhi hua* was published in Taipei.[54]

Translations also continue to appear in journals, most often as part of critical studies. Critical interest in Baudelaire's work has also continued, as the next chapter will show.

"CORRESPONDANCES"

The most frequently translated of Baudelaire's work is the sonnet *"Correspondances."* It is the most famous expression of Baudelaire's poetics of synaesthesia (intermingling of the senses), and some translators rendered only a few lines for discussion. Whether they were interested in Baudelaire's work in general, or in synaesthesia, or in Symbolism, or in the sonnet form, or whether, with Liang Zongdai, they saw in the sonnet the summation of all poetry, numerous poets, critics, and scholars rendered it into Chinese. To give readers of Chinese a sense of the possibilities, twenty full versions are given in appendix 2.

NOTES

1. Hung Chengfu, *Un Siècle*, 114.
2. Zhong Mi 仲密 (pseud. Zhou Zuoren 周作人), "Youzi" 游子 in *Xiaoshuo yuebao* 小說月報 13, no. 6 (1922): 22. "Chuang" 窗 ("Les Fenêtres" ["Windows"]) had appeared earlier in 13, no. 3 (1922): 28. Zhou includes eight of Baudelaire's poems in *Tuoluo* 陀螺 [top—as in the child's toy] (Beijing: Xinchao chubanshe 新潮出版社, 1925), 77–91. He adds a note that he had translated from Arthur Symons's versions in 1918, and had also consulted an unspecified German translation. See also A. R. Davis, "Chi-

na's Entry into World Literature," *Journal of the Oriental Society of Australia* 5, nos. 1–2 (Dec. 1967): 43–50.

3. Mo Yu 莫渝, "'Qiuge' yu 'yixiang ren' Zhongyi cishu zui duo de liangshou Faguo shi" 「秋歌」與「異鄉人」中譯次數最多的兩首法國詩 ["(Verlaine's) 'Chant d'automne' and 'L'Étranger'—Two French Poems Most Frequently Translated into Chinese"], *Yushi wenyi* 幼獅文藝 315 (Mar. 1980): 129–47.

4. Zhang Mo 張默 and Ya Xian 瘂弦, ed., *Liushi niandai shixuan* 六十年代詩選 [*Selected Poems from the Sixties*] (Kaohsiung: Daye shudian, 1961), 123, 199–202.

5. See Mo Yu, "'Qiuge' yu," 140–47.

6. Hung Chengfu, *Un Siècle*, 114. For a translation of Li Bo's poem, see Bynner and Kiang, *The Jade Mountain*, 63. Zhou Zuoren's "Ni zui" 你醉 ["You (Get) Drunk"] is collected in *Tuoluo* 陀螺 (Beijing: Xinchao chubanshe, 1925), 84. Yu Pingbo (俞平伯 1900–1990), "Zuizhe ba" 醉著吧 ["Be Drunk"], and "Wulun nar chu zheige shijie" 無論哪兒出這個世界 ["Anywhere Out of This World"], *Shi* 詩 [Poetry] 2, no. 1 (1923): 4–5, reprinted in *Yu Pingbo shi quan bian* 俞平伯詩全編 [*Complete Edition of Yu Pingbo's Poetry*], ed. Yue Qi 樂齊 (Zhejiang wenyi chubanshe, 1992), 333–35.

7. Zhou Zuoren, "Yueliangde enhui" 月亮的恩惠 ["Moon's Favors"], *Tuoluo* 陀螺 [The Top], 87, offers "yueguang bingzhe" 月光病者 [moonlight-sick-person] in quotation marks, with a footnote indicating that the ancients associated madness with the phases of the moon, adding in Roman letters for his Graecophile readers that this was the meaning of "Seleniazoumenos"; Zhang Dinghuang 張定璜, "Sanwenshi chao" 散文詩抄 ["Selected Prose Poems"], *Yusi* 語絲 [*Threads of Talk*] 23 Feb. 1925): n.p., chooses "Fengkuang ren" 瘋狂人 ["Crazy Person"], which rather spoils the languid mood. Su Zhaolong's "Yueliang juanshu" 月亮眷屬 [Lit. moon and family dependents], 文學週報 *Wenxue Zhoubao* [literary weekly] no. 143 (Oct. 13, 1924), and Xu Weinan's "Yueliangde aichou" 月亮的哀愁 ["Sorrows of the Moon"] are listed in Zhao Jiabi 趙家璧, ed., *Zhongguo xin wenxue daxi* 中國新文學大系 [*Compendium of New Chinese Literature*] (1935, repr. Hong Kong: wenxue yanjiuhui, 1962), 463. Hereafter, *Daxi*.

8. For Li Shangyin's poem, see Bynner and Kiang, *The Jade Mountain*, 58–59, or François Cheng, *Chinese Poetic Writing*, tr. Donald A. Riggs and Jerome P. Seaton (Bloomington: Indiana University Press, 1982), 131

9. Jerome Chen, *China and the West: Society and Culture, 1815–1937* (Bloomington: Indiana University Press, 1978), 84.

10. Xie Zhixi 解志熙, *Mei de pianzhi: Zhongguo xiandai weimei-tuifei zhuyi wenxue sichao yanjiu* 美的偏至：中國現代唯美- 頹廢主義文學思潮研究 [*Study of Modern Chinese Literary Trends of Aestheticism-Decadentism*] (Shanghai: Shanghai wenyi chubanshe, 1998), 265–66, lists three venues in which Zhou Zuoren published his translation of this poem, and posits that it marks Zhou's turn from Realism to Aesthetic-Decadence.

11. Li Liewen 黎烈文, "Sanwen shichao" 散文詩抄 [Selected Prose Poems], *Yiwen* 譯文 [Translated Literature] 1, no. 2 (Oct. 1934): 126–33.

12. Shi Min石民: *Sanwen shi xuan* 散文詩選 (Shanghai: Beixin, 1931) and *Bali zhi fannao* 巴黎之煩惱 (Shanghai: Shenghuo shudian, 1935), advertised in the 1930s, are now listed in Worldcat but were not available through the system.

13. *OC*, 32.

14. Xu Zhimo, "Sishi" 死尸 ["Corpse"], *Yu si* 語絲 3 (1 Dec. 1924): n.p. *Yusi* was founded by Zhou Zuoren to introduce Western literature. Leo Oufan Lee, in *Shanghai Modern: The Flowering of a New Urban Culture in China 1930–1945* (Cambridge, MA: Harvard University Press, 1999), 236–37, finds Xu's version to "exceed the sensory limits of the original." Haun Saussy in "Preface to a Preface: Xu Zhimo 徐志摩, Baudelaire, and the Stakes of Intercultural Reading," *Ex/change* 5 (September 2002): 5–8, has a fuller translation of the preface. Saussy posits that Xu read Baudelaire's poem as an extension of Zhuangzi's idea on transformation. Guo Shaohua, in "Bodelai'er zai Zhongguo," 4, lists a translation of the same poem by Jin Mancheng 金滿成, "Sishi" 死尸 in *Wenxue xunkan* 文學旬刊, 57 (Dec. 1924), and in the same journal two issues later, another translation by Zhang Renquan 張人權, entitled "Fu shi" 腐屍.

15. Tian Han 田漢, "E-mo shiren bo-tuo-lei'er de bainian ji" 惡魔詩人波陀雷爾的百年祭 ["Centenary of Demonic Poet Baudelaire"], *Shaonian Zhongguo* 少年中國 3, no. 4 (Nov. 1921): 1–6, and 3, no. 5 (Dec. 1921): 17–32.

16. Li Sichun 李思純, "*Xian he ji*" 仙河集 ["Seine River Anthology"], *Xue heng (The Critical Review)* 學衡 47 (Nov. 1925): 6447–6510. (Each stanza is printed in one vertical line, with a dot to the right of the character marking the end of a line. I divided the lines for clarity).

17. Ma Yiu-man, "The Reception of French Symbolism in China, 1919–25," in *The Force of Vision 4: Translation and Modernisation: Proceedings of the XIIIth Congress of the ICLA.*, ed. Theresa Hyun and José Lambert (Tokyo: University of Tokyo Press, 1995), 51.

18. Wang Li (Wang Liaoyi) 王力 (王了一), *E zhi hua* 惡之花 (Beijing: Waiguo wenxue chubanshe, 1980). Preface dated 1940. See also Wang Nuo 王諾, "Faguo xianzheng zhuyi shige de yishu tonggan" 法國象徵主義詩歌的藝術通感 ["Artistic Synesthesia in French Symbolist Poetry"], *Waiguo wenxue yanjiu* 外國文學研究 3 (1985): 99. Wang Li was not a "diehard opponent" to writing in the vernacular. His *Hanyu shilü xue* 漢語詩律學 [*Chinese Prosody*] (Shanghai: Xin zhishi chuban she, 1958) is written in lucid and supple *baihua*. The chapters on modern (xiandai 現代) and Europeanized (ouhua 歐化) poetry are omitted in the 1962 edition, and restored in 1978 edition by Shanghai jiaoyu chubanshe). It gives a prominent place to Baudelaire's sonnets on pages 926–50.

19. Wang Li, *E zhi hua*, 65–67.

20. Li Sichun, "*Xian he ji*," 48. (shi ren du zhi, gan mazui, ruo zhong kuang ji 使人讀之。感麻醉。若中狂疾。).

21. Wang Zuoliang, *Degrees of Affinity: Studies in Comparative Literature* (Beijing: Foreign Language Teaching and Research Press, 1985), 107–8.

22. Stephen Owen, "The Anxiety of Global Influence," 28, invokes a friend who uses Classical Chinese "in poetry he writes for his friends," but "his 'new poetry,' by contrast, is what permits him to think of himself as a Poet, what offers him the hope of eventual recognition." The most recent volume of new poems in Classical Chinese in my collection was published in 2004.

23. Bian Zhilin 卞之琳, "E zhi hua lingshi" 惡之花零拾 ["Gleaning from the Flowers of Evil"], *Xinyue* 新月, 4, no. 5 (Mar. 1933): 1–8.

24. Liang Zongdai 梁宗岱, *Yiqiede fengding* 一切的峰頂, repr. in *Liang Zongdai yi shi ji* 梁宗岱譯詩集 [*Liang Zongdai Translated Poems Collection*] (Changsha: Hunan renmin chubanshe, 1983), 24–32.

25. Harry Kaplan, "The Symbolist Movement," 34–35. See chapter 7 below.

26. Wang Zuoliang, "Degrees of Affinity," 102.

27. Dai Wangshu 戴望舒, "E zhi hua zhuiying"《惡之華》綴英 ["Stitched Petals from *Flowers of Evil*"], in *Dai Wangshu juan* 戴望舒卷, ed. Ya Hsien 瘂弦 (Taipei: Hongfan shudian, 1977), 97–118; also in *Li* 笠, 48 (Apr. 15, 1972): 83–102; *Dai Wangshu yi shi ji* 戴望舒譯詩集 [*Dai Wangshu Translated Poetry Collection*] (Changsha: Hunan renmin chubanshe, 1983), 119–53, and Wang Zuoliang, "Degrees of Affinity," 101–2.

28. Dai Wangshu, "Yi hou ji" 譯後記 ["Afterword to Translation"], *Dai Wangshu yi shi ji*, 153–54.

29. Xu Zhongnian 徐仲年, *Faguo wenxue ABC* 法國文學 ABC [*ABCs of French Literature*] (Shanghai: Shijie shuju, 1933), 54–55.

30. Bao Qianyuan, 包乾元 trans., "'Dong Dan xia diyu,' Botelai'er zhu" [董丹下地獄: 波特萊爾著 ["'Don Juan Descends to Hell,' by Baudelaire"], *Zhongyang ribao shikan* 中央日報詩刊 [*Central Daily Poetry Periodical*], (Sunday, 7 Mar. 1937): Sec. 4, 3.

31. Chen Jingrong 陳敬容, "E zhi hua (xuanyi)" 惡之花 (選譯) ["*Flowers of Evil* (Selected Translations)"], *Yiwen* 譯文 7 (1957): 133–43.

32. Chen Jingrong 陳敬容, *Tuxiang yu huaduo* 圖像與花朵 [*Pictures and Flowers*] (Changsha: Hunan renmin chubanshe, 1984), 5.

33. Qin Zihao 覃子豪, *Shijie ming shi xinshang* 世界名詩欣賞 [*Appreciation of World-Famous Poems*] (1956, repr. Taizhong: Putian chubanshe, 1976), 125–26, and in *Qin*

Zihao Quanji 覃子豪全集 (Taipei: Qin Zihao quanji chuban weiyuan hui, 1965–1974), vol. 2.

34. Du guoqing 杜國清 (Tu Kuo-ch'ing), "Xie zai fanyi *E zhi hua* zhi qian" 寫在翻譯「惡之華」之前 ["Written before Translating *Flowers of Evil*"], *Li* 笠 48 (15 Apr. 1972): 75–76.

35. Hu, Pinqing 胡品清, "*E Zhi Hua* xuan yi"「惡之花」選譯 ["Selected Translations from *Flowers of Evil*"], *Zhongguo Yizhou* 中國一週 632 (4 June 1962): 15, and 633 (11 June 1962): 32. Patricia Guillermaz, *La Poésie chinoise des origines à la révolution* (Paris: Seghers, 1957, repr. Verviers, Gérard et cie., 1966), *La Poésie chinoise contemporaine* (Paris: Seghers, 1962).

36. Cheng Baoyi 程抱一, *He Ya Ding tan Faguo shi* 和亞丁談法國詩 [*Chatting about French Poetry with Ya Ding*] (Taipei: Chun wenxue chubanshe, 1970), 1–25. Cheng Baoyi writes in French as François Cheng, cited in chapter 1.

37. Du Guoqing 杜國清 (Tu Kuo-ch'ing), *E zhi hua.*

38. Ma, Yiu-man, "Translating without the Source Text: A Case Study of Liang Tsung-tai's Baudelaire," *Tamkang Review*, 27, no. 1 (Autumn 1997): 91–112. Paul Manfredi, "Writing the Influenced Text: Modern Chinese Symbolist Poetry," *Journal of Modern Literature in Chinese* 5, no. 2 (Jan. 2002): 12–13.

39. Mo Yu 莫渝, *E zhi hua* 惡之華 [*Flowers of Evil*] (Taipei: Zhiwen chubanshe, 1985, 2nd edition 1998).

40. Ya Ding 亞丁, *Balide youyu* 巴黎的憂鬱 [*Paris Spleen*] (Nanning: Lijiang chubanshe, 1982).

41. Qian Chunqi 錢春綺, *E zhi hua* 惡之花 [*Flowers of Evil*] (Beijing: Renmin wenxue chubanshe, 1986). On Qian's background, www.wxread.com/ZJWX/mjft/50.htm (accessed 8 Nov. 2009—no longer accessible).

42. Qian Chunqi 錢春綺, *E zhi hua* 惡之花; *Bali de youyu* 巴黎的憂鬱 [*Flowers of Evil; Paris Spleen*] (Beijing: Renmin wenxue chubanshe, 1991).

43. Guo Hong-an 郭宏安, *E zhi hua: Chatu ben* 惡之花: 插图本 [*Flowers of Evil: Illustrated Volume*] (Guilin: Lijiang chubanshe, 1992).

44. Guo Hong-an 郭宏安, *1846 nian de shalong: Bodelai'er meixue lunwen xuan* 1846 年的沙龙: 波德莱尔美学论文选 [*Salon of 1846: Selection of Baudelaire's Aesthetic Theory*] (Guilin: Guangxi shifan daxue chubanshe, 2002); *Xiandai shenghuo de huajia* 现代生活的畫家 [*Painter of Modern Life*] (Hangzhou: Zhejiang wenyi chubanshe, 2007).

45. Su Fengzhe 蘇鳳哲, *Bodelai'er shi xuan* 波德萊爾詩選 [*Selected Poems of Baudelaire*] (Shijiazhuang: Huashan wenyi chubanshe, 1992).

46. Hu Xiaoyue 胡小躍, *Bodelai'er shi quanji* 波德萊爾詩全集 [*Complete Poems of Baudelaire*] (Hangzhou: Zhejiang wenyi chubanshe, 1996).

47. Qian Chunqi 錢春綺, *E zhi hua; Bali de youyu* 惡之花; 巴黎的憂鬱 [*Flowers of Evil; Paris Spleen*] (Taipei: Guangfu wangji wanglu, 2001).

48. Guo Hong-an 郭宏安, *E zhi hua* 惡之花 [*Flowers of Evil*] (Taipei: Linyu wenhua, 1997).

49. Guo Hong-an 郭宏安, *E zhi hua* 惡之花 [*Flowers of Evil*] (Beijing: Beijing yanshan chubanshe, 2005); (Beijing: Zhongguo shuji chubanshe, 2006).

50. Ya Ding 亞丁, *Bali de youyu* 巴黎的憂鬱 [*Paris Spleen*] (Beijing: Sanlian shudian, 2004); (Taipei: Yuanliu, 2006).

51. Wen Aiyi 文愛藝, *E zhi hua* 惡之花 [*Flowers of Evil*] (Chengdu: Sichuan renmin chubanshe, 2007).

52. Hu Xiaoyue 胡小躍, *Balide youyu* 巴黎的憂鬱 [*Paris Spleen*] (Shanghai: Shanghai wenyi chubanshe, 2006).

53. Qian Chunqi 錢春綺, *E zhi hua Bodelai'er shige jingcui* 惡之花: 波德莱尔诗歌精粹 [*Flowers of Evil: Essence of Baudelaire's Poetry*] (Beijing: Renmin wenxue chubanshe, 2008).

54. K. C. Tu, e-mail message 18 Feb. 2012. See also http://ntupress.pixnet.net/blog/post/84452776.

FOUR
Baudelaire in Chinese Literary Criticism

"Anyone who has paid the slightest attention to modern literature knows the author of *Les Fleurs du mal*, Charles Baudelaire," Li Liewen 黎烈文 wrote in 1934. By 1935, Liang Zongdai could declare that Baudelaire's name was "well known to Chinese readers." In 1980, having surveyed the available translations and critical works, Mo Yu would pronounce Baudelaire the French poet best received by the Chinese.[1]

Baudelaire has been the subject of a wide range of essays and articles appearing in Chinese journals, literary manuals, and anthologies from the 1920s until the present day. These publications played a major role in introducing Baudelaire to Chinese readers, and in forming Chinese images of Baudelaire.

CLASSIFICATION

When Baudelaire was introduced in China the 1920s, critical introductions far outpaced translations from his work. As writers, critics, and scholars rushed to introduce the vast corpus that is "Western" literature, they devoted much attention to the national literary histories as a way to provide an overview. The idea of evolution in literature, if not an article of faith for all of them, was at least a useful contextual and organizational tool. Thus French literature was shown to pass from Classicism, through Romanticism, then Naturalism, Parnassianism, Symbolism, and Surrealism, to arrive at Modernism. Chinese critics hailed Baudelaire as the inventor of the prose poem, and even those who had not read his work, even in translation, knew Baudelaire for his aesthetics of synaesthesia and beauty in ugliness.

As Chinese writers and readers struggled to acquaint themselves and each other with European, English, and American literature, many became preoccupied with classification. Those who followed the judgments of English, American, and Japanese critics viewed Baudelaire as a Satanist, Diabolist, or Decadent. Although many expressed disapproval of the poet on these grounds, others must have seen in his work a reflection of their own iconoclastic spirit. For those who focused on the French literary tradition, it was not difficult to place Baudelaire chronologically, but finding his place within schools and movements proved to be an uncommonly recalcitrant task. Yuzhi 愉之 places him in a section on Naturalism and describes him as an aesthete (*weimei pai* 唯美派), but later adds that through his influence on Verlaine and the Parnassians, he also belonged with the Decadents (*tuisang pai* 頹喪派) and Diabolists (*emo pai* 惡魔派).[2] Li Huang and Liu Yanling follow French sources in placing him in between the Parnassian and Symbolist schools.[3] In a special supplement to the *Short Story Monthly* on French literature, four authors variously present Baudelaire as a founder of Symbolism, as a Parnassian, as the last Romantic, and as the first Modern; they associate him with the "schools" of Decadence, Satanism, and Modernism.[4]

The literary manuals did little to clear up the confusion. Zheng Zhenduo's monumental *Wenxue Dagang* 文學大綱 [*Outline of Literature*] draws the practical conclusion that Baudelaire "belonged to no particular school," but nevertheless classifies him as a "Satanic poet" who shared with the Parnassians "extremely penetrating" descriptions of smell and taste, and as a forerunner of Symbolism through "the decadence and peculiarity of his thought."[5] Yuan Changying's *Faguo wenxue* 法國文學 [*French Literature*] classifies Baudelaire as "the most influential of the Parnassians" and "first of the Symbolists."[6] Mu Mutian's *Faguo wenxue shi* 法國文學史 [*French Literary History*] declares him to be a representative of Romanticism, Parnassianism, Symbolism, and Modernism, and places him in a chapter on Realism.[7]

Many of the critics and scholars who sought to classify Baudelaire simply declared him "strange, odd, or peculiar." Zheng Zhenduo described him as one who went his own "dark peculiar way," "exalted death and sought the new and strange," "took opium and hashish to seek illusory states, and praised things others considered ugly, such as owls, corpses, and ghosts."[8] Xu Xiacun wrote in his *Faguo Wenxuede gushi* 法國文學的故事 [*Story of French Literature*]:

> Baudelaire is a singular figure in French literature, odd in appearance and eccentric of personality; what ordinary people call beautiful, he considered ugly; what ordinary people consider ugly, he contrarily considered beautiful. . . . [H]e often liked . . . to shock the bourgeoisie. . . . [H]is work . . . reveals his special feeling toward color, taste, perfume, and sound, using sound to describe color, using color to describe sound, thus opening the way to Symbolism. He translated Poe,

and . . . like Poe, his mind was always prey to a melancholy imagination, and constantly kept company with the concept of death.[9]

Xu's vocabulary is echoed in two studies from 1965 and 1975, Ge Xianning and Shangguan Yu's *Wushinianlaide Zhongguo Shige* 五十年來的中國
詩歌 [*Chinese Poetry in the Last Fifty Years*] and Wang Zhijian's *Xiandai
Zhongguo shi shi* 中國現代詩史 [*History of Modern Chinese Poetry*]. Presenting Baudelaire as the vanguard of Symbolism and as the master of Symbolism, Decadence, and new poetry, they find him an "odd poet" (怪詩
人):

> What ordinary people consider beautiful, he contrarily considered
> ugly. What ordinary people consider ugly, he contrarily considered
> beautiful. From his strange work, we can see he has a special synesthet-
> ic and Symbolist feeling toward color, sound, perfume, taste, and
> touch, describing sound with color, describing color with sound stimu-
> lating the senses; it is rather peculiar.[10]

In these judgments, Baudelaire's life and work are judged as one.

BIOGRAPHY

"A great work of art cannot be separated from the life of the artist," wrote
Zong Lin in 1933.[11] In the hands of literary critics the life of an artist
inevitably goes through new transformations. Chinese accounts of
Baudelaire's life, by their choice and presentation of details, reveal much
about the Chinese literary scene in which they appear.

In "Baudelaire's Tragedy" Wen Zheng recounts Baudelaire's birth,
youth, adulthood, decline, and death. These are just the external facts of
Baudelaire's life, Wen concedes, but he "has no room" to treat the more
important inner life. Baudelaire's life is a tragedy even though there was
no bloodshed, no murder, he concludes, without attempting to define
"tragedy."[12]

Four articles from the 1930s focus on Baudelaire's private life. Zong
Lin offers a chronological account. Shen Baoji's "Baudelaire's Love Life"
treats the dichotomy between the poet's physical love for Marie Daubrun
and Jeanne Duval, and his idealizing love for Madame Sabatier. Wen
Jiasi, in his "Baudelaire: A Few Loves of Different Colors," gives the
subject more imaginative treatment. No doubt inspired by Rimbaud's
"*Sonnet des voyelles*," Wen assigns a different color to each of the women
in Baudelaire's life. In a second article, "Baudelaire and Women," Wen
divides the women into two groups: "*l'amour de coeur*" [heart's love], and
"*l'amour de sens*" [sensual love], and then adds a third, "*l'amour d'esprit ou
d'imagination*" [spiritual or imagined love], to introduce the poem "*A une
passante*" ["To a Passerby"], which he translates in full.[13] These articles
appear in the publications of the Université franco-chinoise, and were

probably the work of students engaged in the then raging campaign for free love and free choice in marriage. They wrote with enthusiasm for, rather than disapproval of, Baudelaire's many amours.

Curiosity about Baudelaire's life, which threatened to overshadow appreciation for his writings, reached extreme expression in an article entitled "Pathology of Baudelaire," translated from Japanese by Zhang Chongwen. Taking a medical approach, it asserts that Baudelaire had congenital syphilis, inherited from his father. Drawing on letters and comments from Baudelaire's friends, the author traces his symptoms through many years, and then focuses on his final illness and death. The interest in the "pathology" of a writer long dead seems somewhat morbid. But in the context of free love, it can also be seen as an attempt to redeem Baudelaire's love life. If his syphilis was congenital, his many liaisons should not be held responsible for infecting him with it. [14]

As Wang Weike had suggested a few years earlier in 1931 that while Musset was "the poet for youth," Baudelaire is "the poet for the old; we must live a long time, think a long time, and think a lot, before we can understand him." [15] Perhaps this is one reason for young critics to write on his life rather than on his work.

The brief biography accompanying Chen Jingrong's 1957 translations takes a completely different focus. Whereas earlier biographers had stressed the love for art and the aristocratic manners of Baudelaire's father, Chen describes him simply as an artisan (*gongyi huajia* 工藝畫家). Ignoring Baudelaire's early extravagance and dandyism, Chen declares him "penniless and frustrated all his life" (*yisheng qiongchou liaodao* 一生窮愁潦倒). His role in the 1848 revolution was brief, Chen explains, because the newspaper for which he was working, *Le Salut public*, closed in two days due to a lack of funds. Conceding that Baudelaire's life was undisciplined (*sanman* 散漫), Chen redeems him by declaring that "when he labored (*laodong* 勞動), he was very intense; the word 'labor' (*laodong* 勞動) often appears in his poetry; it was not simply an abstraction for him." Whereas earlier critics had emphasized the slimness of Baudelaire's output, Chen praises his overall productivity, pointing out that "when he died in Paris from illness at the age of forty-six after more than twenty years of creative life, he had written the thick volume of *Les Fleurs du mal*, a volume of prose poems, many essays on literature and art, as well as a collection of selections from Edgar Allan Poe that became a model of translation." Writing at a delicate time in Chinese history when workers, *"laodong renmin"* 勞動人民 [laboring people], were glorified, Chen made Baudelaire a worthy member of their ranks by the volume of his production. [16]

For Guo Hong-an, writing in the post-Mao era, Baudelaire was a rebel against bourgeois morality. But that antibourgeois rebellion was doomed to failure, Guo judges, because it was aimed at the rebel's own class. Guo praises Baudelaire's "spiritual labor" (*jingshen laodong* 精神勞動) and "assiduous training" (*keku duanlian* 刻苦鍛煉), using vocabulary that in an earlier era would have referred to hard physical labor (*laodong* 勞動) and forging metal (*duanlian* 鍛煉), but is now accepted in the everyday senses of work and exercise. However, Guo avers, because Baudelaire could not deeply understand the large-scale suffering and struggles of the laboring masses, he was like someone trying to leave the world by pulling at his own hair. With a surprising change of context, Guo concludes that Baudelaire's efforts to escape the world were like turning somersaults on Buddha's palm.[17]

Baudelaire was not a revolutionary, his Chinese critics and biographers were quick to point out. In recasting an earlier article for publication in the People's Republic in 1980, Cheng Baoyi emphasizes this fact. He was a rebel, yes, against bourgeois morality, against his family, and against the pretentiousness and ugliness of society, but he was not a revolutionary. He fought in the street battles in 1848, but for the wrong reasons; his real revolution was in his work. Since he could not achieve revolution in his life full of contradictions, he achieved it in his poetry.[18] Decades earlier, no less a figure than Lu Xun had noted in his "Non-revolutionary's Radical Revolutionary Theorists," "Everyone knows France's Baudelaire is a decadent poet, yet he welcomed the revolution, until the revolution was going to harm his decadent way of life; then he hated the revolution."[19]

DECADENCE

"When Baudelaire is mentioned, the Chinese immediately think of the epithets 'decadent, morbid, demonic poet, etc.,' It seems he represents ugliness." Thus wrote Mo Yu in the 1980 article which demonstrates that Baudelaire is the French poet best received by the Chinese.[20]

The subject of Baudelaire's decadence was developed in numerous articles from the May Fourth era onward. Wen Tian's "Study of Baudelaire" represents most of the judgments on Baudelaire that would become commonplace in Chinese criticism for the next few decades, and supplies much of the vocabulary for those judgments. It is actually a translation of Frank Pearce Sturm's "Charles Baudelaire: A Study."[21]

"We used to hear a deal about Decadence in the arts . . . but Baudelaire *is* Decadence." With this declaration, Sturm takes a step further the judgment of Swinburne, Symons, and others of the time. He dilates on Baudelaire's use of opium and hashish, but deems Baudelaire "quite sincere in his perversion and his decadence." Finding Baudelaire's poetry "sinister . . . the apotheosis of the horrible and grotesque, the perfecting of symbols to shadow forth intellectual sin," Sturm nevertheless places it at "the root of modern French literature and much of the best of English literature."

If this exercise of moral judgment was congenial to the Chinese critics, reflecting as it does a long tradition in Chinese literary criticism that emphasized the moral function of literature (*wen yi zai dao* 文以載道 [literature is to convey the Way]), the more impressionistic comments would have been equally appealing: "His art is like the pearl, a beautiful product of disease, and to blame it is like blaming the pearl." Sturm's article was the more useful in including most of the best known comments on Baudelaire, including Poe's influence, Thierry's comparison of Baudelaire with Dante, and Barbey d'Aurevilly's retort that "Baudelaire came from hell; Dante only went there," as well as Hugo's remark to Baudelaire, "You have created a new shudder." Sturm's translation of Hugo's "frisson" as "shudder" rather than "thrill" again shows his emphasis on what he found perverse and sinister in Baudelaire.

Wen Tian's task in translating Sturm's long, convoluted sentences was no easy one. The article is at once a good source for the vocabulary of Baudelairean criticism: "decadent" is *"tuifei"* 頹廢, "symbolism" is *"biaoxiang"* 表象 or *"xiangzheng"* 象徵, and an example of how impossible it is to translate terms like "morbid," rendered as *"you bing"* 有病 [sick]; "sinister" as *"buxiang"* 不祥 [inauspicious]; and "perverse" as *"diandao"* 顛倒 [reversed, deranged]. Subtlety could be lost with the omission of a single word, such as the word "successful" in translating Sturm's judgment of *"Franciscae meae laudes"* [in praise of my Frances] as "one of the many successful steps in the wrong direction." These difficulties in translation often lent to the Chinese critical articles an air of stark overstatement.

"His brain was clouded with smoke; his blood seethed with liquor," judged Li Sichun, loosely quoting Verlaine.[22] In the brief introduction to Baudelaire that accompanies his selections from *Les Fleurs du Mal*, Li introduces Baudelaire as "the main force of 'Décadence' [sic] and 'Symbolism.'" For Li, Baudelaire "described the truth of Parisian life from his deep observation of the sinful urban life of material wealth. He worshipped ugliness, praised evil, described barbarity, and sketched sweaty filth, all of which caused his readers to feel numbed, as if driven insane." "This suffices," Li concludes, "as an accurate critique of the collection *Les Fleurs du mal.*"[23]

"This 'Master of Decadence' (*tuifei dashi* 頹廢大師) should be forgotten," in 1934 Li Liewen 黎烈文 quoted "some people" (*you xie ren* 有些人) as having said. But for Li Liewen, Baudelaire's "style, sentiment, and harmonious music" redeem the Decadence represented by "melancholy, despair over human life and praise of death and evil."[24]

It was Baudelaire's love for death that led "some people" to call him Decadent, diabolic, or a Satan worshipper, wrote Qin Zihao in 1955. Qin posits that Baudelaire used opium as an escape from suffering caused by practical reality, and that his death was partly due to excessive use of opium, but that death was the only escape from the pain of life. Qin introduces "six tendencies of Decadence," drawing on Max Nordau for five: antiscientific, solipsistic, technical, impassible, and evil. He explains the "antiscientific tendency" as hatred of materialism and the mechanistic point of view and solipsism as "self-worship" (*ziwo chongbai* 自我崇拜). He finds the "technical tendency" in Baudelaire's praise of makeup. Impassibility, which he translates as "without feeling" (*wu ganjue* 無感覺), Qin explains as "the supremacy of art over social morality, religion, customs, systems, etc." The tendency to evil is for Qin "what the Decadents meant by Diabolism." To these Qin adds a sixth tendency: that toward ambiguity. When Naturalists write about the dark and ugly aspects of life, they present them as dark and ugly, but the Decadents contrarily present them as aesthetic (*meigan* 美感). Qin himself seems to associate Satan with death, thus completing the circle.[25]

The focus on death is emphasized in Yuan Changying's entry on Baudelaire in her 1944 survey of French literature:

> his only concept is death. . . . In love with death . . . his only feeling is death; everywhere, always, he thinks of death, sees death, wishes for death. . . . His concept of death is not abstract, but is represented by the flesh on a rotting corpse, visible, palpable, and smellable.

Yuan adds that "Baudelaire is especially sensitive to smell and tactile feeling; his poetry is full of smells and atmospheres that make the flesh crawl." His "main aim was to shock the bourgeoisie, and escape boredom through frightful ugliness."[26]

Decadence and fascination with death are deplored in Lu Yuehua's 1955 handbook *Nineteenth Century French Literature*:

> Baudelaire's misfortune is not solely, as most people believe, that he was deeply morbid and decadent by nature. . . . [H]is excessively acute intelligence stopped the free flow of his emotions, making us doubt the truth of those emotions today. . . . In his work *Les Fleurs du mal* the strange forms, extremely tragic emotions, erudite polish and new music were not sufficient to detach the poems from prose and to spare us from disappointment. It seems that the poet first wrote in prose, and then changed to verse. . . . Those who say he was not in his right mind are correct at least in the obvious characteristics of his thought and language.[27]

Lu's distaste for his subject must have prevented him from closer reading or further research. He is nearly alone in asserting that Baudelaire wrote his verse poems first in prose. Although other scholars may have questioned Baudelaire's state of mind, Lu is nearly alone in questioning the truth of his emotions. His aversion is further reflected in the idiosyncratic transcription for Baudelaire's name as *po-te-lai* 婆特來, which literally means "the crone-especially-comes."

Decadence famously was given a very different definition by Théophile Gautier, who called it "the most mature product of an ancient civilization." This much-quoted definition is taken up in an article by Lie

Weike (the Russian Wilhelm Levik) translated into Chinese by He Ru in
1957.[28] While Chen Jingrong in the same year had redeemed Baudelaire
as one of the workers of the world, He Ru, through Levik, emphasized
hatred of capitalism found in his art reviews. Indicating the same poems
that Chen had translated, He praised *"Crépuscule du matin"* ["Morning
Twilight"] and *"Crépuscule du soir"* ["Evening Twilight"] for their realism, and *"Le Cygne"* ["The Swan"] for showing sympathy for the oppressed. He quotes Gautier and Gorky's view that Baudelaire had lived
in an evil world, but had always aspired to the good and the beautiful.
Yet after carefully having defined decadence as synonymous with "elegant, exquisite, refined," the author seems to return to conventional definitions with the assertion that the nondecadent aspects in Baudelaire's
work are far more significant than the decadent parts.

The decadent, pessimistic, and morbid elements occupy only a small
part of *Les Fleurs du Mal*, according to Guo Hong-an, whose 1981 article
associates decadence with obscenity, abnormality, and immorality.
Drawing on Gorky, Guo states that Baudelaire lived in evil times, but he
loved the good; he did not deny the moral dimension of poetry, but
simply insisted on drawing moral lessons from evil rather than from
good.[29]

Decadence has a broader meaning for Cheng Baoyi, who applies it to
Baudelaire's work as a whole. Rather than a love for death or escape,
Cheng sees in Baudelaire's Decadence a pursuit of life. Taking drugs,
drinking wine, seeking carnal pleasure and longing for death are undeni-
ably decadent, Cheng allows, but Baudelaire also rejected superficial enjoyment and empty ideals; he wished to experience life in the raw, as an
artist. His decadence was part of a profound experience of life with all its
wounds, terrors, and desires. At first people noticed only the dissolute
aspects of Baudelaire's life, but now, a century later, Cheng avers, we see
through his letters, essays, art criticism, and poetry a farsighted, serious
artist.[30]

REDEMPTION

Although Baudelaire's reputation as a "decadent" was firmly established
by 1929, and although decadence was one of the "thirteen kinds of intol-
erable thoughts and ideas blacklisted by the Crescent Moon Society" in
their "rectification campaign,"[31] Baudelaire found a warm reception in
the pages of their journal. An enthusiastic introduction to Baudelaire's
prose poems was published in the *Crescent Monthly* in 1929 by the very
author of the "rectification" manifesto, Xu Zhimo.[32] In a panegyric rang-
ing from Shakespeare to Proust, Xu asserts that "like Flaubert and Walter
Pater, Baudelaire will evoke for posterity the solitary image of one who,
like the saints in the Middle Ages, seeks the light in the bitterness of self-

analysis." He calls Baudelaire "the penitent for the nineteenth century, just as Rousseau was for the eighteenth and Dante for the Middle Ages." This moral dimension, for Xu, is evident in Baudelaire's sympathy for the poor, and in certain passages from *"Les Veuves"* ["Widows"], *"Le Joujou du pauvre"* ["The Poor Boy's Toy"], and *"Les Yeux des pauvres"* ["The Eyes of the Poor"]. He cites in the original French a passage from *"Les Veuves,"* where Baudelaire observes that poor widows must scrimp even on mourning clothes, while the rich, by contrast, wear their mourning in elaborate suits. Xu instead translates the last line as "The rich also wear mourning in this way." By avoiding Baudelaire's irony, Xu strengthens his own conclusion: "They must scrimp even in mourning—can we think of a purer sympathy, a purer style?" and adds, *"This* is the author of *Les Fleurs du mal!"* Then, misquoting Ariel in English, Xu describes how in Baudelaire's hands things "suffer a sea change—into something beautiful and strange." Citing J. M. Murry's statement that Proust is the new sensibility of the twentieth century, Xu claims that each fresh discovery emphasizes the greatness of our forebears. Along with this sense of literary history, Xu also reveals the Chinese critic's predilection for fanciful, impressionistic judgments: Baudelaire's prose poems "have captured the perfume from orchids and phosphorescence from waves." They "have the freshness of flowers in a fairy kingdom, and of dewdrops, where the moon and stars hoard their light." "Before such genius," Xu finally demands, "how can we not be humble?" In this context, it is all the more surprising that the only poem from *Les Fleurs du mal* that Xu Zhimo translated in full should have been *"Une charogne,"* surely Baudelaire's most decadent poem, especially in the literal sense.

SYMBOLISM

Chinese critics who associated Baudelaire with Symbolism were less prone to moral judgment than those who saw him as Decadent. Welcoming the idea of progress in the arts, they presented Symbolism as a step forward from Romanticism and Parnassianism.

Liu Yanling's 1922 article "Symbolism and Free Verse in French Poetry" places Baudelaire between Parnassianism and Symbolism. He explains that Parnassians emphasized meticulous objective description without emotional involvement, exquisite craftsmanship approaching sculpture and painting, and rhythmic sonority. The Symbolists reacted against it, finding objective description inadequate for expressing the complexities of modern life, much less for expressing the human soul and spirit (*hunling yu jingshen* 魂靈與精神), those "treasure troves for the artist." Although *Les Fleurs du mal* retains the Parnassian characteristics of meticulous description, regularity of form, and sonority of tone, Baudelaire broke away from the Parnassians by his description of sentiments,

ugly and evil fantasies, selfish desires, and depression and disgust. For
Liu, Baudelaire having understood that sounds create feeling before
meaning comes through, also preceded the Symbolists in his preference
for sound to sight. In writing on free verse as providing freedom from
formal constraints, Liu nevertheless takes his examples from the highly
formal sonnet "*Correspondances.*" After introducing the major French
Symbolist poets, Liu ends with a plea for individual creation, to be dominated by no "ism." [33]

In the revival of the literary scene in Mainland China after the Maoist
era, Baudelaire reappeared in journal articles associated with Symbolism.
Yuan Kejia's 1985 article "Symbolist Poetry" also presents Baudelaire as a
forerunner of Symbolism, but sees the movement as a reaction against
Romanticism rather than against Parnassianism. Baudelaire's description
of the evils of society and human nature and his revelation of "every kind
of ugliness" in Paris, "that large city he called hell," represent for Yuan a
radical departure from the Romantics' hymns of praise for nature, naive
youth, and sacred love. Although there are few truly Symbolist poems in
Baudelaire's work, Yuan declares, he brought poetic art a step forward by
abandoning ornamentation, and by emphasizing analytical intellect, con-
creteness, and precision to express the "limitless ennui of modern man at
odds with society." [34]

The "Chinese Symbolists" had written on Baudelaire a few decades
earlier. Wang Duqing, a staunch advocate of French Symbolism, wrote in
1927 that in order to become real poets, the Chinese must learn from
Baudelaire, Verlaine, and Rimbaud, to write "pure poetry" (*chuncuide shi*
純粹的詩). [35] The Chinese Symbolists were eager to avow the influence of
French Symbolism in their work. Their relation to Baudelaire will be
explored in another chapter. Their own work would lead to a redefinition
of Symbolism for the Chinese situation.

MODERNISM

Les Fleurs du mal "is generally recognized as the first work of modern
French poetry," according to Cheng Baoyi. Quoting Rimbaud's naming
Baudelaire the first "*Voyant* [clairvoyant]," Cheng remarks that with this
one volume, Baudelaire "pushed French poetry into the modern sphere."
Baudelaire's poems do not seem modern in form—with his preference for
the sonnet, or for poems with four-line stanzas, and for even-numbered
syllables, and his never mixing masculine and feminine rhymes—Cheng
observes, but his diction and imagery are new, and produce a personal
style. Cheng recognizes strong elements of Romanticism in the poems,
but points out that these are not romantic imaginings and sad sighs, but
are founded on solid descriptions of real experience. Cheng also presents

Baudelaire as the poet of Paris, and goes on to describe both the beauty and ugliness of that city in a passage worthy of his subject.[36]

Whereas Cheng Baoyi uses the term "*xiandai*" 現代 for "modern," Mu Mutian, in his *History of French Literature*, uses the term "*jindai*" 近代, perhaps borrowed from his Japanese sources.[37] Mu locates Baudelaire's modernity in the contradictions and assimilation of three tendencies, as pointed out by Paul Bourget: the crisis of religious belief, Parisian life, and the modern scientific spirit. It was this conflict and resolution that led Baudelaire to love what is hazy or obscure in nature (*ziran zhong de menglong* 自然中的朦朧), according to Mu, who pursued the same quality in his own poetry.

In an article published in 1984 on "French Modernist Literature," Luo Dagang reports consulting with a French professor specializing in nine-teenth-century French literature, Professor Henri Behard (Béhar), from whom he learned that there was no school of "*modernisme*" (*xiandai pai* 現代派) in French literature, and that French literary critics preferred the term "*modernité*," which he explains as "*xiandai xing huo xiandai tese*" 現代性或現代特色 [modernity or modern characteristics]. Yet, he points out, many critics inside and outside of France name Baudelaire as the first Modernist (*xiandai pai de chuangshiren* 現代派的創始人 [founder of modernism]). Chronologically, Luo points out, Baudelaire stood between the Parnassians and the Symbolists, but he was neither Parnassian nor Symbolist. Baudelaire's work for Luo forms a bridge between Classic and Modern. "Before Mallarmé, Rimbaud, and Verlaine, and before Moréas's *Manifesto of Symbolism* (1866)," Luo reminds us, "the third line in '*Correspondances*' had already set forth what many critics see as the source of Symbolism." He illustrates this with the line in French and Chinese: "*L'homme y passe à travers des forêts de symboles* (*ren zai nali tongguo xiangzhengde senlin*" 人在那里通過象徵的森林 [man there passes through symbol's forest]). What distinguishes Baudelaire from the Classics, according to Luo, are his dissatisfaction with social realities and his tragic view of life. In his art, the imagery, atmosphere, rhythm, melody, lack of inhibition, and intense emotion all differ from Classicism. Yet, Luo argues, Baudelaire cannot be said to be the first Modern. After all, Villon was "Modern" and "avant-garde" in his time, the fifteenth century. Thus Luo undermines the idea of modernity as a step forward from Symbolism.[38]

Interest in Modernism and modernity continues to draw scholars and critics to Baudelaire. In recent decades his art criticism, which has contributed to the definitions of modernity, also has drawn attention from Chinese critics and scholars.

COMPARATIVE CRITICISM

Chinese scholars, critics, and poets, in their introductions to Baudelaire, overcame tremendous difficulties in translating both linguistic and cultural notions, to bring European ideas and poetics into China. Notwithstanding the comparative acts necessary to achieve this, their view remained primarily Eurocentric, and they made no overt attempts at comparison. This was not the case with three poet critics: Tian Han, Hu Pinqing, and Liang Zongdai, who all brought their analyses into a Chinese context.

Tian Han (田漢 *1898–1968*)

Tian Han, a well-known poet and dramatist and founder of the Creation Society, takes a comparative approach to Baudelaire's "Satanism" in his 1921 two-part article "Centenary of the Demonic Poet Baudelaire."[39] Tian begins the first part with a few lines from Swinburne's "*Ave atque vale* " ["Hail and Farewell"] offered in English without translation, and proceeds to a brief biography that includes "*La Vie antérieure* " ["Past Life"] quoted entirely in French (though with one line unfortunately missing), again without translation. He quotes F. P. Sturm's comments on Baudelaire's use of opium and hashish, and ends with the first quatrain of "*Le Mort joyeux* " ["The Gladly Dead"], which title is mistranslated "*Si zhi huanxi*" 死之歡喜 ["The Joy of Death"]. In the second part of the article, Tian Han is more careful about translating his quotations into Chinese, including Nordau's "Degeneration" and De Quincy's description of the effects of opium. He quotes in full the sonnet "*Correspondances*" in French followed by his own translation, and although he presents the sonnet as having been made under the influence of hashish, he declares its importance for the study of Modernism (given in English and translated "*jindai zhuyi*" 近代主義) as well as "Decadent Symbolism" (in English and translated "*likadan xiangzheng zhuyi* " 醴卡妖象徵主義). Tian Han's transliterations may have been based on Japanese, and were not adopted by other critics.

What makes Tian Han's article interesting, however, is that it is cast in the context of the choice between God and Satan. Asking whether such a choice is really necessary, he suggests that the answer lies in Mahayana Buddhism and the *koan* "If you see the Buddha, kill the Buddha." Tian posits that both Christ and Buddha can be killed if they carry the ropes of bondage; by the same token, those who preach Satanism might also be tyrants who wish to exchange one violence for another; thus Satan must also be killed, for the goal of the artists is to reach that untrammeled state (*zizai jingdi* 自在境地) where he is like a marionette with its strings severed; where he is bound neither to Christ nor to Buddha, nor to Satan; only then can he create the art of the Greater Vehicle. According to Tian

Han, revolt is the key. When Christ "killed" the "devil of polytheism," that was revolt. Christ then set himself in its place for over 1800 years, until Baudelaire publicly raised the sound of revolt; thus Baudelaire's Satanism has life; those who study it should not fall into the Lesser Vehicle. Tian gives particular attention to the section "Révolte" in *Les Fleurs du mal*, quoting and translating at length from the three poems therein, and explaining their source in the Bible. He ends with a discussion of the "artist's religion," citing *"Hymne à la Beauté"* with a complete translation. In finding this aesthetic solution to the question of religion, Tian rejoins many Western critics, but places the question in a Buddhist rather than Christian context.

Hu Pinqing (胡品清 1920–2006)

Hu Pinqing, in an article accompanying her translations, examines *Les Fleurs du mal* from the point of view of a Chinese reader of poetry in her own tradition. The poems, she declares, are new, original, and forceful, especially for readers accustomed to the "tender, soft, honest, sincere" (*wenrou dunhou* 溫柔敦厚) tradition of Chinese poetry. Baudelaire's "cursing and reviling" (*zuzhou tuoma* 詛咒唾罵) are the antithesis of the "delicacy and gentleness" (*xianli wanyue* 纖麗婉約) of traditional poetry. But Baudelaire also has two points of similarity with Chinese poets: both aspire to the highest realms or sublime beauty, and both use the symbol. Hu points out that the symbol has been an important part of Chinese poetry from the earliest times of the *Classic of Poetry* (*Shi Jing* 詩經), and asserts that both for Chinese poets and for Baudelaire, poetry is almost a religious revelation. In terms of modern Chinese poetry, Hu Pinqing, quoting one of Hu Shi's "Eight Don'ts," "Don't groan without being sick," concludes that *Les Fleurs du mal* is most praiseworthy for its expression of reality. Baudelaire's sufferings are real; he is a sacrifice to evil, a man eaten by suffering, and he is our brother. Thus he speaks a universal, eternal language.[40]

In a French language work *Les Fleurs du mal: Une autobiographie en vers* [*Flowers of Evil: An Autobiography in Verse*], Hu Pinqing offers a similar analysis. There, she generalizes more about Chinese poetry, stating that it is essentially preoccupied with the moral and the social, so that it ignores psychology, rigorous thought, and character analysis; it is basically concrete, and ignores the metaphysical. She finds the Classical Chinese poets lacking in imagination, originality, and precision, and their corpora lacking in real love poems. If Chinese poems sometimes develop tableaux of grandeur, they exclude fanaticism, cynicism, furor, and virulence. Such poems as *"Le Mort joyeux"* ["The Gladly Dead"] and *"Le Vin de l'assassin"* ["Murderer's Wine"] could never have been written by a Chinese poet, and *"Bénédiction"* ["Benediction"] is a flagrant violation of filial piety. The Chinese poet does not shock, but expresses himself with sensibility, restraint, and infinite delicacy. He has neither the courage to curse, nor the presumption to consider himself godlike. All this is in clear contrast to Baudelaire's crude realism, sentimental excess, cruel condemnations, powerful imprecations and incantations, and the originality of his images, which transport Hu, as the reader, "to an unknown horizon," to feel the "new shudder."

Hu Pinqing points out parallels between Baudelaire and traditional Chinese poets going beyond concision of expression and use of the symbol. There are, Hu concedes, Chinese poets who do not set themselves to moralizing, but write to evoke a memory, to fix a fugitive sentiment, to eternalize an unforgettable moment; they write for the pleasure of writing, to soothe their anguish, to paint themselves. These she finds akin to Baudelaire. Again quoting Hu Shi's call for sincerity in poetry, Hu lauds *Les Fleurs du mal* for being an autobiography: each of the lines is an evocation of a life intensely lived. Baudelaire is not only a tormented spirit, an afflicted soul, a victim of sin laid low by misfortune, deception, bitterness, furor, hate, remorse, and vain aspiration to higher things, but also a spiritual brother who speaks a sincere, universal, and eternal language for himself and for us all.[41]

Liang Zongdai (梁宗岱 1903–1983)

Liang Zongdai places Baudelaire at the center of an article entitled "Symbolism," and offers examples from poetry Chinese and Western, ancient and modern, in an attempt to define the term.[42] A good poem can be produced through the symbol, Liang proposes, and a symbol is produced when "scene" (*jing* 景) matches "emotion" (*qing* 情); when the subject observes the object, and can say, "There is emotion in the scene, and scene in the emotion." But to reach the "higher realm" of Symbolism requires that the poem is one of which one can say "The emotion *is* the scene, and the scene *is* the emotion;" that is, subject and object must dissolve into one. Drawing on the Six Dynasties poets Xie Lingyun (謝靈運 385–433) and Tao Qian (陶潛 365–427), Liang finds the two basic characteristics of Symbolism to be "harmonious or continuous" (*ronghe huo wujian* 融合或無間), and "implicit or infinite" (*hanxu huo wuxian* 含蓄或無限). The symbol grasps the infinite in the finite, eternity in the moment, dream in reality; it expresses and implies not an insipid abstract concept, but an abundant, complex, profound, spiritual world. The Way of the Symbol (*xiangzheng zhi dao* 象徵之道), according to Liang, can be summed up in one word: "*qihe* 契合."

"*Qihe* 契合" is Liang's translation for the title of Baudelaire's sonnet "*Correspondances*," which he offers in both French and Chinese. For Liang, Baudelaire has fathomed a truth that permits him to "shake hands across the centuries" with Leibniz: "Life is a great harmony. No two leaves on a tree are alike." To explain, Liang paraphrases Baudelaire: "the living pillars in the temple or the forest of symbols at all times emit sounds and echoes—all the colors, perfumes, sounds" and shadows melt into one inseparable, eternal, creative transformation; not a single leaf can fall without sending forth growing ripples, like a drop of water in the ocean. But in the great chain, we forget that we are only links. Only people who are drunk—(again paraphrasing Baudelaire) on wine, on virtue, or on poetry, as you will—can glimpse in a joyous, carefree moment this tenebrous and profound world of harmony. This he finds in lines by the Northern Song Dynasty poet Lin Hejing (林和靖 927–1028):

> *Shuying hengxie shui qingqian*
> *Anxiang fudong yue huanghun*
> 疏影橫斜水清淺
> 暗香浮動月黃昏

[Dappled shade slants across the shallow stream / Dark perfume drifts under the moon at dusk]

where the poet is enraptured in the bosom of nature, or in Li Bo's lines:

> *sanbei tong dadao*
> *yidou he ziran*
> 三杯通大道
> 一斗合自然

[With three cups one knows the way / With a pint one becomes one with nature.]

which have a "meaning beyond words." Liang rejects the psychological explanation of losing inhibitions through drink to find that "material things (e.g., a bell-shaped flower), dreams and trances" can also take us to that "world without 'I'" where the subject, "I," and the object, "the thing known," are indistinguishable. In order to reach this stage, we must give up action, give up knowledge, and gradually sink into a vague, unconscious, almost empty realm (*jingjie* 境界) where our spirit is so quiet that we no longer feel our own body. Just as a fruit cannot be formed until all the petals have fallen from a flower, so we must let go before we can attain the greater life; we must forget our own existence before we can obtain a more real existence. Here he paraphrases Lao Zi: "Wishing to obtain it, one must first give it" (*jiang yu qu zhi, bi xian yu zhi* 將欲取之，必先與之).[43] As he describes how "in this elusive moment, where there is no obstruction or interruption in our being in complete communion with nature, there is a kind of sympathetic rhythm which transcends spirit and flesh, dream and waking, life and death, past and future; we are at one with the universe, and the universe is entirely within us," he comes back to Baudelaire.

In *Les Paradis artificiels* [*Artificial Paradises*] Baudelaire describes how, under the influence of hashish, the poet first projects onto a tree his own desires, passions, or moods, then becomes the tree; or where at first the bird only represents the desire to fly, but subsequently the poet becomes the bird.[44] We must not think, Liang warns us, that this is mental confusion; just as the correspondences of colors, perfumes, and sounds come from our senses reaching their utmost acuity, the same correspondences will bring us to that world of drunkenness and dream, where imagination roams and things are revealed, where we will not only be at one with nature (*yu wanhua minghe* 與萬化冥合), but know, and comprehend, that we have become one with nature. Therefore, Liang concludes, all the best poems will remind us of the two kinds of response expressed in Baudelaire's line: "*chantent les transports de l'esprit et des sens*" [sing the transport of the spirit and the senses]; that is to say, the drunkenness that comes from shedding the body, and the deep awaking that will be everlasting. He finds examples in Goethe's "*Über allen Gipfeln*" ["Over All the Hilltops"] and Basho's famous *haiku* of the frog jumping into the water. Likening the moment of awakening to "returning home," Liang then offers a rhapsody of words, ideas, feelings, and images, some his own and some borrowed, to illustrate this harmony of the universe, which is found "not only in flowers, streams, stars, moon, skylarks, and nightingales, but in a field mouse, a pile of compost, a potsherd," (Zhuangzi's examples of where to find the Tao), that is, in all the smallest, lowliest, most decadent, and even most obscene things. Liang then freely roams back to the West, quoting Blake's "To see a world in a grain of sand . . . eternity in an hour," and Valéry's "*Tout l'univers chancelle et tremble sur sa tige*" [The whole universe totters and trembles on its stem], he finds that they reveal "the same profound and mystical truth" (using here the Taoist term *xuan-ji* 玄機).

Liang further explains that, just as the task of our senses is not solely to tell us to avoid harm in order to protect our fleshly body, but primarily to come into contact with the world of sound, color, light, and perfume in order to cleanse, nourish, and please our souls, so things in the external world coming into contact with us, and vice versa, also have two aspects: when we use our reason or will to analyze or direct them, they are only countless, unconnected, uninteresting, lifeless things, but when we release our reason and will, and entrust ourselves completely to the basic nature of things, letting our imaginations enter the object, and letting the great breath of the universe penetrate our spirits, then two similar lives, in an accidental meeting, in that instant, will reach a tacit understanding and smile. He presents examples of this from Goethe's *Faust*, in Zhuang Zi's dream of the butterfly, from Dante's *Commedia*, and again, from Baudelaire, ending with a paean to the French poet:

> From the point of view of theme, nothing is more incidental, perishable, sometimes—how shall I say it? so ugly and obscene—as the majority of poems in Baudelaire's *Les Fleurs du mal*. But not one poem among them fails to achieve an inner, familiar, imperishable greatness.

Whether it is a bent, crippled old woman, a murderer dripping with fresh blood, two prostitutes caressing each other lasciviously, a corpse suppurating with stinking filth, flies roaring, and worms and maggots swarming, once it passes through his sonorous, sad voice, none fails to emit a strong, gloomy, serious, sadly beautiful, or pure radiance, spreading in our souls a "new thrill"—in that thrill, we are almost walking again the entire course of Dante's *Commedia*, from hell through the Pure Land to Heaven. Because at the end of each of Baudelaire's poems, what we discover is no longer an incidental or instantaneous spiritual world, but an urgent call to eternity for help from a broken, suffering soul, and, relying on the crystallization of this call, to fly up to that creative universe where everything is happy, and breathing is clear and free; where stinking decay is transformed into the miraculous; the low becomes high, the contradictory becomes consistent, the discordant becomes harmonious, the imperfect becomes perfect, the ineffable becomes accomplished.

For Liang, the effect of Baudelaire's poetry seems to combine ascension to heaven with *satori*.[45] His exaggeration notwithstanding, Liang's juxtaposition of the Western and Chinese traditions considerably broadened the scope of Baudelairean criticism in China.

A Mystical Reading

In an article published in 1993, "L'Itinéraire baudelairien à la lumière du *Yi-king*," Lee Seong-Bok uses the sixty-four hexagrams in Chinese classic *I Ching* (*Yijing* 易經) to read *Les Fleurs du mal* and the *Petits Poèmes en prose*.[46] The hexagrams are built from trigrams, which are composed of three broken and unbroken lines, in the eight possible combinations; the broken and unbroken lines in turn represent the *yin-yang* duality. Lee justifies his method by pointing out the "irreducible duality" in Baudelaire's work, opposing the eternal, absolute, and invariable to the transitory, relative, and variable, as well as the real as opposed to the imaginary and mysterious. Lee proceeds to take images and phrases from Baudelaire's poetry and match them up with hexagrams from the *I Ching* (*Yijing* 易經). To an extent, Lee's study is an exercise in exoticism and mystification. The *I-Ching*, often used in fortune-telling and in feng shui siting, is extremely cryptic and open to myriad interpretations. Lee is serious, however. He had earlier presented a thesis interpreting the poetry of Gérard de Nerval using his *Yijing* method at the National University of Seoul; the *Yijing* had been introduced to Korea along with Confucianism, he explains, and was much studied during the Yi Dynasty (1392–1910).[47]

Other Comparisons

Baudelaire has also been the subject of comparison with individual Chinese writers, and specific poems from both *Les Fleurs du mal* and *Petits Poèmes en prose* have been compared with specific Chinese poems. Most of these comparisons assert influence rather than simply posing parallels. As Yuan Hao-yi pointed out in 1983:

> In the eyes of some foreign scholars, influence studies are not as attractive as parallel studies. In the comparative literature of China, however, influence studies have been the main force in the last few years.[48]

Similarly, an anthology of essays published in 1985 bears the English subtitle "The Influence of Foreign Literature upon the Modern Chinese Writers."[49] Modern Chinese poets have been willing to acknowledge influence from abroad openly and readily. These comparisons and assertions of influence will form the basis of discussion in the following chapters.

NOTES

1. Li Liewen 黎烈文, "Sanwen shichao" 散文詩抄 ["Selected Prose Poems"], *Yiwen* 譯文 1, no. 2 (Oct. 1934): 133; Liang Zongdai, *Shi yu zhen* [*Poetry and Truth*] (Shanghai: Shangwu, 1935–1936), 7; Mo Yu, "'Qiuge' yu. . ." 140.

2. Yuzhi 愉之, "Jindai Faguo wenxue gaiguan"近代法國文學概觀 ["Conspectus of Recent French Literature"], *Dongfang zazhi* 東方雜志, 18, no. 3 (1921): 72–73.

3. Li Huang 李璜 "Fa-lan-xi shi zhi gelü ji qi jiefang" 法蘭西詩之格律及其解放 ["French Poetry's Prosody and Its Liberation"], *Shaonian Zhongguo* 少年中國 2, no. 12 (June 1921): 1–9; Liu Yanling 劉延陵, "Faguo shi zhi xiangzheng zhuyi yu ziyou shi" 法國詩之象徵主義與自由詩 ["French Poetry's Symbolism and Free Verse"], *Shi* 詩 1, no. 4 (Apr. 1922); repr. in Sun Langgong 孫俍工, ed., *Xin wenyi pinglun* 新文藝評論 [*Comments on New Literature and Art*] (Shanghai: Zhimin shudian, 1923), 123–25.

4. "Faguo wenxue yanjiu" 法國文學研究 ["French Literature Study"], *Xiaoshuo yuebao* 小說月報 (Subtitle in English: *Short Story Monthly*) 13 haowai 號外 [supplement], (1922).

5. Zheng Zhenduo 鄭振鐸, *Wenxue dagang* 文學大綱 [*Outline of Literature*] (Shanghai: Shangwu yinshuguan, 1927), 4:233–34.

6. Yuan Changying 袁昌英, *Faguo wenxue* 法國文學 [*French Literature*] (Chongqing: Shangwu, 1944), 92.

7. Mu Mutian 穆木天, *Faguo wenxue shi* 法國文學史 [*French Literary History*] (Shanghai: Shijie shuju, 1935), 326–28.

8. Zheng, *Wenxue dagang*, 233.

9. Xu Xiacun 徐霞村, *Faguo wenxuede gushi* 法國文學的故事 [*French Literature's Story*] (Taipei: Shangwu 商務, 1947; preface dated 1942), 130–31.

10. Ge Xianning 葛賢寧 and Shangguan Yu 上官予, *Wushi nianlaide Zhongguo shige* 五十年來的中國詩歌 [*Chinese Poetry in the Last Fifty Years*] (Taipei: Zhengzhong shuju 正中書局, 1965), 58; Wang Zhijian 王志健, *Xiandai Zhongguo shi shi* 現代中國詩史 [*Modern Chinese Poetry History*], (Taipei: Taiwan shangwu yinshuguan, 1975), 183–84. If these two works are similar, it is because Shangguan Yu is Wang Zhijian's pen name.

11. Zong Lin 宗臨, "Chali Bodelai'er" 查理波得萊爾 ["Charles Baudelaire"], *Zhong-Fa Daxue yuekan* 中法大學月刊, 4, no. 2 (Dec. 1933): 111–42.

12. Wen Zheng 文錚, "Bodelai zhi beiju" 波德萊之悲劇 ["Baudelaire's Tragedy"], *Xiandai pinglun* 現代評論 7, no. 159 (1927): 51–55.

13. Shen Baoji 沈寶基, "Baotelai'erde aiqing shenghuo" 鮑特萊的愛情生活 ["Baudelaire's Love Life"], *Zhongfa Daxue yuekan* 中法大學月刊, 3, nos. 2–3 (Sept. 1933): 159–87 and 3, nos.4–5 (Oct. 1933): 181–98. Wen Jiasi 聞家駟, "Bodelai'er—jizhong yanse butongde ai" 波德萊兒—幾種顏色不同的愛 ["Baudelaire—a Few Different Colored Loves"], *Xue Wen* 學文 1, no. 3 (July 1934): 82–90; Wen Jiasi 聞家駟, "Bodelai'er yu nüren" 波德萊兒與女人 ["Baudelaire and Women"], *Xue Wen* 學文 1, no. 4 (Aug. 1934): 111–22.

14. Zhang Chongwen 張崇文, trans., "Botelai'er de binglixue" 波特萊爾的病理學 ["Baudelaire's Pathology"], *Xiandai* 現代 4, no. 6 (1934): 1055–60.

15. Wang Weike 王維克, "Emo shiren Botelai'er"惡魔詩人波特萊爾 ["Demonic Poet Baudelaire"], *Xiaoshuo yuebao* 小說月報 (*Short Story Monthly*) 22, no. 1 (1931): 84.

16. Chen Jingrong 陳敬容, "E zhi hua (xuanyi)" 惡之花 (選譯) [*Flowers of Evil* (Selected Translations)], *Yiwen* 譯文 7 (1957): 133.

17. Guo Hong-an 郭宏安, "Lun 'E zhi hua'" 論《惡之花》["On *Flowers of Evil*], *Waiguo wenxue yanjiu jikan* 外國文學研究集刊 8 (Jan. 1984): 51–98, and 9 (July 1984): 355–91.

18. Cheng Baoyi程抱一, "Lun Bodelaier" 論波德萊爾 ["On Baudelaire"], *Waiguo wenxue yanjiu* 外國文學研究 1 (1980): 58–63. According to the preface, the article was obtained from the author on a visit to France by Xu Chi 徐遲 (1914–1916), the journal's chief editor and a poet in his own right. In the translations accompanying the article, "*Le Soleil*" and "*Une Charogne*" from the earlier version are replaced by "*Spleen*," "*Le Chat*," "*L'Homme et la mer*," and the last part of "*La Mort*."

19. Lu Xun 魯迅, "Fei geming de jijin geminglunzhe" 非革命的急進革命論者 ["Nonrevolutionary Radical Revolutionary Theorists], *Er xin ji* 二心集, quoted in Sun Yushi 孫玉石, *Yecao Yanjiu* 野草研究 [*Study of Wild Grass*] (Beijing: Zhongguo shehui kexue chubanshe, 1982), 207.

20. Mo Yu, "'Qiuge yu. . .'" 140.

21. Wen Tian 聞天, trans., "Botelai'er yanjiu: Shidumu zhu" 波特來耳研究:史篤姆著 ["Study of Baudelaire Written by Sturm"], *Xiaoshuo yuebao* 小說月報, 13, suppl. 號外 (1922): 5–20. From Frank Pearce Sturm's "Charles Baudelaire: A Study," written in 1905 as an introduction to his selection and translation from *Les Fleurs du mal*. For the original, see Frank Pearce Sturm, *The Poems of Charles Baudelaire Selected and Translated from the French, with an Introductory Study*, in *Frank P. Sturm: His Life, Letters, and Collected Work*, ed. Richard Taylor (Urbana: University of Illinois Press, 1969), 215–34.

22. Verlaine's original remark "*son cerveau saturé de tabac, son sang brûlé d'alcool*" [his brain saturated with tobacco, his blood burnt with alcohol], actually referred to *l'homme moderne* [the modern man] who is Baudelaire's reader, rather than to the poet himself. See: Paul Verlaine, "Charles Baudelaire," *Oeuvres posthumes* II (Paris: Albert Messein, 1913), 9.

23. Li Sichun, "*Xian he ji*," 48.

24. Li Liewen 黎烈文, "Sanwen shichao" 散文詩抄, *Yiwen* 譯文 1, no. 2 (Oct. 1934): 133.

25. Qin Zihao 覃子豪, "Botelai'erde tuifei zhuyi ji qi zuopin" 波特萊爾的頹廢主義 及其作品 ["Baudelaire's Decadence and His Work"], in his *Quanji* 覃子豪全集 [*Collected Works*], 2:576–80.

26. Yuan Changying 袁昌英, *Faguo wenxue* 法國文學 [*French Literature*] (1944, repr. Shanghai: Shangwu 商務, 1946), 92.

27. Lu Yuehua 盧月化, "Po-te-lai" 婆特來 ["Baudelaire"], *Shijiu shiji faguo wenxue* 十九世紀法國文學 [*Nineteenth Century French Literature*] (Taipei: Zhonghua wenhua chubanshe, 1955), 2:339–41. Lu Yuehua was a professor in the highly prestigious Foreign Literatures Department of Taiwan National University.

28. He Ru 何如, trans., Lie Weike (Sulian), "Botelai'er he tade 'E zhi hua'" 列維克 (蘇聯), 波特萊爾和他的《惡之花》 ["Levik, (Soviet Union), Baudelaire and his *Flowers of Evil*"], *Yiwen* 譯文 (1957): 162–66. Wilhelm (or Vilgelm) Levik (1907–1982) translated

selections from Baudelaire into Russian, and cited translations of Iakobouvitch-Mel-chine. On this subject see Efrim Etkind, "Baudelaire en langue russe," *Europe*, 456–57 (1967): 252–61, and Adrian Wanner, *Baudelaire in Russia* (Gainesville: University Press of Florida, 1996), 48.

29. Jin Dequan, Shi Kangqiang, and Guo Hong-an 金德全，施康強，郭宏安, "Lun Miaosai, Gedi'ai he Botelai'er" 論繆塞，戈帝埃，和波特萊爾 ["On Musset, Gautier, and Baudelaire"] (three articles by three authors published as one). *Waiguo wenxue yanjiu jikan* 外國文學研究集刊 3 (1981): 57–102. Guo on Baudelaire, 84–102.

30. Cheng Baoyi, *He Ya Ding tan Faguo shi*, 4–5.

31. See Constantine Tung, *The Crescent Moon Society: The Minority's Challenge in the Literary Movement of Modern China*, Council on International Studies, Special Studies No. 11 (Buffalo: State University of New York, 1972), 11.

32. Xu Zhimo 徐志摩, "Bo-te-lai de sanwen shi" 波特萊的散文詩, *Xinyue* 新月 2, no. 10 (10 Dec. 1929); repr. in *Xu Zhimo Quanji* 徐志摩全集 [*Complete Works of Xu Zhimo*], ed. Jiang Fucong 蔣復聰 and Liang Shih-chiu 梁實秋 (Taipei: Zhuanji wenxue chuban-she, 1969), 6:403–7.

33. Liu Yanling 劉延陵, "Faguo shi zhi xiangzheng zhuyi yu ziyou shi" 法國詩之象徵主義與自由詩, *Shi* 詩 1, no. 4 (15 Apr. 1922); repr. in Sun Langgong 孫俍工, ed. *Xin wenyi pinglun* 新文藝評論 (Shanghai: Zhimin shuju, 1923), 121–34. Liu Yanling (1894–1988) was also a poet, and wrote on English literature. For a discussion in English of his comments on Symbolism see Michel Hockx, *A Snowy Morning: Eight Chinese Poets on the Road to Modernity* (Leiden: Research School Centre of Non-Western Studies, 1995), 153–63.

34. Yuan Kejia 袁可嘉, "Xiangzheng zhuyi shige" 象徵主義詩歌, *Waiguo wenxue yanjiu* 外國文學研究 3 (25 Sept. 1985): 90–97 and 4 (25 Dec. 1985): 3–13. Yuan Kejia 1921–2008) was a poet of the "Nine Leaves" 九葉 group. He mainly studied English and American literature; for this article he relied on Dai Wangshu's translations of *Les Fleurs du Mal* and of Valéry's article.

35. Wang Duqing 王獨清, "Zai Tan Shi" 再談詩, *Chuangzao yuekan* 創造月刊 1, no. 1 (Mar. 1926): 5–6.

36. Cheng Baoyi, *He Ya Dingtan Faguo shi*, 4–5.

37. Mu Mutian, *History*, 327.

38. Luo Dagang 羅大岡, "Guanyu Faguo xiandaipai wenxue de jidian chubu ren-shi" 關于法國現代派文學的幾點初步認識 ["Regarding French Modernist Literature: A Few Points of Preliminary Acquaintance"], *Waiguo wenxue yanjiu*外國文學研究 1 (24 Mar. 1984): 8–12.

39. Tian Han 田漢, "E-mo shiren botuolei'er de bainian ji" 惡魔詩人波陀雷爾的百年祭 ["Demonic Poet Baudelaire's Centenary"], *Shaonian Zhongguo* 少年中國 3, no. 4 (Nov. 1921): 1–6 and 3, no. 5 (Dec. 1921): 17–32.

40. Hu Pinqing, *Hu Pinqing yi shi yu xinshi xuan* 胡品清 譯詩與新詩選 [*Hu Pinqing Translated Poems and New Poems Selection*], (Taipei: Zhongguo wenhua chuban shiye she, 1962), 19–40.

41. Hu Pinqing 胡品清, *E zhi hua pingxi* 惡之花評析: *Les Fleurs du mal: Une autobio-graphie en vers* [*Analysis of Flowers of Evil: An Autobiography in Verse*] (Taipei: Zhongguo wenhua daxue chubanshe, 1981), 63–70.

42. Liang Zongdai 梁宗岱, "Xiangzheng zhuyi" 象徵主義 ["Symbolism"], *Wenxue jikan*, 文學季刊 2 (Apr. 1934): 15–25; also Liang's *Shi yu zhen* 詩與真 [Poetry and Truth—from "Dichtung und Wahrheit"], (Shanghai: Shangwu 商務, 1935, 1936), 88–91.

43. Compare chapter 36 of the *Tao Te Ching* (*Dao De Jing* 道德經): 將欲取之，必固與之.

44. See *OC* 419–20.

45. Frederick Mote, *Intellectual Foundations of China* (New York: Alfred A. Knopf, 1971), 78, distinguishes Taoist mysticism from religious mysticism, explaining that the sensory quality of religious mysticism is diminished to nothingness in Taoist mysti-cism.

46. Seong-Bok Lee, "L'Itinéraire baudelairien à la lumière du Yi-King" [Baudelaire's Itinerary in the Light of the *Yijing*], *Travaux de Littérature* 6 (1993): 263–83. The best known translation of the *Yijing* is *The I Ching or Book of Changes* (the Richard Wilhelm Translation rendered into English by Cary F. Baynes), Bollingen Series XIX (1950; Princeton, NJ: Princeton University Press, 1978).

47. Seong-Bok Lee, "L'Itinéraire baudelairien," 263.

48. Yuan Haoyi, "Survey of Current Developments in the Comparative Literature of China," *Cowrie: A Chinese Journal of Comparative Literature* 1, no. 1 (1983): 90.

49. Zeng Xiaoyi, *Zouxiang Shijie Wenxue*, 323–542.

Part II

The Creative Response

In the reception of Baudelaire in China, many poets responded to his work in their own poetry. Some made direct reference to or quoted lines from his works. Some claimed direct influence, and explored similar themes, forms, or imagery. Some were associated with Baudelaire by contemporary critics. Some read Baudelaire's work in French; some read selections in French, or in English, Japanese, or Chinese translation; some seem to have known his work only through conversation and reputation. The purpose here is not to assess the depth of Chinese knowledge of Baudelaire, nor is it to redraw a map of misreading. Instead, the aim is to show the richness and variety of poetic exchange and conversation among those who were interested in Western literature in China in the twentieth century.

In the chapters that follow, writers are grouped by their relation to Baudelaire. Again, the groups overlap and the divisions are perforce arbitrary. This study does not insist on definitions of "Decadents," "Symbolists," and "Modernists," but adopts the terms as applied by previous critics to the writers under consideration. In all cases, the focus is on specific poems by individual poets. The one exception is Yu Dafu, whose short story is the source of comparison.

In Chapter 5, the great pillars of modern Chinese literature, Lu Xun and Xu Zhimo, form a contrastive pair in their response to Baudelaire. One sought to refute and outdo while the other expressed unbridled admiration. One adopted the prose poem form while the other responded in verse. Both had firsthand knowledge of Baudelaire's work.

The "Chinese Decadents" Yu Dafu and Yu Gengyu were associated by their Chinese critics with Baudelaire through themes of sex or death, and through depressive moods in their works. Shao Xunmei made several direct references to Baudelaire, and chose filth and putrescence, sex and sin for his subjects.

The "Chinese Symbolists," so named in many studies in Chinese and Western languages, include Li Jinfa, Wang Duqing, Mu Mutian, Feng-Naichao, Liang Zongdai, and others. Li Jinfa professed his debt to Baudelaire, while the others are associated with Baudelaire through filiations with later European Symbolists. XuYunuo and Qin Zihao wrote poems that have reminded readers of Symbolist poetry.

There is no clear line between "Chinese Symbolists" and "Modernists." Qin Zihao was first associated with Modernism and later associated with Symbolism. Dai Wangshu, Bian Zhilin, and He Qifang were associated with Symbolism in their early work. In their move toward Modernism, they tended to move away from Baudelaire. This chapter also treats briefly Cao Baohua and Chen Jingrong.

The final chapter takes up three very different poets: Wen Yiduo, a close associate of Xu Zhimo, is set apart in this chapter for two reasons: unlike the case of Xu Zhimo, there is no evidence that he read Baudelaire; more importantly, he takes the aesthetic of "finding beauty in ugliness" in a new direction, beyond somber moods and beyond irony, toward social and national conscience. Ai Qing studied in Paris, and like Li Jinfa, he studied art. Most of his poems are at a far remove from anything resembling Baudelaire, yet a critic has found a poem that for him could have been written by Baudelaire. Finally, Duoduo, through his statements and through his poems, shows that the nineteenth-century French poet is still relevant in post-Mao China.

The original texts of poems I have translated can be found in Appendix 3. Excerpts of five or fewer lines are placed in the text.

FIVE

Lu Xun and Xu Zhimo

Lu Xun and Xu Zhimo respectively have been called modern China's greatest writer and modern China's greatest poet. Both responded directly to Baudelaire. One is skeptical, critical, and even sarcastic, while the other is appreciative and enthusiastic.

Lu Xun is best known for devoting literature to social and political missions, after an experience while studying medicine in Japan convinced him that "to cure physical ills was not as important as to cure spiritual ones."[1] His interest in Baudelaire thus seems an anomaly, and critics who read Baudelaire narrowly as a "nihilist" have taken pains to explain away Lu Xun's interest. But closer examination of Lu Xun's prose poems suggests that even when reference to Baudelaire is direct and undeniable, Lu Xun's response was consistent with the themes and values expressed in his other writings.

Xu Zhimo, in contrast to Lu Xun, is known for dreamy, romantic poems, and for pursuit of love and individual happiness rather than political or social change. When he sings of the happiness of a snowflake or the rebirth of spring, his poems also form a contrast with Baudelaire's. Xu's interest in and enthusiasm for Baudelaire have already been introduced in the previous two chapters. Here his response to the French poet will be examined through his own poetry.

LU XUN (魯迅 1881–1936)

> —Ah! misérable chien, si je vous avais offert un paquet d'excréments, vous l'auriez flairé avec délices et peut-être dévoré. Ainsi, vous-même, indigne compagnon de ma triste vie, vous ressemblez au public, à qui il ne faut jamais présenter des parfums délicats qui l'exaspèrent, mais des ordures soigneusement choisies.

[Ah, miserable dog, if I had offered you a packet of feces, you would
have sniffed it with delight and perhaps devoured it. Thus you, un-
worthy companion of my sad life, you resemble the public, to whom
one must never present delicate perfumes that annoy, but carefully
chosen excrement].
—Baudelaire[2]

"Yes, I'm inferior to man. . . . I'm ashamed to say I still don't know how
to distinguish copper from silver, silk from cotton cloth, officials from
common citizens, masters from their slaves; I still don't know. . ."
—Lu Xun[3]

Baudelaire's prose poem, *"Le Chien et le flacon"* ["The Dog and the
Flask"], likens the reading public who cannot appreciate exquisite literature to the dog who would choose a packet of excrement over a bottle of
delicate perfume. Lu Xun's prose poem is entitled *"Goude bojie"* 狗的駁詰
["The Dog's Retort"]. Its narrator relates a dream in which he shouts at a
dog, thinking that it had barked at him because his dress was ragged as a
beggar's. In believing that the dog had decided by the quality of people's
clothes whether to wag its tail or to bark, the narrator took the dog to be a
representative of snobbery. But the dog makes it clear that such snobbery
is a projection of human prejudices.[4] Baudelaire's poem, on the other
hand, disdains the dog for not being able to discriminate according to
human preferences. Whereas Baudelaire's poem is a recrimination
against popular taste, Lu Xun's is an attack on the snobbery that might
lead to such recrimination. Thus his dog's retort is not only to Lu Xun the
dreamer, but to Baudelaire.

Lu Xun, whose original name was Chou Shu-jen (Zhou Shuren 周樹
人), is not primarily known as a poet. His reputation as China's greatest
modern writer rests instead on his short stories and essays, which have
been translated into over fifty languages.[5] A prolific translator himself,
his renditions from Japanese, German, and Russian fill thirty-three volumes, by one count.[6] A profound scholar and critic, his *A Brief History of
Chinese Fiction* is still a standard work, and his "Power of Mara Poetry,"
which traces the influence of Byron and Shelley on Russian and Polish
writers, has won him the title of the first modern Chinese literary comparatist.[7] Although he never joined any political party, he was revered by
the Leftists, while his work was banned for decades in Taiwan.

Lu Xun's prose poems appear in a volume entitled *Yecao* 野草 (*Wild
Grass* is the standard translation for the title, which can also mean
"weeds"), first published in 1927. The twenty-three poems comprising
the collection had first appeared in the journal *Yusi* 語絲 [*Threads of Talk*],
and are individually dated from 15 September 1924, to 10 April 1926.
Numerous scholars have noted parallels and made comparisons with
Baudelaire's *Petits Poèmes en prose*.

Lu Xun did not know French, but he could not have failed to come into contact with Baudelaire's prose poems. In the course of translating from Kuriagawa Hakuson's *Symbols of Agony* 苦悶的象徵, he would have translated Baudelaire's prose poem *"Les Fenêtres"* ["Windows"] around the same time he began writing pieces for *Wild Grass*.[8] Zhou Zuoren, who had published his translations of *"L'Étranger"* and *"Les Fenêtres"* in 1922, was Lu Xun's brother. Lu Xun himself had been the editor in 1925 of *Yusi*, the journal that published Zhang Dinghuang's translations of five of Baudelaire's prose poems that year.[9] *"Le Chien et le flacon"* is among Zhang's selections.

Another of Zhang Dinghuang's selections, *"Laquelle est la vraie?"* ["Which Is the Real One?"], is compared with Lu Xun's *"Mujie wen"* 墓碣文 ["Epitaph"] by Sun Yushi in his book *Yecao Yanjiu* 野草研究 [*Study of "Wild Grass"*], and by Chen Yuankai in an article entitled *"Wild Grass* and Foreign Literature."[10] The two poems are set in cemeteries.

In Baudelaire's poem, the first-person narrator describes a girl, Benedictà, whom he believes to be a "miraculous girl" embodying the Ideal and inspiring him to greatness, beauty, and fame, and "everything which makes us believe in immortality." But she is too beautiful to live long, and dies a few days after they meet. As he buries her, a little person in her exact likeness rises from the grave, tramples on it, laughs, and tells him that she is the true Benedictà, really a notorious slut, and that he is condemned to love her as such. He vehemently refuses, and stamping his foot in protest, becomes caught in the freshly dug earth, which traps him "perhaps forever, at the grave of the ideal."

In Lu Xun's poem the first-person narrator dreams he is standing at a moss-covered, crumbling grave marker inscribed on two sides. One side refers to finding salvation in hopelessness. The other side recounts tearing out the heart to eat it and discover its true taste. But while the heart was fresh, the pain of eating it was too severe to tell its taste, and when the pain subsided, the heart had become stale. As the dreamer turns to leave, a disemboweled corpse he had spied earlier sits up and speaks. The dreamer hurries away, not daring to look back, for fear of seeing the corpse in pursuit.

Sun points out that Lu Xun's piece was written just four months after the publication of Zhang's translation of Baudelaire's prose poem and posits that the artistic conception of meeting with the dead, and the expression of obscure sentiments with dream imagery are clearly influenced by Baudelaire's Symbolism. Sun interprets the story in the French poem to mean that the greatness, beauty, glory, and love that humans seek are permanent only in the grave, and sees it as an example of Baudelaire's nihilism. By contrast, Lu Xun's dreamer, by running away at the end, "moves forward toward revolution."[11] Chen attends more fully to the attitude toward reality expressed at the end of Baudelaire's poem, and also identifies it as nihilism. Like Sun, he concludes that Lu Xun's dreamer surpasses Baudelaire in escaping from nihilism.[12]

But what is "nihilism" in the two poems? In "Epitaph," the corpse had torn out his own heart. The heart is identified as the seat of love and hate, joy and sadness, color and sound in another *Wild Grass* piece called "*Xiwang*" 希望 ["Hope"]. In "Epitaph," when the disemboweled corpse sits up and speaks, presumably even after eating its own heart, what it says is, "When I turn to dust, you will see me smile!" Only when the process of disintegration is complete, when the corpse has returned to dust, when there is no longer any joy or sadness, love or hate, color, sound or taste, only then will the corpse somehow smile, and the narrator will somehow see it smile. But if the corpse has turned to dust, how can it smile? What can its smile mean? As the corpse looks forward to returning to dust, in a twist of dream logic, the narrator fears that it will pursue him. Paradox builds on paradox.

Baudelaire's poem ends with his narrator trapped at the grave, unable to run off. Although his Benedictà had been too good to live long, she nevertheless did live once, and now lies buried. Benedictà's eyes had exuded desire for grandeur, beauty, and glory; such desire could also be a debased mistress, or a "notorious slut" (*une fameuse canaille*). The "notorious slut" rises to trample on the grave. The title of the poem asks, "Which is the real one?" But the grave at which the narrator is trapped is "*la fosse de l'idéal*" [the grave of the ideal]. What lies buried in the grave is not a corpse that has eaten its own heart and then disintegrated into dust. It is the ideal that may be buried, but still has the power to hold on to the narrator. For Baudelaire's narrator to run away would have implied he was running after the "notorious slut" and away from the ideal.

Where the frame of Lu Xun's "Epitaph" is reminiscent of Baudelaire's "*Laquelle est la vraie?*" the scene in Lu Xun's prose poem is more reminiscent of the final stanza of "*L'Héautontimorouménos*" ["The Self-Executioner"] from *Les Fleurs du mal:*

> *Je suis de mon coeur le vampire,*
> *—Un de ces grands abandonnés,*
> *Au rire étenel condamnés*
> *Et qui ne peuvent plus sourire!*

[I am the vampire of my heart, / —one of these great derelicts / condemned to eternal laughter / and who can no longer smile!].[13]

If the corpse in Lu Xun's poem had wished to quote French verse he certainly would have chosen Baudelaire's "*L'Héautontimorouménos.*" He was the vampire of his heart.

"Nihilistic ideas" exist in the Chinese rather than the French poem when Zha Peide compares "*Laquelle est la vraie?*" with Lu Xun's "*Yingde-gaobie*" 影的告別 ["The Shadow's Leave-Taking"]. Lu Xun's poem presents what the shadow might say in farewell when one "has slept to a time when one doesn't know the time." The shadow does not want to go to heaven, or to hell, or to some "future golden world." Darkness would swallow him up, but light also would cause him to disappear. Not wishing to wander between darkness and light, he chooses to "enter the darkness and wander in nothingness." Reading the image of the shadow as "actually the symbol of the poet himself," Zha posits that "although he does not know any better place to go than darkness, he would rather sink into darkness as a kind of revolt against his present status." For Zha this represents Lu Xun's attempt to break away, "unlike Baudelaire who clings to the illusion." [14]

Baudelaire's narrator does not run away. He is trapped, sunk up to his knees in mire, caught forever between the ideal toward which he aspires, and mundane reality, by which he is repelled yet attracted. He could neither bury the one nor reject the other, whom he is "condemned to love."

A similar sense of perpetual unresolved and unresolvable confrontation, represented in the moment frozen in eternity, is presented in the first of Lu Xun's two poems entitled *"Fuchou"* 復仇 ["Revenge"]. There two figures, grasping sharp knives, face each other, neither moving to kill the other in the moment of death that would bring the "transcendent, supreme ecstasy of life." Like the figure in Baudelaire's poem, they are caught in a state that is neither the embrace of life nor the moment of death.

The confrontation in Lu Xun's poem is witnessed by passers-by. They rush up, hoping to see carnage, but as the two figures remain static in their confrontation, the passers-by become bored with the lack of action. Boredom seeps through their pores, until "their throats and tongues become parched, their necks tired"—until they become so atrophied they gradually lose all interest in life. The effect of boredom on the passers-by is a "bloodless massacre" in which the two figures find "the transcendent, supreme ecstasy of life." This enormous boredom resembles Baudelaire's "delicate monster" that could "swallow the world in a yawn:" Ennui, as described in *"Au Lecteur"* ["To the Reader"] in *Les Fleurs du mal.*

Lu Xun's portrayal of the common crowd is no more flattering than Baudelaire's of the reading public. Going far beyond indicting them for lack of taste, Lu Xun portrays them as cruel and indifferent in "Revenge." In a second poem by the same title, *"Fuchou"* 復仇 ["Revenge II"], the passersby look on with hatred and scorn while soldiers beat, spit upon, and mock Jesus as they prepare to crucify him. The indifference of human beings to each other's suffering, or the "inhumanity of man to man" is a constant theme in Lu Xun's work.

Scorn and contempt for other humans is also a theme in Lu Xun's *"Qiuqizhe"* 求乞者 ["The Beggars"], which Li Tiejun compares with *"Assommons les pauvres"* ["Let's Beat Up the Poor"]. [15] Both poems are about beggars.

In Baudelaire's poem the narrator decides to go out for a drink after being shut in for two weeks reading about the public good. He is accosted by a sexagenarian beggar, when a voice, that of either his good angel or his bad demon, whispers in his ear that the beggar is just as good as anyone else. He immediately jumps on the beggar, breaks his teeth, bangs his head against a wall, knocks him to the ground with a vicious kick, then sets to beating him with a tree limb. Somehow, miraculously, the decrepit old bum gathers the strength to get up, grab the tree limb, and beat the narrator to a pulp. At this the narrator expresses great satisfaction, for having reawakened the beggar's sense of life and pride.

Lu Xun's poem also has a first-person narrator. Walking alone, he is accosted by a beggar child. Here, the voice is not that of his own inner angel or demon, but that of the child, and the narrator dislikes both his voice and manner. The narrator walks on, and a second child begs from him. He is filled with disgust, suspicion, and hate. Refusing to give alms, he then goes further to despise alms-givers, and pushing logic to the extreme, he anticipates disgust, suspicion, and hate for those who consider themselves better than the alms-givers. His beggar, unlike Baudelaire's, never has a chance for revenge. The piece ends with dust everywhere, and several people walking alone, after the narrator's declaration: "I shall beg with inactivity and silence. . . . I shall at last receive nothingness."

Lu Xun creates a total image of beggar and narrator, according to Li Tiejun, and a gloomy, cold environment in which he rejects both the act of begging and the society in which beggars exist. Lu Xun's poem is cast as a dream. Here, Li Tiejun finds parallels with Baudelaire, stating that although Baudelaire does not use the phrase "I dreamed," three of his prose poems, *"La Chambre double* ["The Double Room"], *"L'Invitation au voyage"* ["Invitation to the Voyage"], and *"Un Hémisphère dans une chevelure"* [Half a World in a Head of Hair"] form a "dream trilogy." Baudelaire's "double room" is a shabby, untidy room turned lovely in a drug-induced reverie; the "invitation" is to voyage to a land of calm and luxury that is an "Orient of the Occident," and the "head of hair" evokes lovely distant climes created by memory and the imagination. Lu Xun's dreams by contrast more often resemble nightmares. Li suggests that Lu Xun overuses the dream device: nine of the twenty-three pieces in *Wild Grass* are cast as dreams, and seven actually begin with the words "I dreamed."

The words "I dreamed" function to offer rational explanations for dislocation and discontinuity in narration. According to Carolyn T. Brown, Lu Xun was aware of psychological theories that dream reflects "inner reality," and used literary techniques to create the illusion of dreams.[16] But "The Beggars" has a logical coherence so that it does need to be explained away as a dream. The poem begins and ends with the narrator walking alone, and aware of several other people walking, each of them alone. The image of walking alone reminds Li Tiejun of *"Chacun sa chimère"* [To Each His Own Chimera"] where each person walks alone, burdened with his own pet monster.

But if one reads Lu Xun's poem "The Beggars" as a more assertive response to Baudelaire, in the way that "The Dog's Retort" responds to *"Le Chien et le flacon,"* yet another comparison suggests itself. In *"Les Yeux des pauvres"* ["The Eyes of the Poor"], the narrator is seated with a woman companion in a fancy cafe while an obviously poverty-stricken father and his two children gaze through the window with longing admiration. The narrator feels somewhat ashamed of their carafe and glasses, more than they need, but his companion says: *"Ces gens-là me sont insupportables avec leurs yeux ouverts comme des portes cochères! Ne pourriez-vous pas prier le maître du café de les éloigner d'ici?"* [I can't stand those people with their eyes open wide like carriage gates! Couldn't you ask the headwaiter to get them away from here?]. The poet then concludes that communication is impossible even among people who love one another.

In Lu Xun's poem, it is the narrator himself who despises beggars. He is no less cold-hearted and unfeeling than the woman in Baudelaire's poem. But by turning a mirror on himself to despise those who set themselves above alms-givers, Lu Xun's narrator indicts himself, and does not set himself above a woman companion as does the French narrator. Lu Xun once criticized Baudelaire's sympathy for the poor as empty philanthropy.[17] If "The Beggars" is read as a response to *"Les Yeux des Pauvres,"* then Lu Xun seems to be stating the same case, albeit more obliquely, in his prose poem.

As with Baudelaire's poem, Lu Xun's also suggests the impossibility of human communication. But in the latter case, the impossibility is not limited to one man and one woman. Neither beggar has communicated with the narrator, although the first could speak and whine, unlike the second who only stretched out his hand in dumb show. Everyone else on the road is walking alone. No one communicates with another. Lu Xun's poem ends even more bleakly than Baudelaire's, with the narrator realizing that he "will receive nothingness," and with several people walking alone through dust and more dust.

Bleakness intensifies into despair in Lu Xun's *"Tuibai xian de diandong"* 頹敗線的顫動 ["Tremors of Degradation"], which has been compared with Baudelaire's *"Le Désespoir de la vieille"* ["The Old Woman's Despair"]. Leo Lee postulates that Lu Xun constructed his piece from Baudelaire's poem.[18]

In Baudelaire's short poem, an old woman tries to please a pretty child, as fragile, bald, and toothless as herself. But at her approach the child is terrified and begins howling. The old woman retreats to a corner, lamenting that age and lost attraction could disgust even innocent children.

In Lu Xun's longer and more complex poem, an old woman is rejected by her own daughter, whom she had raised with much sacrifice, then by her son-in-law, and then by her grandchild. When the last shouts "Kill!" in her shock she retreats to "a boundless wasteland" and hurls a cry, half-human and half-animal, toward heaven.

Here, rather than offering a retort to Baudelaire's poem, Lu Xun puts forth a broader scope and draws a tighter relationship between the personae. His old woman's anguish is the more intense in that she is rejected by her own offspring rather than by an accidental encounter with a "pretty child." By focusing on human relationships rather than on individual vanity, Lu Xun intensifies the feeling of bitterness in his poem. Like "The Beggars" and "Revenge I," this piece ends in a "vast wilderness." It is cast in a double dream, beginning "I dreamed that I was dreaming."

Lu Xun's "*Guoke*" 過客 ["The Passerby"] also reminds readers of Baudelaire. Michelle Loi speculates that "critics might one day find" that Lu Xun had borrowed the form for "The Passerby" from Baudelaire's "*L'Étranger.*"[19] Leo Lee finds that Baudelaire's "'extraordinary stranger' may have served as a partial basis for Lu Xun's 'Passer-by,' a poetic play much longer and more elaborate than Baudelaire's prose poem."[20] Lu Xun could not have failed to know Baudelaire's piece; his brother Zhou Zuoren had published a translation of it in 1922.[21]

Lu Xun's poem is set in the form of a conversation among the Passer-by, an old man who had already taken the road, and a young girl who has not. The Passerby, like the stranger in the French poem, does not know what his name is or where he is from. But he is asked not what he loves, but where he is going. He does not know. He only knows he has to keep going ahead. The old man tells him that ahead lie only graves. The girl points rather to the roses and lilies on them. They invite him to rest, and give him a cloth to bind his bleeding feet. He is tempted to stay, but in the end, continues westward, toward the sunset.

The two poems share the use of direct discourse and a tentative, mysterious quality. Baudelaire's poem is a dialogue in which neither interlocutor is identified. Lu Xun's characters, though unnamed, are clearly delineated, and are presented in a dramatic situation. Representing three generations and three different points of view, they suggest a very different range of meaning.

"The Passerby," with its background of a road-less wilderness, for Li Tiejun is similar to "*Chacun sa chimère*" ["To Each His Own Chimera"]. He points out that the human figures in both poems carry burdens and appear tired, yet they desire to keep walking. He also underscores the differences: the figures in the French poem walk forward with their strange burdens without questioning why they do so, whereas the Passerby makes a conscious decision not to turn back or to stop walking ahead. For Li the Chinese poem offers a positive element which is lacking in the French one.[22]

But Lu Xun's poem is harsher in mood and his questioning goes beyond aesthetics and personal and social identity to existence itself. His piece is more hermetic than Baudelaire's. It is reminiscent of a Japanese Noh play, and as Leo Lee has suggested, it anticipates Beckett.[23]

Other readers have noted similarities between the two collections without drawing parallels between specific poems. Leo Lee, who has discerned "traces of Baudelaire" in *Wild Grass*, notes that Jaroslav Průšek had found Lu Xun's prose poetry to read "much like" Baudelaire's *Petits Poèmes en prose*.[24] For Průšek, "the emotional atmosphere, complex images and metaphors, and the extraordinary strength of feeling" in Lu Xun's prose poems place them as "an exceptional link in the special chain of modern poetry—poems in prose—which begins with . . . Bertrand's *Gaspard de la Nuit*, continues with Baudelaire . . . Lautréamont . . . Rimbaud . . . , and ends with Mallarmé." After raising the question of whether Lu Xun became acquainted with this type of poetry through Japanese translation or Japanese imitation, Průšek leaves the answer open, and states his preference for the opinion that Lu Xun created the form independently and "succeeded in producing an original parallel to this remarkable trend in European poetry."[25]

In fact, the European prose poem was already well-known in China by 1924 when Lu Xun began writing the pieces for *Wild Grass*. Turgenev's prose poems had been translated as early as 1918. Lu Xun's brother Zhou Zuoren had published in 1919 a piece entitled *"Xiao he"* 小河 ["Small River"], with an introduction stating that it had been inspired by Baudelaire's prose poem form.[26] Liu Bannong and Guo Moruo had used the form in 1920 and 1921.[27] Xu Yunuo had included many prose poems in his 1922 collection, *Jianglai zhi huayuan* 將來之花園 [*Garden of the Future*].[28] Zheng Zhenduo had published a staunch endorsement of the form in the same year.[29] Thus it appears unlikely that Lu Xun invented the form for himself, though neither can it be claimed conclusively that he learned it, directly or indirectly, from Baudelaire. Still, it appears that Lu Xun is the first Chinese writer to have created an entire collection of prose poems.

Having entitled his prose poem collection *Wild Grass*, Lu Xun, in his preface for the English edition, referred to the poems as "small pale flowers at the edge of neglected hell."[30] The association of flowers and hell brings to mind Baudelaire's title *Les Fleurs du mal*. When Lu Xun adds that the flowers "could not of course be beautiful," he again seemed to be making a retort to Baudelaire, who proposed to identify his "flowers of evil" with beauty.

Parallels also have been drawn between Lu Xun's prose poems and Baudelaire's verse poems. Zhang Ting pairs specific pieces from *Wild Grass* and from *Les Fleurs du mal* for comparison.[31]

For Zhang, "Revenge II" and *"Le Reniement de Saint Pierre"* ["Saint Peter's Denial"] are so similar "they can be said to be twin-sister-flowers." Both poems jeer at Jesus in distress. The jeering comes from passers-by and priests in the former, and from the poet himself in the latter.

In Lu Xun's "Revenge II," Jesus suffers in an agony of compassion and contempt for his tormentors. Believing himself the Son of God, he calls out to Him, but is forsaken; he is only the son of man after all. When Lu Xun concludes: "Those who crucify the son of man are more stained and stinking with blood than those who crucify the Son of God," it is a humanist response. For Baudelaire, "Humanity" exists in Jesus' head, which receives the crown of thorns. He imagines God asleep "to the sweet sound of blasphemy," and asks if Jesus on the cross remembers the hopes, ideals, and triumphs of the Garden of Olives and Palm Sunday, and whether he regrets his actions (chasing merchants from the temple). The poet, who would sooner "live by the sword and perish by the sword" to exit quickly from a world where "action is not sister to dream" concludes: "Saint Peter denied Jesus . . . he did well!"

Baudelaire, writing as one steeped in Christianity who now violently rejects it, creates an extremely bitter tone. Not surprisingly, Lu Xun's bitterness is more intense where family relationship rather than Christianity is at issue.

Lu Xun's "Tremors of Degradation," previously compared with Baudelaire's prose poem "*Le Désespoir de la vieille*," reminds Zhang Ting of Baudelaire's verse poem "*Les Petites Vieilles*" ["The Little Old Women"]. For Zhang, the old lady in Lu Xun's poem could be a rural sister of Baudelaire's little old lady. Both poems show tortured, anguished sympathy beneath bitterness and irony that support Zhang's comparison.

Zhang also finds in the two writers' personal lives similarities in family, class, social background, and personal experience. But, he warns, the differences are equally important. Political systems and conditions led Baudelaire to an escapist route in pursuit of abstract ideals of "love" and "beauty" and intoxication in wine, women, and drugs, whereas Lu Xun could join the May Fourth Movement and the revolution; he could face life head-on, breaking with his own class to fight together with the Proletariat, reforming the world as he reformed himself![32]

Chinese critics tend to describe the relation between Lu Xun and Baudelaire as one of influence. Sun Yushi and Zhang Ting variously find positive influences in depth of emotion and self-examination, in concentration and musicality of poetic language, and pursuit of the new and strange, but find negative influence in pessimism and "nihilism." Sun associates "mysticism" with Baudelaire, but then states that Lu Xun "disapproved of mysticism" and was "not interested in" the "*fin de siècle* poet." Both Zhang and Sun emphasize that Baudelaire's influence occupied only a short period in Lu Xun's life and a small part of his work, as he moved "forward to revolution."[33]

The possibility for multiple meanings in the poems, generally appreciated as a positive quality in Baudelaire's poems, is criticized as a negative influence on Lu Xun. "Mysticism" was pernicious because it made it impossible for the reader to articulate the meaning of the poem as a whole. The depressive mood in Lu Xun's poems has also been associated with Baudelaire. As Leo Lee has pointed out, Chinese critics tried to explain those moods away, as their analyses remained "on the social message level." Lee predicts increased interest in *Wild Grass* to follow the "trend toward demythologizing Lu Xun's revolutionary stature."[34]

Lu Xun is one of modern China's most original writers. His relation to Baudelaire can lead to an understanding of influence that is broader, and at the same time more specific. If Lu Xun was inspired by or borrowed certain situations, images, and artistic approaches from Baudelaire, he always transformed them in expressing his own ideas. Whether he expanded upon, contradicted, or retorted to Baudelaire's work, the themes, preoccupations, and attitudes are always Lu Xun's own.

XU ZHIMO (徐志摩 1897–1931)

"Can we think of a purer sympathy, a purer style?" Xu Zhimo had asked with rhetorical drama in his description of Baudelaire's prose poems. Baudelaire's verse poem "Une Charogne" he had described as "strangely poisonous yet strangely fragrant." These two aspects of Baudelaire's work, sympathy for the poor and finding beauty in ugliness, appear in Xu Zhimo's own.

Xu Zhimo was the best known and most admired poet of his generation. His life and death are at least as well-known as his work, and add to his reputation as a thorough Romantic. The only son of a wealthy banker, he was educated in the Chinese classics before attending the Westernized Hujiang University and then Peking University, followed by Clark University in the United States and then Cambridge University in England. His marriages and divorce were the talk of the Chinese literary world, and his death in a plane crash at the Chinese age of thirty-six completed the legend.[35] He left four collections of poetry: *Zhimo de shi* 志摩的詩 [*Zhimo's Poetry*] 1925, *Feilengcui de yiye* 翡冷翠 的 一夜 [*A Night in Florence*] 1927, *Menghu ji* [*Fierce Tiger*] 1931, and *Yun you* 雲游 [*Roaming the Clouds*] 1932. Among his collections of essays, *Bali de linzhao* 巴黎的鱗爪 [*Paris Miscellany*] 1927, the title notwithstanding, has little to do with Paris and nothing to say about French literature.

Xu Zhimo's work is known for its skillful weaving of traditional Chinese poetics with English and European poetic elements. Frequently mentioned influences include Keats, Byron, Shelley, Swinburne, Rossetti, Hardy, and Whitman, as well as the Indian Rabindranath Tagore.[36] Xu had come to know Baudelaire, just as he had become acquainted with so many Western writers, not through any formal introduction, but purely by chance.[37] Well-grounded in traditional Chinese literature, Xu Zhimo did not adhere strictly to vernacular usage, as advocated by Hu Shi, but blended classical diction with colloquial language in a manner that earned praise from contemporary critics.

Most of Xu Zhimo's early poems, and his best known ones, are dedicated to love, nostalgia, aspiration, inspiration, or yearning for the abstract ideals of beauty or freedom. *"Zhe shi yige nuoqie de shijie"* 这是一个懦怯的世界 ["This Is a Cowardly World"] exemplifies some of his major concerns, and shares a theme with Baudelaire's *"L'Invitation au voyage"* ["Invitation to the Voyage"]:

> This is a cowardly world,
> Intolerant of love!
> Let down your hair;
> Bare your feet;
> Follow me, my love;
> Abandon this world;
> Let us die for our love!
>
> I am holding your hand,
> Love, follow me;
> Let thorns pierce our feet;
> Let hailstones break open our heads;
> Follow me,
> I am holding your hand,
> To escape from this prison, and recover our freedom,
> My love!
> The world has already fallen behind us.
> Oh look, is this not the vast white sea,
> The vast white sea,
> The vast white sea,
> Boundless freedom, love, you and me!
>
> Look along my pointing finger,
> That blue of a little star on the horizon
> Is an island, an island with green grasses,
> Flowers, beautiful beasts and birds;
> Come quickly onto this light skiff;
> Let us go to that heaven of ideals,
> Of love, happiness, and freedom,
> and leave this world behind, forever.[38]

There is a pastoral innocence in Xu's invitation to his loved one to loosen her hair and bare her feet. On his island there is no suggestion of civilization, only nature in its pristine state. It is the little blue star on the horizon. As Julia Lin has suggested, "the poetic world of Hsu is of the celestial realm, translucent, ethereal, and abstract."[39] Xu's vision, like that of the Tang dynasty poets, was directed skyward. His favored images were the moon, stars, clouds, flying.

All this puts Xu at antipodes with Baudelaire. *"L'Invitation au voyage"* also invites the loved one to an ideal realm where pleasure and beauty await. But instead of the sea and stars, birds, wild flowers, and grass, Baudelaire imagines "Oriental splendor" in a room with gleaming furniture, rare flowers, amber, rich ceilings, and deep mirrors, where luxury, calm, and order reign. Where Baudelaire found a dream world of "Oriental splendor," might Xu have found the prison of civilization?

Yet when the two poets focus their gaze on the human predicament, they have something in common. An example is Xu's *"Jiaohua huogai!"* 叫 化活該! ["Serves You Right, Beggar!"]:

> "Kind-hearted ladies, virtuous gentlemen,"
> The northeast wind slashes his face like a knife.
> "Grant me a little of your leftover broth."
> A black shadow huddled against the gates.
>
> "Have pity. I am starving to death, wealthy gentlemen."
> Inside the gates, there is happy laughter, warm stoves, jade cups.
> "Have pity. I am freezing to death, fortunate gentlemen."
> Outside the gates the Northwest wind laughs: "Serves you right, beggar!"
>
> I, too, am a trembling huddled black shadow,
> Wriggling wormlike on the front street of humanity.
> I, too, want only a little sympathy and warmth
> To cover my bare bones scraped of flesh.
>
> But at this heavy, tightly-closed gate, who will notice?
> On the street, only the cold wind mocks: "Serves you right, beggar!" [40]

By its irony, its expression of sympathy for the poor, and its view of the difficulty of human communication, this poem is strongly reminiscent of Baudelaire's *"Les Yeux des Pauvres"* ["The Eyes of the Poor"], the very prose poem which Xu had singled out for appreciation, and which also had elicited a response from Lu Xun. Xu's beggar is more abject than the father with two children who gaze in mute admiration into Baudelaire's café, but the contrast between inside and outside in both poems is essentially the same. Xu's poem is heightened in pathos because it is the wind, rather than a human companion, who mocks the beggar. Readers of traditional Chinese poetry might recall Song Yu's *fu* (宋玉"風賦") on the wind, where the conceit is that only pleasant breezes enter palaces, but dusty squalls haunt poor neighborhood lanes, to see double cruelty here. [41] Further, in Chinese, "to drink the northeast wind" is a metaphor for starvation. Finally, Xu goes a step further in explicitly identifying himself with the beggar.

A similar commiseration is expressed in Xu's *"Guguai de shijie"* 古怪的 世界 ["Odd World"]:

From Stone Lake Dike of Pine River,
A pair of old women came on board.
Shakily supporting their bow-shaped bodies,
Thanks to (I guess) Mount Putuo's coiled dragon reeds.

Dark cotton padded coat, black cotton padded suit;
Head half bald, teeth half missing,
Shoulder to shoulder, they sit before the sun-warmed window
Fearfully, murmuring, like a pair of old swallows in the cold.

Trembling, dried up hands,
Trembling, wrinkled dewlaps,
These two old ones! Are they sisters-in-law, or sisters?
Huddled together, in their old eyes, sorrowful tears!

Poor things! Poverty is not lowliness.
In aged decrepitude there is limitless dignity.
What sorrow, what griefs have the old?
Why are they abandoning their homes on this happy New Year's Day?

In the car mingled human voices;
On the rails, rapidly turning wheels;
I alone, alone am pondering: this world is strange—
Who is it playing on the inharmonious pipes of humanity?[42]

The poem is reminiscent of *"Les Veuves"* ["The Widows"], with its description of the loneliness and dignity of poor widows who must scrimp even in mourning, which Xu had praised so highly in his article on Baudelaire's prose poems. Xu's poem also recalls the first part of Baudelaire's verse poem *"Les Petites Vieilles"* with its description of "little old women" as

> *Des êtres singuliers, décrépits et charmants . . . Monstres brisés, bossus / Ou tordus . . . Sous des jupons troués . . . flagellés par les bises iniques, / Frémissant au fracas roulant des omnibus . . . débile . . . fragile . . . Ces yeux sont des puits faits d'un million de larmes.* [43]

> [Odd, decrepit, and charming beings . . . broken, hump-backed or twisted monsters . . . under tattered skirts . . . whipped by wicked north winds, trembling in the rolling din of omnibuses . . . feeble . . . fragile . . . these eyes are wells made of a million tears]

More than sympathy, a sort of curiosity toward the old women, who are observed with a certain detachment, is expressed in both poems. But where Baudelaire contrasts the condition of age with youth, Xu muses about the old women's familial relations. Where Baudelaire's poem is more generalized in time, Xu gains pathos by noting that it is New Year's Day, the traditional day for family reunions in China. Thus, even without place names, Xu's poem belongs solidly in a Chinese context. The objective description of ragged clothes, bowed bodies, and tearful eyes clearly depict poverty, age, and loneliness, and lend both poems their universality.

Xu had stated in his article on Baudelaire: "To show sympathy for the poor is no ordinary matter." To be sure, just as Lu Xun had questioned Baudelaire's real sympathy, the poet-critic Mu Mutian has objected that Xu's sympathy for the poor is that of a comfortable member of the gentry or aristocracy.[44] There is no call to action, and no hint of revolution. This he shares with Baudelaire.

Xu's recognition of the darker side of life was not limited to these poems of social concern. Two antiwar poems appear in *A Night in Florence*. And in *Fierce Tiger*, a poem simply entitled *"Shenghuo"* 生活 ["Life"] reads:

> Gloomy, dark, writhing like a venomous snake,
> Life forces out a narrow passage:
> Once you enter, you can only go forward,
> Hands groping along the slime on its cold walls ,
>
> Struggling inside the demon's bowels,
> Overhead not a single ray of light can be seen,
> This soul, under such fearful oppression,
> Apart from extinction what more can it desire?[45]

For Xu, who had believed with Wordsworth, "We live by admiration, hope, and love,"[46] this poem surely represents an expression of the deepest despair. It is reminiscent of Baudelaire's "Spleen IV" poem *"Quand le ciel bas et lourd pèse comme un couvercle"* ["When the low heavy sky weighs like a lid"], with its second quatrain

> *Quand la terre est changée en un cachot humide,*
> *Où l'Espérance, comme une chauve-souris,*
> *S'en va en battant les murs de son aile timide*
> *Et se cognant la tête à des plafonds pourris;*

[When the earth is changed into a dank dungeon, / Where Hope, like a bat, / Goes beating the walls with his timid wings, / And hitting his head on the decayed ceilings;]

and its ending:

> *—Et de longs corbillards, sans tambours et musique,*
> *Défilent lentement dans mon âme; l'Espoir,*
> *Vaincu, pleure, et l'Angoisse atroce, despotique,*
> *Sur mon crâne incliné plante son drapeau noir.*[47]

[And long hearses, without drums and music, / Pass in slow procession in my soul; Hope, / Vanquished, weeps, and terrible ruthless Anguish, / Plants its black banner on my drooping skull].

Both poems are "gloomy and somber," and refer to dank and moldy enclosed spaces. Both are concerned with the soul. While Xu's poem falls somewhat short of Baudelaire's concrete evocation, it is interesting that Xu, mostly remembered for his ebullient charm, should arrive at similar imagery to express a gloomy mood.

Xu had written some years earlier in the *Xinyue* 新月 [Crescent]:

> We dare not accept aestheticism and decadence, because we do not wish to sacrifice the grandeur of human life to carving a gold and jade-inlaid wine cup. Beauty we respect and love, but to savor the beauty of evil is not as good as reflecting on the eternity of virtue. Going to the seashell to collect coral-colored miracle drugs is not as good as placing oneself in the tumult of the human world, and listening carefully to the serene, somber tones of humanity.[48]

He would take his material from human life. But in the preface to *Fierce Tiger* he declared, "In the past few years, life has not only been mediocre; it has simply reached the depths of distress." Was it in trying to express this new attitude that Xu looked again to Baudelaire? For *Fierce Tiger*, published in the year of his death, ends with his translation of Baudelaire's "*Une Charogne*."[49]

NOTES

1. Lu Xun, "Preface." *Call to Arms*; see Yang Xianyi and Gladys Yang, trans., *The Complete Stories of Lu Xun* (Beijing: Foreign Languages Press, 1981), 2–3.

2. *OC*, 284.

3. Lu Xun, *Ye Cao* (s.l.: s.n., preface dated 1927; poems dated 1924–26). This poem is dated 23 Apr. 1925. See also Lu Xun 魯迅, *Yecao* 野草: *Wild Grass*, trans. Yang Xianyi and Gladys Yang, bilingual edition (Hong Kong: The Chinese UP, 2003), 74–75.

4. OrhanPamuk, in "Turkish Journal: The View and the Dog in the Road," *New Yorker* (5 Mar. 2007), 45, describes "a dog that barked furiously at any poor person passing through but let the rich pass in silence." That dog was not given an opportunity to retort.

5. Irene Eber, "The Reception of Lu Xun in Europe and America: The Politics of Popularization and Scholarship," in *Lu Xun and His Legacy*, ed. Leo Ou-fan Lee (Berkeley: University of California Press, 1985), 242.

6. Yuan Haoyi, "Survey," 93.

7. Lu Xun, *A Brief History of Chinese Fiction* (*Zhongguo Xiaoshuo Lueshi* 中國小說略史), trans. Yang Hsien-yi and Gladys Yang (Beijing: Foreign Languages Press, 1959). Lu Xun, "Moluo shili shuo" 摩羅詩力說, is partially translated by Shu-yingTsau and Donald Holoch as "The Power of Mara Poetry" in Denton, 96–109. Lu Xun as comparatist is introduced in Liu Xianbiao 劉獻彪, *Bijiaowenxue ji qi zai Zhongguo de xingqi* 比較文學在中國的興起 [*The Rise of Comparative Literature in China*] (Nanning: Guangxi renmin chubanshe, 1986), 152–56.

8. Sun, *Yecaoyanjiu*, 207; Leo Ou-fan Lee, *Voices from the Iron House: A Study of Lu Xun* (Bloomington: Indiana University Press, 1987), 92; Lee, in *Shanghai Modern*, 235, indicates that Lu Xun "seems to put more emphasis on the French poet by inserting as an illustration a painting of Charles Baudelaire with a caption in German."

9. Zhang Dinghuang's translations in *Yu Si* are introduced in chapter 3. Xu Zhimo's translation of "*Une Charogne*" appeared in a different issue of the same journal.

10. Sun, *Yecao yanjiu*, 209–11.Chen Yuankai 陳元愷, "*Yecao* yu waiguo wenxue"《野草》與外國文學, *Ershi shiji Zhongguo wenxue yu shijie* 二十世紀中國文學與世界 (Xi'an: Shaanxi renmin chubanshe, 1987), 271.

11. Sun, *Yecao yanjiu*, 215.

12. Chen Yuankai, "*Yecao* yu waiguo wenxue," 271.

13. *OC*, 78.

14. Zha Peide, "Poetic Quality of Prose Poetry: Charles Baudelaire and Lu Xun." *Comparative Literature in Canada* 21–22, no. 2 (1990–91): 83.

15. Li Tiejun 李鐵軍, "Canbai yu youyu: Zai 'feichi de diyu' bianyuan" *Yecao* yu *Bali de youyu* bijiao yanjiu 慘白與憂鬱：在"廢馳的地獄邊沿"—《野草》與《巴黎的憂鬱》比較研究 ["Deathly Pale and Melancholy: At the Edge of 'Neglected Hell': Comparative Study of *Wild Grass* and *Paris Spleen*"], *Waiguo wenxue yanjiu* 文學研究, 10 (1991): 46–53.

16. Caroline T. Brown, "Lu Xun's Interpretation of Dreams" in *Psycho-Sinology: The Universe of Dreams in Chinese Culture* (Washington, DC: Woodrow Wilson Center for Scholars, 1988), 67–79.

17. Sun, *Yecao yanjiu*, 207.

18. Lee, *Shanghai Modern*, 239–40.

19. Loi, *Roseaux*, 95.

20. Lee, *Shanghai Modern*, 239.

21. Zhong Mi (pseud. of Zhou Zuoren), "Youzi." 遊子, *Xiaoshuo yuebao* 13, no. 6 (1922): 22. See chapter 3.

22. Li Tiejun, "Canbai yu youyu," 50.

23. Lee, *Voices*, 101–2.

24. Ibid., 96.

25. Jaroslav Průšek, *The Lyrical and the Epic: Studies of Modern Chinese Literature*, ed. Leo Ou-fan Lee (Bloomington: Indiana University Press, 1980), 56–57.

26. Zhou Zuoren, "Xiao he xu" 小河序 ["Small River Preface"], *Xin qingnian* 新青年 6 (1919): 2. The poem is translated as "Rivulet" and discussed in Michel Hockx, *A Snowy Morning*, 33–50.

27. Sun, *Yecao yanjiu*, 199.

28. Xu Yunuo 徐玉諾, *Jianglai zhi huayuan* 將來之花園 [*Future's Garden: The Garden of Tomorrow and Other Poems by Y. N. Sü*], Chinese Literary Association Series (Shanghai: Shangwu, 1922).

29. Zheng Zhenduo 鄭振鐸, "Lun sanwenshi" 論散文詩, *Wenxue xunkan*, reprinted in Sun Lianggong, ed., *Xin wenyi pinglun* 新文藝評論 (Shanghai: Zhiminshuju, 1923), 89–98.

30. According to the editors of the 1974 English edition of *Wild Grass*, Lu Xun wrote the preface for an English translation by Feng Yusheng, but the translation never appeared in print. Lu Xun later published the preface in *Erxin ji* 二心集, a collection of essays written in 1930 and 1931.

31. Zhang Ting 張挺, "Botelai'er ji qi E zhihua yu Lu Xun ji qi *Yecao* zhi bijiao guan: wei qingzhu jianguo sanshiwu zhounian er zuo" 波特萊爾及其《惡之花》與魯迅及其《野草》之比較觀—為慶祝建國三十五周年而作, ["Comparative View of Baudelaire and His *Flowers of Evil* with Lu Xun and His *Wild Grass*: Written to Celebrate the Thirty-Fifth Anniversary of The Nation's Founding"], reprinted in *Waiguowenxueyanjiu* 外國文學研究 4 (1985): 14–30.

32. Zhang Ting, 23–24.

33. Sun, *Yecao yanjiu*, 208–15; Zhang Ting, "Botelai'er ji qi E zhihua," 27.

34. Lee, *Voices*, 90, 214, 217.

35. Thirty-six is three times twelve, the basic number of the Chinese zodiac. At his death on 19 November 1931, Xu would have been thirty-four by the Western way of counting, but sources disagree on the year of his birth, giving variously 1895, 1896, and 1897. The fullest biographical accounts in English are in Leo Oufan Lee, *The Romantic Generation of Chinese Writers* (Cambridge, MA: Harvard University Press, 1973), 124–74, and Jonathan Spence, *The Gate of Heavenly Peace: The Chinese and Their*

Revolution 1895–1980 (New York: The Viking Press, 1981); see index 460. Xu Zhimo's life was the subject of a television series in 2000, *Renjian siyue tian* 人間四月天 [*Human World April Days*].

36. For comparisons with Western writers, see Hsu, *Twentieth Century Chinese Poetry*, 70; Lin, *Modern Chinese Poetry*, 100–32; Robert Payne, ed., *Contemporary Chinese Poetry* (London: Routledge, 1947), 13, 35; Birch, "English and Chinese Metres," and "Hsü Chi-mo's Debt to Thomas Hardy (Abstract)," *Transactions, International Conference of Orientalists in Japan* 9 (1964): 73–77.

37. *Xu Zhimo Quanji*, 6:403–7, 1:610.

38. *Xu Zhimo Quanji*, 2:40–43. See appendix 3. For other translations, see Payne, *Contemporary Chinese Poetry*, 39–40; Hsu, *Twentieth Century Chinese Poetry*, 78–79; Lee, *Romantic Generation*, 162–63.

39. Lin, *Modern Chinese Poetry*, 107.

40. *Xu Zhimo Quanji*, 2:112–13. See appendix 3. For other translations, see Payne, *Comtemporary Chinese Poetry*, 42; Hsu, *Twentieth-Century Chinese Poetry*, 77–78; Lin, *Modern Chinese Poetry*, 129–30.

41. For Song Yu 宋玉, "*Fengfu*" 風賦 in English, see Burton Watson's translation in Birch, *Anthology*, 1:135–38.

42. *Xu Zhimo Quanji*, 2:81–83. See appendix 3. Mount Putuo is one of the five Buddhist holy mountains. The "I guess" in parentheses is in Xu's original poem. I gratefully acknowledge help for this translation from the late Professor James J. Y. Liu.

43. *OC*: 89.

44. Mu Mutian 穆木天, "Lun Xu Zhimo" 論徐志摩, in *Zuojialun* 作家論 [*On Authors*], ed. Mao Dun 矛盾 (Shanghai: Shenghuoshudian, 1936), 65.

45. *Xu Zhimo Quanji*, 2:448–49. See appendix 3. For another translation see Acton and Ch'en, *Modern Chinese Poetry*, 80. The antiwar poems are "*Dashuai*" 大帥 ["Commander in Chief"] 2:245–49 and "*Da bianshou*" 大變獸 ["Dehumanization"], 2:250–51.

46. *Xu Zhimo Quanji*, 3:663; 6:189.

47. *OC*: 74.

48. *Xu Zhimo Quanji*, 6:277–87, originally published 10 Mar. 1928.

49. *Xu Zhimo Quanji*, 2 :345; 481–87.

SIX

The Chinese Decadents

When Chinese critics labeled Baudelaire a "Decadent," they used it as a pejorative. They regarded with moral disapproval such themes as sex and drugs, depression, decay, and death. They deplored the general mood of pessimism and despair.

The Decadent movement in France occurred in the last two decades of the nineteenth century, when Decadent writers and artists, according to Jean Pierrot, oppressed by the dominant ideas of science and progress, rationalism and determinism, found their religious faith shattered and reality "de-poeticized," dooming them to pessimism and despair. While religious faith remained a nostalgic memory, that vital theme of poetry, love, became suspect as "an unconscious subjection to an instinct aimed at survival of the species," and nature, rather than attending and responding to human beings as it had for the Romantics, became "an unfeeling, pitiless mechanism." In the anguish caused by this conception of human existence, they sought escape by turning inward, to "escape boredom and banality of everyday life through exquisite refinements of sensation," in a desperate quest for "the new, the rare, the strange, the refined, the quintessential in everything." Their quest could be made through the imagination, intoxication, or drugs, as they probed the unconscious, and turned to mysticism and the occult to create "secret, inner paradises for themselves."[1] The literature and art they created out of this exacerbated sensibility formed a new aesthetic. It was an aesthetic that Théophile Gautier had described as "art arrived at that point of extreme maturity shaped by the slanting suns of aged civilizations, ingenious, complicated, learned, full of nuances, etc." And although Gautier had declared that it was "improperly" called the Decadent style, later critics took his statement for their definition of Decadence.[2] Decades later, when Richard Gilman conducted his "experiment in free association" with the

107

word "decadence," *Les Fleurs du mal* sprang to his mind in a list that was "mostly sexual" and "heavily literary."[3] When Chinese critics pronounced Baudelaire a "Decadent," they used the term *"tui-fei"* 頹廢 [decline-waste], with a heavy note of censure. They did not follow Théophile Gautier's reference to style and ancient civilization or the subtle insinuations of Frank Pearce Sturm. The Chinese Decadent School, *"tuifeipai"* 頹廢派, was also known as the *"tui-jia-dang-pai"* 頹加蕩派.[4] The latter term, a transliteration for "decadent" in English and French, suggests the element of Western inspiration in their work. Oscar Wilde, Algernon Swinburne, and Arthur Symons had all become part of their horizon of expectations for Decadence. The Chinese writers who were called "Decadent" by various critics actually did not form a school or movement, and there is little evidence that they knew each other, or even read each other's work. Three Chinese Decadents have been compared with Baudelaire, each on different grounds: Yu Dafu, Yu Gengyu, and Shao Xunmei.

YU DAFU (郁達夫 1896–1945)

Yu Dafu has been called "China's Baudelaire," according to Zhao Cong, because of "the decadent atmosphere of his work."[5] Yu Dafu's collected work covers several volumes, but it is by his early fiction that he is best known. One biographer sums it up: "Yu's early stories are, as he described them, decadent, and they focus on one subject, sex."[6] Yu's early fiction forms the basis of comparison with Baudelaire.

Yu Dafu published his first collection of short stories, *Chenlun* (沉淪 [Sinking]) in 1921. Fiercely attacked by defenders of morals, it was an instant success. Yu was then studying at Tokyo Imperial University, and cofounded the Creation Society with a group of friends in the same year. He spent much of his time reading Western fiction, frequenting cafés, and drinking wine. This was his decadent phase.

"Sinking," the title story of Yu Dafu's collection, has often been taken as an autobiographical account. It is the story of a Chinese student in Japan whose deep feelings of alienation from his host country are conflated with sexual frustrations leading to fantasies, voyeurism, masturbation, and self-disgust. Alienated also from his compatriots, as he wanders about the Japanese countryside with his Emerson and Thoreau, Wordsworth, Heine, and Gissing, the protagonist is more reminiscent of Werther (as suggested by C. T. Hsia)[7] or Rousseau (as suggested by Leo Lee)[8] than of Baudelaire or the personae in his poems. After his visit to a brothel ends in fiasco, the youth walks into the sea, determined to end his lonely, frustrated, self-pitying life.[9]

In a preface to the collection Yu introduces the story as describing "the psychology of a sick youth. It can be called an anatomy of hypochondria. It also describes as a broad theme the suffering of modern man—that is, sexual need and clash between soul and flesh." The "clash between soul and flesh" in this case is not comparable with that experienced by Baudelaire with Madame Sabatier, who ruined the poet's idealizing love by granting him her favors. Yu's soul is not given over to an idealized love, and no sexual fulfillment is involved. With Yu, the clash is between sexual desire and guilt. Where Leo Lee finds in "Sinking" "the first effort by a Chinese literary man to merge sex with sentiment in unveiled and unadorned frankness,"[10] the sentiment that is merged with sex is not love, but guilt.

Yu's exploration of psychology and sexual guilt contributes to the story's modernity. His protagonist suffers agonies of guilt from lust, autoeroticism, and reading pornographic novels. In traditional Chinese literature, including the classic *Dream of the Red Chamber*, specific erotic, homoerotic, and autoerotic scenes are presented frankly, often without so much as a veil of figurative language, and without descriptions or even hints of struggles with conscience or soul. Nor, in traditional China, did brothel visits necessarily bring guilt: in his autobiographical *Six Chapters of a Floating Life*, Shen Fu movingly describes both the mutual love shared with his wife and his brothel visits, both with and without her.[11] There is nothing apologetic, defiant, or embarrassed in the account. C. T. Hsia explains Yu's protagonist's feelings of guilt in Confucian terms, making a contrast with Baudelaire:

> If the decadence of Baudelaire is explicable only in terms of a Christian faith, then, likewise, the guilt and remorse of Yü Ta-fu is to be understood in the framework of a Confucian ethic, which had conditioned his upbringing. Even when engaged in casual amorous pursuits, Yü Ta-fu or his fictional alter ego always suffers from the acute awareness of his truancy as son, husband, and father.[12]

While guilt about visiting the brothel may reflect his role as husband and father, his guilt about autoeroticism could be linked to his role as son. The *Classic of Filial Piety* (孝經) remonstrates against harming the body, because it is received from one's parents. Anxious about his daily masturbation, the youth in "Sinking" "would go to the library and look up medical references on the subject. They all said without exception that this practice was most harmful to one's health." Thus his hypochondria is directly linked to autoeroticism. In recompense, the youth would take a bath and have milk and several raw eggs every day, "but he couldn't help feeling ashamed of himself when taking his bath or having his milk and eggs: all this was clear evidence of his sin."[13] "Sin," the word used in this passage, leads back to the comparison with Baudelaire; the same word is used to translate "mal" in *Les Fleurs du mal*: "*zui'e*" 罪惡.

In Baudelaire's work, the correlation between sin, evil, and sexual guilt is clearest in the section of poems entitled "*Fleurs du mal.*" In "*Les Deux Bonnes Soeurs*" ["The Two Good Sisters], the sisters are Debauchery and Death. In *"Un voyage à Cythère"* ["A Voyage to Cythera"], on the isle of Venus, Goddess of Love, the poet finds not love, but a hideously castrated corpse hanging from a gibbet. The poem ends with a prayer for courage to contemplate his heart and body without disgust, so closely is lust associated with love. In the condemned poems that originally also comprised this section, lesbian lovers are *"Femmes damnées"* ["Women Damned"]; in *"Les Métamorphoses du vampire"* ["The Vampire's Metamorphoses"], the blood-sucking vampire is a desirable woman whose lips turn into a wineskin slimy with pus when the poet tries to kiss her, after which she metamorphoses into a skeleton. In the "clash between soul and flesh," the urges of the flesh lead to castration, debauchery, death, and damnation; sex leads to guilt, fear, and disgust. In Baudelaire's description of a brothel visit, describing a prostitute with whom he spends the night as an *"affreuse juive"* [frightful Jewess], the poet shares the sentiment expressed more baldly by Yu's protagonist after he leaves the brothel and is contemplating suicide: "I'll probably never get the kind of love I want."[14]

In addition to the connection between sexual guilt and evil, the aura of pessimism and decay, the brothel visits, and overindulgence in alcohol all contribute to the idea of "Decadence." All are found in the work of both authors. And both authors' works contain "purple patches" of narcissism and excess.

The Chinese story is a loosely structured, episodic, and overly sentimental first publication by a young man of twenty-five. What makes it possible to compare it with lyric poetry is Yu's method of description, which concentrates not on action but on the mental and emotional states and the inner contradictions of the protagonist. But the ending of Yu Dafu's story draws him far apart from Baudelaire. As the protagonist leaves the Japanese brothel and walks into the sea, he says haltingly: "Oh China, my country, you are the cause of my death! May you become rich and strong soon! . . . Many of your sons and daughters are still suffering!"[15] How did China as a nation become implicated in his feelings of degradation and guilt? Leo Lee offers a plausible explanation:

> To feel himself drawn irresistibly to the fair maidens of a nation which considered him as inferior—especially to succumb to their temptation in brothels—must have been a psychological problem that Yu felt acutely but found it hard to articulate. Hence sex, racism, and even nationalism are all intertwined in his psyche as in his stories.[16]

Even Yu Dafu himself may not have seen the connection so clearly, although in the preface he admits to "a few sketchy touches of nationalism." To be considered inferior without regard to his talent, character, speech, writing, actions, aspirations, or the state of his soul, but simply because of his nationality, was a torment that Baudelaire never had to know.

Going beyond the single story "Sinking," Yu's stories portray dashed youthful hopes; crushing poverty; gloomy, undirected pessimism; hopelessness; self-disgust; and self-pity. Anna Dolezalová points out their "autobiographical truth and sincerity" as well as a certain "masochism" in exposing all his weaknesses, going so far as "merciless mental self-flagellation;" and the "melancholy, pessimism, and cries of hopelessness and grief."[17] The same descriptions can describe the penultimate stanza from Baudelaire's "*L'Héauton-timorouménos*" ["Self-Executioner"]:

> *Je suis la plaie et le couteau!*
> *Je suis le soufflet et la joue!*
> *Je suis les membres et la roue,*
> *Et la victime et le bourreau!*

[I am the wound and the knife! / I am the slap and the cheek! / I am the limbs and the rack, / Both the victim and the executioner!]

The self-flagellation, masochism, and pessimism are common features of literary decadence.

On the matter of decadence, Dolezalová writes:

> Yü Ta-fu's contemporaries often branded his works as decadent, using this term explicitly as a reproach or an abuse without attempting to give support to their views by any deeper considerations. Elements reminiscent of decadent literature may be found in Yü Ta-fu's works in the sense that he focused his attention on the negative aspects of life. In some of his prose works the heroes dissect their suffering with an apparent delight, particularly in the initial stages of his literary writings.[18]

Similarly many of Baudelaire's poems can also be said to "dissect suffering," and even at their gloomiest and most depressed, one can detect a sense of delight in the dissection.

In the end, one can see a ray of optimism in "Sinking," however. While the youth walking into the sea may seem like the depth of nihilism, yet his last thoughts are of his nation. Even though the thoughts of his nation may have been stirred by self-pity, they ultimately have lifted him above dwelling on his physical and sexual body.

Yu Dafu eventually broke with the Creation Society, worked with Lu Xun for a time, and became a cofounder of the League of Leftwing Writers. The biographical record shows that after his return to China, according to McDougall and Louie, "he enjoyed an active social life and considerable success as a writer, editor, and businessman." During the war years he went to Southeast Asia and ironically was executed by Japanese security police in 1945 just after the end of the war.[19]

Yu Dafu also wrote poetry. But for that he chose classical forms, and wrote on such conventional subjects as meditations on history, feelings aroused by the seasons, descriptions of travel, and occasional poems on visits to or parting from friends.[20] The ground for comparison with Baudelaire, then, rests with his stories.

YU GENGYU (于賡虞 1902–1963)

Yu Gengyu's poetry is gloomy and depressed, often taking ghosts and dried bones for its subject; from the names of his collections *Roses on a Skull, Solitary Soul, Devil's Dance*, one can see that he aspired to the French poet Baudelaire.[21]

Yu Gengyu's poems, in the words and between the lines, are filled with the flavor of weariness and depression; they are gloomy and dejected. He often took ghosts and dried bones for his subjects; he probably aspired to the French poet Baudelaire.[22]

Yu Gengyu often took abandoned graves and skeletons as subject; [his poetry] is replete with the flavor of Baudelaire.[23]

Chinese critics have classified both Yu Gengyu and Baudelaire variously as *emopai* 惡魔派 [Demonic School], *xiangzheng pai* 象徵派 [Symbolist School], and *tuifei pai* 頹廢派 [Decadent School]. Unlike Yu Dafu and Shao Xunmei, he did not focus on sex, but was identified with Decadence through the dejected tone and morbid imagery in his poetry. As the poet Ai Qing put it, "Yu Gengyu was so decadent that he entitled his collection of poems *Roses on a Skull*."[24]

Yu Gengyu, like many writers of his generation, wrote most of his poetry as a young man, publishing six volumes between 1926 and 1930. A graduate of Yanjing University in Beijing, he studied at the University of London, toured Western Europe, and then returned to China to take up a lifetime of teaching, translation, and editorial work. His verse and prose poetry collections include: *Chenxi zhi qian* 晨曦之前 [*Before Dawn*] 1926; *Kuloushang de qiangwei* 骷髏上的薔薇 [*Roses on a Skull*], 1927, *Luohua meng* 落花夢 [*Fallen Flower Dream*], 1927; *Moguide wudao* 魔鬼的舞蹈 [*Devil's Dance*], 1928; and *Gu ling* 孤靈 [*Solitary Soul*], 1930. His translations include a volume of selected poems from English, Shelley's *Ariel*, and Dante's *Divine Comedy*. He also edited a volume of world poetry and a history of world literature.[25] There is no evidence of his having had first-hand knowledge of Baudelaire.

The comparisons with Baudelaire are based on depressed moods and graveyard imagery. Xie Zhixi offers an example from *Before Dawn* where the persona in the poem is pacing back and forth between graves, with yellow leaves falling and nightingales singing sadly, but there, among the unswept graves and bleached bones, grows an evil flower (*yiduo e hua*—一朵惡花), fragrant, and seducing ten thousand eyes with its secretive, peach-colored beauty. Xie declares the evil flower to be a duplicate of Baudelaire's "flower of evil" (*e zhi hua* 惡之花).[26]

There are indeed parallel images and phrases, but comparisons scarcely bear close examination. The poem *"Shantou ningsi"* 山頭凝思 ["On the Mountaintop Lost in Thought"] has Yu's favorite images of graves and skeletons:

> Spring has gone; hope still sleeps soundly among the scattered withered flowers,
> For life's desires it tosses all day long on the skeleton's grave mound,
> Now lost in thought in the mountain grove, it bitterly weeps in sunset's fading glow,
> And entrusts its unaging sorrow to the lone goose on its journey through the azure.
>
> The sea birds have gone, from two or three pleasure-boats sound mournful songs,
> In the world ruled by the gods of night, they harmonize with the tolling bells of a funeral service;
> Now in the music of gods and devils I sing alone to a new life
> To satisfy my enemies' hearty laughter I drink my fill in this dark night!
>
> "Madman, open wide your imagination; sing; whip the clusters of stars in the sky!"
> The century has died; exhausted souls have not yet awakened from their absurd dreams;
> There is no one now, the trembling rhymes of the wild woods smile wanly for me in the silence
> Listen to the goose's cry, like the shadows of lost dreams sadly moaning in an ancient well!
>
> Ah sorrow! On the darkling mountain path I am intoxicated, alone, walking alone,
> My irretrievable youth is like a corpse, silent in the night;
> Henceforth I go with a sigh of grief, whether to hell or to heaven,
> I will give my all to the ruins of the human world, to toss and turn on the skeleton's grave mound.[27]

Yu evokes the mood of nostalgia and regret with images common in traditional Chinese poetry: the mountain grove, the lone goose, the boat songs. The persona in the poem drinks alone. When Li Bo drank alone in the Tang dynasty, he imagined that the moon and his shadow became his companions; Yu Gengyu instead imagines the laughter of unspecified enemies. As he wanders around in Nature, the gathering darkness reflects his mood in a manner reminiscent of the European Romantics. In the poem's conclusion, Baudelaire's readers might hear an echo of *"Hymne à la Beauté"* in the indifference to the distinction between heaven and hell, but here it is used simply as cliché to enhance the melodramatically depressed mood, as Yu mourns his irretrievable youth in a poem he published at the ripe old age of twenty-five.

Yu Gengyu also recalls Baudelaire in choosing the prose poem form. *"Moguide wudao"* 魔鬼的舞蹈 ["Devil's Dance"], the title poem of that collection of prose poems, expands on the theme of death and drunkenness:

> This is the great world of night!
>
> The drinking party has dispersed; the heavy red wine has given me unfathomable strength, so that in the remnant ashes of the land of life I can still sorrow, recollect, and weep.
>
> Unbearable to speak of, the life of bygone days is only a floating dream now, lost without a trace in the devil's dance and song! I cannot, cannot bear to imagine the tragic shadow of song and dance; rhythms, steps, are only blurred forms in fading reds and blacks. Smiles and gentleness become unbearable faded reds; anger and violence become painful tragic deep blacks; distant now, hope for life of the mind! It all exists in the drunkenness of this night, staggering along; the poisoned flaming arrows have struck the dead soul.
>
> Stars and moon in the cold dawn, the world sunken in dreams; I lie alone in the grasses along the shore, enduring nature's impassive devastation, injury; enduring the devil's impassive dance and song on my heart. In its staggering steps, in its misty songs, red wine, cigarettes, drugs, meld into the palace of all hope. Ah—the full golden hair of yesteryear has turned white, the apple complexion has turned grey, all, all like a decrepit old man—youth has died; its color is like the dew on withered roses.
>
> Destruction! Throw life into the hideous black stagnant pool, poison it to death in the dead water; no need to be passionately attached to your life of suffering; to be the place where the devil dances and sings! Alas, lone soul, get drunk then, get drunk on smiles, get drunk on death, get drunk on shining palaces, get drunk on river banks; because of this, even if the devils sing and dance in your heart, on your hair, you can still fall into a dead drunk that you cannot recall—like death, forget everything.
>
> Ah, thus carrying on life's rhythms, forever, forever to sink into an unfathomable dream. The drinking party has dispersed; from my drunken state I had a glimpse into this tranquil life. . . .
>
> This is the great world of night![28]

As in many of his poems, here Yu Gengyu mourns the passage of time, dashing of hopes, and the inevitability of death. His description of youth as having "golden" rather than black hair adds a note of exoticism. The exhortation to drink as a source of enjoyment and seizing the day has a long history in Chinese poetry. But the exhortation to "get drunk!" and to do so not necessarily by imbibing wine could well have come from Baudelaire's prose poem *"Enivrez-vous"* ["Get Drunk"] where the reader is exhorted to get drunk on wine, poetry or virtue. And in assigning colors to emotions, could Yu have been making a self-conscious attempt to "aspire to Baudelaire" through synaesthesia?

Skeletons and graveyards, ghosts and demons, wine and poison appear far more frequently in Yu's poetry than in Baudelaire's. Yu did not practice short, concentrated forms. Yu's style, in its mixture of literary and vernacular language and in its technique of blending concepts and images has been compared with Li Jinfa.[29] Li Jinfa is the best known Chinese Symbolist poet; his relation with Baudelaire will be examined in the next chapter.

SHAO XUNMEI (邵洵美 1905–1968)

Shao Xunmei is known as a Chinese Decadent primarily through a single collection of poetry, *Hua yiban de zui'e* 花一般的罪惡 [*Flowerlike Evil*]; its title clearly is a deliberate echo of *Les Fleurs du mal*. K. Y. Hsu aptly translates the title as *The Flowerlike Sin* for reasons that will be discussed below.[30] Like Yu Dafu, Shao wrote about sex and sin. But in Shao's work there is none of Yu's anguished guilt or sense of nationalism. Shao was turned toward England and Europe rather than Japan, and his references to God and Satan brought him closer to Baudelaire.[31]

Born to a prominent wealthy family, Shao Xunmei studied in England and France and traveled in Europe before returning to Shanghai to lead the life of a bon vivant. He was deeply engaged with all aspects of literature: he read widely and wrote prolifically, contributing articles, reviews, and witty essays in Chinese and in English; he established publishing houses, journals, and magazines.[32] His "marriage" to Emily Hahn of the *New Yorker* is described in her book *China to Me*.[33] Already living in reduced circumstances before the regime change in 1949, he was imprisoned in 1958 for three years, emerged with his health broken, and was subjected to persecution thrice more during the Cultural Revolution before his death in 1968.[34]

In a collection of personal reminiscences and ruminations on literature, *Yige rende tanhua* 一個人的談話 [*A One-Way Conversation*],[35] Shao Xunmei tells of his early training in the Chinese classics, and his subsequent interest in American, European, and English literature. He read Longfellow, Dante, and Sappho in his teens, then discovered Swinburne and the Pre-Raphaelites, and later acquired an enthusiasm for what he called French Impressionist poetry (*yinxiang pai* 印象派), and then T. S. Eliot, all of whom he preferred to Shakespeare and Milton. He mentions being in France in 1926, but writes nothing of his studies at Cambridge. Emily Hahn recalls his loyalty to Cambridge, as well as his dedication to new poetry, adding: "Secretly he loved his classics, but he wouldn't admit it." Hahn also recalls that he read French, and often read from and discussed with his friends the works of Baudelaire and Mallarmé.[36]

Like his friend Xu Zhimo, Shao Xunmei had begun writing poetry in Cambridge. His first collection, *Tiantang yu wuyue* 天堂與五月 [*Heaven and May*], published in 1927, is comprised of poems dated 1925–1926 from Cambridge, London, Paris, and Shanghai. In that brief span of one year, Shao's poems progress from the puerile *"Hua Jiejie"* 花姊姊 [Sister Hua], based on the woman warrior Hua Mulan, to increasing sophistication in theme, regularity in form, and density in imagery and complexity in meaning. They also progress toward the eroticism that would earn Shao the epithet of "Decadent." Shao incorporated fifteen of the better poems into his next collection, *The Flowerlike Sin*, in 1928. In 1935 he lamented that he was not really a poet, that his earlier efforts lacked inspiration, and were simply "made up" (*zuochulai de* 做出來的), but he published one more collection in 1936, *Shi Ershiwu shou* 詩二十五首 [*Twenty-Five Poems*]; it includes a poem entitled *"Ni yiwei wo shi shenme ren?"* 你以為我是什么人? ["Who Did You Take Me For?"] which reasserts his status as a poet.[37]

In *Heaven and May*, among poems dedicated to Sappho and Swinburne, Adam and Eve and Venus de Milo, one poem invokes Baudelaire. Entitled in Italian *"Anch' io sono pittore!"* ["I too am a painter!"], the persona in the poem "sees" writers in various scenes and poses: Apuleius surrounded by roses and birds, Sappho strumming her lyre, Swinburne embracing love's light, Goethe weighed down by time, Keats listening to the nightingale, and Beethoven representing music with his symphonies. "I do not see," the poet writes, Byron, Shelley, Shakespeare, or "the ancestor of poetry, Homer." But in the fifth of six quatrains, he "sees:"

> *Dou-ban de yandeng-bian de shi bao-te-lei,*
> *Ni shi bushi tian-shang duoluo de mogui;*
> *Ni ba nide rou nide xue zuo le shi,*
> *Ni zhe yao-er qi ye zai dixia shengchan?*
> 豆般的煙燈邊的是包特蕾，
> 你是不是天上墮落的魔鬼；
> 你把你的肉你的血做了詩，
> 你這妖兒豈也在地下生產？

[Next to the bean-shaped opium lamp it's Baudelaire. / Are you the devil fallen from heaven? / You've made your flesh and blood into poetry; / Could you, this demon, also be produced on earth?][38]

Here Shao sees Baudelaire in devil-demon stereotype, but his view of the French poet would develop beyond it later.

In a 1928 essay on Swinburne collected in *Huo yu rou* 火與肉 [*Fire and Flesh*], Shao gives Baudelaire and Swinburne the highest positions in cultural history, declaring that although both had aroused great uproar and numerous attacks, they would influence not only their contemporaries but posterity. He praised both poets and their poetry as:

revolutionaries, and liberators of all literature imprisoned by religion, morality, and custom. Both are creators; they are protective deities of all poetry of truth, beauty, feeling, music, and sweetness. All of their poetry seeks fragrance from stench, truth from falsehood, goodness from evil, beauty from ugliness, diversion from the depression of living, and happiness from a world of melancholy; in short, they seek "consolation from evil." [39]

Putting Swinburne on the same level as Baudelaire makes Shao's estimation of the English poet's influence appears grossly overblown today. Shao's appreciation is also evident in the poem "To Swinburne" which appears in both *Heaven and May* and *The Flowerlike Evil*. As K. Y. Hsu has pointed out, "Shao admired Swinburne and openly imitated his style, even its rhythm and alliteration." [40] Shao himself later expressed regret at this, realizing that, under the influence of Swinburne and the Pre-Raphaelites, he had often "sacrificed whole lines to the sound of a single word." Well might he regret this influence, too, for Robert Nye's judgment on Swinburne, if cruel, seems just: "Swinburne's reputation as an empty vessel making a lot of meaningless if musical noise relates to only about nine-tenths of his poetic production. The other tenth is worth salvaging." [41] But Shao was more than an imitator of Swinburne. Anthologists and translators have "salvaged" at least a tenth of his poems.

Shao learned of Baudelaire from Swinburne, whose admiration for the French poet was well known, both through a review published anonymously in the *Spectator* in 1862, and through the elegy "*Ave Atque Vale*" written on the report of Baudelaire's death, some months before the French poet actually died. Swinburne, in his review, praised Baudelaire's "sensuous and weighty style," his "mastery of the sonnet form," his "balance of sound and meaning," and his "use of allegory;" but above all, Swinburne found, "there is not one poem of the *Fleurs du Mal* which has not a distinct and vivid background of morality to it." Even Baudelaire protested that Swinburne had exaggerated his moral intentions. [42] The notions of morality and sin provide striking points of comparison between Baudelaire and Shao.

Such a comparison begins and ends with contrasts. Baudelaire, despite his fascination with Classical antiquity and temptation to paganism, is in most of his work governed by a Christian awareness of sin. Shao similarly makes frequent references in his poetry to Greek and Roman antiquity; he also refers to Christianity, Heaven, and Hell. But much of his work draws on Taoist themes and imagery, as is the case with his "*Xuqu*" 序曲 ["Prelude"] which K. Y. Hsu translates as "Preface:"

I, too, have learned: There is an end to everything in the universe;
And in the end, even the yawning of the leaves breaks the solitude of the woods.

Formerly asleep with death, but isn't this instantaneous awakening
Due to the temptation of flesh, the prompting of sounds, and the sin of
motion?

These half-spent lives, soiled and degraded souls,
Strewn on earth at random like abandoned corpses;
Let them sink in the ocean for the fish and vermin to nibble,
Ah, better for them to be charcoal to kindle life, dreary and cold. [43]

The mention of corpses is too casual to recall *"Une Charogne,"* but the
reference to motion recalls Baudelaire's line in *"La Beauté," "Je hais le
mouvement qui déplace les lignes"* [I hate movement which displaces lines].
The poem's central idea of life coming from death is a Taoist one, but
where in Taoism, life and death are related in ceaseless alternation, Shao
does not follow the path back to death. Shao's "instantaneous awakening" similarly recalls Taoism, although the Taoist idea of the "moment of
awakening" is associated with dream: we do not know until that moment
whether we are waking from a dream or whether we had been dreaming
all along that we were awake. In Shao's poem, the moment of awakening
is from death to life. That awakening to life is prompted by "the temptation of flesh" and sound, and "the sin of motion." Hsu notes: "The attitude of the Taoist toward motion is such that, if speaking of 'sin' is
relevant to Taoism at all, he would regard motion as sinful." [44]

Shao's most frequent associations of sin are not with motion, but with
sex and beauty. Hsu's translation of *"zui'e"* 罪惡 as "sin" rather than
"evil" ("Evil" is the dictionary definition for *"zui'e"* 罪惡, while *"zui'nie"*
罪孽 is the dictionary equivalent for "sin"), is justified by the title poem,
"Hua yiban de zui'e" 花一般的罪惡 ["Flowerlike Sin"]. In eighteen quatrains reminiscent of both Keats's "La Belle Dame Sans Merci" and Rossetti's "The Blessed Damozel," Shao describes "an angel of God" as erotic
temptation personified. Her sin is using *"se"* 色, in its double sense of sex
and beauty, to "cheat men of love." She comes from Heaven, bringing
sweetness and marriage, but also separation and death. She confesses
that she has intoxicated men and led them astray, so that many curse her,
but still, some praise her. For her confession, she is offered redemption.
God forgives her, telling her "Suffering is the glory of human life," and
"Everything is an illusion of the self." The possibility for redemption
brings *"zui'e"* from "evil" to "sin." God invites her to return to Heaven,
but she chooses to remain on earth, a "slave to human life." Shao implies
that Evil in the form of suffering, separation, and death is a necessary
part of human life. Thus he subverts both the Buddhist notion that "All
life is suffering" to be escaped through meditation or through the Eight-
fold Path, and the Christian notion of forgiveness following the confession of sin.

In the same poem Shao asks of his "angel of God," "Or is she a demon?" Baudelaire had asked the same question in *"Hymne à la Beauté,"*

whether Beauty, personified as a woman, is "From Satan or from God?" "Angel or Siren?" and had answered rhetorically, "*Qu'importe*?" [What does it matter?] In "*Duoluo de huaban*" 墮落的花瓣 ["Fallen Petal"] Shao writes:

> *meiren shi mogui;*
> *ai le ni,*
> *ta zong zhanwu ni.*
> *yiding de.*
> 美人是魔鬼；
> 愛了你，
> 她總沾污你，
> 一定的。
> Beauty is a devil.
> After loving you,
> She always defiles you.
> That is certain.[45]

Here, beauty is not "*se*" 色 but "*meiren*" 美人 [beautiful woman].

The beautiful woman is similarly destructive in "*yidi xiang xian*" 一滴香涎 [a drop of fragrant saliva]: for a drop of saliva from the legendary beauty Xi Shi, palaces are destroyed, poets live drunk and die of dreams, and strong warriors die in full armor. Both the central image and the theme are reminiscent of Baudelaire's lines in "*Le Poison*:"

> *. . . ta salive qui mord,*
> *Qui plonge dans l'oubli mon âme sans remords*

[. . . your saliva which bites, which plunges my soul into oblivion without remorse]

In the French poem, saliva is compared with wine and opium in leading to oblivion. Similarly, Shao chooses the "poison" without remorse, as the poem concludes:

> *ai ba jinliang de ai ni yao ai de ba,*
> *hao feng-er bu zai qu xie-le de hua jian*
> 愛吧盡量地愛你要愛的吧，
> 好蜂兒不再去謝了的花間。

[Love then, love fully whom you would, / Good bees do not return to withered flowers.][46]

Whereas Baudelaire's poem ends in choosing Beauty to render the universe less hideous and time less heavy, Shao's chooses love and sex to recommend a joyous carpe diem.

Shao makes a more paradoxical connection between sin and sex in the poem "*Women de huanghou*" 我們的皇后 ["Our Empress"] with the line, "*Jing zui jie zhong meiyou bu haose de shengren*" 淨罪界中沒有不好色的聖人 [in the world of pure sin, there are no saints who do not love sex]. This connection is elaborated in his review of D. H. Lawrence's *The Escaped*

Cock. Lawrence's work creates a sexual experience in Egypt for Jesus after resurrection and before ascension. Shao explains that according to Lawrence, imagining sex is a sinful act, but responding to a purely carnal sexual urge is holy. Jesus had sacrificed his carnal life to implement his ideas; only after his resurrection did he realize that the body, too, has its "little life," and beyond that lies the greater life. To remain a virgin is so great a sacrifice that it becomes a form of greed: greed for suffering. Thus in writing this novel Lawrence was not committing blasphemy, but seeking to redress a wrong for Jesus. Shao explains that flesh and spirit each has its province; neither should obstruct the other—that is returning to the most primitive and purest state.[47] Sex here is not sinful, but redemptive.

Baudelaire referred to his poems as "flowers;" it was through these flowers that he would create beauty from what is conventionally considered ugly and vile.[48] In a poem entitled simply *"Hua"* 花 ["Flower"], Shao describes the flower as born of the union of earth and sky; he has the universe for his dwelling, branches and leaves for his companions, and lives in harmony with streams, clouds, rain, wind, sun, and moon. (Shao was being ultra-modern in distinguishing genders in his use of pronouns, using the feminine form for beauty and the masculine form for the flower, which is feminine in French). His flower fears only the complaints of song birds, and pities the lot of man. He drinks the dew of the immortals, and with the perfume of his breath, changes hell into heaven. Shao's flower is thus similarly redemptive.[49]

Shao Xunmei, like Baudelaire, also chose filth and putrescence as subjects for poetry. There are the abandoned corpses in "Preface," and foul-smelling earth and filthy worms in *"Sile you shen anyi"* 死了有甚安逸 ["Death Offers Extreme Comfort"].[50] Its title notwithstanding, the latter poem ends by choosing life, stating that "only live persons can quench the thirst of live persons," and that it is better to kiss a live ugly woman than a dead beautiful one. With Shao, the tension between beauty and ugliness lies on the surface, rather than forming the essence of the poem as with Baudelaire.

Baudelaire's power often comes from what has been called his "simultaneous aspiration toward God and Satan."[51] Shao, on the other hand, is not in search of absolutes. In spite of his repeated references to God and the Devil, to Heaven and Hell, there is no real awe before one or terror before the other. Shao's notion of sin is not associated with ideas of absolute evil or transgression of divine law; rather, it reflects the view from Chinese popular religions, as described by Wolfram Eberhard, where sin is associated with dirt, odor, blood, and pus, as well as with sex, and where Hell reflects life on earth, with its "divine bureaucracy," "divine ministries," and "divine red tape."[52] Like the elite of which he was a member, Shao did not take this religion seriously.

Shao's Occidentalizing was a game: he played with the idea of sin. His chosen Romanization for his given name, Xunmei 洵美, was Sin May. A poem entitled *"Wuyue"* 五月[May] in K. Y. Hsu's translation contains these lines: "A sin is born of a virgin's kiss . . . / If she is not a rose, a rose all white, / then she must be redder than the red of blood." The poem concludes: "Heaven has just opened two large gates, O God, I am not one to enter. / I have already found comfort in Hell."[53]

Shao's admiration for Western literature was indisputably genuine, but his poetic world is Chinese. He did not construct "an Occident of the Orient." While he was avidly reading Western literary works, he also read the Tang dynasty poets Wang Wei (王維 701–761) and Wen Tingyun (溫庭筠 813?–870) to "find some Chinese friends for them." He joined the two worlds in his poetry. Thus his poem *"Madonna Mia,"* its Italianate title notwithstanding, refers to the legendary Chinese beauty Xi Shi. The *"Légende de Paris,"* with its French title and address to Venus, rejoins the Chinese tradition in its treatment of the passage of time, and its view of reality as process.

Shao's sense of affinity with writers outside the Chinese tradition is evident from his poem "To Swinburne" which ends:

> *women cong lanni li lai reng xiang lanni li qu,*
> *women de xiwang bian shi yongjiu zai lanni li.*
> 我們從瀾泥裡來仍向瀾泥裡去，
> 我們的希望便是永久在瀾泥裡。

[We came from mud and will return to mud, / Our hope is to remain in mud forever].

His choice of the word "mud" is more suggestive of filth and dirt than "clay" "ashes" or "dust," and again brings back his affinity with Baudelaire's creation of beauty from ugliness.[54]

Largely because of his self-professed Decadence, Shao Xunmei's poetry has been more often disparaged than admired by his compatriots. Zhou Jin, writing in 1975, went so far as to charge Shao with "sounding the death-knell of formalism" through his "aestheticism and decadence."[55] Shen Congwen instead appreciated praise for life and love in Shao's aestheticism.[56] Shao's consistent embrace of life has led some critics to conclude that he was more Hedonist than Decadent.[57] *"Ai de ding-zhu "* 愛的叮囑 "[Love's Warning"] shows both sides of the question:

You have learned now how I wanted
My jade missive to enter that gold and silver trove!
When it entered, you knew
My becalmed heart had taken the aimless road again.

Why should the proper fish
Want to swim alone in the flooding turbulent waves?
Why should the little lamb

Want to parade alone before the lion's cave, the tiger's den, the wolf's lair, the fox's earth?

Ah, if your beloved
Paces a pit more frightful than a prison,
If you are someone with a soul,
Can you still be tranquil as a lotus leaf bare in the autumn wind?

Bone-tired now,
Dragging joy and care from life's door to the gate of death,
Too many doors are open!
Ask the way no more; crave pity from the enemy.[58]

The eroticism of the poem is the more powerful for the restraint in expression. The poem embraces life, but the final image is of exhaustion. That sense of exhaustion brings us back to the French Decadents.

A better known and frequently anthologized poem, *"Zuori de yuanzi"* 昨日的園子 ["Garden of Yesterday"] also recalls the Decadents with its melancholy tone, its images of decline, withering, and stillness:

Quiet, quiet, dark night comes again;
She wears the grey habit of a nun;
Embracing melancholy and sorrow;
She is the executioner of light.

She has hidden God's abode;
Oxen, horses, cocks, dogs, turtles, men,
Grope in the darkness
And finally find the devil's dwelling.

Here is a garden of yesterday
Green leaves have yellowed;
Fresh flowers have withered;
Lively birds have died.

There is still a pair of lovers,
Embracing each other, kissing,
Without breath, and without sound,
Ah, they are the beloved children of God.[59]

By comparing night with a nun and an executioner, Shao brings the images of nature into the human realm. The human pair of lovers, "without breath and without sound" may well be statues. Here Shao fulfills the European Decadents' goal to "dethrone life, and put art in its place."[60]

Finally, like Baudelaire, Shao chose the city for his subject, and successfully captured its moments of flux. His poem *"Shanghai de linghun"* 上海的靈魂 ["The Soul of Shanghai"], evokes tall buildings, cars, telephone wires, the race track, a theatre, a prostitute . . . and ends, in K. Y. Hsu's translation: "Here there are true illusions, false sentiments; / Here dusk is awake, lights are smiling; / Come, then, here is your burial ground."[61]

Another poem about Shanghai, *Rishenglou xia* 日昇樓下 ["Below Sunrise Pavilion"], is less philosophical, but equally evocative:

> Car sounds, flute sounds, spitting sounds,
> A sudden shaping of smoke,
> A woman's skirt.
>
> Like clouds before the wind, a surge of humanity—
> Stenches of flesh, of blood,
> Stench of sweat—come in waves.
>
> Over the roofs, atop the tower, a clock,
> Ten after ten;
> Among the stars, scattered electric lamps.
>
> I am at the crossroads,
> Trembling with desire,
> I imagine a kiss.[62]

The last six lines of the poem had appeared earlier in a poem of twelve lines entitled *"Tuijiadang de ai"* 頹家蕩的愛 ["Decadent Love"]. The original "Decadent Love" began with white clouds in heavenly beds, but carried a note that it had been written on a tram car. By using only the latter part of the poem to highlight the urban scene in his new poem, and by going beyond visual imagery to evoke smells and sounds, Shao brings the new poem closer both in subject and in technique to Baudelaire's evocations of Paris. If, as Pierrot has it, the "essential line of cleavage between traditional and modern" is the dissociation of art from the imitation of nature,[63] then Shao's poems on the city bring him closer to the modern.

NOTES

1. Jean Pierrot, *The Decadent Imagination, 1880–1900*, trans. Derek Coltman (Chicago: University of Chicago Press, 1981), 10, 14–15, 25–26.

2. Gautier, *Charles Baudelaire*, 28; Havelock Ellis, "Introduction," in *Against the Grain (À Rebours)*, by J. K. Huysmans, trans. J. H. Lewis, (1931, New York: Dover, 1969), xv.

3. Richard Gilman, *Decadence: The Strange Life of an Epithet* (New York: Farrar, Straus and Giroux, 1971, 1979), 12.

4. Lee, *Shanghai Modern*, 233, adds "tuibai" 頹敗 and "tuitang" 頹唐, which he translates as "degradation" and "dejection," rendering "tuifei" 頹廢 as "dilapidation." Lee gives an excellent introduction to Shao Xunmei as Decadent and to the relation of Decadence to modernity. Here I concentrate on relations to Baudelaire.

5. Zhao Cong 趙聰, "Zhongguode Bodelai'er" 中國的「波德萊爾」 ["China's Baudelaire"] *Wusi wentan diandi* 五四文壇點滴 [*Tidbits from the May Fourth Literary Field*] (Hong Kong: Youlian chubanshe, 1964), 181–85.

6. Howard L. Boorman, *Biographical Dictionary of Republican China* (New York: Columbia University Press, 1967–1979), 71.

7. C. T. Hsia, *A History of Modern Fiction* (New Haven, CT: Yale University Press, 1962), 104

8. Lee, *Romantic Generation*, 112.

9. According to Bonnie S. McDougall and Kam Louie, *The Literature of China in the Twentieth Century* (New York: Columbia University Press, 1997), 109, Yu Dafu's early fiction was "modeled on Japanese confessional fiction."

10. Lee, *Romantic Generation*, 111.

11. Shen Fu 沈復, *Fusheng liuji* 浮生六記 is translated by Leonard Pratt and Chiang Su-hui as *Six Records of a Floating Life* (New York: Penguin Classics, 1983).

12. Hsia, *History*, 109.

13. C. T. Hsia and Joseph S. M. Lau, trans., "Sinking," by Yu Dafu, in *Twentieth-Century Chinese Stories*, ed. and trans. C. T. Hsia and Joseph S. M. Lau (New York: Columbia University Press, 1971), 16–17.

14. Ibid., 32.

15. Ibid., 33.

16. Lee, *Romantic Generation*, 90–91.

17. Anna Dolezalová, *Yü Ta-fu: Specific Traits of His Literary Creation* (Bratislava: Publishing House of the Slovak Academy of Sciences, 1971; New York: Paragon Reprint Corporation, 1971), 7, 25, 31, 36.

18. Ibid., 133.

19. McDougall and Louie, *The Literature of China in the Twentieth Century*, 47–48.

20. *Yu Dafu Quanji* 郁達夫全集 [*Yu Dafu Complete Works*], vol. 10 (Hong Kong: Shenghuo dushu, xinzhi, sanlian shudian, 1984).

21. Zhao Jingshen 趙景深, "Preface," *Xiandai shixuan* 現代詩選 [*Modern Poetry Selection*] (Shanghai: Beixinshuju, 1934), 10.

22. Li Yiming 李一鳴, *Zhongguo xin wenxue shi jianghua* 中國新文學史講話 [*Introduction to Chinese New Literary History*] (Shanghai: Shijieshuju, 1943), 71.

23. QiuWenzhi 邱文治, Du Xuezhong 杜學忠, and Mu Huaiying 穆懷英, "Lun Zhongguo xiandai xiangzheng shipai zhi shengchen" 論中國現代象徵詩派之升沉 ["On the Rise and Fall of the Modern Chinese Symbolist School"], *Wenxuepinglun* 文學評論 1 (1987): 119.

24. Ai Qing, "Sixty Years of New Poetry in China," *Chinese Literature* 3 (1981): 98.

25. Biographical dictionaries disagree on the details. The entry in *Zhongguo wenxuejia cidian* 中國文學家辭典 [*Dictionary of Chinese Writers*] (Chengdu: Sichuan reminchubanshe, 1979), 5:14–15, lists four collections, and has him in England in 1931; Yang Li 楊犁 et al.，*Zhongguo xiandai zuojia da cidian* 中國現代作家大辭典[*Large Dictionary of Modern Chinese Authors*] (Beijing: Xin shijie chubanshe, 1992), 578, says he went to London in 1935, and lists seven collections. Both sources date all of his poetry collections prior to his studying abroad.

26. Xie Zhixi 解志熙, *Mei de pianzhi: Zhongguo xiandai weimei-tuifei zhuyi wenxue sichao yanjiu* 美的偏至：中國現代唯美—頹廢主義文學思潮研究[*Extremes of Beauty: Study of Modern Chinese Aesthetic-Decadent Literary Trends*] (Shanghai: Shanghai wenyichubanshe, 1998), 330.

27. Yu Gengyu, "Shantou ningsi" 山頭凝思, from *Kuloushang de qiangwei* 骷髏上的薔薇 [*Roses upon a Skull*], reprinted in *Daxi*, 265–66 and in M. M. Y. Fung et al., ed. and comp., *Xiandai Zhongguo shixuan* 現代中國詩選: *Modern Chinese Poetry: An Anthology 1917–1949* (Hong Kong: Hong Kong University Press, 1974), 370–71. See appendix 3.

28. Yu Gengyu, *Moguide wudao* 魔鬼的舞蹈 (Shanghai: Beixinshuju, 1928) 24–26. See appendix 3.

29. Fung et al., *Xiandai Zhongguo shixuan*, 368.

30. Hsu, *Twentieth Century Chinese Poetry*, 125. Shao Xunmei 邵洵美 , *Huayiban de zui'e* 花一般的罪惡 (Shanghai: Jinwushudian, 1918).

31. Wang Zhijian 王志健, *Xiandai Zhongguo shi shi* 現代中國詩史 [*History of Modern Chinese Poetry*] (Taipei: Shangwu, 1975), 153, compares him with French Decadents; see also Su Xuelin 蘇雪林, "Tuijiadang pai de Shao Xunmei" 頹加蕩派的邵洵美 ["The Decadent School's Shao Xunmei"] in *Er-sanshi niandai zuojia yu zuopin* 二三十年代作家與作品 [*Authors and Works of the Twenties and Thirties*] (Taipei: Guangdong chubanshe, 1980), 148–55.

32. Most notably "Jinwu shudian" 金屋書店 [Golden Room Bookstore] produced deluxe editions, and "Shidai yinshua gongsi" 時代印刷公司 [Modern Press] boasted the most up-to-date equipment; *Lunyu* 論語: *Analects* had Lin Yutang as chief editor, and *Tianxia yuekan* 天下月刊：*T'ien Hsia Monthly* published articles in English.

33. Emily Hahn, *China to Me* (Garden City, NY: Doubleday, Doran and Co., 1944). According to Hahn, the "marriage of convenience" was approved by Shao Xunmei's wife Zoa, since "according to foreign law," they had never been married! It was also a plan to save the press from the Japanese. Wen Xing 文星, "Tuifeishiren Shao Xunmei" 頹廢詩人邵洵美 ["Decadent Poet Shao Xunmei"], Hong Kong: *Mingbao* 明報 (April 5, 1974), states that Shao spent most of his time drinking and gambling, so that Hahn had to sell her books to support him. Hahn's *Mr. Pan* (Garden City, NY, Doubleday, Doran, 1942) tells of Shao's constant borrowing and begging from her—this aspect of his life was overlooked by the biographies provided in English by Jonathan Hutt, "The Sumptuous World of Shao Xunmei," *East Asian History* 21 (June 2001): 111–42, and Lee, *Shanghai Modern*, 241–46.

34. Interview with his son Shao Zucheng: "In the 'New' China, Old Problems Remain," Associated Press, February 16, 2003. *St. Petersburg Times Online.* www.sptimes.com/2003/02/16/news_pf/Worldandnation/In_the_new_China_o.shtml (accessed 28 Jan. 2004, site no longer accessible).

35. Shao Xunmei, *Yige ren de tanhua* 一個人的談話 [*A One-Way Conversation*] (Shanghai: Diyichubanshe, 1935).

36. Hahn, *China to Me*, 20, and personal letter to me dated 13 Feb. 1978. When we met in March 1978, Emily Hahn had not heard of Shao Xunmei's death, though she knew that he had given up opium. Lee in *Shanghai Modern*, 248–49 adds many authors to Shao's "reading list."

37. Shao Xunmei, *Tiantang yu wuyue* 天堂與五月 (Shanghai: Guanghua shuju, 1927), 23–60; the lament is in *Yigeren de tanhua*, 1. *Shi Ershiwu shou* 詩二十五首[*Twenty-Five Poems*] (Shanghai: Shidaitushugongsi, 1936), 36–38.

38. Shao, *Tiantang*, 151–54. "Bean-shaped:"*dou* 豆 [bean] is also the name of an ancient bronze drinking vessel, so the opium pipe can also be called "*dou*-shaped."

39. Shao Xunmei, *Huo yu rou* 火與肉 [*Fire and Flesh*] (Shanghai: Jinwu shudian, 1928), 19–20; Lee, *Shanghai Modern*, 248.

40. Hsu, *Twentieth-Century Chinese Poetry*, 125.

41. Shao, *Yigerende tanhua*, 1; Robert Nye, *A Choice of Swinburne's Verse* (London: Faber and Faber, 1973), 13.

42. Algernon C. Swinburne, *Les Fleurs du Mal and Other Studies*, ed. Edmund Gosse (London: printed for private circulation, 1913), xiii, 11, xii.

43. Hsu, *Twentieth-Century Chinese Poetry*, 127.

44. Ibid., 125.

45. Shao, *Hua*, 21.

46. Ibid., 18–19.

47. Hao Wen 浩文 (pseud. of Shao Xunmei), "Shubaochunqiu" 書報 春秋 [*Books and Newspapers Annals*], *Xinyue* 新月 (1932): 1–4, review of D. H. Lawrence, *The Escaped Cock*, first published in *Forum* 79, no. 2 (1928), 286–96; Shao cites the 1929 printing by Black Sun in Paris.

48. Marcel Ruff, *Baudelaire*, trans. Agnes Kertesz (New York: New York University Press, 1966), 87.

49. Shao, *Hua*, 25–28.

50. Ibid., 33.

51. Ruff, *Baudelaire*, 89–90.

52. Wolfram Eberhard, *Guilt and Sin in Traditional China* (Berkeley: University of California Press, 1967), 13, 21.

53. Shao, *Hua*, 6–7. Hsu, *Twentieth-Century Chinese Poetry*, 126–27.

54. Shao, *Hua*, 23–24. Hsu, *Twentieth-Century Chinese Poetry*, 128, uses "dust," which is "chen" 塵 in Chinese; "dust" has Christian overtones, and "chen" has Buddhist overtones. "Lanni" 瀾泥 or 爛泥, is "mud, slush, mire." Su Xuelin, "Tuijiadang-pai,"150, compares this poem with Baudelaire's *"Une Charogne."* I find the parallels too weak to repeat here.

55. Zhou Jin 周錦, *Zhongguo xin wenxue shi* 中國新文學史 (Taipei: Changge chuban-she, 1976), 433. Zhou's charge is easily refutable: Bian Zhilin published "formalist" poems well into the thirties; Feng Zhi's *Sonnets* appeared in 1941.

56. Shen's judgment is quoted in Wang Zhijian, *Xiandai Zhongguo shi shi*, 153.

57. Loi, *Roseaux*, 139, finds in his work a kind of "Taoist Hedonism." Jonathan Hutt sees him as an "aesthetic Hedonist" rather than a Decadent.

58. Shao, *Hua*, 35–36. See appendix 3.

59. Ibid., 15. See appendix 3. There is another translation by Arno L. Bader and Lucien Mao, "Three Modern Chinese Poems," *T'ien Hsia Monthly* 10, no. 1 (Jan. 1940): 162.

60. Pierrot, *The Decadent Imagination*, 10.

61. Shao, *Hua*, 47–48. Hsu, *Twentieth-Century Chinese Poetry*, 127–28 has a more poetic translation.

62. Shao, *Hua*, 45–46. See appendix 3. Sunrise Pavilion was a teahouse in Shanghai.

63. Pierrot, *The Decadent Imagination*, 11.

SEVEN

The Chinese Symbolists

The Chinese Symbolists (*xiangzheng pai* 象徵派) did not represent a movement or a school. The poets identified as Symbolists in literary histories, anthologies, and criticism shared an interest in French Symbolist poetry; their works have been discussed in connection with French Symbolists in several major studies.[1]

The Symbolist movement in France overlapped with the Decadent movement; French literary histories generally date Symbolism from Moréas's manifesto first published in 1886.[2] Thus some writers were associated with both movements: Verlaine, who embraced the term "Decadence," appears in anthologies and studies of Symbolist poetry. Mallarmé, and later Valéry, became leading figures of the Symbolist school. The Symbolist aesthetic spread from poetry to other literary genres, art, and music, and from France to England, Germany, and other countries, forming a vast movement. A great deal has been written on Baudelaire's relation to the Symbolist movement. Many Chinese critics follow Moréas in declaring Baudelaire to be the true precursor to the Symbolists, while others regard him as a Symbolist *tout court*. They regard his sonnet "*Correspondances*" as the emblem or wellspring of Symbolism.

Most studies of Chinese Symbolists begin with Li Jinfa. Li translated poems from *Les Fleurs du mal,* which he then included in his own poetry collections. Three founders of the Creation Society—Wang Duqing, Mu Mutian, and Feng Naichao—studied in Japan, were dedicated to "art for art's sake," discussed French poetry in their journal, and praised Baudelaire in their pursuit of "pure poetry." Tu Kuo-ch'ing, who has made a study of French Symbolism in Japan and China, identifies three "waves" of Chinese response: Li Jinfa in the first; Mu Mutian, Feng Naichao, and Wang Duqing in the second; and Dai Wangshu in the third.[3] In terms of chronology, the poets were not very far apart: the first four were born between 1898 and 1901, Dai in 1905; their first poetry collections date from 1925 to 1928; Dai's first poem also dates from 1928. A major study of Dai Wangshu's work gives compelling reasons to identify him as a Modernist, so his relationship to Baudelaire will be taken up in the next chapter. This chapter instead will introduce Xu Yunuo, who has not been grouped with the Chinese Symbolists, but whose work has reminded some readers of the Symbolist poetry. It will examine the original poems by Liang Zongdai and Qin Zihao, admirers of Baudelaire whose translations and criticism were introduced in previous chapters, and whose poems have been or can be compared with Baudelaire.

LI JINFA (李金髮 1900–1976)

Known as the first Chinese Symbolist poet, and credited with having introduced French Symbolism into Chinese poetry, Li Jinfa was once called the "Baudelaire of the Orient" (*dongfang zhi Bao-te-lai* 東方之鮑特萊).[4] His penname means "Golden Hair" and indicates how far he went in the direction of Westernization. He later adopted "Li Jinfa" as his regular name, spelling it Ginffa Lee.[5] His fellow poet Ai Qing has gone so far as to call him a "fake foreigner."[6]

Born in 1900 to a Hakka family of some means in Guangdong province and originally named Li Quanxing 李權興,[7] Li Jinfa studied English in Hong Kong from 1917 to 1919 and then joined a large group of students going to France on a work-study program. After studying French in Fontainebleau and then Bruyères in the Vosges, Li decided to study sculpture in Dijon. He soon arrived in Paris, where by 1921 his portrait sculpture was good enough to be entered in the Spring Salon.[8] Well-off compared with other Chinese students in France and not having to work, he nevertheless later recalled living in poverty and spending his time in "humanist and leftist readings," which led to "cynical and misanthropic feelings," and in turn to an interest in "Decadent works." He remembered reading Baudelaire and Verlaine with avid interest, becoming "infatuated with the Symbolist style."[9] Although his knowledge of Chinese poetry was limited, he began to write his own; in a city then alive with literary movements, he found encouragement from only one person, the scholar Li Huang (李璜 1895–1991). He nevertheless sent the poems to Zhou Zuoren, who responded with enthusiasm and promised to see to their publication.[10]

Li Jinfa's three collections of poetry, all written in Europe, were published after his return to China: *Weiyu* 微雨 [*Light Rain*], 1925; *Shike yu xiongnian* 食客與凶年 [*The Long-Term Visitor and Hard Times*] (hereafter, *Hard Times*), 1926; and *Wei xingfu er ge* 為幸福而歌 [*Sing for Happiness*] (hereafter, *Happiness*), 1927. In 1942 appeared *Yiguo qingdiao* 異國情調 [*Exoticism*], a collection of poems, essays, and fiction, and in 1964, *Piaoling xianbi* 飄零閑筆 [*Idle Jottings*], a volume of essays and memoirs. Toward the end of his life, he revealed to Ya Xian that he no longer took interest in American or European poetry, with the sole exception of Baudelaire's *Les Fleurs du mal*, which he read in an English-French edition given to him by a friend.[11]

Li Jinfa's three collections of poetry contain over three hundred poems. He wrote on a great number of themes, the most frequent being love, nostalgia, the passage of time, and the approach of death. Some poems describe nature, especially at twilight or in autumn. Many describe moods and emotions, especially of melancholy, loneliness, and gloom. Nymphs, shepherdesses, and cabaret dancers all find a place, as does the figure of the poet, generally passive and suffering. Although there are more lighthearted poems in *Happiness*, its German subtitle, *Sehnsucht* [longing] (misprinted as "Schusucht"), also indicates part of the contents.[12]

In the epilogue to *Hard Times*, Li comments on the similarities of themes in Chinese and Western poetry, and states his wish to bring the two traditions together in his work. His poems are often sprinkled with foreign words (most frequently French, but also English, German, and Italian). *Light Rain* includes several poems translated from the French. Many of the poems in the later collections carry epigraphs in English, French, or German.[13] Women's names in French and German, and place names going beyond Europe to Saigon and Titiyamatata [*sic*] contribute to the exotic flavor of his poems. In addition *Hard Times* and *Happiness* both contain curious drawings blending Chinese and Western techniques and subject matter (e.g., a faun holding a slant-eyed female nude) which add to their exotic appeal.[14]

Like many Chinese poets of his era, Li wrote most of his poetry as a young man, in his case in the short span of three years before age twenty-five. And like them, he later repudiated his work. He wrote in his memoirs in 1964: "Actually my poetry was a kind of verbal game of youth, with no thought to speak of; some were only childish fantasies, clumsy in technique; nowadays when I read them I really feel embarrassed."[15] Still, his poetry had caused a stir when it first appeared, and in the same memoirs, he regrets not having joined with the other Chinese Symbolists—he names Mu Mutian, Wang Duqing, and Dai Wangshu—had they promoted each other, he thought, they might have succeeded in forming a more impressive movement. But he found the literary scene at the time dominated by Xu Zhimo, whose poetry for him read like translations from Hugo, with rhymes contrived at the end.[16] Ten years later, when Dai Wangshu returned from France, Li Jinfa was too little involved with poetry to join forces with him.

Most descriptions of Chinese Symbolist poetry begin with the work of Li Jinfa. Zhu Ziqing's statement in *Daxi* is frequently quoted:

His poems do not contain ordinary structure; part by part they are understandable, but put together, they are meaningless. What he wants to express is not meaning, but sensations or emotions; they are like strings of beads of various colors and sizes whose string he has hidden; you must string them yourself. This is precisely the French Symbolists poets' technique, and Li is the first to introduce it into Chinese poetry.[17]

In the same work, Zhu summarizes an article by Su Xuelin (蘇雪林 1897–1999) which identifies in Li's poetry four characteristics that she associates with the Symbolists: (1) obscurity, in the sense of hazy and hard to understand; (2) hyperaesthesia; (3) melancholy and decadence; (4) exoticism. Adding that Li's art is peculiar in its association of concepts, and pointing out his liking for personification and compression, Su asserts that such is the secret of Symbolist poetry. But she notes that Li takes it too far, often rendering his writing incomprehensible.[18]

Incomprehensibility and obscurity became hallmarks in definitions of Chinese Symbolism. K. Y. Hsu finds the obscurity in Li's poems due less to their "unusual associations" and "frequent omission of certain links in the chain of association" than to their "studied departure from linguistic conventions, both new and old, both written and spoken."[19] Julia Lin carefully warns that many of the typical Symbolist techniques are equally important in traditional Chinese poetry, but finds Li's "aesthetic and spiritual concept of poetry," "fluctuation between the actual and the ideal," "private set of symbols," "compression," and "effective distribution of words within lines and stanzas" to be closer to Rimbaud and Mallarmé than to the Classical Chinese poets.[20]

The French critic Michelle Loi questions the associations with French poetry and asserts that Li's work derives solely from his own tradition:

> Li Jinfa cultivated obscurity, not only in the enchainment of his images, but in the very expression of his language, which he willingly archaizes ... he truly valued only *wenyan*. He himself says so. Hence the beauty of some of his poems, strange bordering on the fantastic, could be from Li Ho, rather than Mallarmé or Valéry to whom he refers, but from whom it was difficult for him to borrow anything. And with reason! The 'monstrous' poetics of Li Jinfa is the sway of the spontaneous impression, undisciplined down to the most gratuitous forms.[21]

The similarity to Li Ho is corroborated by Tu Kuo-ch'ing, who declares: "With regard to diction, Li Jinfa appears to be a disciple of Li Ho."[22] But if Li Jinfa read Li Ho, he did not mention it in his writings.

Li Jinfa did publish some translations from Mallarmé, accompanied by an introduction to the poet that cites several French sources.[23] But Li's own poetry, written in two to three years to fill three thick volumes, often reveals a haste and carelessness in sharp contrast to Mallarmé and Valéry's experiments and "anguish before the blank page."

It was difficult for Li Jinfa to borrow anything from Mallarmé and Valéry, contends Michelle Loi, because of his inadequate knowledge of the French language. His style is "Occidentalist kitsch," his Chinese sources hidden "under the ornaments of French trumpery:" "Inscribe a couple of lines by Verlaine atop an obscure poem, and the trick is played. Could he even understand Verlaine? Even Verlaine. It is not quite certain.[24] Loi bases her judgment of Li Jinfa's ignorance of French partly on his own statement in his memoirs:

> In my experience, I'm afraid French is the hardest language in the world; the grammatical transformations are so numerous, the pronunciation is so irregular, and the words must be linked together in sound. After living (in France) for a year, most of us were still unable to hold conversations; often Chinese students who have studied in France for four or five years still cannot converse fluently; as soon as they see a Caucasian, they become wide-eyed and tongue-tied; you can imagine the difficulty of the French language. As for English, in less than half a year one can converse fluently, and if one lives in England for two years, one can enter Oxford and Cambridge.[25]

There is no small humor in Li's remarks, and there is a temporal and qualitative difference between conversation and reading. In an interview published in 1935, Li stated that although he could carry on conversations in English and German, French was the only foreign language in which he could read poetry.[26]

Li Jinfa actually wrote two poems entirely in French, published in *Hard Times*. They are simple, and not without grammatical errors, but original. He also made a good many translations from the French, going beyond random selected poems to include Pierre Loti's *Les Derniers jours de Pékin*, serialized in *Qianfeng* 前鋒 [Avant-garde], and Pierre Louÿs's *Chansons de Bilitis* in a complete volume entitled *Gu Xila lian'ge* 古希腊恋歌 [*Ancient Greek Love Songs*].[27]

Evaluating Li Jinfa's style in relation to their own poetical tradition, his compatriots were led not to Li Ho, but to questioning Li's command of Chinese. Rather than finding a "classical Chinese manner" as Loi had, Zhu Ziqing judged that Li's poems read like translations. Zhu wrote that despite Li's frequent use of *wenyan* particles, his grammar was so "Europeanized" that it was hard to judge whether he was "overly eager to create a new language, or whether he was too unfamiliar with his mother tongue." Other critics, including Su Xuelin, Li Jianwu, Gao Zhun, and Cai Yizhong, were less kind, concluding flatly that Li simply did not know the Chinese language well.[28] Nevertheless, studies of modern Chinese Symbolists invariably devote a major portion to Li Jinfa. In 1987 Li's three poetry collections and his work on exoticism were republished in one volume; in his preface essay, Zhou Liangpei cites three sources to question Li's command of Chinese: Bian Zhilin's judgment that Li had no feel for the Chinese language; Sun Xizhen's verdict that not only was Li's French not very good, but that he was guilty of corrupting the Chinese language; and Xu Xiacun's finding from personal experience that Li communicated poorly both in speech and in letter writing. Still, Zhou points out, Li Jinfa has many defenders, primarily because of his association with Symbolism.[29]

"It was indeed Li Jinfa who first introduced French symbolist poetry into China," Bian Zhilin concedes in his 1982 article published in English entitled "The Development of China's 'New Poetry' and the Influence from the West." But, Bian goes on to aver, "his 'translation' from them and his 'imitations' of them mystified [his readers] so that so-called symbolist poetry was considered just a jumble of incomprehensible dazzling words devoid of meaning or logic." "The fact is that his far from adequate knowledge of French and his no less inadequate mastery of his mother tongue, both in *Baihua* (the vernacular) and *Wenyan* (the literary language), did gross injustice to the French Symbolists." But although Bian found Li's influence on China's "New Poetry" to be "pernicious," he nevertheless concedes that Li was not without talent, and that in his poetry he "somehow caught the aroma of the Symbolist poetry of the late Nineteenth Century."[30]

Li Jinfa's staunchest defender so far is Jin Siyan, who has written both in French and in Chinese on the Chinese Symbolists. Li Jinfa occupies nearly half of her book-length study in Chinese; he occupies a smaller proportion in the French version only because half of that study is devoted to categorized lists of the contents of early twentieth-century journals. While Jin acknowledges Verlaine's influence on Li Jinfa's work, it is Baudelaire's that most captures her attention. She finds some of Li's strange diction to be direct translations from the French, and points to a line in French in two separate poems that Li had taken from Baudelaire without attribution.[31] Jin finds shared themes, images, and attitudes to establish that the relationship could not have been accidental. She finds that Li goes beyond imitation and beyond emotional connection to Baudelaire, in being "the first Chinese poet to express spiritual defeat and to hesitate between God and Demon, to sing of the refinements of a moribund civilization, to breathe in the harmful perfume of decayed flesh, and to fall into decadence," and concludes that like Baudelaire, Li Jinfa was a "*poète maudit.*"[32] The conclusion seems to be overdrawn, as Jin's generalizations about the Chinese tradition are too vast, and attention to differences too scant. Her method of proceeding by extracting fragments, images, and lines also leaves room for further exploration.

Li himself had declared that his poetry was influenced by Baudelaire and Verlaine, and named the latter his "honorary teacher" in 1926.[33] In the 1930s he published here and there translations of Baudelaire's prose poems and Verlaine's verse, and at the end of his life, as previously noted, he had returned to *Les Fleurs du mal.*

Li Jinfa's first anthology, *Light Rain*, includes three translations from *Les Fleurs du mal*. His choices do not reflect those made by other translators at the time, and his renderings are completely idiosyncratic. A closer examination of those translations reveals much about Li's methods of work. That he made the translations before and during the writing of his own poetry emphasizes the close relation between them.

Li gives the title *"La fleur de mal"* ["The Evil Flower"] to Baudelaire's untitled poem that begins *"Tu mettrais l'univers entier dans ta ruelle"* [You would let the whole world into your bed]. The original poem reproaches a woman for promiscuity, cruelty, indifference, and evil; in her beauty, she is a queen of sins, a vile animal, filthy, but sublime. The last word in the first line, *"ruelle,"* can refer to the narrow space between a bed and the wall; by translating it in its more frequent sense of *"xiaolu"* 小路 [small road], Li's version suggests a pastoral scene rather than a boudoir.[34] The loss of ambiguity may be inevitable, but his translation of *"cruauté féconde"*[fertile cruelty] as *"canku de bozhong"* 殘酷的播種 [cruel seed-sowing)] implies a gender confusion that is absent in the original. When he ignores the accent mark on *"où"* [where, in which] to read it as *"huozhe"* 或者 [or] it breaks up the link in ideas. And when he translates *"fangeuse"* [filthy] as *"kexi"* 可惜 [too bad; a pity], and *"miroir"* [mirror] as *"jiyi"* 記憶 [memory], it is hard not to question his command of French. He leaves in French *"Grandeur"* (adding the capitalization) and *"râtelier"* [rack—either storage device or torture instrument], the latter rendered the more puzzling as it is misprinted *"Rahelier"* and capitalized. Here, as often in his own poetry, the insertion of foreign words suggests haste rather than art. The poem as a whole becomes like a riddle, conveying only a vague mood of horror and disgust.

For the untitled sonnet *"Avec ses vêtements ondoyants et nacrés"* [with her undulating and pearly garments], Li uses the number 27 as it appears in the original. He conveys well the description of a seductive woman, but translates the woman's *"indifférence"* [indifference] into *"yiyang"* 異樣 [difference]. Where Baudelaire compares the woman's eyes with polished metal, Li breaks the link with metal by rendering *"polis"* [polished] as *"duoqing"* 多情 [passionate]. The sphinx with which the woman is compared becomes the more conventional *"tianshi"* 天使 [angel], and *"la femme stérile"* [sterile woman] becomes the *"wuwei"* 無味 [dull, insipid] woman. Baudelaire's cold stone-like enigmatic figure becomes softer and more human in Li's version, as Li creates a poem of perverse and frustrated love.

Li's third selection is *"Le Mort joyeux"* ["The Gladly Dead"], for which he does not use any title but the number 72. The sonnet is full of the "ugly" images for which Baudelaire was known, and for which Li himself would become known. Li successfully conveys the greasy ground crawling with snails, and crows picking at carcasses, but where the original says the gladly dead would play in the waves like a shark, Li domes-

ticates the effect by rendering "shark" as "*xiaoquan*" 小犬 [puppy]. The
first tercet begins "*O vers!*" which Li renders "*a, shi!*" 呵，詩 [Ah poetry!]
Lexically it is correct, but in the original context, "*O vers!*" is an apos-
trophe to the earless and eyeless black companions, the sons of putrescence to whom the gladly dead would come—"*vers*" in its other sense, of
"worms." Having apparently misread "*le mort*" [the dead one] as "*la
mort*" [death], Li surrounds "*si*" 死 [death] with quotation marks, to indicate Death. In adding this layer of abstract meaning, Li loses the unity of
the original poem.

Li's translations thus take on the characteristics of his own poetry.
Striking images remain, but the meaning of entire poems becomes obscure. For "*Tu mettrais . . .*" he has "hidden the string" by ignoring the
grammar of the original. For "*Avec ses vêtements . . .*" by rendering "*indifférence*" as "difference," he breaks the thread that binds the woman's
indifference to the comparisons with metals, sphinxes, and sterility. For
"*Le Mort joyeux*," by translating "worms" as "poetry," he breaks the connection between the corpse and worms that would eat it. Li's own poem
"*sizhe*" 死者 ["Dead One"], which would be "*le mort*" in French, departs
too widely from Baudelaire's poems on death to invite comparison. Jin
Siyan has compared it with "*Hymne à la Beauté*."[35]

Many scholars and critics have compared specific poems by Li Jinfa
with Baudelaire. "*Qi fu*" 棄婦 ["Abandoned Woman"], the first poem in
Light Rain, is perhaps the best known and most frequently anthologized
of Li's poems.[36] Its topic, technique, and imagery recall several poems by
Baudelaire for Vincent Yang, who concludes that Li derived a technique
of symbolic representation from Baudelaire's "*Spleen*" poems in which
symbols shift constantly, and cites Auerbach to declare: "The data are of
so little importance that the symbols can be changed without loss."[37] Tu
Kuo-ching analyzes the same poem with reference to Su Xuelin's criteria
for Symbolism and finds that it fulfills all but that of exoticism.[38] Wang
Zuoliang quotes the lines:

> *xiyang zhi huo buneng ba shijian zhi fanmen*
> *huacheng huijin*
> 夕陽之火不能把時間之煩悶
> 化成灰燼

[The setting sun's fire cannot turn the Ennui of time / into ashes]

and notes that the limitless Ennui (Wang gives "Ennui" in parentheses
for "*fanmen*" 煩悶) and the visual imagery combining time, setting sun,
and ashes are "pure Baudelairean style."[39]

Another of Li's poems which has been compared with Baudelaire, "*Ye
zhi ge*" 夜之歌 ["Night Song"], owes a more obvious debt. It begins with
imagery reminiscent of "*Une Charogne*":

women sanbu zai si chao shang
beifen jiuchan zai xixia.

fenhong zhi jiyi
ru dao pang xiu shou, fachu qichou
我們散步在死草上，
悲憤糾纏在膝下。

分紅之記憶
如道旁朽獸，發出奇臭。
We stroll on dead grass,
Grief and anger entangle our legs.

Pink memories
Like decayed animals by the road, emitting stench . . .

But here Li's dead animal is "just part of the scenery," as Paul Manfredi aptly points out, whereas Baudelaire's carrion achieves a "great shock effect" by its central situation in a love poem.[40] Li's poem continues several lines later:

dashen! qi ni de tiemao,
wo fanyan zhu shengwu zhi hanqi.
大神！起你的鐵錨，
我煩厭諸生物之汗氣。
O God! Weigh your steel anchor,
I'm tired of the sweat-smell of all living beings.[41]

echoing Baudelaire's "*Le Voyage*":

O Mort, vieux capitaine, il est temps. levons l'ancre!
Ce pays nous ennuie, ô Mort! Appareillons!
[Oh Death, old captain, it is time. Let's weigh anchor!
This land bores us, oh Death! Let's set sail!]

The lines are, as David Jason Liu puts it, "one of the clearest homages Li pays to Baudelaire."[42]

Images of death and ugliness in other poems are parallel to various lines from Baudelaire for Song Yongyi and Jin Siyan. For Harry Kaplan, "*Chun cheng*" 春城 [Spring City] from *Light Rain* recalls Baudelaire's "*La Vie antérieure*" ["Former Life"], in that both poems have "a recollected vision of primitive innocence, spoiled in the end by a return to the banal reflections of the subject."[43]

Titles in French that Li Jinfa gave to some poems also suggest French sources. There are two poems each entitled "*Spleens*" [sic] in *Hard Times*. Each is appropriately steeped in melancholy. One, mourning the passage of time, carries an epigraph by the Symbolist poet Henri de Régnier, "*L'âge est venu sournois, furtif*" [The era has arrived sly, sneaky]; the poem opens and closes with an exhortation to drink up the golden cup. The other, a wish for escape, ends not with "Anywhere out of the world," as with Baudelaire, but with a pang of homesickness. Li apparently has appropriated only the title, "*Spleen*," which had also been adopted by Symbolists and Decadents from Pierre Louÿs to Ernest Dowson, although not in the plural form.

Among the epigraphs in *Happiness*, two are taken from *Les Fleurs du mal*, and the poems themselves bear a more interesting relation to Baudelaire. "*Sheng zhi yanhuo*" 生之炎火 ["Flame of Life"] quotes from Baudelaire's prologue poem "*Au lecteur*" ["To the Reader"]:

> La sottise, l'erreur, le péché, la lésine,
> Occupent nos esprits et travaillent nos corps

[Stupidity, error, sin, stinginess, / occupy our minds and overwork our bodies].

Li's poem continues:

> I see demons
> Leaping on the head of golden years;
> Fangs open about to bite,
> And then I am roaming,
> And receive a blow on the head.
>
> I am roaming,
> Tempering this weak heart,
> Like snowflakes sighing in stone moats,
> Hand in hand we will call on this marvel.
> The sea waves are groaning
> Turbulently to where the rocky bank breaks off;
> They harmonize a while,
> Produce countless green-white bubbles,
> Wipe away tears of "the river's banks alas!"
> Then collapse and go away.
> But how many comings and goings!
> What has it taken away?
>
> I wish to smell the flavor of life,
> Then cheat all the bad men who puppet me,
> The future is long,
> The few red petals in my heart,
> Will they just scatter like this?
> The distant swan
> Its cry flows with blood,
> What a pity Diana is sound asleep,
> I want to stroke its long neck,
> Indulge in indolent games (Ah, nature's beloved wife)
> Obstructs my future,
> Loveable, of course,
> A patch of red copper sunlight;

> The river flows to reflect,
> Ancient pines lying pliant like goddesses,
> But the result of this poetry
> Will stop the rhyme in the heart.
> The eyes lose their light,
> The corners of the mouth flow with saliva.
>
> I wish to smell the flavor of life,
> Then cheat all the bad men who puppet me,
> I need a spread of clear land.
> The oily parts produce many-colored snails;
> Nourished in the shade of leaves
> The ants are too swarming,
> The worms tedious!
> A few blades of grass are enough![44]

The poem typifies Li Jinfa's style in its strengths and weaknesses. The subjects of his verbs are often omitted, as they are in Classical Chinese; the resulting ambiguity can add resonance, but in Li's poem, more often simply puzzles the reader. The sudden interpolation of "The river's banks, alas," a quotation from the *Shi Jing* 詩經 [*Classic of Poetry*], may have been intended to contribute a timeless aspect. But where nouns and verbs, and the senses of smell and taste are confounded, the devices Li uses differ from those of Classical Chinese poetry: the first is not a result of parataxis or hypotaxis, and the second not achieved through synaesthetic images. Modern syntax forces their interpretations, at once striking and irritating in their departure from normal expectations. The two lines repeated at the beginning of the third and fourth sections of the poem illustrate this:

> *wo yu yu wen sheng zhi ziwei,*
> *sui qipian yiqie kueilei wo de huairen*
> 我欲與聞生的滋味，
> 遂欺騙一切傀儡我的壞人
>
> [I - wish - give/with - hear/smell - life - *de* - taste/flavor
> Then - cheat - all - puppet - I/me/my - *de* - evildoers]

The *de* used in both lines is a grammatical marker of possession or modification. In the first line "*yu*" 與 can mean either "give" or "with," but in either case it needs a grammatical object; by not providing one, Li forms a construction that reflects neither literary nor vernacular grammar. The word "*wen*" 聞 usually refers to hearing or smell; but whereas "*sheng*" 聲 means sound, which would form a logical object for "*wen*" 聞, Li uses the homophonous "*sheng* 生" for "life," repeating the line in the next section since it expresses the poem's theme. Li's synaesthesia is expressed as an unfulfilled wish to smell a flavor or taste. To make sense of the second line quoted above, placing a caesura after "*kueilei*" 傀儡 to arrive at its normal usage as a noun would yield the equally nonsensical "Then cheat every puppet, my evildoer." Reading the line as one sentence, "*kueilei*" 傀 儡 [puppet] must be a verb. One could perhaps interpret the line to read "Then cheat all the bad people who treat me like a puppet."

The Chinese language, with its lack of inflection and often fluid grammatical categories, accommodates wide ranges of meaning, but it does not permit the kind of arabesques in sentence structure found in Baudelaire or Mallarmé. Still, Li achieves a movement between the images that succeeds in leaving the impression of aimlessness and bewilderment, yearning and resolution, alternating in the face of life.

It is in his use of the swan image that Li Jinfa moves closest to the French Symbolists. The swan is gazed at from afar. Its cry flowing with blood refers to the belief that swans only sing at the moment they die. The poet's wish for the huntress Diana's wakeful presence is a wish for the swan's death, as well as for closer proximity to this creature who in the next line moves back to life, indulging in indolent games with the poet-Leda. If the poet is not to become nature's handmaiden and scatter his forces like red petals, then he must also welcome death. The beauty of the natural scene, representing life, creates a poem in the poet's heart; the poem is in turn represented by the swan-song that will be his death. The alternation of life and death are again reflected in the images of the river's flow (life) and the ancient pines (death: pines and cypresses are associated with graveyards in China). The movement between life-nature and death-poetry echoes the movement of the waves in the second portion of the poem. It is not impossible that this represents also a partial response to Baudelaire's poem, "*Le Cygne*" ["The Swan"], with its references to rivers, trees, and Greek myth. From a Chinese context one can see that all five of the elements of life are embodied in Li's poem: the gold of the years, the waters of the sea, the fire of life, the wood of the pines, and the soil to which the poem returns in the last section. Like the soil in Baudelaire's "*Le Mort joyeux*," Li's land is greasy with snails. The snails, ants, and worms shock the reader, and take him back to the epigraph.

The poem from which the epigraph is taken is far gloomier than Li's, the images less pretty, having no red petals and no swans, presenting instead jackals, vultures, snakes, scorpions, mongrels, and apes, and comparing life's few moments of pleasure to a debauched old pauper's biting and kissing the breasts of an old whore. The sixth stanza of Baudelaire's poem points out most clearly the similarities and differences between the two poems:

> *Serré, fourmillant, comme un million d'helminthes,*
> *Dans nos cerveaux ribote un peuple de Démons,*
> *Et, quand nous respirons, la Mort dans nos poumons*
> *Descend, fleuve invisible, avec de sourdes plaintes.*

[Packed in, swarming, like a million intestinal worms, / In our brains carouse a mob of Demons, / And, when we breathe, Death into our lungs / Descends, an invisible river, with muffled complaints].

Baudelaire does not see his demon's fangs; they are in his own brain; his river is death, flowing down into the lungs with every breath. In Li's poem, the river is not death but life; his sea waves also moan, but their going and returning, his river's flow, and the repetition of the word "flow," all emphasize the continuity of life. Li's swarms are of ants, not intestinal worms. They are external, not internal. His worms may suggest death, but in them he finds boredom. Baudelaire had written that the most frightful demon of all is Boredom, whose acquaintance is shared by his "hypocritical" reader.[45] For Li, boredom seems to wait only in the grave. Elsewhere, he had written *"shengming bian shi / sishen chunbian/ de xiao"* 生命便是 /死神唇邊/ 的笑 [Life is /a smile/ on the lips of Death],[46] but here, having escaped his demons in the first lines, he seems to be affirming, even celebrating life.

Li Jinfa's use of Baudelaire as a source for another poem is equally complex. *"Wo ai zhe canzhao de wuli"* 我愛這殘照的無力 ["I Love the Feebleness of This Evening Glow"] is a poem in prose. It begins with an epigraph from *"Ciel Brouillé"* ["Murky sky"], in which the sky is identified with a woman's eyes:

> On dirait ton regard d'un vapeur couvert;
> Ton oeil mystérieux (est-il bleu, gris, ou vert?)
> Alternativement tendre, rêveur, cruel,
> Réfléchit l'indolence et la pâleur du ciel .

[One would say your gaze was covered with a haze; / Your mysterious eye (is it blue, grey, or green?) / Alternatively tender, dreamy, cruel, / Reflects the indolence and pallor of the sky]. (I have replaced the accent marks, whose omission might have been printer's errors).

Li misquotes the first line, using the indicative *"dit"* for the conditional *"dirait."* This suggests that he may have learned the lines by heart, but was not sensitive enough to French prosody to notice when the line fell a syllable short. His own poem reads:

I

Oh, I love the feebleness of this evening glow.

Whether it slumbers beneath ancient walls, or recklessly dyes the leaves atop dense woods, oh, I love the feebleness of this evening glow. Since the sea entered the region of tranquility, not even a faint uneven breath can be heard; only trust the wind to urge black clouds together, to form some unrecognized external shapes. Sunbeams pass one by one over their brows, casting a few reflections on a thatched hut, but those behind the woods form broken patches, and groan on the grass, lacking courage to retreat to the horizon and defend it. (Oh, I love the feebleness of this evening glow); copper-hued sky, gold-hued clouds, lead-hued mountain peaks, lacquer-hued ocean, ochre-hued lake, orange-hued pine branches, dark-green vegetable gardens, are all subdued in the feebleness of the evening glow.

II

The eastern corner turns murky red; it should flee now; the night colors advance step by step, with even less strength to make the clouds transparent; in only a moment, the evening will die of old age on the ancient mound. Oh, I love the feebleness of this evening glow; a chimney emits a whitish puff; it hurries straight to the horizon, as if wishing to report an emergency, but this city is tired; before my eyes it is falling asleep; and is murmuring with weary voices, like the deep sound of the beat of distant sea waves, like the roar of bustling crowds. Oh, I love the feebleness of this evening glow; then it buries its head in its arms and falls asleep.

Let us remain a little while longer, ah, a little while! The last sun rays will mingle our reflections; perhaps we can leave unforgettable traces on this unfamiliar land; yet I grow afraid; whence the low woods that can hide my limbs; oh, I love the feebleness of the evening glow. Whence the fog that can dim my sharp eyes?[47]

As was the case with "The Flame of Life," Li returns to the epigraph at the end of his poem. The fog (*wu* 霧) seems to be a deliberate echo of Baudelaire's *"brouillé"* [murky], which is derived from the same original root as *"brouillard"* [fog]. But Li's reference is to his own eyes, which are sharp and penetrating, and cannot be dimmed by fog. Whereas in Baudelaire's poem, the description of nature and its effect on the poet are artfully equated with the woman's eyes and their effect, Li uses the device, more conventional in Western poetry, of personifying nature: the clouds have brows; sunbeams groan and lack courage, and the day buries its head in its arms and sleeps. Indeed, Li's poem bears a stronger resemblance to the first two sections of one of Baudelaire's prose poems, *"Crépuscule du soir"* ["Evening Twilight"]:

> *Le jour tombe. Un grand apaisement se fait dans les pauvres esprits fatigués du labeur de la journée; et leurs pensées prennent maintenant les couleurs tendres et indécises du crépuscule.*
>
> *Cependant du haut de la montagne arrive à mon balcon, à travers les nues transparentes du soir, un grand hurlement, composé d'une foule de cris discordants, que l'espace transforme en une lugubre harmonie, comme celle de la marée qui monte ou d'une tempête qui s'éveille.*

[Daylight falls. A great relief comes over the poor minds wearied with the day's toil, and their thoughts now take on the tender and uncertain colors of the twilight.

And yet from the mountain's height comes to my balcony, across the transparent evening clouds, a great howl, composed of a host of discordant cries, which space transforms into a mournful harmony, like that of a rising tide or of an awakening tempest].

Li's poem also refers to the transparency of clouds, and to the sounds of waves or tides, and compares the evening noises to the roar of a human crowd, but when Baudelaire goes on to describe how the night brings out the madmen, Li does not follow. Both Baudelaire's prose poem and Verlaine's "*Nocturne parisienne*," of which Li published a translation in 1926, concentrate on the human sphere, on human noises and human cares.[48] For Li, man occupies but a small part in a natural scene, and here, he is closer to his own tradition than to the West.

Li has been credited, though erroneously, with being the first to introduce the prose-poem form into China.[49] Here his choice of the prose poem form is somewhat puzzling, as his repetition of the exclamation "*yu, wo ai zhe canzhao de wuli*" 吁，我愛這殘照的無力 [Oh, I love the feebleness of this evening glow], with its strong rhythm and used like a refrain, is more to be expected in verse. His phrases, separated only by commas, differ from Baudelaire's in that they easily can be divided into individual lines without requiring enjambment. Since none of Li's verse poems have even line lengths or end rhymes, printing this as a prose poem probably reflected Li's wish rather than a typesetter's decision.

The many close parallels to French poetry that can be found in Li Jinfa's work have raised the question of whether many of his poems were actually imitations or adaptations. An example from *Light Rain* gives useful clues.

A poem entitled "*Gei xingren*" 給行人 ["For a Traveler"] bears the epigraph, "By chance read Pierre Louÿs's '*Dialogue au soleil couchant*' ["Dialogue in the Setting Sun"]; loved it deeply; changed its form and completed this."[50] In Louÿs's tale, Arcas, a "goatless goatherd," seduces the shepherdess Melitta. At first she resists, citing her mother's warnings, but then weeps in confusion as he continues to speak. As darkness descends, they go into the woods, so deep that even the gods are afraid, and satyrs and nymphs are never seen. An old tree forms their nuptial palace, the sound of palms their cortege, and the stars their torches. So they are married by the Olympians, protectors of shepherds.[51] In Li Jinfa's version, the poet looks back at what has occurred. Melitta's role is cast in the first person: she is twenty, rather than thirteen, as in Louÿs's tale. Unlike Louÿs's Melitta, who cites her mother's warnings with little understanding of the words, the woman in Li's poem has already learned to distrust men, saying, "Those who can say the sweetest words are the least reliable people." Both poems allude to the passage from autumn to spring, but in Li's it is only in an epilogue after the man has gone and left the woman behind. What had attracted Li Jinfa to the tale was clearly not the air of innocence that Pierre Louÿs conveyed. Li's description of his "I"-Melitta's hibiscus-like beauty, drinking from the pure springs and enjoying clear breezes, could come from the Chinese tradition rather than from Louÿs, as could his concluding image of Melitta as the abandoned woman. In short, Li has simply taken a few images from Louÿs and responded with a work of his own.

It seems clear that if Li confused the issue of influence, it was not by making false claims, as Michelle Loi charged, or by direct borrowing and adaptation or by purposeful misreading, but by resorting to a large number of sources and using them in a variety of ways. In this, he differed from his contemporaries only in that he studied in France rather than in England or the United States. Li read, and misread, a good deal of French poetry, especially French Symbolist poetry. It must have echoed in his mind as he composed his own poems. This is strongly suggested in a poem entitled "X," from *Hard Times*:

> My soul is a bell-sound in the wilderness:
> It comprehends the traces of spring,
> And the reason golden autumn weeps bitterly,
> The whispers of young girls on the grass;
> Planets are reflected on the shallow waves,
> They discuss their own beauty,
> And souls haughtily pass by.
>
> Only time has moved,
> The roar of the tide
> Deafened her ears;
> Distant fog
> Has blurred both her eyes;
> So she stopped this inspection.
>
> Ah, let us leave this country of suffering,
> To rescue the crippled soul,
> Place her on the Qiantang River's bank—
> How many oars ply to and fro—
> The night, too, will quiet down.[52]

Li's comparison of his soul to a bell-sound recalls Baudelaire's sonnet "*La Cloche fêlée*" ["The Cracked Bell"], where the quatrains evoke the sound of bells heard in the fog, and the old bell that sounds out vigorously like an old soldier, despite its age. The tercets then compare the poet's soul to a bell that is cracked, and when it wishes to sound out, lines 11–13 read:

> *Il arrive souvent que sa voix affaiblie*
> *Semble le râle épais d'un blessé qu'on oublie*
> *Au bord d'un lac de sang, sous un grand tas de morts.*
> [It happens often that its weakened voice
> Resembles the thick death rattle of a wounded person forgotten
> At the edge of a lake of blood, under a big pile of the dead.][53]

The line "*Semble le râle épais d'un blessé qu'on oublie*" was one of Li's favorites; he used it without translation in two separate poems in *Light Rain*.[54] In this poem, however, Li's wounded soul would not be forgotten underneath a great pile of dead bodies; his "I" would rescue her (he uses the feminine form of the pronoun) and place her on a river bank. The last lines of Li's poem, which Kaplan describes as "appeals from clemency from the world," remind him of the first lines of Baudelaire's *"Recueille-ment"*:

> *Sois sage, ô ma Douleur, et tiens toi plus tranquille.*
> *Tu réclamais le soir, il descend; le voici;*

[Be good, oh my sorrow, and quiet down / You demanded evening; it is descending; it is here].[55]

Li's poem creates a haunting, elusive, faintly erotic atmosphere, permeated with tender sadness. His soul is sensitive and understanding, but alone; having passed through the seasons, time, and distance, and having experienced love and sorrow and known beauty, it is weary, and longs for rest. The last stanza, by making a direct reference to an actual river in China, situates the poem in reality. By bringing up the theme of home-sickness, it rejoins the Chinese tradition.

Li Jinfa's work was neglected and nearly forgotten for several decades. He settled in the United States in 1951, and occasionally published writings in Taiwan, where his earlier work was unavailable, except for the small fraction of poems that had been anthologized.[56] On the Mainland, when interest revived in East-West literary relations in general and in Symbolism in particular, Li Jinfa's work also was revived. The collection of his poetry published in 1987 is incomplete (e.g., the poem "X" discussed above is missing); his prose writings have not been collected. But he appears in nearly every history of Chinese Symbolism, and nearly every study mentions his relation to Baudelaire. This includes two works in English: Mi Jiayan devotes a third of his 2004 study to Li Jinfa.[57] Paul Manfredi wrote an MA thesis on the poet, in which he makes a valid plea to go beyond tracing sources to find the "relative integrity" of Li's poetic work. But surely he goes too far when he proposes "to understand Li's work as a creative field as capable of generating 'Baudelaire' as Pound and Judith Gautier are the creators of 'China.'"[58]

Li Jinfa was self-admittedly and indisputably inspired by Baudelaire. Although he was also inspired by a great number of other European poets, far from feeling anxiety at the influence, he might well have been pleased at being called "The Baudelaire of the Orient." He was the chief editor of the journal in which the epithet appears.

WANG DUQING (王獨清 1898–1940)

Wang Duqing's best-known poem, *"Wo cong café-zhong chulai"* 我從 café 中出來 [I Come Out of a Café] has been associated with Baudelaire:

I come out of a café,
My body loaded with
Intoxicated
Fatigue.
I do not know
Which way to go, to find my
Temporary home.
Ah, chill silent streets,
Dusk, fine rain.

I come out of a café,
Loaded with wine,
Wordlessly
Walking alone
In my heart
Feeling the sorrow of a wanderer
About to lose his native land.
Ah, chill silent streets,
Dusk, fine rain.[59]

The original poem has the word "*café*" in French. Vincent Yang relates its final lines to Baudelaire's "*Spleen*" poem "*Quand le ciel bas et lourd . . .*" ["When the low and heavy sky . . ."]. Conceding that the French poem describes rain heavy enough to resemble prison bars while the Chinese poem describes quiet misty rain through which one would wander, Yang asserts that what is more important is Baudelaire's use of the rain as a symbol that "presages the tears at the end." Having translated "*huanghun*" 黃昏 [twilight] as "sunset," Yang draws a parallel with Baudelaire's line from "*Le Voyage*": "*La gloire des cités dans le soleil couchant,*" for which he selects the translation "Cities resplendent in the setting sun." The contradiction between the images of heavy rain and resplendence leads Yang to conclude that "the rain is more of a mental picture than an actual scene." Wang Duqing himself had indicated that the poem was inspired by Verlaine's "*Chanson d'automne*" ["Autumn Song"]. Yang's comparison seems the more forced as he explains: "Verlaine was actually following Baudelaire in using this image to represent an inner mood."[60]

Wang's writings on poetics reveal his great admiration for Baudelaire, but set greater value on experience and emotion than on cerebral qualities in poetry. Wang was not always the most reliable guide to his own poetry, however, as some of the following will make clear.

Wang's autobiography and correspondence place him at the crossroads between Chinese and French poetry. Born to an ancient family of scholar-officials in the ancient capital city Chang'an (now Sian, or Xi'an), Wang received a traditional education from his poet-painter father, and began writing poetry at age eight or nine. He took his pen name, "Duqing" 獨清 [alone clear] from his favorite poem in the *Chu Ci* 楚辭 (*Songs of the South*).[61] In 1910, following the death of both his parents, he began to acquire a modern education in science and English. By age fifteen he had become chief editor of a radical local newspaper. When the newspaper was shut down by the government, Wang went to study science in Japan, where he became acquainted with the future members of the Creation Society. Returning to China after the May Fourth Incident in 1919, he worked as a journalist in Shanghai, then went abroad to study in France.

The second volume of Wang's autobiography, *Wo zai Ouzhoude shenghuo* 我在歐洲的生活 [*My Life in Europe*] is rich in anecdote. Although he is remembered as being plain and plump, resembling Balzac in physical appearance, Wang describes a series of amorous adventures, including one in an unnamed village on Lake Geneva that seems to have come straight out of Rousseau's *Confessions*. Despite his frequent complaints of poverty, Wang found the means to travel widely in Europe, visiting Florence and Rome on one trip, Madrid, Venice, Pompeii, and Naples on another, living briefly in Lyon, London, Berlin, and in that unnamed village on Lake Geneva.[62]

Wang spent most of his European sojourn in Paris. He describes his life there as "romantic and decadent," with days and nights spent in cafés drinking to excess. Through a Robert Bollier, met in one such café, he met Pierre Loti and Anatole France. He describes himself at the time as a misanthrope, suffering from *neurasthénie* [*sic*]. He read philosophy and poetry, apparently having abandoned all interest in science. In Paris Wang began a new creative life. He would later describe the poems from that time as "stiff" "world-weary," and "all having the color of death." French newspaper accounts of the May Thirtieth Incident prompted him to return to China in 1925.

After returning to China Wang published eight volumes of poetry between 1926 and 1932. Among them, *Shengmuxiang qian* 聖母像前 [*Before the Image of the Holy Mother*], *Aijiren* 埃及人 [*Egyptians*], and *Weinishi* 威尼市 [*Venice*] all have a strong element of exoticism, but do not refer directly to his experiences in France. Joining the Creation Society in 1926, he became chief editor of the *Creation Monthly* (*chuangzao yuekan* 創造月刊).

Wang translated widely from European poetry. In his autobiography he alludes to studying Latin, Greek, Italian, Spanish, and German as well as French, though his rarely mentioned knowledge of Japanese must also have contributed to his translations. In his published volume of translations, he notes having culled from over two hundred poems and includes selections from Anacreon, Sappho, Dante, Ronsard, Desbordes-Valmore, Burns, Byron, Shelley, Hugo, Musset, Goethe, Ulland, Pearse, Maeterlinck, and Verlaine.[63] Although he gave Baudelaire a high place in his criticism, he apparently did not translate from his works.

Wang Duqing's ideas on poetry appear in the inaugural issue of the *Creation Monthly* in the form of a letter to Mu Mutian and Zheng Boqi following discussions with Guo Moruo.[64] Basing his remarks on French rather than on Chinese poetry, Wang states his preference, in descending order, for four French poets: Lamartine for his *"émotion,"* Verlaine for his *"yin"* 音 [sound], Laforgue for his *"force"* [*li* 力], and Rimbaud for his *"se"* 色 [color]. (Wang leaves the poets' names and the words "Emotion" and "Force" in French). Together, they provide the following formula:

$$(qing + li) + (yin + se) = shi$$
$$(情 + 力) + (音 + 色) = 詩$$
$$(\text{emotion} + \text{force}) + (\text{sound} + \text{color}) = \text{poetry}$$

Wang goes on to quote Verlaine's *"De la musique avant toute chose"* ["Music above Everything"].

It is here that Wang states that his poem "I Come Out of a Café" was inspired by Verlaine's *"Chanson d'automne."* He gives a close analysis of the meter, rhyme, and line lengths of his own poem, showing how the two nine-line stanzas balance each other, and commenting that the uneven lines and rhymes of his poem befit the mood of the intoxicated author, and that it was in pursuit of "pure poetry" that he limited the number of words. Curiously, in his translation of Verlaine's poem, Wang transforms the eighteen three- and four-syllable lines of the French into six decasyllabic Chinese lines rhyming aa, bb, cc.[65] Compared with the traditional five- and seven-syllable lines, the ten-syllable line in Chinese seems as much too long as the three- and four-syllable French lines seem too short compared with the alexandrine.

It is with what he calls *"poésie pure"* [*sic*] that Wang Duqing associates Baudelaire. In order to become real poets, he states in the same letter, the Chinese must learn from Baudelaire, Verlaine, and Rimbaud, to be poets of "art for art's sake" (*weimei de shiren* 唯美的詩人). Baudelaire's spirit (*jingshen* 精神) is that of a true poet, he asserts, for not only should poetry avoid explanation, it should avoid seeking comprehension. A poet who seeks people's comprehension is a seller of songs, not a pure poet! Incomprehensibility already had become one of the defining characteristics of Chinese Symbolist poetry.

Wang's own poetry avoids seeking comprehension partly through being sprinkled with words from various European languages. Aside from *"café,"* and most frequently, *"marronniers"* [chestnut trees] from French, he has used *"populus"* [for poplars] from Latin; *"gondola, Rio, Rialto,"* and others from Italian; and "nostalgia" from English. He defends this use of foreign language as one practiced by European poets, and as one that adds an *"exotic"* [*sic*] beauty. He gives as example four lines from his long poem *"Dongshen guiguode shihou"* 動身歸國的時候 ["When Starting Out for the Homeland"] where not a single Chinese word appears:

Assez vu! sur les boulevards, les gens lents ou gais,
Assez vu! toutes les longueurs des ponts et des quais,
Assez vu! devant Notre-Dame, les yeux des filles éclatants de flammes,
Assez vu! sur les Champs Elysées, la vive volupté du pas des femmes.

[Seen enough! On the boulevards, slow or cheerful people, / Seen enough! All the lengths of bridges and docks, / Seen enough! In front of Notre Dame cathedral, girls' eyes flashing with flames, / Seen enough! On the Champs Elysées, the lively pleasure of women's steps].[66]

"Assez vu" also begins each of the first three lines of Rimbaud's *"Départ"* ["Departure"], published (entirely in French) decades earlier, but the rest of the lines are original with Wang.

Wang Duqing does not always admit to his use of French sources, however, even when he imitates or copies entire lines without trying to cover his tracks. As previously noted, part of his "autobiography" reads like a pastiche of Rousseau's *Confessions*. His *"Zuihoude libairi"* 最後的禮拜日 ["The Last Sunday"] takes whole lines from Jules Laforgue's *"L'Hiver qui vient"* ["Coming Winter"], with *"Ton ton, ton taine, ton ton!"* left in the original French. Other lines from the same poem, *"Oh, tombée de la pluie! Oh ! tombée de la nuit, / Oh ! le vent ! . . . / La Toussaint, la Noël et la Nouvelle Année . . ."*[Oh, falling of the rain! Oh, falling of the night! Oh! the wind! . . . All Saints Day, Christmas, New Year's . . .] reappear in Wang: "那些 *fêtes exotiques ! Toussaint* 呀, *Noel* 呀 . . ./ 哦雨！哦風！哦風！哦雨"[Those exotic festivals ! Like All Saint's, like Christmas . . . /Oh rain! Oh wind! Oh wind! Oh rain!]. Laforgue's line *"Vous nous avez gâté notre dernier dimanche! "* [You have spoiled our last Sunday!] also provides the title for Wang's poem. Wang himself points out these parallels in his published letter to Mu Mutian and Zheng Boqi, but he asserts that he had written his poem before reading Laforgue![67]

As for Baudelaire, in spite of Wang's laudatory remarks, there is little in his poetry to recall that French poet. He professes admiration for Verlaine's line, which he quotes in French *"De la musique avant toute chose"* [Music above all things], but confesses that he finds it extremely difficult to achieve with the Chinese language. He admires Rimbaud's color alphabet poem, and strives to use color, but the results become overly obvious.[68] He shares with Laforgue the use of onomatopoeia, repetition, and exclamation, but none of the irony. Thus, even when his subject was the poor people of Paris, as in the following poem, his outcries and sentimentality are at far remove from French models he admired:

Winter Night on the Seine

Cold cruel winter night has covered all of Paris,
The bustling capital gradually becomes quiet;
Buried under the grey of this modern civilized area
The wind swirls wails and howls.
Now on the sparsely populated banks of the Seine,
A few poor people sleep among the fallen leaves.

By the dim moonlight,
These few human shadows can faintly be seen;

All are thin in appearance,
All are disheveled,
All are wrapped in short ragged garments,
Sleeping motionless as if dead.

Ah, ah, brothers, are you cold?
Did you toil hard for others for a whole day,
To buy a bottle of red wine and sit on the ground to drink your fill,
And after crazily yelling and singing,
To fall down into a dead drunk without awakening?
Ah, poor brothers!
They have prohibited absinthe!
You'll never again have such good strong liquor
To send you safely into a long sweet dream!

Do you still remember that last war?
How you have sacrificed for your native land!
Pools of blood stained your hands;
Cannon smoke blackened your temples. . . .
Now when they all roar out "La Marseillaise" to celebrate victory,
Who will bother about you suffering demobilized soldiers?

Ah, brothers, wake up then!
Prick up your ears and listen carefully,
Where is that lewd laughter coming from?
The electric fire in the night café bears witness:
They are being wayward and licentious,
The coquettes are obscenely hugging and squeezing,
The short-haired half-naked black slave is playing the sexually rousing *Chica* to advance the merriment . . .
Ah, poor brothers,
Listen! Listen!

The wind ceaselessly wails so!
I find this capital of civilization merely a deep pit of evil!
Brothers, wake up, wake up,
Ay! I see you cannot wake from your deep sleep!
I would as soon learn from Nero of Rome,
And burn down this bustling Paris![69]

The references to wine, sexual license and sympathy for the poor and downtrodden recur in many of Wang's poems, and might be vaguely associated with Chinese views of Baudelaire. However, the exclamations, apostrophes, widely varying line-lengths, and direct moral statements that also typify his style are seldom found in Baudelaire's poems.

Wang's better poems integrate his sources, as in "*Diao Luoma*" 弔羅馬 [Mourning for Rome], wherein he juxtaposes Rome with his old home,

Chang'an, former capital of the Tang dynasty. The long poem has double epigraphs from Qu Yuan 屈原 and from Goethe in the original German, and is encrusted not only with foreign words, but with Classical allusions, both Western and Chinese. Wang's predilection for this practice might also go back to his childhood experience. He recalls being enchanted by the poem *"Da zhao"* 大招 ["Great Summons"] from the *Chu ci* 楚辭 (*Songs of the South*—the collection from which he later took his pen name). Asked to explain the extremely obscure poem by his father, he could only respond by asking his father whether he understood all that went into the herbal potion he was drinking. The mystery of the unknown words had already greatly appealed to the young Wang Duqing.

Wang did not have the chance to develop in this poetic direction. After his return to China, Wang's political and social consciousness engulfed even his poetry. Thus his poem *"Shanghai de youyu"* 上海的憂鬱 ["Shanghai's Melancholy"], which might be translated "Shanghai Spleen," is composed of lines like:

> *xiongdimen, tuo ya, tuo ya!*
> *Hanshui shi liubianle nimen de quanshen,*
> *Nimen de qi ye chuande shangxia bu xiang-jielian.*
> 兄弟們，拖呀，拖呀！
> 汗水是流遍了你們底全身，
> 你們底氣也喘得上下不相接連。
>
> Pull, brothers, pull!
> Your bodies are covered in sweat,
> You can hardly catch your breath.

And:

> *xiongdimen, tuo ya, tuo ya!*
> *Zheixie mutou shi wei neige zibenjia qu jianzhu gongsi,*
> *Haishi wei neige weiren qu xiugai gongguan?*
> 兄弟們，拖呀，拖呀！
> 這些木頭是為那個資本家去建築公司，
> 還是為那個偉人去修蓋公館？
>
> Pull, bothers, pull
> Is this wood going to build a company for some capitalist,
> Or is it going to build a mansion for some great man?[70]

But even with such class-conscious rhetoric in his poetry, he did not go far enough in the direction of "revolutionary literature" to satisfy his friends at the Creation Society. While the Nationalists censored his works, the leftists regarded him as a "Trotskyite."[71] At the outbreak of the war with Japan, Wang returned to his old home in Chang'an, and died there of illness in 1940.

Wang Duqing is regarded as a Symbolist by many Chinese critics, and his poetry fits the characteristics they associate with Symbolism: obscure, hypersensitive, sentimental, decadent, and exotic.[72] But compared with French Symbolism, as Harry Kaplan points out, Wang's poems address the reader too transparently and too directly to be considered Symbolist.[73] Zhu Ziqing finds that among the poems that are comparable with the Symbolists, Wang's are more obvious than obscure, more powerful than subtle, and that the larger number of his poems resemble those of Hugo or Byron.[74] Wang was probably more on the mark with his self-assessment as a "Romantic turned Decadent."[75] He had noted Byron's to be the strongest influence on his *"Diao Luoma"* 弔羅馬 ["Mourning for Rome"]; similarly, his *Aijiren* 埃及人 [*Egyptians*], sighing over lost culture and pride, recalls European Romantics rather than Symbolists. He shared with the Romantics his preoccupation with emotions, with love, and with ruins, and in his poems he described himself as a pale poor consumptive. He shared with Decadents his obsession with death and decay, but his political consciousness was too strong to allow him to devote his life completely to aesthetics. In spite of Vincent Yang's strenuous effort, Wang's link with Baudelaire seems extremely tenuous.

MU MUTIAN (穆木天 1900–1971)

Mu Mutian translated Baudelaire's sonnet *"Correspondances"* and placed it at the center of his 1935 article *"Shenme shi xiangzheng zhuyi"* 什麼是象徵主義 ["What Is Symbolism?"].[76] He had been introduced to French literature in Japan a decade earlier, and majored in that subject at Tokyo Imperial University. He was fascinated with the Symbolists and Decadents, and recalls reading Remy de Gourmont, Samain, Rodenbach, Verlaine, Moréas, Maeterlinck, Verhaeren, and others, as well as Baudelaire.[77] His first volume of poetry, *Lü xin* 旅心 [Traveler's Heart], was published by the Creation Society in 1927 after his return to China. Several poems from the collection have been compared with that of Baudelaire and the French Symbolists.

Mu Mutian, from a once-wealthy Manchu family in Northeastern China, showed an early talent for mathematics which earned him a scholarship to study mathematics and chemistry in Japan before he turned to literature. He later blamed poor eyesight for abandoning mathematics and science, but claimed that his basic nature remained that of a scientist, while his relationship to literature was that of an Amateur (sic).[78] Nevertheless, he devoted the rest of his life to teaching literature, writing poetry, essays, and criticism, and translating French, and later Russian literature.

Mu's early views on poetry appear in the form of a letter to Guo Moruo, in indirect dialogue with Wang Duqing in the inaugural issue of the *Creation Monthly*.[79] Declaring poetry's "basic elements" to be "unity" (*unité* in the original) and "continuity," he offers examples from Vigny, Poe, Moréas, and the Late Tang poet Du Mu (杜牧 803–852). He explains what he calls his "physics" point of view, that a poem can contain silences, yet achieve continuity; just as when one walks by a stream, the sound of water sometimes seems to disappear, but this does not mean that the sound of water has ceased; if it had ceased, one would have to hear a new sound when it starts up again.

Like Wang Duqing, Mu Mutian calls for "pure poetry" ("The pure poetry" in English in his text), which requires suggestion and delicacy (*Délicatesse* in the original). Poetry must avoid philosophizing and conceptualizing; it must use finite words to reveal the infinite world; it must suggest, not state. Poetry is woven from mist and copper wires. The stuff of poetry comes from movements of thought that seem to be felt yet not felt, the sounds that seem to be heard yet not heard, and feelings that seem expressible yet are inexpressible. To achieve close relations between form and content, poetry must join mathematics to music. A prose poem is formed when the melody of the phrase cannot be divided into shorter lines. Positing that one must *Penser en poésie, to think in poetry* (both French and English in the original text), Mu mistakenly faults Baudelaire for having first composed in prose, then translating into verse.

In the same article, Mu also discusses "*Correspondances*," (using the French spelling), by which he means an individual's response to beauty in different places and times. Due to the different *Correspondances* of their souls (to place), he would write about the snow-laden fields of the northeast plains while his friend Feng Naichao would look to his native south. Through their shared *Correspondance* (to time), they both feel nostalgia for the past, and wish to make the "*antan mort*" [dead yesteryears] into a "*passé vivant*" [living past]. (Again Mu leaves the terms in French). Mu also gives term a political interpretation: the life of a nation and that of the individual must have *Correspondance* [sic] for either to exist. In a later critical piece, Mu refers to Baudelaire's sonnet "*Correspondances*" to describe Zang Kejia's use of the sunset to symbolize society's decline.[80]

In his 1935 article "What Is Symbolism?" Mu Mutian defines "*Correspondances*" as the primary characteristic of Symbolist poetics. There are complex correspondences between the manifestations of nature and the human soul, and subtle similarities between sounds, colors, perfumes, form, and the state of the human soul that can be suggested through poetry. The rhythm and music in that poetry can suggest the correspondences in the poet's mind or heart.

"*Correspondances*" in Mu Mutian's own poetry is clearest from his most famous poem, "*cangbaide zhongsheng*" 蒼白的鐘聲 ["Pale Bell Sound"]. Mu uses no punctuation in the poem, but separates words and phrases with blank spaces to suggest silences amid sound. The device does not work as well with alphabetical languages as with the square blocks of Chinese characters, but is reproduced in the following literal rendering:

Pale   bell-sounds   decayed   hazy
Scattered   exquisite   desolate   mist-laden   in the valley
— Withered grasses   thousand times   ten-thousand times
Listen   forever   fantastic   ancient bell
Listen   thousand sounds   ten-thousand sounds

Ancient bells   disperse   on the waves'   gleaming-white
Ancient bells   disperse   on ash-green   poplar-tree tops
Ancient bells   disperse   in the wind-sounds'   soughing
— Moon-shadows   carefree   carefree
Ancient bells   disperse   on white clouds'   floating

One strand   another strand   rank-fragrance
Sea water's edge   dried grasses   desolate-path   nearby
— Past years' sorrow   everlasting   longing for   new wine cup
Listen   one sound   another sound   desolation
From ancient bells   drift   drift   not know where   misty land
Ancient bells   dissipate   into silk-like   floating vapor

Ancient bells   unstirring   enter   sleeping water's   ripples   murmuring
Ancient bells   unstirring   enter   faint   distant   cloud-clad hills
Ancient bells   drifting about   enter   vastness   between the four seas
— Growing dark   past years   eternal joy   misery

Soft   ancient bells   soar following   waves of moonlight
Soft   ancient bells   continuously   enter   ribbons of the Milky Way
— Ah   from afar   ancient bells   echo   song of ancient home
From a distant past   ancient bells   reflect   songs of ancient home
From afar   ancient bells   enter   boundless land   nothingness

Listen   decayed   ancient bells   in the ash-yellow   valley
Enter   limitless   vastness   dissipate   delicate
Dried leaves   withered grass   follow   senseless   north wind
Listen   thousand sounds   ten thousand sounds   misty   misty
Fantastic   vast   decadent   eternal   bell-sound   of   home
listen   in   dusk's   deep valley[81]

The poem's title, describing sound through a visual image, illustrates Synaesthesia. The entire poem is permeated with the sense of sound, while each of the other four senses is evoked in turn: the visual with dried grasses, the olfactory with "rank perfume," the gustatory with "new wine," and the tactile, as "soft" in the fifth stanza is *"ruanruande"* 軟軟的 [literally, soft to the touch]. Mu also makes use of the visual possibilities of Chinese characters, as *"piaosan"* 飄散 [disperse] and *"piaodang"* 飄蕩 [drift] both show the wind radical with *"piao"* 飄. while *dandan* 淡淡 [faint], *"mangmang"* 茫茫 [vast], *"piaoliu"* 漂流 [waft], *"chanchan"* 潺潺

[murmur, babble], and so on all use characters with the water radical. Mu's description of perfume as *"xing"* 腥 [rank] might also represent a deliberate effort to suggest the idea of beauty in ugliness.

The central image of *"guzhong"* 古鐘 [ancient bell] is a homophone for *"guzhong"* 谷中 [in a valley]; the repetition of the phrase echoes the deep tolling of a bell; the sounds *"-ong," "-eng,"* and *"-ang"* repeat throughout the poem in deliberate echoes, with *"menglong"* 朦朧 [hazy, misty obscure], *"linglong"* 玲瓏 [delicate, exquisite], *"mengmeng"* 濛濛 [drizzly, misty], *"qianchong, wanchong"* 千重，萬重 [a thousand times, ten thousand times], *"qiansheng wansheng"* 千聲，萬聲 [a thousand sounds; ten thousand sounds], and so on. The sound is reminiscent of Verlaine's *"sanglots longues des violons"* [long sobbing of violins], but even more of Laforgue's *"L'Hiver qui vient"* ["Coming Winter"] that had inspired Wang Duqing, and of which Mu had quoted in his 1926 article the lines describing hunting horns going off into the distance, *"Les cors, les cors, les cors— mélancoliques! . . . / Mélancoliques! . . . / S'en vont, changeant de ton, / Changeant de ton et de musique, / Ton ton, ton taine, ton ton! . . . / Les cors, les cors, les cors! . . . / S'en sont allés au vent du Nord* [the horns . . . melancholic! . . . Go away, changing in tone, changing in tone and music, toot toot, the horns . . . have gone away with the north wind]." Mu's poem also refers to the north wind. But most of Laforgue's imagery (e.g., the white sun lying like spittle in a tavern) offers sharp contrast with the pastoral beauty of Mu Mutian's scene. Mu's use of the *"-ong"* sound is more effective, in that it lies closer to the sound of a large bell than of violins or hunting horns.

To weave together "mist and copper wire," Mu interweaves water, mist, and clouds with the hard resistant image of the ancient bell. The five senses all describe the sound of the bells, and form a *"correspondance"* with the poet's sensibility, with his "eternal joys and sorrows," and nostalgia for his homeland. Thus Mu's poem reflects Baudelaire's sonnet where "perfumes, colors and sounds respond to each other like long echoes from afar in a tenebrous and profound unity," and achieves his criteria of unity, connectedness, delicacy, and suggestion.[82]

Two other poems by Mu Mutian remind Harry Kaplan of Baudelaire. Kaplan associates *"Xian shi"* 獻詩 ["Dedicatory Poem"] of *Traveler's Heart,* with its "spiraling succession of repeated phrases" with *"L'Harmonie du soir"* ["Evening Harmony"]. In *"Shuisheng"* 水聲 ["Water Sound"], as in Baudelaire's with *"L'Invitation au voyage,"* there is direct address to a sister, although *"meimei"* 妹妹 in Chinese can also mean lover. Kaplan describes the poem's "motif of escape through a voyage by water," as "Baudelairean," but concedes that it is "also an established theme in Classical Chinese poetry."[83]

Drawing a more distant parallel, I find Mu's *"Jiming sheng"* 雞鳴聲 ["Cock's Crow"] vaguely reminiscent of Baudelaire's prose poem *"L'Étranger"* ["The Stranger, or "The Foreigner"]:

Cock's crow
Cannot awaken
Real
Sorrow
I do not know
Where home is
Where country is
Where my lover is
Where I should return
Ah   fading lamp   decadence

Cock's crow
Cannot arouse
New
Grief
I do not know
Where brightness is
Where darkness is
Where obscurity is
Where I should escape
Ah   decadent fading   lamp.[84]

The form of the poem, Mu indicates in his reminiscences, was inspired by
Wang Duqing's "I Come Out of a Café."[85] The two Chinese poems also
share melancholic moods and the feeling of being lost. The theme of exile
and wandering occurs frequently in Mu's poems, both reflecting and
predicting his life. The persona in Mu's poem, like Baudelaire's
"*L'Etranger*," does not know where his home country is. Instead of responding to a string of questions, Mu's persona responds to a cock's
crow, which is meant to awaken people from dreams and announce the
end of night. Unlike Baudelaire's *Étranger*, Mu's persona does know who
his lover is. He just doesn't know where she is. The drifting clouds that
occur in so many of Mu's other poems and that are the only things that
Baudelaire's *Étranger* loves, are not evoked in this poem. Both poems are
dominated by the sense of vagueness, where things named are absent.

Mu Mutian did not often achieve his ideal of suggestiveness, however. Too often, the correspondence between the scene and the self are too
openly stated. For example, in "*ye miao*" 野廟 ["Wild Temple"], three
stanzas of four lines set a lovely misty scene of a decayed temple. But
these are followed by three stanzas stating "*wo yuan*" 我願 [I want] to be
that temple, that bell, that Buddha's statue, and so forth. In a poem actually entitled "*Wo yuan*" 我願 ["I Want"], ten of the sixteen lines begin
with those two words. Zhao Jingshen, having counted twenty-four occur-
rences of "I want" in the thirty poems of *Traveler's Heart*, rather wickedly
dubs Mu "*wo yuan shiren*" 我願詩人 [The "I Want" Poet], and points out
that the frequent repetition of "I want" destroys the suggestibility and
delicacy of Mu's poems.[86]

The single collection of poems *Traveler's Heart* also marked the end of Mu's Symbolist period. Giving up completely the "perfume of exotic countries" and the "stagnant waters and decayed cities" that had been his poetic landscape, no longer attempting to make *"l'antan mort"* into *"passé vivant"* [living past from dead yesteryears], he devoted himself to *"littérature engagée,"* writing in 1932:

> women bu pingdiao lishi de canhai,
> yinwei na yi chengwei guoqu.
> women yao zhuozhu xianshi,
> gechang xin shijide yishi.
> 我們不憑吊歷史的殘骸，
> 因為那已成為過去。
> 我們要捉住現實，
> 歌唱新世紀的意識。

> We do not ponder the wreckage of history
> Because that has already become the past.
> We want to seize reality, and
> Sing the consciousness of the new age. [87]

FENG NAICHAO (馮乃超 1901–1983)

Feng Naichao is known for a single volume of poetry, *Hong sha deng* 紅沙燈 [*Red Gauze Lantern*], comprised of forty-three poems and published in 1928. The poems are preoccupied with death and decay, evening and autumn, mist and rain, pale and faded colors, moonlight and candle light. Many are pervaded with nameless grief and an air of exhaustion. Like Mu, Feng omitted punctuation, made deliberate use of empty spaces, and fully exploited the musical qualities of the language. His vocabulary is often recherché; his poems do not yield to quick comprehension. His style has been compared with Baudelaire by Zhou Bonai, and Marián Gálik has compared a specific poem with Baudelaire. [88]

Feng was born in Japan to a Chinese family, and learned Classical Chinese at home while he concentrated in science at school. He later changed to philosophy, then studied aesthetics and art history at Tokyo Imperial University, where he became friends with Mu Mutian, and wrote most of the poems by which he is known. Arriving in China in 1927, he became the chief editor of the *Creation Monthly*, which he took in an increasingly leftist political direction. He joined the Chinese Communist Party in 1928 and was one of the founders of the League of Leftwing Writers in 1930. Aside from *Red Gauze Lantern*, Feng published some fiction and some translations from the Japanese. A collection *Jinri zhi ge* 今日之歌 [*Songs of Today*], scheduled for publication in 1930, was seized and never appeared. [89]

Feng Naichao's views on poetry are generally extrapolated from Mu Mutian's letter to Guo Moruo, in which Mu refers several times to conversations with Feng. Feng is said to share Mu's goals of pure poetry, suggestiveness and musicality, and creating a *passé vivant* from *l'antan mort* [living past from dead yesteryears]. Zhao Jingshen finds in Feng the "misty obscurity" that Mu Mutian had failed to achieve.[90] Marián Gálik describes Feng's work as possessing a sad, sensuous atmosphere and a "decadence proper to Moréas," but judges it to be "devoid of the erotic passion of Ernest Dowson" or the "splenetic vitriol of Baudelaire."[91]

The Feng poem that Gálik compares with Baudelaire is "*Xiaochen de gu jialan*" 消沉的古伽籃 ["Sunken Ancient Buddhist Temple"]. "*Jialan*" 伽籃 in the title is the Chinese transliteration of the Sanskrit term *sangharama*, meaning a Buddhist temple and its grounds. For "sunken," "*xiaochen*" 消沉 is composed of the characters for "vanish" and "sink," which as a compound usually means "despondent, dejected, and depressed." Marián Gálik, who translates the title "The Silent Old Sangarama," notes:

> The title of the poem points to an affinity with the masterpiece of C. Debussy, but also with Ch. Baudelaire's "temple" of nature depicted in his famous poem *Correspondances*. In fact the forty-eight lines . . . represent twenty-four "analogies," that is relationships between "things and our senses."[92]

Claude Debussy's masterpiece, "*La Cathédrale engloutie*" ["The Submerged Cathedral"], was in turn a response to Gerhardt Hauptmann's "*Die versunkene Glocke*" ["The Sunken Bell"]. Feng's poem is literally about a temple, and begins with "the forest's secret language," which also evokes Baudelaire's sonnet "*Correspondances*."

"The Sunken Old Buddhist Temple" first appeared in the *Creation Monthly*, typographically disposed in two columns separated with a line down the middle; divided into three sections, each with six pairs of five-syllable lines alternating with two-syllable lines:

I

The forest's secret language	The sinking of the setting sun
Murmurs	Dark red
The fragrance of evening clouds	The drifting wanderer's heart
Hazy	Grieving
The ancient pagoda of a distant temple	Wave after wave of nostalgia
Scrapes the void	Evening bell

II

The despondent mood	The flavor of dusk

Deep blue	Decayed
The beauty of the heavens	The cadence of myriad sounds
Sorrowful	Declines and dies
The seclusion of the prayer hall	The sunken ancient temple
Boundless	Deeply hidden

III

The soaring of eternity	Vague meditation on the past
Sinks down	Without end
The beliefs of a quiet night	The ardor of old stories
Buried alive	In ashes
Wordless silence	Memory of the grave
Hangs back	Youth

The even-numbered lines in the first section all rhyme in "*-ong*," in the second section in "*-ang*;" the third section rhymes "*-un, -ün, -ün, -in, -in, -un*" (abbcca, all in near-rhymes). The musical effect is enhanced with vowel sounds within the lines. Each two-syllable line describes and extends the image evoked by the line that precedes it, with the exception of first and last pairs of the third section, where there is a contrary motion between soaring and sinking, and a contrast between the grave and youth.

The stillness of the poem suggests a complete absence of motion for M. Gálik, who finds that "There is no suggestion of any activity. The world is extremely quiet, nearly dead but beautiful." He goes so far as to assert that "the whole poem is written without a single verb.[93] But the difference between verbs and substantives cannot always be so clearly drawn in Chinese grammar. Reading some of the two-syllable lines as verbs, one finds a motion in the poem from sorrow, to decline, finally subsiding into silence.

The sad mood, quiet tone, and descent of evening are reminiscent of Baudelaire's "*Recueillement*": "*Tu réclamais le Soir; il descend, le voici*" [You demanded evening; it descends; here it is].[94] In the French poem, the past, wearing an outdated dress, leans down from the balcony of heaven; in Feng's poem the past is evoked through the ancient temple and its grounds, and through old literature, with the term "*huaigu*" 懷古 [meditate on the past] referring to a traditional theme, and with "*chuanqi*" 傳奇 [transmit the strange] referring to a traditional genre (here translated "old stories"). Feng's poem thus has a historical dimension that brings it close to such poems from his own tradition as Li Shangyin's "*Leyouyuan*" 樂遊原 [Leyou Heights]:

Xiang wan yibushi
Qu ju deng gu yuan
Xi yang wu xian hao
Zhi shi jin huanghun
向晚意不適
驅車登古原
夕陽無限好
只是近黃昏

[Toward evening feeling ill at ease / I drive my chariot up to the ancient heights.
The setting sun is infinitely fine; / Only, it is approaching dusk].[95]

Li's poem has traditionally been interpreted as a lament for the decline of the Tang dynasty: the title refers to a park that overlooks the entire city of Chang'an; the once glorious capital would fade into history, just as the sun would decline and fade into night. In Feng's poem the ancient Buddhist temple seems to sink with the setting sun. Both Chinese poems ruminate on life and death, time and eternity, with an aching sadness. But Feng's poem does not end with sinking. Youth could be just a memory, but its occurrence in the last line, reversing the order between youth and the grave, suggests reversal and endless alternation.

In mood and technique, Feng's poem also recalls Ma Zhiyuan's famous *"Qiusi"* 秋思 ["Autumn Thoughts"] of which the first three of five lines read:

ku teng lao shu hun ya
xiao qiao liu shui ren jia
gu dao xi feng shou ma
枯藤老樹昏鴉
小橋流水人家
古道西風瘦馬

Withered vines, old trees, evening crows,
Small bridge, flowing water, human homes,
Ancient path, west wind, lean horse[96]

The juxtaposed images form a painting in words. The pictorial quality in poetry summed up by the Chinese phrase "詩中有畫" [there is painting in poetry] is a characteristic Feng shares with the Chinese traditional poetry, as Sun Yushi has pointed out.[97] Through its historical dimension and through its "analogies," Feng's poem goes beyond Mu Mutian's prescription, and makes a dead past into a living present.

In another of Feng Naichao's poems, *"Mo"* 默 ["Silence"], many of the same images appear, combined with more modern and exotic elements:

Light mist shrouds the pond's peaceful slumber
Deep silence withers the sleeping lotus in the dream

Winter comes to the roots of the exhausted grasses
Quietly slaying the pallid smile
Sunlight hides in the lissome mist
Not shining on the sorrows in the trees' shadows

The languid weary withered branches complain
The golden early autumn has also aged
Long silver hair soaking in the water
Lightly sweeps the vexations of the ripples

I can hear some raucous mocking
Ugly old crows fly cawing in the treetops
Deep-red fallen leaves have filled the empty heart
Why thank that merciless mischief

Midwinter's solemnity far surpasses prayer
Without the annoyances of the religious martyr
Melancholy Holy Mother appears silently in the sky
To watch over this waning day of the soul[98]

The poem carries some of the favorite themes of Chinese painting: mists, ponds, lotuses, withered branches, and crows. But the silver hair in the pond and the figure floating in air recall rather the water colors of the Pre-Raphaelites and Gustave Moreau. The "Holy Mother" in the penultimate line can refer only to Mary, mother of Jesus. She is invoked in another poem, "*Si de yaolanqu*" 死底搖籃曲 ["Death's Lullaby"], treated in Marián Gálik's article.[99] Feng's references to Christianity, like his references to Buddhism, contribute to a vaguely religious atmosphere that is part of his aesthetic landscape.

There is no evidence that Feng Naichao had a direct knowledge of French poetry. The occasional words in the Latin alphabet that appear in his poems are in English rather than in French. Looking at a larger sampling of his poems, resemblances to Verlaine seem more striking than those to Baudelaire. For example, Feng's "*bei'ai*" 悲哀 ["Sorrow"] and "*yueguang xia*" 月光下 ["Beneath the Moonlight"] are like variations on Verlaine's "*Clair de lune*" ["Moonlight"]; Feng's "*Shengming de aige*" 生命 的哀歌 ["Sad Song of Life"] recalls Verlaine's "*deuil sans raison*" [mourning without cause]. The insistent music of much of Feng's verse also recalls Verlaine.[100]

Feng's poetic concerns, his creation of vaguely religious atmosphere, interplay of color and sound, appearance and disappearance, reality and imagination, can perhaps best be illustrated by the title piece of his collection, "*Hong sha deng*" 紅沙燈 ["Red Gauze Lantern"], composed of six couplets:

In the center of the somber dark deep deep temple

In the heart of midnight faintly flickers an ancient red gauze lantern.

Worried silence groans in the middle of the night shadows' slumber
I hear the footfalls of ghosts and demons dancing in midair

Clusters of black clouds hide the albumen-colored moon
A river of white silk flows like naked corpses lying on the edge of the wild

The ancient red gauze lantern slowly gradually grows brighter
The somber dark temple is suffused with solemn gold

Anxiously silently a black-clad nun steals across the long veranda
How long each step each sound lasts and how it disappears without a trace

I see in the sanctuary of the somber dark temple
Flickeringly dispiritedly shimmers the light of a red gauze lantern. [101]

Although nothing in the poem is directly reminiscent of Baudelaire, if we take the ghosts and demons as suggested by shadows viewed, the persona "hearing" their footfalls would be a case of synaesthesia. The "gothic" elements and quasi-religious atmosphere are shared with European inheritors of Baudelaire.

XU YUNUO (徐玉諾 1894–1958)

Lightly holding aloft those odd little poems,
I slowly walk into the woods;
The little birds nod to me silently;
The little worms cast sidelong glances.
Walking deeper into more mysterious woods,
I secretively place those odd things on the sodden grass,

Oh look, in these woods!
Each little worm extends its face;
Each little leaf opens its eyes;
The music is confusedly beautiful.
In the woods here, there
Everywhere is weaving strange, mysterious strands of poetry. [102]

In this most frequently anthologized piece by Xu Yunuo, simply entitled "*Shi*" 詩 ["Poem"], nature is active, alive, responding to the poet and his poetry. The attitude in the poem is reminiscent of Baudelaire's "*Correspondances*," where man walks through a forest of symbols that observe him. It also recalls Baudelaire's lines from "*Elévation*:" "*Heureux celui qui . . . / . . . comprend sans effort / Le langage des fleurs et des choses muettes*! "[Happy he who . . . understands without effort / the language of flowers and of mute things].[103] Michelle Yeh has made two translations of Yu's poem, in which she detects "an unmistakably Symbolist air."[104]

Another poem by Xu Yunuo, entitled "夜聲" ["Night Sounds"], reads:

> *zai hei'an erqie jimo de yejian,*
> *shenme ye bu neng kanjian;*
> *zhi tingde . . . sha sha sha . . . shidai chizhe shengming de shengyin.*
> 在黑暗而且寂寞的夜間，
> 什麼也不能看見；
> 只聽得 . . . 殺殺殺 . . . 時代吃着生命的聲音.

> In the dark and lonely night,
> Nothing can be seen;
> One only hears . . . sha sha sha . . . the sound of the times eating life.[105]

Reading the poem biographically, Liu Jixian interprets it as a description of bandits coming in the night.[106] But taking "the times" in the broader sense of time itself, one is reminded of Baudelaire's "*L'Ennemi*," where "Le Temps mange la vie" [Time eats life], and of "*Chant d'automne*," where it is also sound, there the thumping of wood being laid by for winter that begins to sound like nails being driven into a coffin, that reminds the poet of the swift passage of time made meaningful by our final ending in death. The sound in the Chinese poem, "*sha sha*," is usually written with the characters (沙沙) to denote "rustle." Xu Yunuo chooses the character 殺 [to kill], thus achieving the effect with a masterful economy of means.

In our inevitable passage toward death, Baudelaire tells us in "*Au lecteur*" ["To the Reader"], frightful sins, errors, stupidity, devils, monsters and a whole menagerie of vices swarm through our brains and descend into our lungs with each breath we take, but the most frightful of all is *l'ennui*. In *Spleen II*, *L'ennui* is "*fruit de la morne incuriosité*" [result of dull lack of curiosity]. Baudelaire's "*ennui*," when it is translated at all, is most often translated as "boredom." In its ordinary usage, the word also means vexation, annoyance, and worry.

Ennui takes on many forms in Xu Yunuo's poems. In "*Mei yiyide rensheng*" 沒意義的人生 ["Meaningless Human Life"], a man roams the earth searching for meaning; he searches high and low, at crossroads and in the mud at the bottom of lakes; in the end, despondent and fatigued, he "moans his last and can no longer sing the boring tune." Here, ennui is "*wuliao*" 無聊 [boring, senseless, silly, stupid].[107] Ennui is "*mei quwei*" 沒趣味 [lacking interest, flavor] in a poem by that title, consisting of only three lines:

> *rensheng hui neng dedao xinxian quwei ma?*
> *zai xianshi de shishi,*
> *ye zai meng zhong de shishi.*
> 人生會能得到新鮮趣味嗎？

在現實的事實，
也是在夢中的事實。

Can human life acquire new fresh interests?
The facts in practical reality
Are also the facts in dreams. [108]

If new interests signal the defeat of ennui, but dream and reality lie in the same facts, how can they create new interests? Can there be escape from boredom even in dreams? In the poem *"Kepa de zi"* 可怕的字 ["Frightful Word"], when the poet utters *"mei quwei"* 沒趣味 [lacking interest, flavor], the words immediately take on the form of a miserable, deformed, mangy dog. The dog fixes the poet with a wily, evil stare, and when the poet tries to dismiss it, it makes as if to pounce. At this, the poet hits it with his palm, thinking it would close its eyes or move its head, but instead, its brains splash out all over the poet. The poet loses consciousness, and wakes to hear his mother complain "It's going to be awfully hard to wash off, this mischief." [109] Dream, reality, and hallucination merge to intensify the meaning of *"mei quwei"* 沒趣味 which takes on the meaning of annoyance as well as boredom here.

"Ennui" in a different sense occurs in *"Gensuizhe"* 跟隨著 ["Follower"], which Xu Yunuo describes as a long snake that follows him everywhere: "When I am walking I see its tail; when cutting grass I see its middle, red mottled with black; when sleeping, I see its head. . . . [I]t never leaves me for a moment," though sometimes it takes the shape of many little snakes. He identifies the follower as *"fannao"* 煩惱, that is, "ennui" in the sense of vexations, cares, sorrows, suffering. [110]

Xu Yunuo perhaps comes closest to Baudelaire's sense of ennui in the poem *"Chuan"* 船 ["Boat"], which equates boredom with human life:

lüke shang zai chuanshang, shi ba shengming quan jiaogei jiqi le:
zai wubian wuji de bolangshang yaobaizhe,
tamen duiyu tamen qiantu de guancha, jihua, nuli, ji xiwang quan gui wuxiao.
a, yuzhoujian meiquwei zai moguo rensheng le!
旅客上在船上，是把生命全交給機器了：
在無邊無際的波浪上搖擺著，
他們對於他們前途的觀察，計劃，努力，及希望全歸無效。
呵，宇宙間沒趣味再莫過人生了！

The passengers on the boat have completely given up their lives to the machine;
Rocking on the vast boundless waves,
All their observations, plans, strivings and hopes for the future are useless.
Ah, for boredom in the universe, nothing surpasses human life! [111]

Once again "boredom" is *"mei quwei"* 沒趣味 [lacking interest, flavor]. In traditional Chinese poetry, the drifting boat is often the symbol of mystical union with nature, achieved by giving oneself up to the movement of the stream. But here Xu's boat is not the "untethered" one of yore, drifting along nature's currents. The boat is now run by machine; its passenger can arrive only at an ultimate sense of helplessness, for which boredom and *"mei quwei"* 沒趣味 are pale translations. It is the state of mind arrived at when one realizes the impossibility of union with nature, that is union with the Tao, or reaching the "Absolute." In this sense, Xu's description of "boredom" comes very close to Baudelaire's Spleen, which lies at the opposite end from the Ideal.

In *"Le Mort joyeux"* ['The Gladly Dead"], Baudelaire imagines digging a deep ditch where he can stretch out his old bones and sleep in forgetfulness, providing a free and joyous corpse for worms. Similarly, Xu Yunuo writes that mankind's shame and weakness are not being able to *"tongkuai de si"* 痛快的死;[112] that is, to die in a manner where *"tongkuai"* 痛快 can mean "joyfully" as well as "free and unrestrained." Xu imagines and welcomes his own death in *"Xiao shi"* 小詩 ["Little Poem"]:

dang wo ba shenghuo jiesuan yixia, fajuele si de menjing shi,
si de men jiu ga de yisheng kai le.
bu qiran de, jiu you ge xiaogui lizai menhou, momo de xiang wo shiyi;
wo lishi ye juede si zhi mei le.
當我把生活結算一下，發覺了死的門徑時，
死的門就嘎的一聲開了。
不期然的，就有個小鬼立在門後，默默的向我示意；
我立時也覺得死之美了。

When I reckoned up my life and discovered the key to death,
Death's door opened with a creak.
Unexpectedly, a little demon standing behind the door silently motioned to me;
I immediately also felt the beauty of death.[113]

Having found beauty in death, Xu could be even more "gladly dead" than Baudelaire, as his cemetery is full of flowers, rather than greasy with snails. In *"Mudi zhi hua"* 墓地之花 ["Cemetery Flowers"], he addresses the dead beneath the graves, exclaiming "How soft your beds are, how comfortable your pillows!" and asking why they do not beckon to others. The poem ends "I slowly lift my feet and walk toward the deepest part of the grave."[114]

In a poem of only two lines, again simply titled *"Shi"* 詩 ["Poem"], Xu writes:

zhei zhi bi shishikeke zai weixiaozhe;
sui zai xiezhe heizhuo de si-mu-zhong de juzi.
這枝筆時時刻刻在微笑着；
雖在寫着黑濁的死墓中的句子。

This pen is smiling all the time;
Even though it is writing dark funereal lines.[115]

The poem only suggests the theme of death, but expresses fully an ironic consciousness of the poet and his craft. That consciousness is also shared with Baudelaire.

Like Baudelaire, Xu has been characterized as *"guairen"* 怪人 [odd person, eccentric], and *"emo shiren"* 惡魔詩人 [monstrous, satanic, or demonic poet]. Both have been said to have a "special feeling for beauty, finding it in darkness, loneliness, mystery, sorrow, the strange and bizarre, and in terror."[116] Xu Yunuo entitled his single collection of poetry *Jianglai zhi huayuan* 將來之花園 [*Future's Garden*], thereby suggesting flowers, albeit not of evil. As in Baudelaire's poems, prostitutes, gamblers, and drunkards appear.[117] Xu Yunuo was also one of the first practitioners of the Chinese prose poem.

Could Xu Yunuo have borrowed forms, themes, images, or attitudes from Baudelaire? There is no evidence whatsoever that he knew of the French poet, even indirectly.

Xu Yunuo has not been classified among the Chinese Symbolists. No foreign words occur in his poetry. No foreign place names. No Europeanized syntax. As with other "pioneers" of the vernacular movement, his language is simple, colloquial Chinese. There are no real allusions to Classical literature, no pedantic locutions, no shocking neologisms. His imagery is plain and often ordinary. His collection, subtitled *Garden of Tomorrow* in English, was published in 1922. He was also one of eight poets who contributed to a collection entitled *Xue Zhao* 雪朝 [*Snowy Morning*] published in the same year. After publishing a few more poems sporadically in various journals, he seems to have disappeared from the literary scene after 1926.[118]

Xu's poems range over a great number of forms and themes, from small poems of one, two, or three lines to stanzas composed solely of onomatopoeic repetition, to dramatic monologues, dialogues, and narratives. He wrote quickly, generally without revision, sometimes leaving orthographic mistakes. His themes go beyond ennui, disillusionment, and death to include love, hope, life, dreams, nature, children, and his old home. Some poems recall traditional Chinese poetry in describing rustic scenes and idyllic childhood juxtaposed with outcries against the hard life of the farmer and the rapaciousness of creditors and tax collectors. Poems exploring the boundaries of dream and waking are reminiscent of Zhuangzi. Poems asking the meaning of life and wondering about death have been compared with his contemporaries Bing Xin and Tagore.[119]

As a member of the Association for Literary Studies, Xu Yunuo would have been dedicated to "art for life's sake" in place of the "art for art's sake" advocated by the Creation Society. His life provided rich material for poetry. Born to a poor peasant family in an area embroiled in local warfare and overrun by bandits, as a boy Xu had tended cows, cut kindling, and worked the land. He also attended school, however, and after graduating from a teacher's college, he worked variously as a primary school teacher and principal, and as editor, tailor, and guerilla leader in more than forty places in China. If drunks, prostitutes, gamblers, opium addicts, and bandits appear in Xu's poetry, it was because he had kept company with them, according to his friend Ye Shengtao, who later wrote a short story based on Xu's life.[120]

Escape from the coils of life through dream and imagination is also a recurrent theme in Xu's work. In his *"Wen xiejiang"* 問鞋匠 ["Asking the Cobbler"], Xu allows the cobbler to make dream shoes to escape the modern world full of thorns, mud, and ulcers. The poem ends "Brother Zhang, come. Brother Li, come. Let's put on the dream shoes together!" This attempt to be brotherly backfired, however. The leftist Qu Qiubai wrote a disapproving rejoinder: "Brother Zhang, awake! Brother Li, awake! / Why not all work together?"[121]

Michelle Yeh and Yang Changnian both find Xu Yunuo close to the Symbolists, and Gong Xianzong believes he influenced the Chinese Symbolist-Modernist Dai Wangshu.[122] Indeed, by his divergent route, going his own way through his own experience, Xu Yunuo's poems often come closer to those of European Symbolists than many of the self-confessed imitators of European poetry.

LIANG ZONGDAI (梁宗岱 1903–1983)

Liang Zongdai, whose translations from and appreciation of Baudelaire were introduced in previous chapters, published a collection of original poems, *Wandao* 晚禱 [*Vespers*], in 1924. One of the poems has been compared with Baudelaire by Harry Kaplan, who describes it as "a liturgy for a Symbolist Vespers," and offers this translation:

> If you won't play it, that's all right,
> Despite this demure, lachrymose piano
> As impalpable as the scent of orchid
> Tossing in a cool breeze.
> All your griefs and depressions
> Dissolve upon this broad plain of tranquility,
> Darkness without limit
> Has descended, along with the peace-bearing canopy of love.
> Causing the faint beat which calms the heart
> To sing solemn praise of
> The gentle, solemn mercy of the Creator Host.[123]

Kaplan finds synaesthesia in "an impression of sunset described visually (darkness), in terms of music (piano), the visceral sense (cool), and an olfactory sensation (the scent of the orchid)."[124] By describing the scent as "impalpable," Kaplan adds to the mingling of senses. He further indicates that the "magical expansion of the soul beyond its daily worries (griefs and depressions) at the point of change from day to night," later

frequently found in French Symbolist poetry, had their source in Baudelaire's *"Recueillement."* The French poem, later translated by Dai Wangshu, as Kaplan notes, "was a favorite of the Chinese Symbolists."[125]

Liang's poem is the first of two *"Wandao"* 晚禱 ["Vespers"] in his
collection by the same title. Kaplan's comparison suggests the affinities
that would draw Liang, a full decade later, to *Les Fleurs du mal* and to
Symbolism.

However, a different reading of the poem is possible. The arresting
image of the "lachrymose piano" is Kaplan's invention. Liang uses *"piao-
miao"* 縹緲, which is "dimly discernible or misty, and *"chanyuan"* 潺湲,
which describes slowly flowing music rather than tears. While the context of the poem justifies translating *"qinr"* 琴兒 as "piano," it could
equally refer to a Chinese lute or zither. There is a period printed after
"qinr" 琴兒, on which Kaplan bases a comparison with Mallarmé. But
without it, and with the verb in the sixth line used as a causative, the
poem would be more coherent; the first four lines would flow into the
next two to describe the music of Vespers. The poem would then read:

> If you won't play it, it's all right,
> Although this lute clear and sweet, softly flowing
> Lingering gently swaying
> As faint as the scent of orchids
> [Lets] all worry, grief, and unhappiness
> Dissolve into the quiet wilderness;
> Boundless darkness
> Descends with harmonious adoration.
> Let the heart's joyful pulse
> Sing deep songs of praise to
> The Creator's warm and majestic love.[126]

The music calms the heart, and all nature joins the soul in singing praises
to the Creator. It would seem to be a rather religious poem, rather than
one that attempts, as the Symbolists were said to do, to dethrone religion
and put art in its place.

The second *"wandao"* 晚禱 [vespers] poem was translated into English
by Liang himself, and entitled "Vespers." It is clearly a devotional prayer,
with a direct address in the second line: "In this dimness of the twilight,
Lord," and ending "In the warm penitent light of the evening star, / I
shall complete my evening prayer."[127]

Liang's collection as a whole does not evoke Baudelaire. A poem on a
traveling stranger *"moshengde youke"* 陌生的遊客, is a dialogue in verse
with an enigmatic stranger, but it is not reminiscent of Baudelaire's prose
poem, as the stranger replies at the end of each stanza, "I didn't come to
pick the flower."[128] There are a few prose poems, with apostrophes to
Mother, and with dreams of home and family. There are many simple
poems, some consisting of only two or three lines, written on flowers,

moonlight, starry skies, morning sparrows, and love, coy, shy, budding, or disappointed and frustrated. A poem on death describes it as night washing away the fatigue and dust from life's journey. There is a postface in French, quoting six lines without title, by Albert Samain. Samain (1858–1900) was a French Symbolist poet known to be influenced by Baudelaire, but the journey from Baudelaire to Liang Zongdai is too distant to follow.

Liang Zongdai knew and translated from several European languages. He studied French in Geneva and Paris, German in Heidelberg, and Italian in Florence. He also translated poems by Valéry, with whom he had studied in Paris. He translated poems by Tao Qian (陶潛 372?–427), as well as one or two of his own poems into French. He no doubt knew English as well, as he published translation of sonnets from Shakespeare.[129] His study of Symbolist aesthetics is the subject of a 2004 monograph.[130] In the end, Liang Zongdai's engagement with Baudelaire does not seem to have gone beyond the few translations and the article on Symbolism.

QIN ZIHAO (覃子豪 1912–1963)

Qin Zihao, whose critical treatment of and translations from Baudelaire are introduced in the previous chapters, published four volumes of his own poetry. Born in Sichuan, Qin had attended the Université Franco-chinoise in Beijing, and then studied in Japan, returning to China when the war began. After working as a journalist and a businessman, in 1947 he took up a bureaucratic post in Taiwan that left him time to be an active leader on the Taiwan literary scene. His complete works, including uncollected poems, translations, criticism, and correspondence, were published by friends after his death.[131] A co-founder of the Blue Star Poetry Society, which according to Michelle Yeh "championed lyricism based on traditional poetry,"[132] Qin nevertheless has been judged "a poet leaning more heavily on modern French poetry than on the Chinese tradition."[133]

Qin Zihao was associated with Modernists before he arrived in Taiwan, but was pronounced a Symbolist by Zhang Mo 張默, Shang Qin 商禽, Zhang Hanliang 張漢良, and others at a conference article commemorating the fifteenth anniversary of his death in Taiwan.[134] Mo Yu, who has pointed out that Qin himself professed to have been influenced by Parnassian and Symbolist techniques, identifies two predominant images in Qin's poetry: the sea, and hair.[135] Both images are associated with Baudelaire.

The two images of hair and the sea are linked in Baudelaire's prose poem *"Un hémisphère dans une chevelure"* ["A Hemisphere in a Head of Hair"], which begins:

Laisse-moi respirer longtemps, longtemps, l'odeur de tes cheveux, y plonger tout mon visage.

[Let me breathe in for a long, long time the smell of your hair, to plunge my whole face in it.]

and continues in the fourth paragraph:

Dans l'océan de ta chevelure, j'entrevois un port fourmillant de chants mélan-coliques, d'hommes vigoureux de toutes nations et de navires de toutes formes.

[In the ocean of your hair I glimpse a port teeming with sad songs, vigorous men of all nations, and ships of every shape.] [136]

The same association of sea and hair occurs in his verse poem *"La Cheve-lure"* [the head of hair]:

> *Fortes tresses, soyez la houle qui m'enlève!*
> *Tu contiens, mer d'ébène, un éblouissant rêve*
> *De voiles, de rameurs, de flammes et de mâts :* [137]

[Strong tresses, be the swell that takes me away! / You contain, ebony sea, a dazzling dream / of sails, of rowers, of pennants and of masts].

Here the hair becomes an entire sea complete with sailing ships.

Qin expresses a similar wish to plunge his face into the loved one's hair in *"fengkuangde shike"* 瘋狂的時刻 ["Hour of Madness"]

> *Cang bange miankong zai ni de facong li*
> *Kuei leyuan zhi wai bange qiyi de shijie*
> 藏半個面孔在你的髮叢裡
> 窺樂園之外半個奇異的世界

[Hiding half a face in your hair, / Peeping at the strange world outside the Garden of Eden] [138]

The hair is the paradise into which the poet has plunged his face.

And in a poem simply entitled *"Fa"* 髮 ["Hair"], Qin blends the subject of hair and the ocean. Rather than Baudelaire's evocation of "men of all nations," however, Qin's poem treats the man without a nation, The Flying Dutchman, both the man and the ship, in the third section of the poem:

The reflection on the wall is my broken shadow
I can tell it is the modern melancholic portrait
Of the Flying Dutchman wandering in the Twentieth Century
He will burn the vessel
To be buried in the tranquility of your thick hair
With the happy sprites
Listen as the sound of your heartbeat foretells the happy omen of death. [139]

Qin's poem might be a meditation on a painting, or on more than one painting, although this poem was not included in his *Hualang* 畫廊 [*Gal-*

lery] collection. The Flying Dutchman is condemned to sail the seas forever with a crew of dead men, but the poet can hope for release, if not through love, then through death. The sea thus symbolizes both Qin's sense of exile and the hope for release. The hair symbolizes both love and death. Added to the similarities in association of images, the blending of abstract and concrete is one of the qualities Qin had praised in Baudelaire's poetry.

Like Baudelaire, Qin associates freedom with the sea. Qin writes in "*Ziyou*" 自由 ["Freedom"]:

> *haiyang a! zai nide mianqian*
> *wo liaojiele ziyou de yiwei le*
>
> *wo jiang chiluozhe, xiang baise de tian'e*
> *yueru lanse de botao*
> 海洋啊！在你底面前
> 我了解了自由的意味了
>
> 我將赤裸着，像白色的天鵝
> 躍入藍色的波濤

[O Ocean! Before your countenance / I have understood the meaning of freedom / I will go naked, and like a white swan / Leap into the blue waves]. [140]

Baudelaire's "*L'Homme et la mer*" ["Man and the Sea"] begins: "*Homme libre, toujours tu chériras la mer!*" [Free man, always you will cherish the sea]! Then, having presented the sea as a mirror, the free man is told, "*Tu te plais à plonger au sein de ton image*" [You enjoy plunging into the bosom of your image]. Qin's poem leaves aside the narcissistic image, but his poetic persona similarly plunges into the waves. In another poem, "*Zhuiqiu*" 追求["Pursuit"], the sea suggests immensity and eternity.

Qin creates a new meaning for the association of hair and the sea in one of his best known poems, "*Guo Heifa qiao*" 過黑髮橋 ["Crossing Black Hair Bridge"]:

> A knife in his belt the mountain man walks across Black Hair Bridge
> The sea breeze dishevels his long black hair
> A flash of black
> Like a bat fleeing into the twilight
>
> The black-haired mountain man returns
> A soaring white-crested egret fills the sky
> A pure white feather floats down
> One white strand of my hair
> Melts into the antique-bronze-colored mirror
> And twilight is the barber on the bridge
> Setting my black silken hair ablaze

One white strand of my hair
Melts into the antique-bronze-colored mirror
And I walk alone
In the no-man's land between mountain and sea

The port lies beyond the mountains
Spring is tied to the forest of black hair
At the hour when bats are blind
On the sea of dawn will be floating
Ships loaded with love [141]

The "mountain man" (*shandi ren* 山地人) refers to the aboriginals of Taiwan. The speaker of the poem stands aside as an observer at first, while the mountain man seems to belong in the landscape, much as the bat belongs. The knife in his belt emphasizes his ability to survive on the land, and foreshadows the image of the barber. The image of the black bat disappearing into the twilight and reemerging as a white egret suggests the quick passage of time. Years have passed. The poet's own hair is turning white. He expresses at once the personal experience of the poet exiled from his homeland, and the general feeling of nostalgia for home, for youth, and for distant beloved landscapes. Despite its novel juxtaposition of images, Qin's poem rejoins the Chinese tradition by its themes of exile and nostalgia.

NOTES

1. The sources are listed in my introductory chapter.
2. Jean Moréas, "Un Manifeste littéraire," *Le Figaro*, Sept. 18, 1886. Now available online at: www.berlol.net/chrono/chr1886a.htm (accessed 30 Nov. 2011). Pierrot, 5, takes issue with the common view that the Decadent movement was just a short transitory stage to Symbolism, and traces their coexistence.
3. Tu Kuo-ch'ing, "The Introduction of French Symbolism into Modern Chinese and Japanese Poetry," *Tamkang Review* 10 (1980): 355, 357, 359.
4. Huang Sandao 黃參島, "Weiyu ji qi zuozhe" 《微雨》及其作者 ["*Light Rain* and Its Author"], *Meiyu Zazhi* 美育雜志 2 (Dec. 1928): 211.
5. Kaplan, "The Symbolist Movement," 104. Kaplan interviewed Li Jinfa's son for biographical details, and cites "Ginffa Lee, a Sculptor, Diplomat, and Poet, Dies in Long Island City," *New York Times* (31 Dec. 1976): 8.
6. Du Xuezhong 杜學忠, Mu Huaiying 穆懷英, and Qiu Wenzhi 邱文治, "Lun Li Jinfa de shige chuangzuo" 論李金髮的詩歌創作 ["On Li Jinfa's Poetic Creation"], *Zhongguo xiandai wenxue yanjiu congkan* 中國現代文學研究叢刊 1 (1983): 61. The authors report that Ai Qing 艾青 called Li "jia yangguizi" 假洋鬼子 [fake foreign devil], an epithet made famous by Lu Xun's "The True Story of Ah Q." Ai Qing does not go quite so far in his article "Sixty Years of New Poetry in China," *Chinese Literature* 3 (1981): 98, noting only that "many of [Li's] poems were written abroad and read as if written by foreigners."
7. Other sources give Shuliang 淑良 or Jinfa 金發 as Li's original name. Kaplan, "The Symbolist Movement," 104, learned from Li's son Oliver that Li was one of five brothers each of whose names bore the character 權.
8. By his own account in "Wode Bali yishu shenghuo" 我的巴黎藝術生活 ["My Artistic Life in Paris"], *Renjianshi* 人間世 22 (20 Feb. 1935): 14.

9. Li Jinfa, "Wenyi shenghuo de huiyi" 文藝生活的回憶 ["Recollections of a Life in Literature and Art"], in *Piaoling xianbi* 飄零閒筆 (Taipei: Qiaolian chubanshe, 1964), 5. Huang Sandao, 214, says Li was smart about money; other students often asked him to handle theirs. Yang Yunda 楊允達, "Li Jinfa de pingjia zhi er: mi yiban de shengping" 李金髮的評介之二：謎一般的生平 ["Evaluation of Li Jinfa 2: A Riddle-Like Life"], *Ming Bao* 明報 18, no. 2 (Feb. 1983): 84, states that Li Jinfa had brought with him an equivalent of 3,000 francs and did not have to work, whereas Zhou Enlai worked in a Renault factory for 6 francs a day, and lived on 100 francs per month. Others worked for as little as 2 francs a day making paper flowers. Perhaps Li had higher expectations because of his wealthy background; or perhaps his complaint about poverty was a pose: poets are supposed to be poor.

10. Tu Kuo-ch'ing, "The Introduction of French Symbolism," 353, based on Li Jinfa's own reminiscence in *Piaoling Xianbi*, 34–35.

11. Li Jinfa, "Da Ya Xian xiansheng ershi wen" 答瘂弦先生二十問 ["Responding to Mr. Ya Xian's Twenty Questions"], *Chuangshiji* 創世紀 39 (Jan. 1975): 6.

12. Li Jinfa, *Wei xingfu er ge* 為幸福而歌 [*Singing for Happiness*] (1926, Shanghai: Commercial Press, 1931), 297.

13. Epigraphs are taken from Baudelaire, Verlaine, Hugo, Corbière, Goethe, Heine, D'Annunzio, H. de Régnier, Tagore, Verhaeren, Chateaubriand, Wordsworth, Shakespeare, Shelley (misspelled Schelley), Ronsard, Musset, and, less known, Lerberghe, Spies, Kinon, Noir, Benoît, Sienkiewiez, Ch. Grandmougin.

14. Kaplan, "The Symbolist Movement," 116–17, identifies the drawings from both volumes to be the work of Li's first wife; the ones in the first volume are signed Que Dan 卻旦 (his first wife's Chinese name); those in the latter are signed Biao 髟, which constitutes the top part of "fa" 髮 in "Jinfa" 金髮. The satyr-nymph drawing is between pages 52 and 53 of *Happiness*. Zhao Jingshen, in *Xiandai shi xuan*, 188, identified the illustrator as his wife 卻但. Sun Yushi, *Chuqi*, 69, gives 卻但 and in parentheses (展姐). Kaplan has identified her original name as Gerta Scheuermann, and ascertained from Li's son Oliver that she was German, not French. Kaplan, "The Symbolist Movement," 117.

15. Li, *Piaoling xianbi*, 1.

16. Ibid., 6.

17. *Daxi*, 8:7–8.

18. *Daxi*, 8:7–8. Su Xuelin's article first appeared in *Xiandai: Les Contemporains* in 1933.

19. Hsu, *Twentieth-Century Chinese Poetry* , xxvii.

20. Lin, *Modern Chinese Poetry*, 153–64.

21. Loi, *Poètes*, 16–17.

22. Tu Kuo-ch'ing, "Li Chin-Fa and Kambara Ariake: The First Symbolist Poets in China and Japan," in *Essays in Commemoration of the Golden Jubilee of the Fung Ping Shan Library (1932–1982)* (Hong Kong, 1982), 334.

23. See "Malamei shichao—fu ji"馬拉美詩抄—附記 ["Mallarmé Poetry Extract: With Supplement"], *Xin wenyi yuekan*, 新文藝月刊 1, no. 2 (Oct. 1929): 249–59. Li warns his reader that his translations are unreliable (kaobuzhu de 靠不住的).

24. Loi, *Poètes*, 16–17. In a note, Loi identifies the American and English critics as Julia Lin and K. Y. Hsu. She notes that "Li Jinfa is the typical 'Occidentalist" in the sense "defined by Mao Zedong in Yan'an," and declares it "a vogue, a daubing which he had the 'genius' to launch as French Symbolism. Nothing more."

25. Li, *Piaoling xianbi*, 4.

26. Du Geling 杜格靈 and Li Jinfa, "Shi wenda" 詩問答 ["Poetry Questions and Answers"], *Wenyi huabao* 文藝畫報 1, no. 3 (15 Feb. 1935), repr. in *Shifeng* 詩風 79 (Dec. 1978): 14–16.

27. Li Jinfa, trans., *Gu Xila lian'ge, biliti zhu,*古希腊恋歌, 碧麗蒂著, 李金髮譯 [*Ancient Greek Poems by Bilitis*, translated by Li Jinfa] (上海: Kaiming shudian, 1928). Bilitis is a fictional ancient Greek poet created by Pierre Louÿs (1870–1925).

28. *Daxi*, 8:8. Su Xuelin 蘇雪林, in *Wentan huajiu* 文壇話舊 [*Reminiscences of Literary Circles*] (Taizhong: Wenxing shudian, 1967), 158, states: "Li Jinfa is not without poetic talent, but his training in Chinese is insufficient." Liu Xiwei 劉西渭 (penname of Li Jianwu 李健吾, who also translated from French) in *Ju Hua Ji* 咀華集 [*Ruminations on China*] (Shanghai: Wenhua shenghuo chubanshe, 1936, repr. 1938), 129; Gao Zhun 高準 (Paul C. Kao), *Zhongguo xin shi de fazhan lun* 中國新詩的發展論: *Critique on Modern Chinese Poetry* (Yangmingshan: Huagang chubanbu, 1973), 17; Cai Yizhong 蔡義忠, "Zhongguo xiangzhengpai de chuangshizhe—Li Jinfa ji qi shi de pingjia" 中國象徵派詩的創始者—李金髮及其詩的評價 ["Chinese Symbolist Poetry's Pioneer: Evaluation of Li Jinfa and His Poetry"] in *Cong Chen Duxiu de wenxue geming dao Li Jinfa de xiang-zhengpai xin shi* 從陳獨秀的文學革命到李金髮的象徵派新詩 [*From Chen Duxiu's Literary Revolution to Li Jinfa's New Symbolist Poetry*] (Taipei: Qingliu chubanshe, 1973), 204.

29. Zhou Liangpei 周良沛, "'Shiguai' Li Jinfa" '詩怪' 李金髮 ["'Odd Poet' Li Jinfa"], *Li Jinfa shi ji* 李金髮詩集 [*Li Jinfa Poetry Collection*] (Chengdu: Sichuan wenyi chuban-she, 1987), 10, 12. Bian Zhilin 卞之琳, "Dui benguo de yuyan, wulun shi baihua haishi wenyan, meiyou ganjue li" 對本國的語言，無論是白話還是文言，沒有感覺力 ["Toward our country's language, whether it's the vernacular or the literary, he had no force of feeling"]. Sun Xizhen孫席珍, "Baihuai yuyan, ta shi zuikueihuoshou" 敗壞語言，他是罪魁禍首 ["In Corrupting the Language, He Was an Arch-Criminal"]; Xu Xiacun 徐霞村, "Bu zhidao wei shenme, yige xie shi de ren, hua shuo bushun, xin xie butong" 不知道為什么，一個寫詩的人，話說不順，信寫不通。["I don't know why, a person who writes poetry could not speak smoothly, and could not communicate in correspondence"]. Unfortunately Li's correspondence with Xu was destroyed during the Cultural Revolution.

30. Bian Zhilin, "The Development of China's 'New Poetry' and the Influence from the West," *Chinese Literature: Essays, Articles, Reviews* 4 (1982): 154.

31. Jin, *Wenxue Jieshou*, 258–60.

32. Jin, *Métamorphose*, 327, 333.

33. Du Gelin and Li Jinfa, "Shi wenda," 16. Li Jinfa, "Bali zhi yejing" 巴黎之夜景 ["Paris Nocturne"], *Xiaoshuo yuepao* 小說月報 17, no. 2 (10 Feb. 1926): 4. Li noted at the same time that he preferred reading Lamartine, Musset, and Samain, whom he found closer to him in personality.

34. Translating meaning rather than words, Tu Kuo-ch'ing chose "fangjian" 房間 (room); Su Fengzhe chose "shalong" 沙龍 (salon); finding equivalents for "boudoir," Mo Yu chose "guifang" 閨房, and Qian Chunqi "guige" 閨閣.

35. Jin, *Wenxue jieshou*, 222.

36. For translations of this poem, see Hsu, *Twentieth Century Chinese Poetry*, 175–78; Lin, *Modern Chinese Poetry*, 159–61; for analyses, see Du Xuezhong et al. "Lun Li Jinfa," 56–58; Lin Huanzhang 林煥彰, "Cangqi de chuanr ruhe chuanzhe qiao—du Li Jinfa *Wei xingfu er ge* yougan" 藏起的串兒如何穿著瞧—讀李金髮「為幸福而歌」有感 ["The Hidden String and How to See It Connected—Comments on Reading Li Jinfa's *Singing for Happiness*"], *Shifeng yuekan* 詩風月刊. 7, no. 7 (1 Dec. 1978): 49; Yang Changnian 楊昌年, *Xinshi Shangxi* 新詩賞析 [*Appreciation of New Poetry*] (Taipei: Wen shi zhe chu-banshe, 1982), 242–44, and Vincent Yang, "From French Symbolism to Chinese Symbolism: A Literary Influence," *Tamkang Review*, 17, no. 3. (Spring 1987): 221–44.

37. Yang, *Xinshi Shangxi*, 233.

38. Tu Kuo-ch'ing, "Li Chin-fa and Kambara Ariake" (1982): 333. Su Xuelin's four criteria were based on her review of Li Jinfa's *Light Rain*.

39. Wang Zuoliang 王佐良, "Zhongguo xin shi zhong de xiandaizhuyi—yige hui-igu" 中國新詩中的現代主義——個回顧 ["A Look Back at Modernism in New Chinese Poetry"], in Cao Shunqing 曹順慶, ed. and comp., *Zhong xi bijiao meixue wenxue lunwen ji* 中西比較美學文學論文集 [*Essays on Comparative Aesthetics East and West*] (Chengdu: Sichuan wenyi chubanshe, 1985), 209.

40. Paul Manfredi, "Writing the Influenced Text: Modern Chinese Symbolist Poet-ry," *Journal of Modern Literature in Chinese* 5, no. 2 (Jan. 2002): 21.

41. For a translation of the entire poem, see Hsu, *Twentieth Century Chinese Poetry*, 175–76, "A Nocturnal Song."

42. *OC*, 134; David Jason Liu, "Chinese 'Symbolist' Verse in the 1920s: Li Chin-fa and Mu Mu-tien," *Tamkang Review* 12, no. 1 (Fall 1981): 42.

43. Song Yongyi 宋永毅, "Li Jinfa: Lishi huiyu zhong de cunzai" 李金髮：歷史毀譽中的存在 ["Li Jinfa: Existence in History's Praise or Blame"], in Zeng, 391, 396; Jin, *Wenxue jieshou*, 222–34; Kaplan, "The Symbolist Movement," 145.

44. Li Jinfa, *Happiness* 201–4. See appendix 3.

45. *OC*, 6.

46. Li Jinfa, "Yougan" 有感 ["Thoughts"], in *Happiness*, 107–8. See Hsu, *Twentieth Century Chinese Poetry*, 171–72, Lin, *Modern Chinese Poetry*, 157, Liu, "Chinese 'Symbolist' Verse," 39–40. Jin, *Wenxue jieshou*, 180–82 compares the poem with Verlaine's "Chanson d'automne" for their references to dead leaves.

47. Li Jinfa, *Happiness*, 264–66. See appendix 3.

48. Li Jinfa, trans., "Bali zhi yejing" 巴黎之夜景 ["Paris Nocturne"], *Xiaoshuo yuebao* 小說月報, 17, no. 2 (10 Feb. 1926): 1–4.

49. Li Mu 李牧, *Sanshi niandai wenyi lun* 三十年代文藝論 [*Art and Literature of the Thirties*] (Taipei: Liming, 1973), 162.

50. Li Jinfa, *Light Rain*, 141.

51. Pierre Louÿs, "Dialogue au soleil couchant" ["Dialogue in the Setting Sun"], in *Oeuvres complètes* (1929–1931; Geneve: Slatkine Reprints, 1973), 7:53–63.

52. Li Jinfa, *Hard Times*, 3–4. Kaplan, "The Symbolist Movement," 152–53, finds the poem "rich in bizarre images," and "one of Li's most difficult poems to unravel." The poem, offered in appendix 3, is missing from the 1987 collected poems, *Li Jinfa shi ji* 李金髮詩集.

53. *OC*, 71–72.

54. See Jin, *Wenxue jieshou*, 259.

55. *OC*, 140–41; Kaplan, "The Symbolist Movement," 154.

56. Kaplan, "The Symbolist Movement," 128, counted only 22 poems out of over 300 originally published.

57. Mi Jiayan, *Self-Fashioning and Reflexive Modernity in Modern Chinese Poetry, 1919–1949* (Lewiston, NY: The Edwin Mellen Press, 2004), 85–148.

58. Paul Manfredi, "Writing the Influenced Text," 24. Manfredi's MA thesis is entitled "Quest for the Missing String: On Li Jinfa's 'Symbolist' Poetry" (Indiana University, 1998).

59. See Fung et al., *Xiandai Zhongguo shixuan*, 281–82, and appendix 3. For other translations, see Hsu, *Twentieth-Century Chinese Poetry* , 194; Michelle Yeh, "'There Are No Camels in the Koran': What Is Modern about Modern Chinese Poetry?" in *New Perspectives on Contemporary Chinese Poetry*, ed. Christopher Lupke (New York: Palgrave Macmillan, 2008), 18. Yeh uses this poem to "illustrate . . . new possibilities in syntax, semantics, tone and cadence" that distinguishes Modern from Classical poetry, ibid., 19.

60. Vincent Yang, "From French Symbolism to Chinese Symbolism: A Literary Influence," *Tamkang Review* 17, no. 3 (Spring 1987), 228–33. Wang Duqing, *Chang'an chengzhong de shaonian* 長安城中的少年 [*Youth in Changan City*] (Shanghai: Guangming shuju, 1935), 7.

61. Wang, "Wo wenxue shenghuo de huigu" 我文學生活的回顧 ["Retrospective of My Literary Life"] (dated June 1933), in: *Wang Duqing xuan ji* 王獨清選集 [*Selections from Wang Duqing*], ed. Ye Wangyou 葉忘憂 and Xu Chensi 徐沉泗 (Shanghai: Zhongyang shudian, 1947), 1. For *Chu Ci*, see David Hawkes, trans., *Ch'u Tz'u: The Songs of the South* (1959, Boston: Beacon Press, 1962).

62. Wang Duqing, *Wo zai Ouzhoude shenghuo* 我在歐洲的生活 [*My Life in Europe*], 2nd ed. (Shanghai: Daguang shuju, 1936). According to the preface, the manuscript was completed in December 1931. The comparison with Balzac was made by Zhao Jingshen, quoted in Ya Xian 瘂弦, "Chang'an caizi Wang Duqing" 長安才子王獨清

["Chang'an's Talented Scholar Wang Duqing"], in *Zhongguo xinshi yanjiu* 中國新詩研究 [*Study of New Chinese Poetry*] (Taipei: Hongfan Shudian, 1981), 80.

63. Wang Duqing, *Duqing yi shi ji* 獨清譯詩集 [*Duqing Translated Poems Collection*] (n.p: s.n., 1937). Kaplan, "The Symbolist Movement," 299, gives the original publication date as 1929.

64. Wang Duqing, "Zaitan shi—ji gei Mutian Boqi" 再譚詩—寄給木天伯奇 ["Chatting about Poetry Again: Sent to (Mu) Mutian and (Zheng) Boqi"], *Chuangzao yuekan* 創造月刊 1, no. 1 (Mar. 1926): 95–104.

65. Wang, *Duqing yi shi ji*, 111–12.

66. Wang, "Zaitan shi," 104. For the full poem, see *Wang Duqing xuan ji*, 29–39. K. Y. Hsu has a partial translation, "About to Sail for Home," *Twentieth Century Chinese Poetry*, 196–98, but omits the lines in French.

67. Wang, "Zaitan shi," 101–2, and *Ouzhou*, 157. Hsu, *Twentieth Century Chinese Poetry*, 194–95, has a partial translation of this poem.

68. Fung et al., *Xiandai Zhongguo shixuan*, 279, cite the poem "Meiguihua" 玫瑰花 ["Roses"] for its use of color. See Hsu, *Twentieth-Century Chinese Poetry*, 193, "A Faded Rose." Jin Siyan, in *Wenxue*, 312, and *Métamorphose*, 445, indicates that Wang alone of the Chinese Symbolists showed interest in Rimbaud.

69. Wang Duqing, *Duqing shi xuan* 獨清詩選 (Shanghai: Xin yuzhou, 1931), 46–49. See appendix 3.

70. Wang, *Wang Duqing xuan ji*, 24.

71. Kaplan, "The Symbolist Movement," 177–78, quotes Xie Bingying's reminiscences on this point. See also Marián Gálik, "Ten Venetian poems by Wang Duqing: Chinese Entry into Literary Decadence," *Asiatica Venetiana* 1 (1996): 62.

72. Critics who regard Wang Duqing as a Symbolist include Zhu Ziqing, K. Y. Hsu, Tu Kuo-ch'ing, Wang Zhijian, Gao Zhun, Zhou Bonai, Sun Yushi, and Jin Siyan.

73. Kaplan, "The Symbolist Movement," 192.

74. *Daxi*, 8:8. Li Yiming, *Zhongguo xin wenxue shi jianghua*, 77–79, also finds Wang closer to Romantics, as do Ya Xian in "Chang'an caizi Wang Duqing," 79, and Zhou Bonai 周伯乃 in *Zaoqi xin shide piping* 早期新詩的批評 [*Criticism of Early New Poetry*] (Taipei: Chengwen chubanshe, 1980), 147.

75. Wang Duqing, "Chuangzaoshe: Wo he ta de shizhong yu tade zongzhang" 創造社：我和他的始終與他底總賬 ["My Beginning and End and Final Accounts with the Creation Society"], in *Wang Duqing xuan ji*, 174.

76. Mu Mutian, "Shenme shi xiangzheng zhuyi" 什麼是象徵主義 ["What Is Symbolism?"], in *Mu Mutian wenxue pinglun ji* 穆木天文學評論選集 [*Mu Mutian Literary Criticism Selection*], ed. Chen, Dun 陳惇 and Liu Xiangyu 劉象愚 (Beijing: Beijing shifan daxue chubanshe, 2000), 98–99, repr. from Zheng Zhenduo 鄭振鐸, Fu Donghua，傅東華, *Wenxue bai ti* 《文學百題》 [*A Hundred Literary Topics*], (n.p.: Shenghuo shudian，1935).

77. Mu Mutian, "Wo yu wenxue" 我與文學 ["Literature and I"], in *Pingfan ji* 平凡集 [*Ordinary Collection*] (1936, repr. Hong Kong: s.n., 1975), 142.

78. Mu Mutian, "Wode shige chuangzuo de huigu" 我的詩歌創作的回顧 ["Retrospective of My Poetic Creation"], in *Xiandai* 現代 4, no. 4 (Feb. 1934): 717–26.

79. Mu Mutian, "Tan shi" 談詩 ["Chatting about Poetry"], *Chuangzao yuekan* 創造月刊 1, no. 1 (Mar. 1926): 1–9.

80. Mu Mutian, *Pingfan ji* 113.

81. Fung et al., *Xiandai Zhongguo shixuan*, 305–7. See appendix 3. Hsu, *Twentieth-Century Chinese Poetry* , 188–90, links the images into meaningful sentences.

82. Loi, *Poètes* 73, appends a note to her translation "Cf. Baudelaire, Spleen II, *Les cloches*." Bells are not mentioned in "Spleen II," however, and in "Spleen IV," they suddenly jump and ring wildly rather than tolling mysteriously.

83. Kaplan, "The Symbolist Movement," 205.

84. Mu Mutian, *Lüxin*, 103–5. See appendix 3.This poem is selected for appreciation by Gao Mu 高穆, who contrasts its accessibility with Feng Naichao's "huise" 晦澀 [difficult, obscure] poems, in his "Feng Naichao lun—Zhongguo xiandai shiren ping-

shu zhi wu" 馮乃超論—中國現代詩人評述之五 ["On Feng Naichao: Fifth Commentary on Modern Chinese Poets"], in Li Weijiang 李偉江, ed., *Feng Naichao yanjiu ziliao* 馮乃超研究資料 [*Materials for the Study of Feng Naichao*] (Sian: Shaanxi renmin chubanshe, 1992), 265–66.

85. Mu Mutian, "Wode shige chuangzuo de huigu," 723.

86. Zhao Jingshen 趙景深, "Feng Naichao yu Mu Mutian" 馮乃超與穆木天 in *Xiandai wenxue za lun* 現代文學雜論 [*Modern Literature Miscellany*] (Shanghai: Guangming shudian, 1932), 125.

87. Sun, *Chuqi*, 193.

88. Zhou Bonai 周伯乃, *Zaoqi xinshi de piping* 早期新詩的批評 [*Critique of Early New Poetry*], (Taipei: Chengwen chubanshe, 1980), 150. Marián Gálik, "The Red Gauze Lantern of Feng Nai-ch'ao," *Asian and African Studies* (Bratislava), 10 (1974): 69–98, and "Feng Nai-ch'ao's *The Red Gauze Lantern* and French Symbolism," in *Milestones in Sino-Western Literary Confrontation (1898–1979)*, Asiatische Forschungen Band 98 (Wiesbaden: Otto Harrassowitz, 1986), 135–51. Hereafter, *Milestones*.

89. *Zhongguo wenxuejia cidian*, 6:106.

90. Zhao Jingshen, "Feng Naichao yu Mu Mutian," 128.

91. Gálik, *Milestones*, 141, 146.

92. Gálik, *Milestones*, 137. Kaplan renders the title "The Submerged Old Sangharama."

93. Gálik, *Milestones*, 137, 138.

94. *OC*, 140.

95. Bynner & Kiang, *Jade Mountain*, 73, translate Leyouyuan 樂遊原 as "Lo-yu Tombs," and make the link with dynastic decline quite clear. Liu, *The Poetry of Li Shangyin*, 160, finds the historical interpretation "unnecessary," and reads the poem as "the perfect symbol of an emotional mood," and a meditation on beauty.

96. For a translation of the complete poem, see Sherwin S. S. Fu, in Liu and Lo, ed., *Sunflower Splendor*, 420.

97. Sun, *Chuqi*, 204.

98. *Daxi*, 3738–39; Fung et al., *Xiandai Zhongguoshixuan*, 513–14; Sun, *Shixuan*, 211. See appendix 3.

99. Galík, *Milestones*, 147.

100. Feng, "bei'ai" 悲哀 [sorrow] and "yueguang xia" 月光下 [beneath the moonlight] are cited by Zhou Bonai, 148–51; "Shengming de aige" 生命的哀歌 ["Sad Song of Life"] is in Fung et al., *Xiandai Zhongguoshixuan*, 517–25.

101. Zhao Jingshen, *Xiandai shi xuan*, 211–12; Sun, *Shixuan*, 210. See appendix 3.

102. Xu Yunuo, *Jianglai zhi huayuan* (hereafter *JH*), 91–92. See appendix 3.

103. *OC*, 10–12.

104. Michelle Yeh, *Modern Chinese Poetry: Theory and Practice since 1917* (New Haven, CT: Yale University Press, 1991), 23, and *Anthology*, 4.

105. Xu Yunuo, *JH*, 60.

106. Liu Jixian 劉濟獻, *Xu Yunuo shi xuan* 徐玉諾詩選 [*Selected Poems of Xu Yunuo*] (Zhengzhou: Henan renmin chubanshe, 1983), 129–30.

107. Xu Yunuo, *JH*, 57–58.

108. Ibid., 84.

109. Ibid., 62–63.

110. Xu Yunuo, *Xue zhao* 雪朝 [*Snowy Morning*], with Zhou Zuoren, Yu Pingbo, Ye Shaojun, Zheng Zhenduo, Zhu Ziqing, Liu Yanling, Guo Shaoyu. Chinese Literary Association Series (Shanghai: Shangwu, 1922), 62–75 hereafter *XZ*). "Fannao" 煩惱 is used to translate "die Leiden" in Goethe's *Die Leiden des jungen Werthers*, which has been rendered into English both as "The Sorrows" and as "The Sufferings" of young Werther). Hockx, who has translated and analyzed the entire anthology, renders "fannao" 煩惱 as "worry," *A Snowy Morning*, 58.

111. Xu Yunuo, *JH*, 3.

112. Xu Yunuo, *XZ*, 101.

113. Xu Yunuo, *JH*, 39–40.

114. Ibid., 75–77.

115. *Ibid.*, 46.

116. See, for example, Shu Lan 舒藍, *Wusi shidaide xin shi zuojia he zuopin* 五四時代的新詩作家和作品 [*Authors and Works of New Poetry from the May Fourth Period*] (Taipei: Chengwen chubanshe, 1980) 234; Yang Changnian 楊昌年, *Xinshi pinshang* 新詩品賞 [*Appreciation of New Poetry*] (Taipei: Mutong, 1978), 214–18; Liu Jixian, *Xu Yunuo shi xuan*, 127.

117. E.g., in Xu Yunuo, "Lushang" 路上 ["On the Road"], *XZ*, 85–87; "Yu yuben de laodongzhe" 與愚笨的勞動者 ["For the Clumsy Laborer"], *JH*, 13–14.

118. Lu Xun, writing in 1934, wondered what had become of the poet, according to Wang Yao 王瑤，in "Bu gai bei wangji de shiren—*Xu Yunuo shi xuan—xu*" 不該被忘記的詩人—《徐玉諾詩選》序 ["A Poet Who Should Not Be Forgotten—Preface to *Xu Yunuo Poem Selections*], in Liu Jixian, *Xu Yunuo shi xuan*, 2. Xu Yunuo apparently published in 1956 a collection of poems on land reform and the Korean War, but none of those poems appear in Liu Jixian's 1983 selection.

119. Liu Jixian, *Xu Yunuo shi xuan*, 125, 139.

120. Ye Shaojun 葉紹鈞, "Yunuo de shi" 玉諾的詩, *JH*, 113–14. Ye Shaojun (1894–1968) is also known as Ye Shengtao 葉聖陶. For Ye's short story "Huozai" 火災 ["Conflagration"] see *Ye Shaojun xuanji* 葉紹鈞選集 [*Selected Works of Ye Shaojun*], ed. Xu Chensi 徐沉泗, Ye Wangyou 葉忘憂, et al. (Shanghai: Wanxiang shuwu,), 96–103. For further biographical anecdotes, see Zhang Mosheng 張默生, "Ji guai shiren Xu Yunuo" 記怪詩人徐玉諾 ["Remembering the Odd Poet Xu Yunuo"], in *Yixing zhuan* 異行傳 [*Extraordinary Biographies*] (Shanghai: Dongfang shushe, 1947), 103–19.

121. *JH*, 77–78. Qu Qiubai *wenji I*, 232–234, quoted in Hockx, *Snowy Morning*, 71.

122. Yeh, *Modern Chinese Poetry*, 23. Yang Changnian 楊昌年, *Xiandai shi de chuangzuo yu xinshang* 現代詩的創作與欣賞 [*Creation and Appreciation of Modern Poetry*], (Taipei: wen shi zhe chubanshe, 1991), 219; Gong Xianzong 龔顯宗, *Nian-sa niandai xinshi lun ji* 廿卅年代新詩論集 [*New Poetry from the Twenties and Thirties, Discussion Collection*] (Tainan: Fenghuangcheng tushu gongsi, 1982), 256–57.

123. Kaplan, "The Symbolist Movement," 34.

124. Ibid.

125. Ibid., 35. "*Recueillement*" is one of the rare poems to have an entire article devoted to it in Chinese. See Shi Deyi 史德義, "Fenxi Botelai'er de 'jingsi'" 分析波特萊爾的'靜思' ["Analyzing Baudelaire's 'Recueillment"], *Waiguo Wenxue* 外國文學 2, no. 5 (Oct. 1973): 102–10.

126. Liang Zongdai, *Wan dao* 晚禱 [*Vespers*] (1924; Shanghai: Commercial Press, 1933), 49. See appendix 3.

127. Liang Zongdai, "Two Poems: Souvenir and Vespers," *T'ien Hsia Monthly* 2 (1936): 85–86.

128. Liang Zongdai, *Wandao*, 62–63.

129. Fung et al., *Xiandai Zhongguo shixuan*, 118; Yang Li et al., *Zhongguo xiandai zuojia da cidian*, 279–80.

130. Zhang Taisheng 張太勝, *Liang Zongdai yu Zhongguo xiangzheng zhuyi shixue* 梁宗岱與中國象徵主義詩學 [*Liang Zongdai and Chinese Symbolist Poetics*] (Beijing: Beijing Shifan Daxue chubanshe, 2004).

131. Qin Zihao 覃子豪, *Qin Zihao Quanji* 覃子豪全集 [*Complete Works of Qin Zihao*] (Taipei: Qin Zihao quanji chuban weiyuanhui, 1965–1974), 4 vols.

132. Yeh, *Anthology*, 56.

133. Chi Pang-yuan et al., *An Anthology of Contemporary Chinese Literature: Taiwan: 1949–1974*, 2 vols. (Taipei: National Institute for Compilation and Translation, 1975), 1:9.

134. "Yige wei jian de linghun kuashang le shijian de kuaima—jinian Qin Zihao shiren shishi shiwu zhounian (一個偉健的靈魂跨上了時間的快馬—紀念覃子豪詩人逝世十五周年 [A Great Spirit Mounted the Swift Steed of Time—Commemorating the Fifteenth Anniversary of the Poet Qin Zihao's Death])," in Xiaoxiao 蕭蕭, *Xiandai*

mingshi pinshang ji 現代名詩品賞集 [*Appreciation of Famous Modern Poems*] (Taipei: Putian chubanshe, 1979), 190.

135. Mo Yu 莫渝, "Lun Qin Zihao" 覃子豪論 [On Qin Zihao], *Li* 笠, 89 (Feb. 1979): 55–80.

136. *OC*, 300–301.

137. Ibid., 26.

138. Qin Zihao, *Qin Zihao Quanji*, 1:428–29.

139. Ibid., 1:426. See appendix 3.

140. Ibid., 1:113.

141. Black Hair Bridge is the name of a bridge on the way from Taidong to Xingang. Qin Zihao, 1:434–35. See Appendix 3. The poem was one of three selected for discussion on the fifteenth anniversary of Qin's death. See Xiao Xiao, 159–96. Yeh, *Anthology*, 59–60, sees a whole flock of egrets, rather than a single one that fills the sky only symbolically.

EIGHT

From Symbolism to Modernism

Although Baudelaire is often named a forerunner of Modernism, there was no real "Modernist" movement in France. Nor can it be said to have been a real "Modernist" movement in China. Chinese poets who have been identified as "Modernist" are often the ones who moved forward in time from Baudelaire to take their inspiration from more contemporary sources. Comparisons with Baudelaire have been and can be made with their earlier work.

Dai Wangshu and Bian Zhilin are most often classified as Symbolists in literary histories. Both translated from *Les Fleurs du mal*, and both were inspired by European Symbolist poetry in their own work. Dai Wangshu first became known as a "Modernist" through his association with the journal *Xiandai* 現代, with its French subtitle *"Les Contemporains."* Dai read and translated the Spanish Modernists. Gregory Lee, in his book on Dai Wangshu's life and poetry, decisively pronounces him to be a "Chinese Modernist."[1] Bian Zhilin, who has been identified with Modernism (現代主義) by Wang Zuoliang and Sun Yushi, among others,[2] has written about his own poetry, and indicated its relation to Baudelaire.

He Qifang has not been associated with any particular school, but there are clearly European influences in his poetry. Bonnie McDougall has published a full article on those influences, and as she and Kam Louie point out, "He Qifang's poetry gives an unusually vivid depiction of the author's progress through romanticism, symbolism, neo-romanticism, modernism, and Russian futurism."[3] He and Bian were lifelong friends and shared many poetic leanings.

This chapter concludes with brief attention to two lesser-known poets, Cao Baohua and Chen Jingrong. Cao Baohua, according to McDougall and Louie, "resembles Dai Wangshu in his progress from symbolism to modernism and eventually to patriotic verse during the War against Japan."[4] Chen Jingrong was not particularly associated with Modernism in her work, but in her life, she was Cao Baohua's student, and associated with Bian Zhilin, He Qifang, and Liang Zongdai.[5] Her translations from Baudelaire were introduced in chapter 3. Her own poetry spans from 1935 to 1986.

DAI WANGSHU (戴望舒 1905–1950)

Dai Wangshu, whose translations from Baudelaire were introduced in chapter 3, published four collections of his own poetry: *Wode jiyi* 我的記憶 [*My Memories*], 1929, *Wangshu Cao* 望舒草 [*Wangshu's Drafts*], 1933, *Wangshu shigao* 望舒詩稿 [*Wangshu's Poetic Drafts*] 1937, and *Zainande suiyue* 災難的歲月 [*Years of Disaster*] 1948. The four collections, comprised of ninety-some poems, occupy a mere 182 pages in his collected works of over 2,300 pages, the majority of which are translations. Although his poems span only two decades, critics generally divide them into three periods, and classify his earliest works as "Symbolist."[6]

Dai Wangshu's most famous and most frequently anthologized poem is "*Yuxiang*" 雨巷 ["Rainy Lane"]. To this day he is known as the "*yuxiang shiren*" 雨巷詩人 [rainy lane poet]. There are many translations of the poem; the following is my own rendition:

> Holding an oil-paper umbrella, alone
> Pacing the long, long,
> And lonely lane in the rain,
> I hope to encounter
> The girl who holds her grief
> Like a spray of lilac.
>
> She has
> The color of lilacs,
> The fragrance of lilacs,
> The sorrow of lilacs,
> Grieving in the rain
> Grieving and wandering
>
> She strolls in this lonely lane in the rain
> Holding an oil-paper umbrella,
> Just like me,
> Just like me,
> Silently pacing,
> Aloof, alone, and melancholy.
>
> She silently walks near,
> Walks near, and casts
> A sigh-like glance,
> She drifts by

Like a dream,
Sad and bewildered like a dream.

Drifting by as in a dream,
Like a spray of lilac,
By my side passes this girl:
She silently draws away, away
To the broken fence hedge,
To the end of this rainy lane.

In the sad song of the rain
Vanished her color;
Scattered her perfume,
Scattered and vanished, even her
Sigh-like glance,
Her lilac-like melancholy.

Holding an oil-paper umbrella, alone
Pacing the long, long
And lonely lane in the rain,
I hope will drift by
The girl holding her grief
Like a spray of lilac.[7]

The lines of irregular length have a natural rhythm of their own; the rhyme in *-ang* is repeated throughout, in end rhymes and internal rhyme as well as in the repetition. Pinyin spelling underlines this in lines like:

Dingxiang yiyangde yanse,	丁香一樣的顏色
Dingxiang yiyangde fenfang,	丁香一樣的芬芳
Di ngxiang yiyangde youchou ,	丁香一樣的憂愁

    [lilac-like color, lilac-like fragrance, lilac-like melancholy]

The poem is symmetrical: in the first three stanzas, the poet hopes to encounter the girl; they meet and pass each other in the fourth stanza; in the fifth and sixth, the girl draws away, and in the final stanza, the poet returns to his hope. The first and final stanzas are identical except for the verb in the fourth line: *"fenzhe"* 逢著 [encountering] becomes *"piaoguo"* 飄過 [drift by], as the image fades and becomes more indistinct at the end.

The poem has yielded many readings. Many readers have compared it with Baudelaire and the French Symbolists.

The "interplay of diverse sense impressions" in specific lines recalls for Julia Lin the lines from Baudelaire's sonnet *"Correspondances,"* *"Comme de longs échos qui de loin se confondent / . . . les parfums, les couleurs, et les sons se répondent"* [Like long echoes which mingle in the distance / . . . perfumes, colors, and sounds respond to one another]. Lin finds in the poem "some distinctive features of symbolism: suggestive indefinite-

ness, musical nuances, synaesthesia, and the intermingling of the imaginary with the real"; and "an atmosphere permeated with effeminate
charm, languorous grace, and mellifluous music that is worthy of [Dai's]
poetic guide, Paul Verlaine."[8]

A similarity in theme recalls for Michelle Loi Baudelaire's "*À une
passante*" ["To a Passerby"], although Loi adds that the theme is also
found in many Chinese fairy tales, where the flower fairy carries an umbrella, "umbrella" (*san* 傘) being a homophone for "disperse," (*san* 散)
which symbolizes the fairy's eventual disappearance. She also recalls
Gérard de Nerval's various stories where girls are glimpsed walking in
parks and disappearing among ruins. Loi finds more specific echoes in
Nerval's "*L'allée du Luxembourg*," where the poet thinks a passing girl
carrying a flower might be the only one he could have loved; in Jammes's
"*Tristesses*" ["Sorrows"], where the poet thinks he might have loved a girl
seen carrying dampened lilacs; and in Carco's "*l'Ombre*," where the poet
passes without recognizing the girl whose shadow is the color of rain.[9]

Loi's comparison with "*À une passante*" fails upon closer examination.
It is based on the sonnet's last line: "*O toi que j'eusse aimée, ô toi qui le
savais!* " [Oh, you whom I might have loved, oh you who knew it!]. But
Baudelaire's "*passante*" is glimpsed in the midst of a deafening crowd.
Strikingly elegant, she is tall, slim, and dressed in heavy mourning; the
poet looks into her eyes before she disappears into the crowd. Walter
Benjamin, citing this poem to discuss Baudelaire's role as *flâneur*, points
out: "The delight of the city-dweller is not so much love at first sight as
love at last sight."[10] The city setting, the appearance of the woman, the
boldness of the poet in drinking pleasure from her eyes, and the perverse
delight in her disappearance in Baudelaire's poem all contrast with Dai
Wangshu's dreamy, wistful melancholy and the longing for pastel beauty
in his poem. In musicality and mood, Dai's poem is far more reminiscent
of Verlaine.

The girl represents the poem itself for Vincent Yang, who posits that
the girl "is only a figure of the speaker's imagination; he has not realisti-
cally encountered her," and that "the encounter between the speaker and
the girl is essentially an illustration of the poet's creative process." Yang
translates "*piaoguo*" 飄過 [drift by] into the past tense and renders the last
three lines: "I hope there drifted by / A lilac-like / Girl who bears sorrow
and grief," to indicate that the girl passing by had only been a hope. He
then concludes that at the end, "the speaker indicates with modesty the
wish that he has successfully composed a symbolist poem of his original
intent." Yang also compares some images in this poem with Verlaine's
"*Voeu*" [wish] and "*L'Allée*" [the lane].[11]

Implying agreement that the girl could have been imagined, Gregory
Lee finds the source for the "lilac-colored girl" in Francis Jammes, whose
"references to lilac occur in poems dealing with imaginary or evasive
female characters." While Chinese critics have traced the association of

dampened lilacs with sorrow to lines by the late Tang poets Li Shangyin and Li Jing (李璟 916–961), Lee is on the mark in pointing out that the "great attraction and contemporary popularity" of the poem "was surely based on its assimilation of Western Symbolist techniques."[12]

"Inconceivable as it may seem, there is little to suggest that Dai had been influenced by or even read Baudelaire at the time of writing 'Rainy Alley,' and nothing in the poem itself would indicate otherwise," contends Lee, who dates the genesis of the poem to 1927. Dai's translations of Baudelaire's poems were published a full twenty years later. Dai's schoolmate at l'Université l'Aurore in Shanghai, Shi Zhecun (施蟄存 1905–2003), recalls that while Dai had read Hugo, Lamartine, and Musset for class, he hid Verlaine and Baudelaire under his pillow for his own reading. But Lee questions this memory, and argues that "had Dai read Baudelaire earlier, he would certainly have translated him, and Dai's friends would have been aware of the fact."[13]

In his "assimilation of Western Symbolist techniques," it seems equally "inconceivable" for Dai not to have read Baudelaire. He had published in 1926 a detailed review of Li Sichun's *Xianhe Ji* 仙河集, with its ten selections from Baudelaire.[14] Lee also diminishes the possibility of Baudelaire's influence by mistakenly associating "*correspondances*" with Proust rather than with Baudelaire.[15] Nevertheless, he acknowledges that Baudelaire's "*Spleen*" poem "*J'ai plus de souvenirs . . .*" may have inspired Jammes's "*La Salle à manger*" ["Dining Room"], which in turn may have provided the form and subject matter of Dai Wangshu's later poem "*Wode jiyi*" 我的記憶 ["My Memory"].[16]

Such indirect influence may have been at work in Dai Wangshu's own "*Spleen*" poem in five couplets, which first appeared under that title, and then as "*Youyu*" 憂鬱 in later editions:

> I have grown weary now of the color of the rose,
> Letting her coy blush spread over her boughs.
>
> My heart's vernal flowers no longer bloom;
> Somber spleen has entered my happy dream.
>
> My lips are shriveled; my eyes dried;
> I am inhaling fire; I hear phantoms whisper.
>
> Go, lovely deceitful dreams, deceitful illusions,
> How can the common person imagine heaven's boughs!
>
> I sadly stroll in the slowness of days,
> I am a weary man; I am waiting for rest.[17]

The first three couplets repeat the adverb "*yi*" 已 [already] to emphasize that everything has passed; the fourth couplet uses two related words for "illusion," "*huanxiang*" 幻像 and "*chixiang*" 痴想; the latter, translated "imagine" above; can also mean "idiotic idea." In the last couplet, "sad-ly" is "*tuitang*" 頹唐 [dejected, dispirited]. Leonid Cherkassky finds that this poem is "an obvious imitation of Baudelaire's poem of the same name."[18] But in form, Dai's use of couplets reflects Verlaine's practice rather than Baudelaire's. The undirected melancholy and vexation are reminiscent of Verlaine's "*deuil sans raison*" [grief without cause]. Indeed, Gregory Lee traces this poem not only to Jammes, but to Verlaine's "*Spleen*," in Ernest Dowson's translation. Dai translated Dowson with Shi Zhecun in 1927, but there is little reason to suppose that he would not have read Verlaine in the original, as Du Heng recalls he did.[19]

Parallels with Baudelaire can be found in other, quite different, poems. "*Liulangren de yege*" 流浪人的夜歌 ["Vagabond's Night Song"], with its owls, graveyards, and broken tombstones, recalls the images frequently associated with Baudelaire, especially by his Chinese critics. But Gregory Lee, who has treated this poem in detail, convincingly associates it with the "French Romanticists" rather than with Baudelaire or the Symbolists.[20] Dai's "*Gu shen si qian*" 古神祠前 ["Before the Ancient Temple"] reminds Michelle Loi of the first line of Baudelaire's "*Eléva-tion*," but she admits that the association is questionable. For "*Duiyu tian de huaixiangbing*" 對于天的懷鄉病 ["Nostalgia for the Sky"] Loi finds the closest parallels in Jammes, but also notes "Cf. Baudelaire," possibly for the association of melancholy with pipe smoking in "*La Pipe*."[21] For a poem simply entitled "*Shisi hang*" 十四行 ["Fourteen Lines" or "Sonnet"], Michelle Loi finds "Rimbaldian images" and parallels with Supervielle and César Moro, but suggests that the theme of hair might be "more or less inspired by Baudelaire" although it had been used by other poets before Dai Wangshu.[22] I believe that parallels between this sonnet and Baudelaire go much further:

> A fine drizzle lights on your flowing hair,
> Like small pearls scattered amid dark kelp,
> Or dead fish tossed about on the waves,
> With a mysterious and melancholy gloom,
>
> Luring and bringing my dark soul
> To rest in the dreamland of love and death,
> There the air is gold and the sun purple,
> There pitiful creatures weep tears of joy;
>
> Like a decrepit thin black cat,
> I stretch and yawn and wither in the gloom,
> And pour forth all my pride false and true;
>
> And then, staggering after it in the murky mist,
> Like a bubble of pale-red wine floating in an amber glass,
> I will hide my sentimental eyes in somber memories.[23]

The poem moves from sensation to memory and from exterior to interior scenes, ending in the poet's mind. An interplay of colors moves throughout the poem; the word used to describe both kelp and the poet's soul is *"qingse"* 青色, which can mean green, blue, azure, or black. The silver fish, golden air, purple sun, pale-red wine, and amber glass reinforce the decadent atmosphere. The "gloom" in lines four and ten are *"youguang"* 幽光 [dim light], which Julia Lin renders variously as "shimmering" and "mystic light," and which K. Y. Hsu translates as "gleam" and "soft twilight." The *"you"* 幽 suggests something hidden or secluded; *"youguang"* 幽光 enhances the feeling of indefiniteness by suggesting not color, but nuance, an ideal Dai adapted from Verlaine's *"Art Poétique."* [24]

In Baudelaire's poem *"La Chevelure"* [head of hair], as in Dai Wangshu's sonnet, a head of hair inspires meditation on the part of the poet. Although Baudelaire's associations are with southern ports, and Dai's end in a homelike interior, both use the image of the sea. Baudelaire's poem in seven quatrains compares the hair to an "ebony sea" or a "black ocean" (Cf. stanza 3, line 4: *"Tu contiens, mer ébène, un éblouissant rêve"* [You contain, ebony sea, a dazzling dream]; stanza 5, line 2 *"Dans ce noir océan où l'autre est enfermé"* [in this black ocean where the other is imprisoned]. It also describes the hair as blue, like the azure of the skies (stanza 6, lines 1–2: *"Cheveux bleus, pavillon de ténèbres tendues, / Vous me rendez l'azur du ciel immense et rond"* [Blue hair, pavilion of shadows stretched out, / You bring me back the azure of the immense round sky]. The equivalence of black, blue, and azure are summed up by *"qing"* 青 in Chinese. In the last stanza of the French poem, the persona proposes to scatter rubies, pearls, and sapphires in the head of hair. The Chinese poet perceives as pearls what nature has formed in the beloved's hair. The French poem ends with drinking the wine of memories; wine, though not imbibed, also appears at the end of the Chinese poem.

The image of the cat also recalls Baudelaire, who describes cats in *"Les Chats"* as *"puissants et doux, orgueil de la maison"* [powerful and sweet, pride of the house]. To enhance their mystery, *"Ils cherchent le silence et l'horreur des ténèbres"* [they seek the silence and horror of shadows]. Dai, likewise, finds his cat in the gloom, or "mystic light," and follows it into "murky mist" (*qingwu menglong* 輕霧朦朧). Baudelaire compares his cats to sphinxes *"Qui semblent s'endormir dans un rêve sans fin"* [who seem to sleep in an endless dream]; Dai Wangshu's cat leads him to *"you'an"* 幽暗 [mystic and dark] memories, and memory is the sister of dreams.

Whether or not Dai Wangshu's poem was directly inspired by Baudelaire, it achieves the Symbolist ideals of succinctness and suggestiveness. While its musicality is not as obvious as that of "Rainy Lane," it follows a regular rhyme scheme (aabb / xabb / ccc / ddd); the uneven lines generally present a pleasing succession of tones (*pingze* 平仄), though without any obvious patterns. In this poem the poet successfully leads his reader into a world of sensation, imagination, and dream.

Baudelaire stands astride Romanticism and Modernism. If he had any influence on Dai Wangshu's early poems, it is from the former more than from the latter. Lacking Baudelaire's use of irony, Dai's early poems describing feelings, moods, and small events often become overly sentimental; his love poems, including those from his middle period, sometimes threaten to cloy.

Like the other "Chinese Symbolists," Dai Wangshu later moved away from his early inspiration. Dai's "poetics" are generally represented by seventeen fragments culled from his notebooks by his friend Shi Zhecun shortly after his departure for France in 1932. Published in *Xiandai* 現代 (*Les Contemporains*), they repudiate the poetic practice of his earlier and best-known poems, renouncing the element of music in poetry to aim at a simpler, more colloquial tone through experimentation with free verse. Dai studied in France, published six original poems in French in the *Cahiers du Sud* in 1935, and translated from French for the rest of his life.[25] On his return to China he was active in the Shanghai literary scene; in 1938 he fled to Hong Kong to avoid the Japanese occupation and was active in anti-Japanese activities there. After the war, he moved to Beijing and was head of the French language section of the Bureau of International Information at the time of his death.

Poems from Dai's last period emphasize social and political consciousness. He seems to have abandoned the themes and subjects of his youth. But his translations of Baudelaire were published only three years before his death. Was he going back to an earlier source of inspiration or finding a new one? Had he lived longer, would Baudelaire have played a different role in his poetry? For his attempt to fuse Western and Chinese poetic elements, a more fitting valedictory might be his four line poem entitled "I think," which joins thought with dream, Descartes with Zhuangzi:

> *wo sixiang, gu wo shi hudie . . .*
> *wannian hou xiao hua de qing hu,*
> *touguo wu meng wu xing de yunwu,*
> *lai zhenhan wo banlan de cai yi.*
> 我思想，故我是蝴蝶…
> 萬年後小花的輕呼，
> 透過無夢無醒的雲霧，
> 來震撼我斑斕的彩翼.

> I think, therefore I am a butterfly . . .
> Ten thousand years from now the soft call of a small flower
> Coming through the dreamless, wakeless mist,
> Will shake my lovely multicolored wings.[26]

BIAN ZHILIN (卞之琳 1910–2000)

"I translated Baudelaire. Of course I was influenced by him," Bian Zhilin stated during a visit to the United States in 1980.[27] Introduced in chapter 3 for his translations from Baudelaire, Bian is not classified as a Symbolist in Chinese literary histories. K. Y. Hsu groups him with Feng Zhi (馮至1905–1993) as a "metaphysical" poet.[28] Lloyd Haft, in his complete study of Bian's life and work, concedes that some of Bian's poetry is reminiscent of the English Metaphysical poets, but points out that Bian preferred the French Symbolists, finding their work closer to the Chinese tradition. Allowing that "his most obvious Western affinity is with the French poets generally called Symbolist," Haft demurs: "it would be going too far to call him a Symbolist *tout court.*"[29] Jean Monsterleet does just that. In his French anthology of modern Chinese poetry, he identifies Bian with "*le Symbolisme*" as he does Xu Zhimo with "*le Romantisme*" and Wen Yiduo with "*le Parnasse.*"[30] Shao Xunmei found "the sensual purity of Baudelaire . . . everywhere within the covers of his book *Yumu ji* 魚目集 [*Fish Eye Collection*]," adding "and the use of an unfamiliar vocabulary and incoherent strange images, does that not remind us of Mallarmé and the French Symbolists?"[31] Bian himself has indicated images, lines, and forms borrowed from, inspired by, or modeled on Valéry, Verlaine, and Baudelaire. But then he has also acknowledged influence from traditional Chinese poets such as Li Shangyin and Jiang Baishi (Jiang Kuei 姜夔 1155?–1235?) as well as the English Modernists Eliot, Yeats, and Auden. Kang Peichu has suggested that Bian properly belongs with the Modernists.[32]

Bian Zhilin's major poetic work, four collections of lyric poetry, appeared in the 1930s: *Sanqiu cao* 三秋草 [*Drafts of Three Autumns*], 1933; *Yumu ji* 魚目集 [*Fish Eye Collection*], 1935; *Luye chuan* 蘆葉船 [*Reed-Leaf Boat*], 1936; and *Hanyuan ji* 漢園集 [*Han Garden Collection*], 1936. *Yumu ji* particularly attracted critical attention. Bian chose the title with typical modesty, as fish eyes suggest false pearls. His own contribution to the critical discussions only reinforced the impression that his poems were difficult and obscure. His fifth collection, *Shinian shicao* 十年詩草 [*Ten Years' Poetic Drafts*], is comprised of untitled love poems composed in 1937 and a small selection from his previous collections.[33]

Bian's 1940 collection, *Weilao xinji* 慰勞信集 [*Letters of Gratitude*], represents a change in poetic direction inspired by his visit to the Communist base in Yan'an, which resulted in the attempt to writing simpler poems describing "real people and real events." After the war Bian studied in England, and returned to a new China in 1949, to begin what he called a "new era" in his life and work.[34] His poems from the fifties were unsuccessful, both from the view of the peasants, who wanted something simpler, and from the view of his earlier aesthetic sophistication and formal polish. Sent to the countryside for reeducation from 1964 to 1972, Bian was able to return to his earlier poetic concerns only in 1976, which year marked for him a "Second Liberation" and a "Second Awakening" for poetry.[35]

For the "Second Awakening," Bian Zhilin culled seventy poems from the 1930s, and published them in a new collection in 1979, with the self-mocking title *Diao chong ji li* 雕蟲紀歷 [*Record of Carving Insects*]—like the fish eyes that represent false pearls, insects are substituted here for dragons, carving dragons being the usual metaphor for literary craftsmanship. For a second edition in 1980 he added thirty poems from the 1930s. Ever his own harshest critic, Bian criticizes his earlier poems for being "sensitive to small things but fuzzy about large issues, full of nostalgia for the past and for remote things and people," and dismisses his later poems as "propagandistic, crude and ephemeral."[36]

Bian Zhilin devoted his entire life to literature, as writer, translator, editor, and teacher. Aside from a 1934 poetry collection entitled *Xi chuang ji* 西窗集 [*Windows on the West*], Bian's translations from the French include Gide's *Les Nouvelles nourritures* and Constant's *Adolphe*; his translations from the English include James Joyce and Virginia Woolf. His verse version of *Hamlet* became a standard college text. He also translated his own poems into English, including fourteen selections in Harold Acton and Chen Shih-hsiang's 1936 anthology, and sixteen in Robert Payne's 1947 anthology.[37]

Bian's translations, criticism, and original poems all demonstrate painstaking attention to prosody and form. Thus Wang Li's study on Chinese prosody, *Hanyu shilü xue*, 漢語詩律學, could choose sonnets from *Letters of Gratitude* to compare with rhyme schemes of sonnets from *Les Fleurs du mal*.[38] Lloyd Haft agrees that the rhyme schemes sometimes correspond, but posits that Bian's choice of the octosyllabic line rather than the alexandrine appears to be in conscious imitation of Valéry.[39]

In theme and image, Haft has drawn a specific comparison with Baudelaire, finding Bian's sonnet *"Deng chong"* 燈蟲 ["Insects at the Lamp"] to be "evidently a thematic expansion of two lines from Baudelaire's *'Hymne à la Beauté'*":

> *L'éphémère ébloui vole vers toi, chandelle,*
> *Crépite, flambe et dit: Bénissons ce flambeau!*

[The dazzled mayfly flies toward you, candle, / Sizzles, flames, and says, "Let us bless this torch!"]

At the moment of death, the mayfly, whose life was already ephemeral, would praise the flame which destroyed it, because in that moment, Beauty was created. The two lines come from the same poem (in seven quatrains) that asks whether Beauty comes from Heaven or Hell, from Satan or from God. Bian's sonnet refers to the Golden Fleece and Helen, and also to the Buddha. In Haft's translation, it describes insects "falling in droves" at the lamp who "In a flash of brilliance reaching death's fairyland / To paint a halo on the very Buddha!" This suggestion of spiritual awakening leads to the final tercet where the poem's persona physically awakens to everyday reality and blows away the insect remains. Bian published an English version of the sonnet as "Tiny Green Moths" in his 1979 collection, but the original poem gives better support to Haft's comparison, and is arguably a better poem.[40]

Parallels between two other poems are yet more striking, in sharing form and imagery as well as theme: Bian Zhilin's *"yige heshang"* 一個和尚 ["A Monk"] and Baudelaire's *"Le Mauvais Moine"* ["The Bad Monk"]. Baudelaire's sonnet reads:

> Les cloîtres anciens sur leurs grandes murailles
> Étalaient en tableaux la sainte Vérité,
> Dont l'effet, réchauffant les pieuses entrailles,
> Tempérait la froideur de leur austérité.
>
> En ces temps où du Christ florissaient les semailles,
> Plus d'un illustre moine, aujourd'hui peu cité,
> Prenant pour atelier le champ des funérailles,
> Glorifiait la Mort avec simplicité.
>
> —Mon âme est un tombeau que, mauvais cénobite,
> Depuis l'éternité je parcours et j'habite;
> Rien n'embellit les murs de ce cloître odieux.
>
> Ô moine fainéant! quand saurai-je donc faire
> Du spectacle vivant de ma triste misère
> Le travail de mes mains et l'amour de mes yeux?

[Ancient monasteries on their great walls / Display the holy Truth in paintings / Whose effect warmed pious entrails, / And tempered the cold of their austerity. / / In those days when the seeds of Christ flowered, / More than one renowned monk, little known today, / Taking the cemetery for his workshop, / Would glorify Death with simplicity. / / — My soul is a tomb which, wicked cenobite, / I have rambled and dwelt in for all eternity; / Nothing embellishes the walls of this odious cloister. / / Oh slothful monk! When will I learn to make / Of the living spectacle of my misery / The work of my hands and the love of my eyes?][41]

Bian's poem is also a sonnet:

> Striking his bell day after day,
>   A monk is dreaming a deep pale dream:
>   The traces left by so many past years
> In memory appear only like the smoke of incense that
>
> In the crumbling temple incense suffuses everywhere,

Burnt ends of sorrow remain in the censer
Keeping company with the suffering of devout men and women,
And boredom forever wafts round and round in the Sutras.

Sleepy dream talk dribbles from his mouth,
His head nods in time to the wooden fish,
    Head and wooden fish both empty, both heavy;

One sound after another, lulls hills and streams to sleep,
The hills and streams lazily fall asleep in the evening mist,
    As he tolls the funeral bell of another day. [42]

Both sonnets have regular line-length and rhyme schemes. Baudelaire's is abab, abab, ccd, eed, Bian's abba, abba, ccb, ccb; Bian's lines are eleven-syllables, Baudelaire's twelve.

Both poems are haunted by memory and by emptiness. Striking the wooden fish to keep time with reading the Sutras is, according to K. Y. Hsu, "a gesture demanding the monster to disgorge the Word." [43] But as the monk completes what is by now an empty gesture, the monk's head is as empty as the wooden fish he strikes. In Baudelaire's poem, the meaning of the paintings and martyrdom have faded in memory, and emptiness reigns, too, for the monk, who despairs at the emptiness of the walls of the tomb that is his soul. That the monk in one poem is Christian while the other is Buddhist thus seems to be merely incidental. Endless repetition, reinforced by the circular structure, dominates the Chinese poem; its mood is reminiscent rather of Baudelaire's "*Spleen*" poem, which begins: "*J'ai plus de souvenirs que si j'avais mille ans.*" [I have more memories than if I had lived a thousand years], and especially the lines:

Rien n'égale en longueur les boîteuses journées
Quand, sous les lourds flocons des neigeuses années,
L'ennui, fruit de la morne incuriosité,
Prend les proportions de l'immortalité. [44]

[Nothing equals in length those limping days / When, under the heavy flakes of years of snow, / Ennui, formed from dreary lack of curiosity, / Takes on the dimensions of immortality]

Although Bian's poem is not about memory, it also suggests the idea of days dragging on and on into years, and perhaps even into immortality. In the preface of his *Record of Carving Insects*, pointing to the rhyme in "-*ong*" that was intended to express the monotonous sound of the bell, Bian refers to this poem as a "conscious parody of second- or third-rate French Symbolists from the latter part of the nineteenth century." [45]

Commenting more generally on his poetry from the 1930s, Bian states that although he wrote lyric poems, he was reluctant to reveal private sentiments, so that he expressed feelings through scenes, things, and events; he fictionalized, depersonalized, and dramatized his poems so that "you" and "I" are interchangeable.[46] Here is his greatest difference from the author of "*Le Mauvais moine*." Baudelaire is the bad monk of his own sonnet, so that his wish to embellish the walls would make his art, that is, his poem, a religious devotion. Bian characteristically takes the stance of an observer rather than of one baring his soul. His poem creates a mood and a scene, and makes a powerful statement about an enduring human experience. As Michelle Loi puts it, in spite of a large number of occidental references and his choice of the sonnet form, Bian Zhilin remains classically Chinese.[47]

Chinese critics have used the same vocabulary to describe Bian's poems as they used for Baudelaire in the 1930s: they are "obscure" (*menglong* 朦朧) and "difficult" (*nandong* 難懂). Wang Yao, for example, faults Bian for "thinking that he could make the rotten into the miraculous," or bad into good (*hua fuxiu wei shenqi* 化腐朽為神奇), and that if he did this with originality, it would provide the material for poetry. Wang criticizes his pessimistic attitudes and writing on suffering and melancholy for having a bad influence on readers. He is "weak and morbid," "dissatisfied with reality but helpless in [its] pursuit." Here Wang offers as example two lines from Bian's "*Fashao ye*" 發燒夜 ["Fevered Night"]: "*shui ba, yiqie de xiwang, shui ba, yiqie de suanxin*" 睡罷，一切的希望，睡罷，一切的酸辛 [Sleep then, all hope; Sleep then, all grief].[48] The lines recall Baudelaire's "*Recueillement*": "*Sois sage, ô ma Douleur . . . / Tu réclamais le Soir...*" [Be good, my Grief . . . , you called for Evening], a poem that Bian had translated.[49]

When Bian Zhilin compares his own work with Baudelaire, however, he guides his readers to a very different type of poem. His 1981 article in English "About My Poems" states: "In the poetry I wrote in the earliest period about the desolate scenes of Beiping streets can be seen images of the paupers, the aged, and the blind, of Paris as described by Baudelaire."[50]

One such poem is "*Jige ren*" 幾個人 ["Several People"]:

> The hawker cries his wares: "Candied haws!"
> Swallowing a mouthful of dust as if he didn't care;
> The man carrying a birdcage gazes at white doves in the sky,
> And with carefree steps crosses the sandy stretch,
> While a young man muses in the deserted street.
> The radish vendor idly waves his sharpened knife,
> His load of radishes grin foolishly in the setting sun,
> While a young man muses in the deserted street.
> The short beggar stares entranced at his own long shadow,
> While a young man muses in the deserted street:
> Some people holding a bowl of rice in both hands sigh,
> Some people listen to others sleep-talking in the night,
> Some people wear a red flower in their white hair,
> Like holding the setting sun at the edge of a snowy field . . .[51]

Bian's own translation leaves the candied haws *"bing-tang-hoo-loo"* 冰糖
葫蘆 in transliteration, perhaps because the sound of the hawker's cry is
more important than the object he sells, skewers of candied haws (Chinese hawthorn berries that are like crabapples). The young man in the
street, evoked three times, calls attention to the fact that the observer in
the poem is not lost in thought, but is nevertheless quite detached from
the scene. The sense of desolation is enhanced by the lack of communication among the figures—the listener hears only people talking in their
sleep. In the last line, Bian uses the verb "tuo" 托, which can mean "to
hold in the palm," with the setting sun, so that it seems to be holding off
the moment of the sun's disappearance, just as the red flower against the
white hair in the previous line seems to be defying old age and death.
Whereas the Chinese version of the penultimate line repeats "some people" without specifying gender, Bian's own English version evokes only
one person, pinning a scarlet flower in "her" hair, thus adding a touch of
coquettishness that might have relieved the bleakness of the poem. But
the hair's comparison with snow in the last line makes any suggestion of
coquettishness seem pathetic. Bian's images of ordinary people, including paupers and the aged, are vividly drawn. This poem, as well as two
others that Bian translated for the Acton and Ch'en anthology, "The
Dream of the Old Village," and "The Heart of the Old City,"[52] do recall in
a general sense some of the poems in the *Tableaux parisiens*. But the reader
does not get a sense of Bian wandering down the streets or through
arcades; his is not a *"fourmillante cité"* [teeming city], and he is a far more
detached observer than Baudelaire.

Not all the Bian Zhilin poems that recall Baudelaire describe Beijing
street scenes. Bian's *"Yuanxing"* 遠行 ["Long Journey"], which evokes
camel riders in the desert, is reminiscent of Baudelaire's *"Bohémiens en
voyage"* ["Gypsies on the Road"], one of the poems Bian had translated.[53]
In another of Bian's poems also appears the story of the cat's eyes, though
there is little reason to suppose that he had to borrow it from Baudelaire.[54] An early poem of the type Wang Yao deprecated, *"Moguide serenade"* 魔鬼的 Serenade ["The Demon's Serenade"], was not included in
Bian's collections. It ends with the following stanza:

> *Kuai qilai ba, wo di ai!*
> *Women jiao chixiao changge,*
> *Hai jiao pozhong qiao paizi,*
> *Women yikuair tiaowu!*
> 快起來罷，我底愛！
> 我們叫鴟鴞唱歌，
> 還叫破鐘敲拍子，
> 我們一塊兒跳舞！
>
> Quickly arise, my love!
> We'll tell the owls to sing,

> And the cracked bell to strike the beat,
> Together we shall dance![55]

Owls and the cracked bell both occur in *Les Fleurs du mal*, and here contribute to the decadent atmosphere created in the title. Bian had translated this poem for Acton and Chen's anthology, adding "advance" in the first line to rhyme with "dance" in the last, and "pleasure" to the second line to rhyme with "measure" (for beat) in the second and third lines, resulting in an abba rhyme scheme that does not exist in the Chinese.[56] Two stanzas earlier, the demon had sung:

> *Women qu zuokan yueliang*
> *Zai xitian bianshang bingdao,*
> *Ta sile ye bu yaojin,*
> *Women you linhuo zhaoyao.*
> 我們去坐看月亮
> 在西天邊上病倒,
> 她死了也不要緊,
> 我們有燐火照耀。

> We'll go sit and watch the moon
> Sicken in the western sky,
> No matter if she should die,
> We will have a jack-o-lantern.[57]

Bian's own translation also rhymes "sky" and "die." With the direct address, unhealthy twilight, and even the rhyme irresistibly recalling the first lines of T. S. Eliot's "The Love Song of J. Alfred Prufrock," Bian has taken a clear step toward Modernism.[58]

HE QIFANG (何其芳 1912–1977)

> *"wo ai na yun, na piaohu de yun . . . "*
> *wo zi yiwei shi Bodelai'er sanwenshi zhong*
> *nage youyu de pianqi jingzi*
> *wangzhe tiankong de yuanfang ren.*
> "我愛那雲,那飄忽的雲..
> 我自以為是波德萊爾散文詩中
> 那個憂鬱地偏起頸于
> 望着天空的遠方人。

[I loved those clouds, those drifting clouds . . . / I regarded myself as the man from afar / Who in Baudelaire's prose poem cranes his neck / Melancholically to gaze at the sky].[59]

He Qifang invokes Baudelaire by name in this poem where he makes a direct allusion to the prose poem *"L'Etranger."* He Qifang's early poems, graceful and refined, are known for sophisticated diction, ambiguous meanings, and gentle, sensuous, evocative, polyvalent imagery, on themes of romantic love and confusion between dream and reality. Thoroughly grounded in the Chinese classics, He read widely in Western literature, both in English and in Chinese translation. He later recalled being drawn first to the nineteenth-century English Romantics, then to what he called the "post-Parnassian" French poets. [60] Michelle Loi and Marián Gálik have pointed out Baudelaire's role among the Western influences on his work, as has Bonnie McDougall, who has written a full critical biography and translated much of his work into English. [61]

He Qifang is not known as a Modernist. According to McDougall and Louie, his poetry "gives an unusually vivid depiction of the author's progress through romanticism, symbolism, neo-romanticism, modernism, and Russian futurism." [62] His early work is represented by four volumes: prose poems in *Huamenglu* 畫夢錄 [*Records of Painted Dreams*], and verse poems in *Yan ni ji* 燕泥集 [*Swallow's Nest*], which was his section of the joint anthology with Bian Zhilin and Li Guangtian, *Hanyuan ji* 漢園集 [*Han Garden Collection*]; both were published in 1936. *Keyi ji* 刻意集 [*Painstaking Work*], containing both verse and prose, appeared in 1937, and *Huanxiang riji* 還鄉日記 [*Diary of a Journey Home*], in prose, appeared in 1939.

The lines referring to Baudelaire begin a poem entitled *"Yun"* 雲 ["Clouds"], published in 1937. It continues in the next stanzas to describe his experience in the countryside, where the honest peasants had lost their land, and were left with only a bundle of tools and stone bridges for their beds, while at a seaside resort, empty summer homes stand waiting "like prostitutes for fat merchants." In the fourth stanza, He resolves:

> *cong ci wo yao jijizhazha fa yilun:*
> *wo qingyuan you yige maocao de wuding,*
> *ye bu ai yun bu ai yue*
> *ye bu ai xingxing.*
> 從此我要嘰嘰喳喳發議論：
> 我情願有一個茅草的屋頂，
> 不愛雲不愛月，
> 也不愛星星。

[From now on I will twitter and chirrup my comments: / I would rather have a thatched roof; / I will not love the clouds; I will not love the moon; / And I will not love the stars]. [63]

Other translators have translated "twitter and chirrup," simply as "expressing my opinions," or making "loud comments," which enhances the sense of resolve on the part of the poetic voice. But He Qifang uses the onomatopoeic *"jijizhazha"* which usually describes birds chirping, and eliminates any hint of pomposity. In any case, the poem stands as a farewell to the gentle, dreamy poems of He's earlier work. At the same time, it is a farewell to Baudelaire.

He Qifang makes a similar allusion to Baudelaire in another poem whose title, *"Zui ba"* 醉罷 ["Get Drunk"], is the equivalent of *"Enivrez-vous"* (from *Petits Poèmes en prose*). He's poem reads:

> To those who are softly singing
> Get drunk. Get drunk.
> The true drunkards are blessed,
> For paradise belongs to them.
>
> If alcohol and books
> And honey-dripping lips
> Cannot conceal human suffering,
> If from dead-drunk to half-sober
> You finally become fully sober,
> Would you still keep your hat askew,
> Your eyes half closed,
> And play a little drunk all your life?
>
> The fly trembling in the cold wind
> Flutters its wings on the paper window pane,
> Dreaming of corpses,
> Dreaming of midsummer's watermelon rinds,
> Dreaming of a dreamless void.
>
> In the last sounds of my jeering
> I heard my own shame:
> "You too only buzz, buzz, buzz,
> Like a fly!"
>
> If I were a fly,
> I'd await the sound of a flyswatter
> Smacking my head.[64]

McDougall, noting that Baudelaire's prose poem could have been a source of inspiration, compares the "level of disgust and bitterness" that He Qifang reaches during this period with that of Baudelaire.[65] In addition, the fly's dream of corpses might remind one of *"Une Charogne"* ["Carrion"], and the final lines might recall those of *"Spleen IV"* where anguish plants a black flag on the skull of the poet. In the context of He Qifang's later career, the poem clearly represents his rejection of his earlier work and even of his earlier self.

That the two poems by Baudelaire to which He Qifang refers, *"L'Étranger"* and *"Enivrez-vous,"* both available to him in Chinese translation, should be the very ones Hung Cheng-fu had pointed out as being Chinese in spirit, lends some irony to He Qifang's own criticism of his earlier poetry as being "too Europeanized." Gálik notes that in He's two poems, he "stood up face to face to Baudelaire," "taking contact with the message" of Baudelaire's poem, but "also negating it."[66]

He Qifang's direct reference to Baudelaire in these poems of farewell would suggest that the French poet played a major role in his earlier poetry. Such is not the case. Bonnie McDougall contrasts Baudelaire's "celebrated sensualism . . . concerned with gleaming jewels, heavy brocades and exotic perfumes," with He Qifang's "more natural and gentle imagery," and suggests that "perhaps the sexual timidity which is characteristic of He's poetry inhibited his entry into this world of complete sensual abandonment." Both poets "used the city as a theatrical backdrop," McDougall notes, but finds the Chinese poet "unable to observe or enjoy the grim degradation that Baudelaire loved to depict in poems like 'Les Sept Vieillards' and 'Les Petites Vieilles.'"[67] Ironically, it was "grim degradation" of life observed in the seaside village that drove He to bid farewell to the French poet.

He Qifang's most famous poem is "Yuyan" 預言 ["Prophecy"]. Readers have found different themes and sources to arrive at different readings. K. Y. Hsu finds "a thorough blending of [He's] sensitive appreciation of nature and his baptism in nineteenth-century Western romanticism."[68] McDougall finds its central symbol to be the Young God from Valéry's *La Jeune Parque*, who "could be a symbol for Love . . . or for Inspiration, as in a prose poem by Turgenev, 'Stay!'" Alternatively, he could stand for Beauty; McDougall quotes He Qifang as having written the following year, "Beauty which is only achieved at the sacrifice of friendship and comfort."[69] Gálik adds the possibility of Valéry's *Narcisse parle* as source, and suggests that the poem is sung by "the unnamed Echo . . . the picture of a woman striving to win a man's love through her loquacity [and] excessive solicitude."[70] Another reader finds in it "the subdued melancholy of Keats and of his anxiety about his poetic gift," while its organization and imagery are "reminiscent of certain sections of 'Nine Songs' (from *Chu Ci*) in which poet-priests draw down gods & goddesses from heaven" with descriptions of feasts and delights, and warnings of dangers ahead, and end by lamenting the brevity of their ecstatic contact with the divine."[71] A Chinese critic, reading in the context of popular culture, posits that the voice in the poem is a fairy condemned to await the young god and try to detain him with her song because she has violated a commandment of the Jade Emperor.[72]

To place the poem in a Baudelairean context, my rendering represents some alterations from existing translations, but without finding a better equivalent than "god" for "神," which can also mean "goddess," or "spirit:"

> The heart stirring day has finally arrived.
> Your approaching footfalls like sighs in the night
> I can clearly hear are not the leaves whispering with the night wind,
> Or the faint patter of deer darting across a mossy path.
> Tell me, in your singing voice of a silver bell tell me,
> Are you the young god in the prophecy?

You must come from the lush, warm south;
Tell me of the moonlight there, the sunlight there,
Tell me how the spring breeze blows open the hundred flowers,
How enraptured the swallows are with the green willows!
I shall close my eyes and sleep in your dream-like singing,
That warm fragrance I seem to recall yet seem to forget.

Please stop, stop your long journey's flight;
Come in, here is a tiger-skin rug to sit on,
Let me light on fire every fallen leaf gathered in autumn;
Listen while I softly sing my own song,
The song will dip and soar like flames,
And like flames will tell the story of the fallen leaves.

Don't go forward; ahead is the boundless forest;
Ancient trees take on the spots and stripes of savage beasts;
Half-dead, half-alive, vines twist like pythons and snakes,
Through the dense leaves not one star can peep;
You will be too timid to take a second step
When you hear the empty echo of the first.

Must you go? Wait for me to go with you;
My feet know every safe path;
I shall unceasingly sing songs that dispel weariness,
Then offer you again the comfort of a hand;
When night's thick darkness separates us
You may fix your unwavering gaze on mine.

My urgent song you still do not heed,
Your feet still do not pause for my trembling;
Like a quiet, somber breeze floating across this dusk,
Your proud footfalls fade away, dissolve . . .
Ah, have you finally come, as told in the prophecy, without a word,
And gone without a word, young god?[73]

Young God or god or goddess or spirit, Love, Inspiration, or Beauty, we know only that the arrival has been prophesied and long awaited. The voice in the poem, presumably that of the poet, associates the spirit with everything beautiful and poetic: with nature, with music, with the South, with spring, with autumn, with fire, with the breeze. The spirit seems to be in a hurry to be on its way, and the poet urges it to stay, first by offering comfort, warmth, music, and beauty, then by warning of dangers ahead. The forest image occurs in each of the first four stanzas. But more than representing nature, the seasons, fire, and the frightening aspect of the unknown, the forest has perhaps another layer of meaning.

Reading He Qifang's poem with a memory of Baudelaire brings an echo of that most famous sonnet, "*Correspondances.*" There Nature is a temple of living pillars that speak, and it is only the poet who has the power to decipher its words, through forests of symbols. Baudelaire's is a poem on poetry. He Qifang's introduces the forest image in the fourth stanza, and in the fifth, the poet offers to guide the spirit through this forest. It is he, not the spirit, who knows the paths. The second quatrain of "*Correspondances*" sets forth the notion of synaesthesia: perfume, color, and sound correspond; in the tercets, perfumes sing. In the second stanza of He's poem, sound, touch, and perfume correspond in the spirit's voice, which is a warm fragrance. The many references to song in "Prophecy" reinforce the idea that the voice in the poem, the "I" is the poet in his role of singer-poet. The two poems share a vaguely religious air, through the image of the temple in one, and the parallels to shamanistic practices in the other. Both poems use auditory and olfactory imagery more than visual or tactile ones, heightening the sense of ephemerality. The spirit prophesied in the Chinese poem, by the ephemeral quality of its appearance, by its mystery, and by its association with everything beautiful and poetic, could very well be the spirit of poetry, encompassing Love, Beauty, Inspiration, and Music. If the prophecy is of poetry, its position at the head of the collection is the more appropriate.

The parallels notwithstanding, it would be going too far to say that He Qifang's poem derives from Baudelaire's sonnet.[74] The singing and the departure of the spirit at the end of the poem are too reminiscent of Keats's nightingale. The parallels with the *Chu Ci* are also too compelling. He Qifang truly succeeded in blending Western and Chinese elements into his own style.

"Prophecy" was He Qifang's favorite poem.[75] He chose it for the title piece of his selected works published in 1945. In his autobiographical play, "*Xia ye*"夏夜 [*Summer Night*], the character representing the author tells his girlfriend after she reads part of the poem: "That was also at dusk. I was strolling in a forest on a summer night, and by chance wanted to write a poem like that." The genesis of the poem was like the arrival of the young god: vague and mysterious. But the young god is not simply a symbol of poetic inspiration: to the question whether he has ever played the role of the "young god," the poet answers "yes, but it was a failure." Asked why the young god in the poem is not moved to stay by the song, the poet answers, "Vanishing is more beautiful, gentler."[76] This aesthetic is shared by the French Symbolists.

He Qifang once described writing as requiring agonizing efforts to put into words his experiences of colors and patterns.[77] He started not with an idea or an unforgettable adventure, but with an evanescent experience. He acknowledged the importance of craftsmanship in capturing that experience. He valued memory, to the extent that when he compiled his own selected works, he included only those that he could reproduce from memory, as a measure of their worth. Literary memories undoubtedly also joined experience in the original composition of the poems. All this puts him close to Baudelaire and the French Symbolists.

When He Qifang bade farewell to Baudelaire, he also repudiated his earlier devotion to form, and questioned the value of his own experience. He wrote in 1938: "We believe that a literary work, no matter what its form, cannot become great if it is divorced from human life, the times, and the masses that are suffering, fighting, and dying for the freedom of the race."[78] He tried to "re-educate" himself by studying folksongs and by following Mao's prescription to describe the life of workers, peasants, and soldiers. By 1940 he professed: "I have taken a complete farewell of my former unhealthy and unhappy thinking; and like a small cog in a huge machine, with countless other cogs alongside me, I spin and whir in happy regulation. I am already lost among them."[79]

He's new phase may be represented by his 1941 poem *"Shenghuo shi duome guangkuo"* 生活是多麼廣闊 ["How Vast Life Is"]:

> How vast life is;
> Life is an ocean.
> Wherever there is life there is happiness and treasure.
>
> Go join the chorus; go put on a play;
> Go build a railroad; go become an airplane pilot;
> Go sit in a research laboratory; go write poetry;
> Go ski on the high mountain; go pilot a boat bumping on the waves;
> Go explore the North Pole; go collect plants in the tropics;
> Go sleep under the stars in a tent;
> Go spend ordinary days;
> Go open your eyes wide at ordinary objects;
> Go light another's fire with your own spark;
> Go discover a heart with your heart.
>
> How vast life is.
> And how fragrant life is.
> Wherever there is life there is happiness and treasure.[80]

The poem is successful in so as far as it became part of the high school curriculum in the People's Republic.[81] But for his earlier admirers, it surely represents an enormous sacrifice of erudition and talent. He published no more poetry until 1954. His poem "Reply," explaining the reasons for his silence, was attacked for its ambiguity and lack of optimism.[82]

He Qifang's life has more than once been taken as representative of his entire generation.[83] He devoted himself to "serving the masses" as teacher and bureaucrat. During the Cultural Revolution, He was attacked as a "class enemy," renamed "Qi chou" 其臭 ("his stench"—Qifang can mean "his fragrance"), forced to clean latrines, then "sent down" to feed pigs. Throughout the ordeals, he steadfastly insisted: "I believe in the

Party. I believe in the People."[84] Finally allowed to return home in late 1971, he began to translate Heine (praised by Engels) and Weerth (the first German proletarian poet), having learned German through self-study for the purpose of reading Marx and Engels in the original. True to his wish to revise his style for the common people, he would read his translations to the neighborhood children.[85] Bian Zhilin, editing the translations after He's death, noted that both Heine and Weerth wrote formalist poetry; he found that He Qifang was still searching for a suitable prosody for vernacular Chinese.[86] For his own poetry, He Qifang returned to the classical forms of the Tang dynasty, composing a number of poems in seven-syllable regulated verse. He never returned to Baudelaire.

CAO BAOHUA （曹葆華 1906–1978)

Cao Baohua was born in Leshan, Sichuan Province, and went north to study foreign languages at Tsing-hua University, where he became associated with the Beijing literary scene. He published original verse first in the *Crescent Monthly* (*Xinyue yuekan* 新月月刊), later in *Xiandai* 現代: *Les Contemporains*; and then five collections between 1929 and 1937. Cao was a prolific translator; in 1927 he published a volume of Valéry's poetics; his translations from English include Shakespeare's plays and literary criticism by I. A. Richards and by Herbert Read.[87] He went to Yan'an in 1939 and joined the Communist Party in 1940. His later translations include Gorky, Marx, Engels, Lenin, and Stalin on art, as well as works on politics and philosophy.[88]

There is no evidence that Cao Baohua was particularly engaged with Baudelaire. But a poem in Cao's 1937 *Wuticao* 無題草 [*Untitled Drafts*] begins,

> *poxiao cong leng meng li xinglai*
> *yuanchu you yizhen jumu sheng*
> *haoxiang mangzhe xiuzao guancai*
> *dengdaizhe wo, zheige guairen*
> *yisheng he yin ziji de naozhi*
> 破曉從冷夢裡醒來
> 遠處有一陣鋸木聲
> 好像忙着修造棺材
> 等待着我，這個怪人
> 一生喝飲自己的腦汁

> At dawn waking from a cold dream
> From afar bursts the sound of wood being sawn
> It seems busily building a coffin
> Waiting for me, this strange person who
> Throughout life drinks his own brains[89]

The lines are reminiscent of Baudelaire's *"Chant d'automne,"* where the sound of wood being chopped to lay by for winter suggests the nailing of a coffin somewhere (*quelque part*). In Cao's poem, the sound of sawing wood also comes from an unidentifiable distance, to suggest an earlier stage in building the coffin. Baudelaire's poem asks *"Pour qui?"* For whom is the coffin being prepared? Cao answers, "For me." In both poems, the idea of coffin-building exists mainly in the poet's head. Both poems express the anxious awareness of time that Tu Kuo-ch'ing had pointed out in his comparison of Baudelaire's poem with Li Ho's "Suffering from the Shortness of Days." But Cao's imagery came from Baudelaire rather than from Li Ho. He well could have read *"Chant d'automne"* in Liang Zongdai's 1934 translation, discussed in chapter 3.

Cao was "not the most gifted nor the most accomplished of the Modernists," as M. M. Y. Fung has pointed out.[90] Like so many of his compatriots who became socially and politically engaged, Cao apparently turned away from poetry after 1937.

CHEN JINGRONG (陳敬容 1917–1989)

Chen Jingrong, whose translations and criticism were discussed in earlier chapters, also published original poetry. She was born in Leshan, Sichuan Province, where Cao Baohua was her teacher. At his instigation, according to Shiu-Pang Almberg, she went to Beijing, audited classes at Peking and Tsinghua Universities, and became involved in the Beijing literary scene, listening in as Bian Zhilin, He Qifang, and Liang Zongdai discussed poetry.[91] Chen devoted most of her life to literature, variously as writer, translator, and editor. Like so many writers of her generation, Chen led a peripatetic life, going back and forth from Sichuan to Beijing and Shanghai, and even to the then rural backwater Lanzhou. She was "sent down" to the countryside during the Cultural Revolution, but returned to Beijing and began a new period of creativity in 1979. A posthumous collection of her works contains about thirty uncollected poems from 1932 to 1978, and three times that many from 1979 to 1987.[92]

Chen published two poetry collections in Shanghai in 1948: *Yingying Ji* 盈盈集 [*Limpid*],[93] comprised of poems written between 1935 and 1945 in Sichuan and Beijing, and *Jiaoxiang Ji* 交響集 [*Symphony*] written from 1946 to 1948 in Shanghai. Leaving Shanghai in haste in 1948, she lost a lot of translations she had made there.[94] Other poems of Chen's from the 1940s were collected in a joint anthology *Jiu ye ji* 九葉集 [*Nine Leaves*] so that she is sometimes identified as a "Nine Leaves poet." But it is "at best a tentative epithet" according to Almberg, who adds that Chen cannot be classified as Traditionalist or Modernist, Symbolist or Modernist."[95]

Chen Jingrong published nearly forty poems of Baudelaire translated over the course of nearly forty years. It seems reasonable to expect some echo of the French poems in Chen's own work.[96] Leafing through her collected poems, there is little that is reminiscent of Baudelaire. But in one poem, *"Ye xing"* 夜行 ["Night Journey"] appear "flowers of evil":

> Under the night sky dyed red by neon lights
> The city is spurting out its flowers of evil
> We are like primitives on patrol
> Strolling across the clamorous main street
> Speaking of things the world refuses to listen to respectfully
>
> Ah, world, our dignity
> Is just like your stubborn stupidity
> Our hearts bleed for you in vain
> We have our vastness
> And you have your confines[97]

The neon lights clearly set forth an urban scene. Red as the dominant color suggests danger and blood, leading to the "flowers of evil" in the second line. The personae in the poem, "we" do not seem to belong to this cityscape; "we" are too primitive, as "we" casually stroll across the busy main street, not heeding the dangers of traffic. "We" are set off from "the world," which refuses to listen attentively to what "we" have to say. The second stanza continues the tension between "us" and the world, which becomes personified as "you." The world with all its hustle and bustle seems very important, but "we" know something of which "we" can speak, and the unheeding world, by refusing to listen, cannot reach the breadth that can be created in the mind.

The poem is analyzed by Zhang Yaxin in a volume on *menglong shi* 朦朧詩["misty" poetry]. Zhang points out that the city should be civilized, but it is full of evil. "We" are the citizens of the city, but "we" are in conflict with "the world;" "the world" is illuminated by "evil," and it is still night; "the world" refuses to listen to "our" truth. The imagery creates tension between civilization and evil on one side, truth and loneliness on the other.[98]

Although "misty poetry" became associated with the period immediately after the Cultural Revolution, Almberg dates this poem to 1948, when Chen was engaged in translating Baudelaire. Almberg states: "This poem from Shanghai resounds directly to the Paris of *Les Fleurs du mal*, to which there is also an overt allusion in the second line." However, she adds: "The self-righteous 'we,' on the other hand, is anything but Baudelairean."[99] Whether or not one reads the "we" as "self-righteous," it is hard to disagree that the poem does not seem "Baudelairean." Chen's city of Shanghai does not invite comparisons with Baudelaire's Paris, especially since neon lights did not exist until the twentieth century. Chen states too directly, and fails to convey any sense of anguish or anger at a world that refuses to listen. The world's personification as "you" notwithstanding, it remains an abstraction.

Another of Chen's poems, *"Guocheng"* 過程 ["Process"], has the type of images Chinese readers often associate with Baudelaire: maggots, decay, flies, and blood. The poem dates from 1946 and reads:

> The earth has rotted;
> Maggots crawl out
> To suck up the flavor steaming from garbage piles
> The flies gluttonously
> Watching the corpses on the battlefield,
> Lick their lips.
>
> The earth has rotted,
> Blood flows out
> Forming rivers, forming seas,
> Flooding cities and villages
> Washing away both candor and innocence.
> "Big sale—the world's conscience!"
> On the lone boat a hawker loudly calls.
>
> Rot.
> Agonizing process.
> The times are gasping and waiting,
> Waiting for the corruption to be fully ripe:
> Then the blood of evil will congeal,
> New flesh will grow up beneath the scabs,
> When the scars are at last healed,
> Here, give you back a new face! [100]

Almberg appreciates the "dynamic lines and rhythms, reflecting an "anarchistic energy waiting to break through," letting "the drama enact itself through the poetry," resulting in "one of the strongest utterances in modern Chinese verse." [101] McDougall and Louie find in the same poem "despair lead[ing] to melodrama with its maggots, garbage, flies, and scabs." [102]

Chen's use of "ugly" images suggests the aesthetic that Chinese critics associate with Baudelaire, of "creating beauty from ugliness." But in Chen's poem, there is no paradox. Rather than letting the medium be the message, the poem makes direct statements: "The earth has rotted" or "is rotten;" it is an "agonizing process." The blood washing away candor and innocence makes the connection between physical and spiritual and political corruption overly obvious. The poem goes on to describe how the blood dries and forms scabs, and then new flesh forms. The final word, *"mianmu"* 面目 [face], connotes not only superficial appearance, but "sense of shame, self-respect, and honor." Thus the poem ends in hope and renewal. The idea of renewal from corruption is reminiscent of

Wen Yiduo's "*Sishui*" 死水 ["Dead Water"]. Almberg finds the two poems "much akin in thought-contents," but prefers Chen's "dynamic and unruly" treatment to Wen's "neat package of nine-syllable lines."[103] But Wen's "neat package" comes closer to Baudelaire's aesthetics, and will be taken up in the next chapter.

NOTES

1. Gregory Lee, *Dai Wangshu: The Life and Poetry of a Chinese Modernist* (Hong Kong: The Chinese University Press, 1989).
2. Wang Zuoliang, "Zhongguo xinshi zhong de xiandai zhuyi—yige huigu," 208–29; Sun Yushi, *Chuqi*, 36.
3. Bonnie McDougall, "European Influences in the Poetry of Ho Ch'i-fang," *Journal of the Oriental Society of Australia*, 5, nos. 1–2 (December 1967): 133–51; McDougall and Louie, *The Literature of China*, 77.
4. McDougall and Louie, *The Literature of China* , 70.
5. Shiu-Pang E. Almberg, *The Poetry of Chen Jingrong: A Modern Chinese Woman Poet* (Stockholm: Skrifter Utgivna av Föreningen för Orientaliska Studier 21, 1981), 5–6. Almberg speculates that Chen Jingrong listened in on discussions of art and literature among these older poets.
6. Zhu Ziqing, K. Y. Hsu, and Julia Lin all classify Dai as Symbolist. Michelle Loi, who has devoted all but a fraction of her book *Poètes chinois d'écoles françaises* to Dai Wangshu, has indicated many French sources and parallels in his work.
7. Fung et al., *Xiandai Zhongguo*, 243–46. See appendix 3. *Dai Wangshu Quanji* 戴望舒全集 [*Complete Works of Dai Wangshu*], ed. Wang Wenbin 王文彬 and Jin Shi 金石 (Beijing: Zhongguo qingnian chubanshe, 1999), 41–43, dates the original publication to August 1928. For other translations, see Hsu, *Twentieth-Century Chinese Poetry*, 180–81, Lin, *Modern Chinese Poetry*, 165–66, Loi, *Poètes*, 85–86, Bian Zhilin, *Chinese Literature* 3 (1981): 66–67, Lee, *Dai*, 140–41, Wai-limYip, *Lyrics from Shelters*, 75–76, Yeh, *Anthology*, 31–32.
8. Lin, *Modern Chinese Poetry*, 166.
9. Loi, *Poètes*, 85, *Roseaux*, 276.
10. Walter Benjamin, *Charles Baudelaire: A Lyric Poet in the Era of High Capitalism*, trans. Harry Zohn (London: Verso, 1983), 45.
11. Vincent Yang, "From French Symbolism to Chinese Symbolism: A Literary Influence," *Tamkang Review*, 17, no. 3 (Spring 1987): 234–40.
12. Lee, *Dai*, 150. Lee traces the main influence to Francis Jammes, *Dai*, 144–51. Chinese critics: Xia Zhongyi 夏仲翼, "Dai Wangshu: Zhongguohua de xiangzhengzhuyi" 戴望舒：中國化的象徵主義 ["Dai Wangshu: Sinicized Symbolism"], in Zeng Xiaoyi, *Zouxiang shijie wenxue*, 463; Sun Yushi 孫玉石, *Dai Wangshu mingzuo xinshang* 戴望舒名作欣賞 [*Appreciation of Dai Wangshu's Literary Masterpieces*] (Beijing: Zhongguo Heping chubanshe, 1993), 53. Bian Zhilin, "Xu" 序 ["Preface"], in *Dai Wangshu shi ji* 戴望舒詩集 [*Dai Wangshu Poetry Collection*] (Chengdu: Sichuan renmin chubanshe, 1981), 5. Lee, *Dai*, 148–49. On "assimilation of Western techniques," see Lee, *Dai*, 150. See also Gregory Lee, "Western Influences in the Poetry of Dai Wangshu," *Modern Chinese Literature* 3, no. 1 (1987): 1112.
13. Lee, *Dai*, 128–29. Shi Zhecun 施蟄存, "Xu" 序 ["Preface"], in *Dai Wangshu yi shi ji* 戴望舒譯詩集 [*Dai Wangshu's Translated Poems*] (Changsha: Hunan renmin chubanshe, 1983), 2. Another schoolmate, Du Heng 杜衡, "Wangshu cao xu" 《望舒草》序, ["Preface to Wangshu's Drafts"] in *Dai Wangshu juan*, 155, recalls that Dai was reading the works of Verlaine, Fort, Gourmont, and Jammes, but does not mention Baudelaire.
14. See chapter 3 and Lee, *Dai*, 4–5.
15. Lee, *Dai*, 208.

16. Lee, "Western," 14–15; Lee, *Dai*, 161. All three poems have memories stuffed into drawers.

17. Dai Wangshu, *Wode ji yi* (1929, repr. *Dai Wangshu shi ji* 戴望舒詩集, Chengdu: Sichuan renmin chubanshe, 1981), 24. See appendix 3.

18. Leonid Cherkassky, "Dai Wangshu: 'Wode Jiyi' ('My Memory'), 1929," in *A Selective Guide to Chinese Literature 1900–1949: Vol. 3, The Poem* , ed. Lloyd Haft (Leiden: Brill, 1989), 83.

19. Lee, *Dai*, 13–14, 157–58; Du Heng 杜衡, in *Dai Wangshu juan*, 155.

20. Lee, *Dai*, 133–38.

21. Loi, *Poètes*, 87, 94. For translations of Dai's poem into English, see Yip, *Lyrics from Shelters*, 76–77; Acton and Chen, *Modern Chinese Poetry*, 150.

22. Loi, *Poètes*, 82.

23. Dai, *Wode Jiyi* 我底記憶 (1929, repr. Ya Xian, 1977), 28–29. See appendix 3, also Hsu, *Twentieth-Century Chinese Poetry*, 182; Lin, *Modern Chinese Poetry*, 168; Loi, *Poètes*, 82.

24. Verlaine, *OC*, 207 "*Pas la Couleur, rien que la nuance!*" Dai leaves "nuance" in alphabetical letters: "shi zui zhongyao de shi shiqing shang de nuance, er bushi ziju shang de nuance 詩最重要的是詩情上的 nuance, 而不是字句上的 nuance." [What is most important to poetry is the nuance of poetic emotions, not the nuance of words and expressions], Ya Xian, 144.

25. Dai Wangshu's French poems are reprinted in Lee, *Dai*, 335–38. For biography, see Shao Ren 紹仁, "Neng shi neng wen de Dai Wangshu" 能詩能文的戴望舒 ["Able in Poetry and Prose Dai Wangshu"], *Ming Wan* 明晚 (April 19, 1970), repr. in *Dai Wangshu ziliao ji* 戴望舒資料集 [*Collected Materials on Dai Wangshu*] (Hong Kong? s.n., 1976), 39. Dai also translated, in collaboration with Xu Xiacun 徐霞村, from French translations of literature in other languages.

26. Loi, *Poètes*, 5, translates the first line "Je pense, autrefois je fus un papillon," [I think that I was once a butterfly] taking "gu" 故 as "formerly" rather than "therefore." I believe, with Wang Zuoliang, 211, that Dai Wangshu meant for his poem to be a comment on Descartes' *Cogito ergo sum*, combined with Zhuangzi's dream of a butterfly, which would become "Je pense, donc je suis un papillon." See also Lee, *Dai*, 253–54. Yeh, "There Are No Camels," 19–20, sees this poem as "a testimonial to the lasting beauty" of poets "who were physically destroyed in the turbulent times of modern China."

27. Bian spoke at a small gathering at the home of James J. Y. Liu.

28. Hsu, *Twentieth-Century Chinese Poetry* , 159–60.

29. Lloyd Haft, *Pien Chih-lin: A Study in Modern Chinese Poetry* (Dordrecht: Foris Publications, 1983), 63.

30. Jean Monsterleet, *Sommets de la littérature chinoise contemporaine* (Paris: Editions Domat, 1953), 121–42.

31. Shao Xunmei, "Poetry Chronicle," *T'ien Hsia Monthly* (1936): 266.

32. Kang Peichu 康培初, *Wenxue, zuojia, shidai* 文學作家時代 [*Literature, Writer, Era*] (Hong Kong: wenxue yanjiu she, 1973), 68.

33. Bian Zhilin, *Luye chuan* 蘆葉船 [*Reed-Leaf Boat*] is comprised of early poems that had been praised by Xu Zhimo and Shen Congwen, and was to have been published by Shao Xunmei, but Xu's death, and then the Mukden Incident intervened. *Hanyuan ji* 漢園集 is a joint anthology published with his friends He Qifang 何其芳 and Li Guangtian 李廣田 from Peking University, and named for the street on which the University was located. Bian contributed to the discussion of his poems in Liu Xiwei, *Ju hua ji*, 153–82; Zhu Ziqing 朱自清, *Xinshi zahua* 新詩雜話 (1944, repr. Hong Kong: Taiping shuju, 1965), 6.

34. Bian Zhilin, "About My Poems," *Chinese Literature* 8 (1981): 93.

35. Bian Zhilin, "The Development of China's 'New Poetry' and the Influence from the West," *Chinese Literature Essays Articles and Reviews*, 4 (Jan. 1984): 152–57.

36. Bian, "About My Poems:" 91.

37. Acton and Chen, *Modern Chinese Poetry*, 118–35; Robert Payne, *Contemporary Chinese Poetry* (London, Routledge, 1947), 81–92.

38. Wang Li 王力, *Hanyu shilü xue* 漢語詩律學 [*Chinese Prosody*] (Shanghai: Jiaoyü chubanshe, 1979), second edition, 926, 930, 942–43. Wang Li's translations from *Les Fleurs du mal* were discussed in chapter 3.

39. Haft, *Pien Chih-lin*, 33–34.

40. *Diaochong jili: 1930–1958* 雕蟲紀歷 [*Record of Carving Insects*] (Beijing: Renmin wenxue chubanshe 人民文學出版社, 1979), 123. Mary M. Y. Fung, "Editor's Introduction," in Fung and David Lunde, *The Carving of Insects: Bian Zhilin* (Hong Kong: The Chinese University of Hong Kong Research Centre for Translation, 2006), 33, dates the poem to 1937 and relates it to Bian's love poems and to the Buddhist idea of Nirvana. Haft, *Pien Chih-lin*, 55–56.

41. *OC*, 15–16. See also Barbara Gibbs's translation in Mathews and Mathews, *Charles Baudelaire*, 18, and Kendall Lappin's in *Dead French Poets Speak Plain English: An Anthology of Poems* (Paradise, CA: Asylum Arts, 1997), 127.

42. I have reproduced the spacing from Fung et al., *Xiandai Zhongguo*, 713–14. See appendix 3. For other translations see Hsu, *Twentieth-Century Chinese Poetry*, 161, Fung and Lunde, *The Carving of Insects*, 55, Arno L. Bader and Lucien Mao, "Three Modern Chinese Poems," *T'ien hsia Monthly* 10, no. 1 (Jan. 1940), 163.

43. Hsu, *Twentieth-Century Chinese Poetry* , 161.

44. *OC*, 73.

45. Bian Zhilin, "Xu" 序 [preface], in *Diaochong jili*, 17. Bian might have been indirectly targeting Mu Mutian's "The Sunken Bell."

46. Bian Zhilin, "About My Poems," *Chinese Literature*, 8 (1981): 89.

47. Loi, *Roseaux*, 31. "Malgré tant de références occidentales . . . concis et obscur, il est tenté par le sonnet, mais réussit le miracle d'y rester très classique (chinois)."

48. Wang Yao 王瑤, *Zhongguo xin wenxueshi gao* 中國新文學史稿 [*Draft History of New Chinese Literature*] (Shanghai: Xin wenyi chubanshe, 1954), 1:199.

49. *OC*, 140–41. Bian Zhilin, "Ruding" 入定 in *E zhi hua ling shi*, 7. (See chapter 3). This poem was also evoked in my discussions of Li Jinfa, Feng Naichao, and Liang Zongdai.

50. Bian, "About My Poems:" 95. (Beijing was called "Beiping" during the war against Japan, when the capital was moved south to Nanjing—"Beijing" means "northern capital").

51. Bian Zhilin 卞之琳, *Shi nian shi cao* 十年詩草, 1942 (Hong Kong: Mee Ming Book Centre, n.d.), 9. Bian's own translation is in Acton and Ch'en, *Modern Chinese Poetry*, 129. For other translations, see Hsu, *Twentieth-Century Chinese Poetry*, 164; Fung and Lunde, 74.

52. Acton and Ch'en, *Modern Chinese Poetry* , 118, 127. See also Hsu, *Twentieth-Century Chinese Poetry* , 166, Fung and Lunde, *The Carving of Insects*, 82, 84.

53. In He Qifang 何其芳, Li Guangtian 李廣田, and Bian Zhilin 卞之琳. 漢園集, *Hanyuan ji*, (1936, Hong Kong: Mee Ming Book Centre, 1975?), 120. *OC*, 18. For translations, see Hsu, *Twentieth Century Chinese Poetry*, 161–62; Fung and Lunde, *The Carving of Insects*, 52. Bian, "Liulang de Boximi ren" 流浪的波希米人, in *E zhi hua ling shi*, 7.

54. Bian, "Huan xiang" 還鄉 ["Returning to One's Native Place"], *Hanyuan ji*, 178. Bian translated the poem as "The Return of the Native" in Acton and Ch'en, *Modern Chinese Poetry*, 119–20. Fung and Lunde, in *The Carving of Insects*, translate it as "Homecoming," 79–80.

55. Bian Zhilin, "Mogui de Serenade" 魔鬼的Serenade [Demon's Serenade], *Shi kan* 詩刊1 (1931), 74–77.

56. Acton and Ch'en, *Modern Chinese Poetry* , 133.

57. Ibid., 70. Bian's translation in ibid., 132, does not rhyme the first and last lines of this stanza. He renders "linhuo 燐火" as "jack-o-lantern," in preference to the less eerie possibilities of "phosphorescence" and "will-o'-wisp."

58. Bian's translation was published in 1936. Fung and Lunde, *The Carving of Insects*, 17, date to 1934 Bian's "shift of interest to Modernist poetry of the 1920s in England

and Europe," when he translated T. S. Eliot's "Tradition and the Individual Talent." By 1947 Robert Payne commented in *Contemporary Chinese Poetry*, 81, that Bian "has a disturbing adoration for Auden, and a respect for Yeats and Eliot which approaches divinology."

59. He Qifang 何其芳, *Yuyan* 預言 (Shanghai: Xin wenyi chubanshe, 1957), 77–78. See Bonnie McDougall, *Paths in Dreams: Selected Prose and Poetry of Ho Ch'i-fang* (St. Lucia: University of Queensland Press, 1976), 126; Marián Gálik "Ho Ch'i-Fang's *Paths in Dreams:* The Interliterary Relations with English, French Symbolism, and Greek Mythology," *Milestones*, 176 ; Hsu, *Twentieth-Century Chinese Poetry*, 216; Yeh, *Anthology*, 66, Yip, *Lyrics from Shelters*, 116.

60. He Qifang 何其芳, "Yanni ji houhua" 燕泥集後話 ["Afterword to *Swallow's Nest*"] in Fung et al., *Xiandai Zhongguo*, 618. See also Bian Zhilin, "He Qifang wannian yi shi—dai xu" 何其芳晚年譯詩—代序 ["He Qifang's Later Years Translated Poems: In Place of a Preface"], in *He Qifang yi shi gao* 何其芳譯詩稿 [*He Qifang's Translated Poetry Drafts*] (Beijing: Waiguo wenxue chubanshe, n.d.), 2.

61. Loi, *Roseaux*, 169, states: "C'était, en effet, Baudelaire qui marquait le plus ses premiers poèmes" [Baudelaire had the greatest effect on his first poems]. McDougall, *Paths*, 228. See also Marián Gálik, "Early Poems and Essays of Ho Ch'i-Fang," *Asian and African Studies* (Bratislava) 15 (1979): 59, and *Milestones*, 175.

62. McDougall and Louie, *The Literature of China* , 77.

63. He Qifang 何其芳, *Yuyan* 預言 (Shanghai: Xin wenyi chubanshe, 1957), 77–78. *He Qifang wenji* 何其芳文集 [*Collected Works of He Qifang*] (Beijing: Renmin wenxue chubanshe, 1982), 59–60.

64. McDougall, *Paths*, 125, translates the title "Let's Get Drunk," and uses the first person pronoun rather than the second. Gálik 173, suggests that a third poem from this period, "Song zang" 送葬 ["Funeral Procession"], which includes the image of Gérard de Nerval walking his lobster on a leash, marks the symbolic act of He Qifang's own death. McDougall, "European," 149, calls Nerval "the lunatic suicide." See appendix 3.

65. McDougall, "Influences," 140.

66. Gálik, *Milestones*, 176.

67. McDougall, "Influences," 140. McDougall "Influences," 157, also finds "the form and content of [He Qifang's prose poem] 'Dusk' very close to prose poems by Baudelaire," but I have not found specific parallels.

68. Hsu, *Twentieth Century Chinese Poetry* , 215.

69. McDougall, *Paths*, 226.

70. Gálik, *Milestones*, 162.

71. Boorman, *Biographical Dictionary* , 58. For "Nine Songs," see Hawkes, trans., *Ch'u Tz'u*, 35–44; 101–2.

72. Jin Qinjun 金欽俊, ed., "He Qifang *Yuyan* shangxi—yiduan shenqing de yong-tan—du Yuyan" 何其芳(預言)賞析— 一段深情的詠嘆—讀«預言» ["Appreciation of He Qifang's 'Prophecy': A Song of Deep Feeling; Reading 'Prophecy'"], in *Zhongguo Xin Wenxue Dashi Mingzuo Shangxi Congshu*, 中國新文學大師名作賞析叢書 [*Collectanea of Appreciations of Masterpieces by Great Masters of New Chinese Literature*] (Taipei: Haifeng chubanshe, 1990), 25.

73. He Qifang, "*Yanni ji*" 燕泥集, in *Hanyuan ji* 漢園集 (1936, Hong Kong: Mee Ming Book Centre, n.d.), 4–7. For other translations, see Hsu, *Twentieth-Century Chinese Poetry*, 218–19; McDougall, *Paths* 32–33; Yeh, *Anthology*, 61. Gálik cites McDougall's translation, but changes "prophecy" to "oracle."

74. The parallels do, however, argue against McDougall's assertion in "Influences," 140, that Baudelaire's verse "did not find a response from Ho until 1935, and its influence is only obviously apparent in the Laiyang poems" (1936–1937).

75. McDougall, *Paths*, 226.

76. He Qifang, "Xia ye" 夏夜 ["Summer Night"], *Keyi ji* (1938, Hong Kong: Mee Ming Book Centre, n.d.), 39–40.

77. He Qifang, "Mengzhong daolu" 夢中道路 ["Paths in Dreams"], in *Keyi ji*, 77; Fung et al., *Xiandai Zhongguo*, 618.

78. He Qifang, "Lun gongzuo" 論工作 ["On Work"], in *Xinghuo ji* 星火集 [*Sparks*] (Shanghai: Qunyi chubanshe, 1949), 7. Essay dated 5 March 1938. McDougall, *Paths*, 131.

79. McDougall, *Paths*, 172.

80. *He Qifang wenji*, 174. See appendix 3. For verses later added online, see http://zhidao.baidu.com/question/16955341(accessed 12 June 2010).

81. Yin Zaiqin 尹在勤, *He Qifang pingzhuan* 何其芳評傳 [Critical Biography of He Qifang] (Chengdu: Sichuan renmin chubanshe, 1980), 71.

82. Yin, ibid., 72, blames the critics of this poem for the paucity of He Qifang's creative output from this time on.

83. McDougall, "Influences," 151. Chen Shangzhe 陳尚哲, "He Qifang de shige chuangzuo ji qi fazhan" 何其芳的詩歌創作及其發展 ["He Qifang's Poetic Creation and Its Development"], *Zhongguo xiandai wenxue yanjiu congkan* 中國現代文學研究叢刊 14 (Mar. 1983): 67–93.

84. Bian, "He Qifang wannian yi shi—dai xu," 2. According to Bian, He Qifang did not "awaken" to the misdeeds of the "Gang of Four" until the "Criticize Lin Bian and Confucius" campaign of 1974.

85. Mou Jueming 牟決鳴, "Guanyu He Qifang yi shigao de yidian shuoming" 關于何其芳譯詩稿的一點說明 ["A Little Explanation of the Drafts of He Qifang's Poetry Translations"], (postface to *He Qifang yi shi gao*), 142. Mou is He Qifang's widow.

86. Bian, "He Qifang wannian yi shi—dai xu," 5–6.

87. Fung et al., *Xiandai Zhongguo*, 759.

88. Yang Li et al., *Zhongguo xiandai zuojia da cidian*, 39–40.

89. Wai-lim Yip, *Lyrics from Shelters*, 115, first drew my attention to this poem.

90. M. M. Y. Fung, "Cao Baohua," in Haft, ed., *A Selective Guide*, 71.

91. Almberg, *The Poetry of Chen Jingrong*, 5–6.

92. *Chen Jingrong Shi wen ji* 陳敬榮詩文集 [*Chen Jingrong Collected Poetry and Prose*], ed. Luo Jiaming 羅佳明 and Chen Li 陳俐 (Shanghai: 復旦大學出版社, 2008), 293–535.

93. *Yingyingji* 盈盈集 is translated as "*Poems of Grace*" in McDougall and Louie, *The Literature of China*, 277, and in Haft, *Selective Guide*, 71–72, where Angela Palandri indicates that "盈盈" was first used in the *Nineteen Ancient Poems* 古詩十九首 to describe the "'charming and graceful appearance' of the lady upstairs." But without that context, "Poems of Grace" sounds Christian to me, although nowhere has it been suggested that Chen was Christian. Almberg, *The Poetry of Chen Jingrong*, 9, suggests "Overflow" for 盈盈 while Julia Lin uses "Brimming" in *Women of the Red Plain: An Anthology of Contemporary Chinese Women's Poetry* (New York: Penguin Books, 1992), 28. Zhao Yiheng 趙毅衡 in the second preface to *Chen Jingrong shi wen ji*, 5, suggests that the collection brims with tears.

94. Chen Jingrong 陳敬容, "Preface," in Chen Jingrong, *Tuxiang yu huaduo* 圖像與花朵 Changsha: Hunan renmin chubanshe, 1984, 3.

95. Almberg, *The Poetry of Chen Jingrong* , 10.

96. As Palandri states in Haft, *Selective Guide*, 72, "she has translated some poems of Baudelaire and Rilke, which may have had some impact on her own poetry."

97. *Chen Jingrong Shi wen ji*, 342. See appendix 3. For another translation, Almberg, *The Poetry of Chen Jingrong* , 156.

98. Zhang Yaxin 章亞昕 and Geng Jianhua 耿建華, *Zhongguo xiandai menglong shi shangxi* 中國現代朦朧詩賞析 [*Appreciation of Modern Chinese Misty Poetry*] (Guangzhou: Huacheng chubanshe, 1988), 112–14.

99. Almberg, *The Poetry of Chen Jingrong* , 156.

100. *Chen Jingrong shiwen ji*, 168–69. See appendix 3, also Almberg, *The Poetry of Chen Jingrong* , 120.

101. Almberg, *The Poetry of Chen Jingrong* , 120.

102. McDougall and Louie, *The Literature of China* , 277.

103. Almberg, *The Poetry of Chen Jingrong* , 120.

NINE

Other Comparisons

The foregoing chapters have explored the reception of Baudelaire by various poets roughly grouped according to their own poetics and their relations with the French poet. Three more comparisons will be discussed below. Wen Yiduo, Ai Qing, and Duoduo were not associated with each other. The relation of the first two poets with Baudelaire is based more on aesthetic ideas than on specific poems or images. They bring sharper focus to the types of comparisons that Chinese critics have made of their contemporaries' work with that of Baudelaire. Duoduo's relation to Baudelaire brings together many facets previously treated in this study, and suggests new directions for future study of the reception of Baudelaire in China.

WEN YIDUO (聞一多 1899–1946)

Wen Yiduo's best known poem, the title poem of his 1927 collection *Sishui* 死水 [*Dead Water*], is "clearly influenced by Baudelaire" according to Lan Dizhi.[1] The poem in elegant form, with nine-syllable rhymed couplets forming five quatrains, describes "a ditch of hopelessly dead water," stagnant and full of debris, where one "might as well" throw in more metal and food scraps to see if the metal can become gems and the food become wine. The last quatrain reads in K. Y. Hsu's rhymed translation:

> Here is a ditch of hopelessly dead water—
> a region where beauty can never reside,
> Might as well let the devil cultivate it—
> and see what sort of world it can provide.[2]

What Hsu translates as the "devil" is made up of the characters for "ugly" and "evil," (*chou'e* 醜惡).[3] It is not the specific images in the poem, but the aesthetic of finding "beauty in ugliness" that reminds readers of Baudelaire. But rather than letting the poem itself stand for beauty, Wen explicitly treats the possibility of transformation into beauty from ugliness, adding a moral dimension.

Wen Yiduo "introduced into Chinese verse the aesthetics of the grotesque as practiced by French symbolists such as Baudelaire," according to McDougall and Louie, who find in Wen's "Laundry Song" the "operation of this principle . . . dirt, sweat, stains, blemishes . . . all are concrete but imply wider meanings."[4] In theme and structure, Wen's "Laundry Song" resembles more closely Thomas Hood's 1843 "The Song of the Shirt" than any Symbolist poem; K. Y. Hsu flatly declares Wen's poem "an imitation of Thomas Hood."[5] Again, Wen's poem contains a moral element: stains are attributed to greed (*tanxin* 貪心) and desire (*yu huo* 慾火), and when Wen uses "*zui'e*" 罪惡 to describe sweat-stained shirts, he is using the word translated as "evil" in "Flowers of Evil." The laundrymen of the poem are described as being away from their home country and taking up a job that others disdain, thus conveying a social and political message quite missing from poems like "*Une Charogne*." But the use of "ugly" images to create a beautiful poem is an aesthetic that Chinese readers associate with Baudelaire.

Wen Yiduo's two collections, *Hongzhu* 紅燭 [*Red Candle*], 1923, and *Sishui* 死水[*Dead Water*], 1927, established him as a major poet. Like his fellow members of the Crescent Moon Society, Wen advocated and achieved metrical regularity and rhyme in *baihua* poetry. He had attained a strong foundation in the Chinese classics before attending Tsinghua, at that time a school preparing students to study abroad. Wen studied art in the United States from 1922 to 1925, and devoted himself to literature, teaching, and research after his return to China. During the war he fled with Tsinghua University first to Changsha and then to Kunming, walking with students and colleagues for sixty-eight days to arrive there. One of the few Chinese poets able to combine aesthetics with politics, Wen eventually began to suit action to the word, and fell to assassins' bullets as he exited from a political meeting in 1946.[6]

Wen Yiduo's life and work suggest that if he knew of Baudelaire, it was indirectly. His friend and fellow founder of the Crescent Moon Society, Xu Zhimo, had published his translation of and comments on "*Une Charogne*" in 1924, three years before the publication of "Dead Water." Among other parallels, the lines quoted in chapter 2 of this current study, where Wen begs to be drowned in the loved one's eyes, are addressed to a loved one whose silence, immobility, and sphinx-like cruelty is reminiscent of Baudelaire. The poem is entitled "Death" (*Si* 死).

But Wen's deeper literary interests lay with Chinese poetry from the Tang dynasty and English poetry from the nineteenth century. His poetry reflected his life; the "Laundry Song" grew out of his experience of Americans asking if his father was a laundryman, that being the most common occupation for Chinese in America at the time. Similarly, Wen's poem "Dead Water," read in the context of his life and work, is not a meditation on beauty or on poetry, but an expression of despair about the China in his time, which resembled a ditch with filthy, stagnant water. The poem gains in meaning and resonance as a work of *littérature engagée*. If Baudelaire had indeed played a role in this aesthetic, his reception in China would also gain in meaning and resonance.

AI QING (艾青 1910–1996)

Ren jiang shuo: "women dou shi yongbaozhe
Women de tongku de jidu."
Women shenzhe liangpian hong chun
Shun wen women xinzhong liuchu de gun xue.
Wo feijiehe de nuan huafang ya,
Nali zai 150° de wendu shang,
Cong zidingxiang-ban de feiye,
Wo tuchu le yan qi de honghua.
人將說："我們都是擁抱著
我們的痛苦的基督。"
我們伸著兩片紅唇
吮吻我們心中流出的滾血。
我肺結核的暖花房呀,
那里在150º的溫度上,
從紫丁香般的肺葉,
我吐出了艷凄的紅花。

[People will say: "We are all embracing / Our suffering Christ." / We extend our two red lips / To suck the blood boiling out from our hearts. // In our tubercular hothouse, / It is over 150 degrees, / From lilac-like lung lobes, / We spit out cold red flowers.]

"This poem is not by Baudelaire," writes Huang Ziping after quoting these lines, as though any reader would have assumed that they indeed had been written by the French poet. The images are shocking: there is blood; there is disease; at 150 degrees, one might well be in Hell. There are flowers, and there is evil. But, Huang continues, it was Ai Qing who wrote the lines, in prison in 1934.[7]

Ai Qing, originally named Jiang Haicheng 蔣海澄, has been called the greatest poet of the People's Republic of China.[8] Originally a student of painting, which he studied in Paris, he published his first poetry collection, *Da Yan He* 大堰河 [*Big Weir River*] in 1936, after his imprisonment for "subversive" activities from 1932 to 1935. Thereafter he moved around to various cities before joining the Communists in Yan'an, where he played a major role in the 1942 "Forum on Literature and Art." He published several volumes of poetry during the war, and later became a literary bureaucrat under the new regime. During the anti-rightist campaign in 1957 he was sent to labor in the countryside, not to return to Beijing until 1975. He called 1976 a "second liberation,"[9] and quickly resumed a prolific literary life. He was presented with the French medal "Chevalier des Arts et des Lettres" by the French ambassador visiting China in 1984,[10] and remained active until his death.

Ai Qing had begun to write poetry during his first sojourn in Paris, 1929–1932, when he was studying painting and supporting himself by working in a small factory. He recalls reading Russian literature in Chinese translation as well as modern French poetry.[11] His *"Bali"* 巴黎["Paris"], dated 1937, is a love poem to the city, which he called a "lascivious hysterical whore."[12] The poem describes the trolleys and people in constant motion among buildings and monuments which it names; it names historic events (revolutions, rebellions, the birth of the Commune), and names as its denizens "idiots, gamblers, pimps, drunks, pot-bellied merchants, adventurers, boxers, dreamers, and speculators." In a preface, Ai Qing describes his sojourn in Paris as that of a penniless student; that is the Paris one sees here. The poem ends with a vow to return some day with a conquering army to enjoy her charms.

A second poem to the city, *"Ai Bali"* 哀巴黎 ["Mourning Paris"] translated as "Lament for Paris" in Eugene Eoyang's bilingual anthology, deplores the German occupation. Again it names monuments, this time leaving the *Panthéon* and *Invalides* in the original French. Evoking its "glorious history" and deploring the cowardice of current leaders, the poem expresses faith that the "courageous people" will rise up and struggle against their enemies to create a Second Commune.[13]

These poems on Paris could hardly be more different from Baudelaire's. In contrast with the dense and compact French poems, the 195 lines of "Paris," some as short as a single syllable, the longest extending to thirteen, gush forth with energy and verve. The 106 lines of "Lament for Paris" are filled with overt political statements; "Hitler, Goebbels, Goering" in Chinese transliteration occupy one line. Other lines, such as *"bu"* 不 [no!], *"er tamen"* 而他们 [yet they], and *"dang cike"* 当此刻 [at this moment], contribute to movement in the poem.

In 1980 Ai Qing revisited Paris and wrote a third poem on the city. Again simply titled *"Bali"* 巴黎 ["Paris"], it is prefaced: "Someone asked me: You have been away from Paris for 48 years; now that you're here again, what changes do you see—what has appeared? What has disappeared?" The poem begins:

> *wo kanjian—*
> *Dai-gao-le guoji jichang*
> *wo kanjian—*
> *Peng-pi-du wenhua zhongxin*

我看見一
戴高樂國際機場
我看見一
蓬皮杜文化中心

I see—
DeGaulle International Airport
I see—
Pompidou Cultural Center

and continues the forty-one-line poem with youths on motorcycles and girls on crosswalks, the many Chinese restaurants run by war refugees from Indochina, gargoyles on Notre Dame de Paris aghast at pollution in the Seine, the Eiffel Tower become a radio sending station, cobblestone streets washed clean by the rain, eucalyptus trees reminiscing like old ladies, a ballet audience coming out, neon lights, tourists from all over the world, hippies, and girls flashing "ambiguous smiles."[14] This Paris is a calmer, more prosperous city than the one Ai Qing described in the 1930s. The poem shows no more attachment to the city than is found in poems on other cities Ai Qing visited during his trip, including Rome, New York, Chicago, and San Francisco.[15]

Ai Qing is not a poet of the city. His favorite Francophone poet was the Belgian Émile Verhaeren, whose work he admired for revealing "how the limitless expansion of the metropolis in the capitalist world was leading to the imminent destruction of the countryside."[16] Ai Qing's deeper concern is with the countryside, with the land and people of China, as expressed in such poems as "I Love This Land," "Old Man," "The Woman Mending Clothes," and "Boy Reaping," depicting with great sympathy a hunchbacked farmer, a woman sewing by the side of the road, and a tiny boy, all dignified in their hard labor.[17]

Among Western influences on Ai Qing's poetry, the most frequently mentioned are Verhaeren, Mayakovsky, and Whitman. Eugene Eoyang finds Whitman "the most apposite: his sympathies and his sensibilities are Whitmanesque—but there is one important difference—Ai Qing lacks Whitman's all-encompassing ego."[18] In political statement, in form, and in tone, there are strong resemblances to Mayakovsky's poems in Chinese translation.[19] Hardest to find are resemblances to Baudelaire, although in a poem dedicated to Apollinaire, he had written, in K. Y. Hsu's translation: "I'm madly in love with your Europe / The Europe of Baudelaire and Rimbaud."[20] Yet Huang Ziping is not without grounds for comparing Ai Qing with the French poet. Ai Qing was a realist poet, Huang Ziping concludes, but considering the times in which he lived, it was not possible always to be positive and optimistic. Thus he could write a poem like the one quoted above, with its references to Christ, and blood, and fever, and its depressive tone. It is the depressive tone that Huang traces to Baudelaire, and to the poem "*L'Albatros*" ["The Albatross"], where the poet is compared with an albatross stranded on land and mocked by the crowd. Huang notes that Ai Qing had shown sympathy for the poor and downtrodden from his very earliest poems. He understood their melancholy. But he was ultimately able to draw strength from suffering. In the positive-spirited literary world promoted in 1980s China, Baudelaire was for some a reprehensible example of negativity and "nihilism."

DUODUO (多多 1951–)

Duoduo, also spelled Duo Duo, was originally named Li Shizheng 栗世征. Born in Beijing shortly after the founding of the People's Republic, he moved to the Baiyangdian 白洋淀 countryside in 1969 during the Cultural Revolution, and became associated with the "Baiyang Marshes Poetry Group."[21] He also has been identified with the "Misty Poets," although he was not part of the group, and when he published in their journal *Today* 今天 it was under different pennames.[22] His earliest published poems date from 1972. In 1982 he took as his penname the name of his daughter after she died in infancy.[23] He was involved in the protests at Tiananmen in 1989, but by coincidence left for a previously arranged poetry reading tour on the very day the shooting started.[24] He lived abroad in voluntary exile for a number of years, in England, the Netherlands, and Canada, before returning to China in 2004 to take up a post at Hainan University.

Duoduo's poetry became known to English language readers in 1989 with the publication twice in quick succession of translations by Gregory Lee and John Cayley, with introduction by Gregory Lee.[25] The American poet Donald Finkel, working with Chinese collaborators, published seven selections from Duoduo in 1991.[26] A thorough study with translations into English by Maghiel van Crevel was published in 1996, by which time Duoduo's work had been translated into several European languages and Japanese.[27] In 2002 Gregory Lee published an additional volume of revised and new translations, with the Chinese on facing pages.[28] In 2007 Huang Yibing published an essay in English analyzing Duoduo's work in the contexts of revolution and Modernism.[29]

Duoduo's poems are complex, elliptical, and suggestive. Unlike many of his contemporaries, he does not write poems on political issues to post in public places. He finds such posting to be a "sacrifice" of his work, which he does not dash off in fits of inspiration. Instead, he told an interviewer in 2005, he might work a single poem seventy times (*wo yishou shi yao xie 70 bian* 我一首詩要寫70遍). In answer to the question "What type of poetry do you seek?" he answered that his favorite poets are always changing, and he begins the list with Baudelaire.[30]

Duoduo's poem, *"Cong siwang de fangxiang kan"* 從死亡的方向看 ["Looking Out From Death"] gives its title to the anthology of translations by Gregory Lee and John Cayley, *Looking Out from Death*. In his introduction to the volume, Lee declares the poem to be "modern [and] totally authentic," and judiciously compares its theme and central image with Baudelaire's *"Le Mort joyeux"* ["The Gladly Dead"].[31] Duoduo's poem is at once more defined and more ambiguous than Baudelaire's. It reads:

> From the direction of death one will always see
> People one should not see all one's life
> One will always bury oneself at some random site
> Take a random sniff, and bury oneself there
> Bury oneself in the site that they can hate
> They will shovel soil onto your face
> You must thank them. Thank them once more
> Your eyes will then never again see enemies
> From the direction of death will arrive
> Their howls when they fall into enmity
> You will never again be able to hear
> That is entirely the howl of suffering![32]

In both poems, the persona chooses a burial site. But whereas Baudelaire expresses the wish to dig his own grave in fat soil crawling with snails, to lie there feeling free and happy while the worms eat his corpse, Duoduo writes that any site would do. His choice is *"suibian"* 隨便, meaning casual, random, careless, wanton, doing as one pleases. And whereas Baudelaire uses the first person pronoun, Duoduo leaves the subject ambiguous until the sixth line, when "they" pour the shovelful of soil in "your" face. "They" are the enemies that "you" should not have seen in your lifetime. The poem continues with when the enemies meet with enmity themselves, "you," looking out from the direction of death, will never again hear "their" screams of agony. Whereas in traditional poetry poetic ambiguity comes from omission of personal pronouns, Duoduo uses the omission and contrasting use of *"ni"* 你 [you] and *"tamen"* 他們 [they or them] to chilling effect. Readers familiar with the horrors of the Cultural Revolution in China will be doubly chilled by the image of seeing unnamed and unnamable enemies shoveling soil onto their faces, and then being grateful for not being able to see them again or to hear their screams. The ambiguity of subject returns in the last line: is it "their" howl that "you" will never again hear, or are "you" howling because "you" can never again hear? Or both? The only punctuation is the exclamation mark at the very end of the poem. Duoduo's poem is even more ironic than Baudelaire's, where the poet contentedly lies in the grave and expresses disdain for the judgment of posterity.

Baudelaire is invoked in connection with Duoduo in another context, although it is in connection with Duoduo's absence. Richard King, in his review of an anthology of post–Cultural Revolution poetry, calls Duoduo "another of the symbolists now living and writing outside China," and states that "the new symbolism offers a cultural reaffirmation through its rural images and traditional (particularly Taoist) way of thought, even as it inherits the techniques of Baudelaire and earlier Chinese symbolists like Dai Wangshu."[33] King is deploring the omission of Duoduo from the anthology under review. Although King puts "symbolist" in lowercase, Duoduo's poetry has more in common with the European Symbolists than that of the poets generally identified as "Chinese Symbolists." Those qualities include density of expression, suggestiveness, serious consciousness of the self as Poet, and poems that are about poetry. As with Bian Zhilin and Dai Wangshu, Duoduo may be closely associated with Modernism.

To illustrate what he describes as Duoduo's "darkly mysterious" and "powerful" poetry, King quotes four lines from the poem "Night" ("*Ye*" 夜) in Gregory Lee's translation:

> On a night full of symbols
> the moon is like a sick person's pallid face
> like a mistaken, shifting time
> and death, like a doctor standing before the bed[34]

Illness, death, and the moon in poetry have all been associated with Baudelaire, but here, Duoduo's comparison of the moon with a sick person is more evocative of T. S. Eliot's likening the evening sky to an etherized patient. Duoduo thus goes a line further into Eliot's "The Love Song of J. Alfred Prufrock" than Bian Zhilin had taken in his "Demon's Serenade," discussed in chapter 8.

A poem is presented as "Baudelairean" by Joseph R. Allen in his review of Donald Finkel's translation. Allen quotes the last poem of the seven-poem sequence "Gallery":

> Oh yes, the night
> has hidden your face
> and altered your voice
> I can feel
> our love now,
> gliding silently
> like a sleigh
> across a wound.[35]

The poem is indeed reminiscent of poems in *Les Fleurs du mal* that had attracted earlier Chinese poets such as Shao Xunmei and Li Jinfa: poems that show love as inflicting wounds, and the woman as enigmatic and cruel ("*Tu mettrais . . .*"), whose saliva can bite ("*Le Poison*"), and whose indifference can inflict pain ("*Avec ses vêtements . . .*").[36] Chinese critics have long associated Baudelaire with poems on cruelty, death, the night, pessimism, autumn, and dusk, all of which can be found in Duoduo's work.

A closer filiation with Baudelaire is drawn by Huang Yibing in his analysis of Duoduo's very long (seventy-two-line) poem in two parts entitled *"Ma-ge-li he wo de lüxing"* 瑪格麗和我的旅行 ["Marguerite and My Travels"].[37] The first part of the poem invites Marguerite to travel with the poet to Paris, to the Caribbean, to Spain, to the Black Sea, to the tropics—anywhere out of the Chinese world. But the second part invites Marguerite back to China, to look at the poverty and suffering of the Chinese peasants. Huang compares the first part of Duoduo's poem with two specific poems from *Les Fleurs du mal*, *"L'invitation au voyage"* and *"Sonnet d'automne,"* analyzing differences as well as similarities. He points out that the name Marguerite, clearly transliterated from a Western language, is "actually borrowed from Baudelaire." Huang was given access to a private manuscript archive containing a group of Duoduo's love poems dedicated "to the Great Baudelaire: '—Oh, my so innocent, so cold Marguerite.'" In a letter to Huang, Duoduo had given great weight to his reading Baudelaire in Chen Jingrong's 1957 translations.[38] Duoduo's embrace of Baudelaire is also clear from a statement he made in 1992:

"My boyhood was but a gloomy thunderstorm. . . ." In 1972 I first read poetry by Baudelaire. Well then, had *my* boyhood been but a note in the eulogy for Mao Zedong? While we sang each day: "Chairman Mao is like the sun," Baudelaire said, "The sun is like a poet."[39]

The relation of the sun and the poet is found in the final lines of *"Sonnet d'automne"*:

> *Comme moi n'es-tu pas un soleil automnal*
> *Ô ma si blanche, ô ma si froide Marguerite?*

[Like me, aren't you an autumnal sun, oh my Marguerite, so white and so cold?]

It reads, in Chen Jingrong's translation:

> *ni bu ye ru wo shi yi lun qiu yang,*
> *a, wo ruci chunjie, ruci wuqing de Ma-ge-li*
> 你不也如我是一輪秋陽，
> 呵，我如此純潔，如此無情的瑪格麗

[Are you not like me, an autumn sun,
Oh, my Marguerite so pure, and so cruel?]

Chen had focused on the emotion more than on the scene: in rendering *"blanche"* [white] as *"chunjie"* 純潔 [pure, clean, and honest], she omits the physical sense of color, and in using *"wuqing"* 無情 [merciless, ruthless, heartless, unfeeling] for *"froide"* [cold] she only gives the emotive sense, but not the physical sensation of cold. The association with the autumnal sun, which is cooler than the summer sun, is weakened but not entirely lost. In this poem both Marguerite and the poet are like the autumnal sun.

The simile of the sun being like a poet is given stronger expression in Baudelaire's "*Le Soleil*" ["The Sun"]:

> *Quand, ainsi qu'un poète, il descend dans les villes,*
> *Il ennoblit le sort des choses les plus viles,*

[When, like a poet, it descends into cities, / It ennobles the fate of the vilest things]

"*Il*," which could be "he" or "it" refers to the sun of the title. "*Le Soleil*" is not among the nine poems included in Chen Jingrong's 1957 selection that Duoduo read in 1972. Her 1984 *Tuxiang yu huaduo* 圖像與花朵 [*Pictures and Flowers*] does contain the poem, however, and renders the lines as:

> *fangfu shi yi wei shiren, ta manyou chengxiang*
> *dui mei he chou fuyu de yiyi tongyang gaoshang*
> 髣髴是一位詩人，他漫游城鄉，
> 對美和醜賦予的意義同樣高尚[40]

[Like a poet, it roams city and country, Endowing beauty and ugliness with equally noble meaning]

Chen has added a lot of interpretation to the second line, but Duoduo seems to have responded mainly to the part of the poem that does reflect the original. Was it truly because he and Baudelaire were "kindred souls," as he appears to have suggested in an article quoted in Huang's study?[41]

Duoduo also expressed a love for clouds, shared with the figure in that prose poem most frequently translated into Chinese, "*L'Étranger*." In a 2004 interview, Duoduo stated: "I think that cloudy sky inspires me most, when the wind fast carries clouds along it. Clouds mean freedom, travels. I can see many things in the clouds, since when I was a child I stared long time watching clouds changing shapes." He goes on to state that being Chinese, coming from generations of peasants, he "naturally adore[s] earth." But when asked with which natural element he would compare his own poetry, he did not name earth, but replied: "Clouds. It isn't fire, it isn't water, it isn't wood, it isn't metal; it isn't air. It's a cloud."[42] Here again he seems to have found a "kindred spirit" in Baudelaire.

To return to Duoduo's poem "Night," of which only the first half in Gregory Lee's translation was presented earlier, the poem ends:

> *yixie wuqing de ganqing*
> *yixie xinzhong kepa de biandong*
> *yueguang zai wuqian de kongchang shang qingsheng kesou*
> *yueguang, anshizhe chuchu zaimu de liufang*

一些無情的感情
一些心中可怕的變動
月光在屋前的空場上輕聲咳嗽
月光，暗示着楚楚在目的流放

Some impassive feelings
Some frightening changes in the heart
Moonlight in the front yard softly coughs
Moonlight, hinting at exile clearly faced

Duoduo's play on words, *"wuqing de ganqing"* 無情的感情 [literally, un-feeling feelings] is reminiscent of Baudelaire's sphinx in *"La Beauté."* The moon shining on the ground, and its hinting at exile, it is reminiscent of Li Bo and Du Fu, but its mystery, cold, and personification, are more reminiscent of Baudelaire. As with traditional Chinese poetry, when the poem ends, the meaning goes on, while at the same time the poem invites us back to dwell in it.

Huang Yibing's assessment is persuasive. He wrote: "Duo Duo may not be the first poet in modern China to identify himself with Baudelaire, although he might be the one who eventually stands closest to that French poet in the genealogy of Chinese modernism."[43]

Duoduo's self-professed relation to Baudelaire demonstrates how a Chinese poet can be inspired by another poet who is worlds away in time and place, to create new poetry that does not fall into imitation or derivative pastiche. Without inserting foreign words and images into a poem like "Night," Duoduo allows readers the pleasure of finding filiations with other poetic experiences, and gives new meaning and direction to the idea of "world poetry." In 2010 he was awarded the Neustadt International Prize for Literature, a biennial award sponsored by the University of Oklahoma and World Literature Today.[44]

NOTES

1. Lan Dizhi 藍棣之, "Wen Yiduo—zou jinqu, zai zou chulai" 聞一多－走進去，再走出來 ["Wen Yiduo: Walking In, Then Walking Out"], in Zeng, *Zouxiang shijie wenxue*, 370. Many others have pointed out this parallel, but Lan's is the only one I have found in print thus far.

2. Hsu, *Twentieth-Century Chinese Poetry*, 66.

3. Yeh, *Anthology*, 17, follows Hsu in rendering "chou'e" 醜惡 as Devil, but with a capital *D*; Tao Tao Sanders, in *Red Candle: Selected Poems by Wen I-To* (London: Jonathan Cape, 1972), 34, translates it as "ugliness."

4. McDougall and Louie, *The Literature of China in the Twentieth Century*, 56. Hsu, *Twentieth-Century Chinese Poetry*, 55–56.

5. Hsu, *Twentieth Century Chinese Poetry*, 48.

6. Ibid., 50; McDougall and Louie, *The Literature of China in the Twentieth Century*, 261–62. For a full literary biography, see Kai-yu Hsu, *Wen I-To*, Twayne's World Author Series (Boston: G. K. Hall, 1980).

7. Huang Ziping 黄子平, "Cong caise de Ouluoba daihui le yi zhi ludi" 從彩色的歐羅巴帶回了一支蘆笛 ["From Colorful Europe Brought Back a Reed"], in Zeng, *Zou xiang shijie wenxue*, 487.

8. Wilt Idema and Lloyd Haft, *A Guide to Chinese Literature*, Michigan Monograph in Chinese Studies (Ann Arbor: Center for Chinese Studies, The University of Michigan, 1997), 282. Canadian Broadcast Corporation, *China Rises*, video documentary, 2006, makes the same assertion.

9. Ai Qing 艾青, "Zuozhe zixu" 作者自序 ["Author's Preface"], in Eugene Chen Eoyang, ed. and trans., *Selected Poems of Ai Qing* (Bloomington: Indiana University Press in association with Beijing: Foreign Languages Press, 1982), 5–12, 228–34.

10. "Ai Qing et la France," http://french.people.com.cn/french/200401/29/fra20040129_65100.html (accessed 27 Feb. 2010). The site incorrectly names the medal "Chevalier des Arts et de la Culture."

11. Eoyang, *Selected Poems of Ai Qing*, "Author's Preface," 5.

12. Ibid., 31–36; 251–58.

13. Ibid., 100–104, 335–39.

14. Yang Liu 杨柳 and Mo Wenzheng 莫文征, eds., *Ai Qing Shi Quan Bian* 艾青詩全編 [*Complete Poems of Ai Qing*] (Beijing: Renmin wenxue chubanshe, 2003), 3:1364–66.

15. See Eoyang, *Selected Poems of Ai Qing*, 178–205; 421–54. (This includes a poem on Iowa, where Ai Qing visited the Writer's Workshop).

16. Ibid., 5, 228.

17. See Ibid., 67, 110, 52, 109; "*Wo ai zhe tudi*" 我愛這土地 ["I Love This Land"], 298; "*Laoren*" 老人 ["Old Man"], 346, "*Bu yifu*" 補衣婦 ["The Woman Mending Clothes"], 279, "*Yicao de haizi*" 刈草的孩子 ["Boy Reaping"], 345.

18. Ibid., 5.

19. Mayakovky in Chinese can be found online at several URLs by searching "mayakefusiji shixuan" 马雅可夫斯基诗选.

20. Hsu, *Twentieth Century Chinese Poetry* , 293. See also, 295–319, for translations of Ai Qing's poems.

21. Hong Zicheng, *A History of Contemporary Chinese Literature*, trans. Michael Day (Leiden: Brill, 2007), 248.

22. McDougall and Louie, *The Literature of China in the Twentieth Century* , 439.

23. Gregory Lee, "Introduction," *Looking Out from Death: From the Cultural Revolution to Tiananmen Square—The New Chinese Poetry of Duoduo*, trans. Gregory Lee and John Cayley (London: Bloomsbury, 1989), 9, and Maghiel van Crevel, *Language Shattered: Contemporary Chinese Poetry and Duoduo* (Leiden: Centre of Non-Western Studies Research School, 1996), 102–3.

24. Gregory Lee, "Introduction," *Looking Out from Death*, 13; van Crevel, *Language Shattered*, 103.

25. Gregory Lee and John Cayley, trans. *Statements: The New Chinese Poetry of Duoduo* (London. Wellsweep Press, 1989) was published shortly before *Looking Out from Death*; Lee explains the circumstances in the "Introduction" to the latter, p. 13.

26. Donald Finkel, ed. and trans., *A Splintered Mirror: Chinese Poetry from the Democracy Movement* (San Francisco: North Point Press, 1991).

27. van Crevel, *Language Shattered*, 348–49.

28. Gregory B. Lee, *The Boy Who Catches Wasps* (Brookline, MA: Zephyr Press, 2002).

29. Huang Yibing, "Duo Duo: An Impossible Farewell, or, Exile between Revolution and Modernism," in *Contemporary Chinese Literature: From the Cultural Revolution to the Future* (New York: Palgrave Macmillan, 2007), 19–63.

30. "Duoduo, wo zhuzhang jieshi huanhun" 多多：我主張借詩還魂 ["Douduo: I Advocate Reincarnation through Poetry"], ed. Li Xueqin 李雪芹. Available on several websites, including www.douban.com/group/topic/8897634/ and http://big5.xinhuanet.com/gate/big5/news.xinhuanet.com/book/2005-04/14/content_2822471.htm (accessed 21 October, 2011). After Baudelaire, Duoduo names Marina Tsvetaeva and René Char.

31. Lee, *Looking Out*, 12–13; *Statements*, 10–11.

32. Lee, *Boy*, 50. www.chinapoesy.com/XianDaiD0F589BC-D3CD-4CE6-B923-2E0CDB5F99F6.html (accessed 30 Nov. 2011). See appendix 3.

33. Richard King, review of *The Red Azalea: Chinese Poetry since the Cultural Revolution*, ed. Edward Morin, trans. Fang Dai, Dennis Ding and Edward Morin, in *Pacific Affairs* 64, no. 1 (Spring 1991): 400–401.

34. King quotes from Lee's *Statements*, 34. In *Boy*, 9, Lee retranslated "sick person" as "invalid." See also Finkel, 33.

35. Joseph R. Allen, review of *Splintered Mirror* by Donald Finkel, in *World Literature Today* 65, no. 3 (Summer 1991): 547. The poem is in Finkel, 36.

36. *OC*, 48, 27, 29. See chapters 6 and 7.

37. Huang, *Contemporary Chinese Literature* , 44–48. The original poem is online at www.chinapoesy.com/XianDai4FF7948B-73EA-4113-AB4F-1BA6ECEA2257.html (accessed 20 Oct. 2009). See also van Crevel, *Language Shattered*, 140–42

38. Huang, *Contemporary Chinese Literature* , 45, 196, and 194, note 16, quoting a letter addressed to him by Duoduo.

39. Ibid., 25, quoting van Crevel, *Language Shattered*, 42–43.

40. Chen, *Tuxiang*, 34.

41. Huang, *Contemporary Chinese Literature* , 25, 194.

42. Fabio Grasselli, "Interviewing Duo Duo, the Poet of the Clouds, Haikou, 11 Oct. 2004," www.cinaoggi.it/english/culture/duo-duo-interview.htm (accessed 18 Jan. 2008). Duoduo has added the Greek element of "air" to the traditional "five elements" of water, fire, earth, wood, and metal.

43. Huang, *Contemporary Chinese Literature* , 29, 38–39.

44. See www.ou.edu/wlt/neustadt-prize.html (accessed 21 Oct. 2011).

Summary and Conclusions

> — *Hypocrite lecteur, —mon semblable, —mon frère !* [1]
> —Baudelaire, *"Au Lecteur"*

When Baudelaire addressed the first poem in *Les Fleurs du mal, "Au Lecteur,"* to the reader and ended the poem with "my likeness, my brother," he implied that his reader can understand his poetry because they are alike; they are spiritual brothers. He little could have imagined that spiritual brother to reside in China, the country that in his own poetry represented supreme distance. Yet throughout the past century and into this one, Chinese readers have responded to his work.

The Chinese reader of Baudelaire's poetry, setting aside the language barrier, would have found familiar elements from the Chinese tradition. Most of the poems in *Les Fleurs du mal* are short concentrated lyrics, using rhyme and regular line lengths. Many explore classical themes, such as love, beauty, or the passage of time, and exhibit "the classical qualities of definiteness, harmony, and restraint." [2] These familiar elements are what made it possible for readers and critics to compare poems from Baudelaire's work with classical Chinese poets, as introduced in chapter 1. With Li Bo, he shared the night, autumn, the moon, indistinct dreamy longing, wine drinking, and drunken raptures. With Du Fu, he shared the deep consciousness of the suffering of others, and heightened emotion through restraint in expression. With Li Ho, he shared the sense of horror at the swift passage of time rushing toward impending death. His descriptions of rich interiors, perfumes, and languor find parallels in Li Shangyin.

Yet the sense of familiarity also leads back to Baudelaire's original line, in which he addresses his reader as a "hypocrite." The reader who claims not to know "ennui," the subject of the poem, is a hypocrite. That line can be extended to all poetry. That a number of the poems were condemned as being "harmful to morals" leads to the question: Does understanding not require recognition and knowledge? Would a truly innocent and naïve reader recognize or find interest in those "harmful" passages about taking drugs and seeking carnal pleasure, or know the difference between a portrait of post-coital lesbians and one of nudes at bath in a Classical painting? Baudelaire implies that it is the person who shares and mirrors his experiences who will be his dedicated reader. As A. C. Graham put it, his reader will recognize sin, because he finds it at the bottom of his own heart. [3] The same recognition may have provoked

those critics who condemned Baudelaire's pessimism and "nihilism."
The comparison falters, however, on the level of Christian ideas of original sin and the search for the Absolute; the non-Christian reader is unlikely to feel the same shudder at hearing blasphemy, or the same agony
at not finding the Absolute. But shared across cultures are recognition of
good and evil, beauty and ugliness, love and hate as opposite pairs.

When Baudelaire wrote of evil or hatred or chose ugly images in
poems of surprising beauty, in a sense he was bringing together the union of opposites, a concept already familiar to the Chinese through
Taoism. For the reader of Zhuangzi, who tells us that the Tao (Dao) can
be found in shit and piss—it is not too far a stretch to find beauty in a
rotting body by the wayside. Baudelaire brought the idea into lyric poetry, with his "*Une Charogne*" ["Carrion"] offering a new aesthetic. Xu Zhimo might not have had this in mind when he wrote his paean to Baudelaire, but he reflects Zhuangzi in his "horizon of expectations" when he
points out that "each fresh discovery emphasizes the greatness of our
forebears."[4] Thus recognizable or familiar elements could work simultaneously with the "new thrill" to draw Chinese readers to Baudelaire.

Most Chinese readers of Baudelaire know his work only through
translation. Translators play a central role in this reception both through
the selection of works for translation and through their renderings. In the
nineteen-twenties, translations from Baudelaire's prose poems served the
development of the prose poem form in China. The *Petits Poèmes en prose*
was completely translated into Chinese by the 1930s, while selections
from *Les Fleurs du mal* appeared only sporadically for the next four
decades. But Baudelaire's reputation rested more strongly on his verse
collection. Chinese poets developing in their own poetry formal elements
of rhythm and rhyme in the colloquial language—including Bian Zhilin,
Liang Zongdai, Dai Wangshu, and Chen Jingrong—were drawn to
Baudelaire's use of traditional prosody. Baudelaire's prosody also drew
the attention of the philologist Wang Li, who included Baudelaire's sonnets in his study of prosody. For his own translations of *Les Fleurs du mal*,
Wang took up the challenge of finding in Classical Chinese language
equivalents for topics that had not existed in serious traditional Chinese
poetry. Ultimately, however, translations into Classical Chinese played at
best a very minor role in the reception of Baudelaire in China. More
influential were the full translations by Tu Kuo-ch'ing, published in 1977,
followed nearly a decade later by Mo Yu's in 1985; both were published
in Taiwan, with Tu relying on English and Japanese versions, while Mo
Yu translated directly from the French. In 1986 Qian Chunqi's full translation appeared in the People's Republic, and became the most frequently
quoted version. New translations of the complete collection have appeared every few years since then, as noted in chapter 3.

Chinese critics have played equally important roles in introducing
Baudelaire to Chinese readers, as outlined in chapter 4. Beginning with

early attempts to find Baudelaire's place in world literary history, critics later created images of Baudelaire that mirrored their preoccupations. In the 1920s readers found in Baudelaire a role model for their striving toward free love; their rebellion against traditional values probably also contributed to the fascination with his "finding beauty in ugliness." Both Baudelaire's "*Spleen*" and "*Idéal*" found readers: some focused on his "*L'invitation au voyage*," declared by Hung Cheng-fu to resemble Tang poetry, to find a romantic and idealistic poet; others focused on the four "*Spleen*" poems and those in the "*La Révolte*" section to find a tormented soul. Li Sichun in 1925 quoted unknown persons as saying "this master of Decadence should be forgotten," less than a year after Xu Zhimo had declared Baudelaire to be a saint and redeemer. While Liang Zongdai declared in 1935 that Baudelaire had found life to be a great harmony, other critics excoriated the French poet for pessimism and nihilism. During the years of war in the 1940s and 1950s readers found his work permeated not with beauty or love, but with death. While readers who were devoted to political revolution found Baudelaire deficient in that regard, in 1957 Chen Jingrong emphasized his role in the 1848 revolution and found a way to present him as a laboring hero. Cheng Baoyi would point out in 1980 that Baudelaire's real revolution was in his work. For critics who saw literary history as a linear progression, Baudelaire was seen as the father of Symbolism and the grandfather of Modernism. Although Liu Yanling had pleaded for attention to individual creation rather than "isms," it remains easiest to find references to Baudelaire in articles and books on Symbolism, and occasionally on Modernism.

When Chinese critics named Yu Dafu "China's Baudelaire," or Li Jinfa the "Baudelaire of the Orient," they implied that the French poet's "likeness" and "brother" could be found in China. Their epithets placed these Chinese writers into the context of French literature and simultaneously brought Baudelaire into the nexus of Chinese literature. Only by focusing too narrowly on sex in the case of Yu Dafu, and on incomprehensibility in the case of Li Jinfa, they failed to contribute to deeper understanding of either the French poet or the Chinese writers. The broader aim of introducing world literature into Chinese discourse and integrating Chinese literature into world literature was achieved better in Zheng Zhenduo's 1927 four-volume *Outline of Literature*.

When Chinese critics categorized their compatriots' works and made comparisons with Western literature, national pride played a role. In the twentieth century, China's lesser development vis-à-vis the West in economic, military, scientific, technological, and political spheres led Chinese intellectuals to question their cultural development overall, and led them to a sense that the Chinese literary world had to "catch up" to the West by going through similar stages of "development" and "progress." But the same intellectuals also had the exhilarating sense of creating a new national literature. They were not adrift in a galaxy of "universals."

Instead, they were contributing to the rapid development of a Chinese literature that could stand as equal to Western literary traditions. When they admired French literature for the length and breadth of its tradition, they simultaneously, or by implication, were admiring salient features of their own tradition. Perhaps the unspoken awareness of this contributed to their willingness to receive and embrace foreign literatures.

The Chinese reception of Baudelaire, as with the reception of any Western European writer, cannot be viewed apart from the eventful political history of twentieth-century China. The change from Classical literary language to modern vernacular is associated with the May Fourth movement, named for political demonstrations begun May 4, 1919 against terms of the Versailles Treaty. The successive series of political events that affected writers, briefly outlined in chapter 2, includes the May Thirtieth Incident, the White Terror, the rise of the Communist Party, the War of Resistance against Japan, and the following civil war that divided the Republic of China and formed the People's Republic. The most famous statement on the relationship of politics to literature is found in Lu Xun's preface to his first collection of short stories published in 1923. There he relates how, as a medical student in Japan, he saw a lantern slide of able-bodied Chinese men looking on apathetically as their compatriot was beheaded by the Japanese for spying for the Russians during the Russo-Japanese war. This is the experience that led him to abandon medicine for literature, to save the spirit rather than the body.[5] While his social and political aims are less evident in his poetry, Lu Xun wrote scathing essays and compelling stories to explore the sense and limits of cultural and national pride.

National pride also may have played a role in the scantiness of references to Japanese sources in studies on the reception of Western literature in China. In the 1920s the Chinese frequently translated books and articles on Western literature from Japanese scholarship: Lu Xun's translation of Hakuson, and Tian Han's article for Baudelaire's centenary are just two examples. In the same decade the Creation Society was established in Japan. Yet in their published correspondence, Wang Duqing, Mu Mutian, and Feng Naichao referred not to Japanese translations, but to the anthology of van Bever and Léautaud.[6] Only Mu Mutian's 1935 *History of French Literature* acknowledges Japanese sources along with a Russian source.[7] Lu Xun died in 1936, a year before the War of Resistance against Japan started. His brother Zhou Zuoren, who made so many valuable contributions to the reception of Western literature in China as editor, translator, critic, and writer, either is reviled or ignored in current Chinese sources because he collaborated with the Japanese during the war. But it would be going too far to say that Japanese roles in the study of Baudelaire were erased only by revisionist history. Tu Kuo-ch'ing has shown that even in the 1920s, while the Japanese Symbolist poets relied on Japanese translations, the Chinese Symbolist poets did not do so, but "all went to France to absorb their knowledge individually."[8] But in preparing the first full translation into Chinese of *Les Fleurs du mal* in 1977, Tu Kuo-ch'ing did rely on Japanese as well as English sources. That he had access to four Japanese versions can be taken as evidence of how far ahead of China Japan was in this area of Comparative Literature.

People who have lived in Taiwan for generations do not express the same animus against the Japanese as that expressed by Mainlanders who fled there after China's civil war, perhaps because the Japanese occupation of Taiwan was so much more civil than their occupation of the Mainland. Taking over Taiwan in 1895, they developed irrigation, power, roads, railroads, and schools. While their requirement that the Japanese language be taught in Taiwan's schools might be politically objectionable, it later did allow Chinese scholars and critics to surmount a major barrier to Japanese scholarship. In literary criticism there is the example of Cheng Ch'ing-mao (Zheng Qingmao), who published in Taiwan in 1965 a study of the Ming Dynasty poet Wang Cihui. His article begins with a quotation from the Japanese writer Nagai Kafu (1897–1957), whose comparison of Wang Cihui with Baudelaire dates from 1917,[9] some years before Chinese references to the French poet began to appear.

Chinese critics have been far less reluctant to acknowledge Western language sources in critical as well as creative writing. In writing of the reception of English and European literature in China, they freely use the word "influence." "Influence" is a capacious word. Literary influence can include imitation, appropriation, adaptation, pastiche. All these were in play as Chinese writers imitated or adapted foreign models, adopted forms and metrics, appropriated themes and images, named specific authors, and made direct references to specific works. Whether they represent homage, paraphrase, parallel, or pastiche may depend primarily on how the reader regards the resulting Chinese creations.

In the case of Baudelaire, the prime example is found in the "Chinese Symbolist" Li Jinfa. Li acknowledged in print Baudelaire's influence, translated poems from *Les Fleurs du mal* into Chinese, and incorporated in his own poems lines from Baudelaire's original French. Many Chinese critics have pointed out this relationship, and some have juxtaposed lines from his poems with those Baudelaire's in Chinese translation.[10]

Like Li Jinfa, Shao Xunmei, Bian Zhilin, He Qifang, and Duoduo all have acknowledged in print their debt to Baudelaire. Shao Xunmei played with the idea of sex and sin as being beautiful. Bian Zhilin created portraits of Beijing that were inspired by the *Tableaux parisiens*. He Qifang compared himself with Baudelaire's *Étranger* and bade farewell to the French poet in a poem that was also a farewell to refined poetry. Duoduo, the most recent poet represented in this study, professed to be inspired by the idea of the Poet being like the sun that he found in a poem by Baudelaire in Chen Jingrong's translation. More than any of his predecessors, Duoduo has "hidden the string;" but rather than hiding the string that makes his poem cohere, as with Li Jinfa, he has hidden the string that ties him to Baudelaire. Yet the "hiding" cannot be ascribed to the "anxiety of influence," else why would Duoduo repeatedly point out his debt to the French poet?

Chinese critics have also made comparisons without asserting influence. Such is the case with "China's Baudelaire," Yu Dafu. The critics, knowing Baudelaire at least by reputation as a "Decadent," and associating with that epithet the subject of sex, could thus compare the Chinese writer's fiction with the French writer's poetry. Their putting Baudelaire and Shao Xunmei together as "Decadent" had a stronger basis, as Shao had named his collection *Hua yiban de zui'e* [*Flowerlike Evil*] after *Les Fleurs du mal*, and sex is the topic in many of its poems. Yet when Shao Xunmei as a critic in turn found Baudelairean qualities in Bian Zhilin's work, he did not refer to "Decadence" or sex or sin, but rather, to "sensual purity."

In literary reception going beyond influences, similarities, and parallels, the Chinese poetic tradition has a long history of writing a new poem in response to a previous one. As they continued this practice in the twentieth century, poets could draw on a wider pool of models than before. As they came into contact with poetry from different times and places, their horizon of expectations expanded to receive it. By adopting and adapting Western models, Chinese poets received Western literature into their own literary world, and created a place for their works in an ever-expanding world literature. Many of the poetic values of Symbolism, including the use of synaesthetic imagery and preference for condensed lyricism and suggestiveness, were shared by traditional Chinese poetry. The challenge for the Chinese poets was to "make it new." As this effort moved them toward modernity, Baudelaire continued to serve as inspiration.

The creative works of Chinese writers are the focus in Part II, with critical works serving as guides and reference. Lu Xun's direct response to Baudelaire's *Petits Poèmes en prose* continues the tradition of writing a new poem in response to another poet's work. Lu Xun adopts the prose poem form, new in China at the time. But Lu Xun also breaks with tradition: rather than writing response poems as a polite pastime, he takes the impolite approach of attack, refutation, and irony. The gloomy mood in many of Lu Xun's prose poems have led Chinese critics to ask how he could have departed so far from his goal of healing China's spiritual ills. Almost diametrically opposite to Lu Xun in his response to Baudelaire, Xu Zhimo greeted the French poet with enthusiastic admiration in his translations and criticism. But Xu Zhimo also made a gloomy poetic response in contrast with his famous ebullient personality. His and Lu Xun's creative response is the subject of chapter 5.

Xu Zhimo had compared the sound and color of *Les Fleurs du mal* with "shadows reflected in the last glow of the evening sun," and with "the last echo of a wounded cuckoo." These images of decline are found throughout the poems of Yu Gengyu, and associate him with Decadence in a sense different from Yu Dafu or Shao Xunmei. The three are presented as Decadents in chapter 6.

In offering the images as symbols of decline, Xu Zhimo does not simply name the sunset and the dying cuckoo, and he goes beyond visual images to describe them as "reflected shadows" and "echoes." Suggesting through the senses rather than naming or describing emotions, events, or moods is a major part of Baudelaire's aesthetics and closely associated with Symbolism. For Baudelaire, the senses often intermingled: sounds are described through sight, smells through touch, and so forth, as "synaesthesia." The most famous expression of synaesthesia is found in the sonnet *"Correspondances ,"* where perfumes are compared with children's flesh, oboes, and prairies; and scent, color, and sound respond to each other.

Suggestion and synaesthestic imagery were often used in traditional Chinese poetry, but in modern Chinese literature, they became associated with the "Chinese Symbolists." The "Chinese Symbolists" did not form a school or a movement that included art, music, drama, and fiction as well as poetry in the way that European Symbolists did; they did not publish a manifesto. Although suggestion and synaesthetic imagery were not part of Chinese Symbolism as first defined by Zhu Ziqing and Su Xuelin, they were frequently employed by the poets examined in chapter 7, who either are identified as Symbolist, or are associated with Symbolism through readers' responses.

Chinese Decadents and Symbolists were drawn to Baudelaire's dark and morbid imagery, and the associated mood that he brought into lyric poetry, a mood that he variously identified as *"Ennui"* and *"Spleen."* *"Ennui,"* sometimes translated "Boredom," goes far beyond the ordinary meaning of boredom, to a sense of horror of and fatigue with life that can allow it to "swallow the world in a yawn." As Li Jinfa puts it, "I'm tired of smelling the sweat of all forms of life." Similarly, *"Spleen"* goes beyond the gentle melancholy of earlier poetry to include anger and anguish (although in its milder forms, *"Spleen"* represents a mood that my generation might have called a "blue funk"). Baudelaire entitled four of his verse poems *"Spleen,"* and subtitled his prose poem collection *Le Spleen de Paris.* This mood is recreated in the Chinese Decadent and Symbolist poems. Chinese poets like Li Jinfa and Dai Wangshu, whether they borrowed directly from the French or indirectly from Ernest Dowson, adopted the title in its original language for their own poems.

Chinese Symbolism was at first largely defined from Li Jinfa's 1925 poetry collection *Wei yu* 微雨 [*Light Rain*]. Many critics drew on Zhu Ziqing's definition of its irregular verse against free verse and formalist verse as "Symbolist," along with Su Xuelin's list of the four qualities that she found in the collection: obscurity, hypersensitivity, decadence, and exoticism. Li's "Symbolist" poetry, more than three hundred poems all written in three years before the age of twenty-five, reveal a haste and carelessness at complete variance from his French models. His assaults on grammar are saved by arresting imagery, exoticism (from his use of European languages and allusions), and intense moods. He professed to have taken his inspiration from Verlaine and Baudelaire, and stated that toward the end of his life, he was still devoted to *Les Fleurs du mal*. Li's fascination with Baudelaire's lines describing the death rattle of a wounded soldier under a pile of bodies could well place him alongside Yu Gengyu as a Decadent.

In the "second wave of French Symbolism in China," as Tu Kuo-ching names it,[11] Mu Mutian, Feng Naichao, and Wang Duqing created a different type of Chinese Symbolism. Like the French Symbolists, they discussed poetry among themselves. They sought ways to express indefinite moods through their poetry. Wang's expression was the most direct; Mu used sounds and silences to convey meaning, and aspired to make poetry from "mist and copper wires;" Feng explored light and shadow to create mystery and fleeting moods, and tried to make the "dead past" into a "living present."

By some definitions of Chinese Symbolism, Zhou Liangpei has pointed out, even a poem by Hu Shi could be considered Symbolist.[12] But the Chinese definitions did not form the basis for the choice of the remaining poets treated in chapter 7. Rather, Xu Yunuo, Liang Zongdai and Qin Zihao's poetry have reminded other comparatists of Symbolist poetry. Dai Wangshu, Bian Zhilin, and He Qifang have also been associated with Symbolist poetry in this way, but more recent studies have identified the first two with Modernism.

Given the difficulties of defining "Symbolism" and "Modernism," one might wonder whether another type of organization would have been preferable. One possibility would be to use the Chinese literary societies.[13] Xu Zhimo and Wen Yiduo were founders of the Crescent Moon Society, while Shao Xunmei associated with the group after it moved from Beijing to Shanghai. Xu Zhimo saw to the publication of Bian Zhilin's early poems, and Bian edited the *Crescent Monthly* for a time, but he later also became associated with the Modernists through publication in the journal *Xiandai: Les Contemporains*. Dai Wangshu also published in *Xiandai*, but there is no record of his having discussed poetry with Bian Zhilin. Wang Duqing, Mu Mutian, Feng Naichao, and Yu Dafu were members of the Creation Society. But both Wang and Yu broke with that Society when it gave up "art for art's sake" for "all art is propaganda." Yu Dafu later became a member of the Association for Literary Studies, whose slogan was "art for life's sake." Li Jinfa was also a member, although some of his poetry seemed to be "art for death's sake." Xu Yunuo, who probably never met Li Jinfa, was also a member, along with Lu Xun, who was also a member of several other societies. These ambiguities and crossings, while interesting, would have shifted the focus away from Baudelaire's reception in China.

While Baudelaire's dark and morbid images drew the attention of Chinese Decadents and Symbolists, at the same time, Baudelaire's Poet could soar above the sordidness of life. Although he could be like an albatross, at home in the clouds but clumsy and helpless on land, he could also ascend above the clouds, and even beyond the sun, and beyond Ennui and worries, as he does in the poem *"Élévation."* Rising aloft in his thoughts, the Poet could comprehend effortlessly "the language of flowers and of mute things." In another poem, as Duoduo noted, the poet is the sun. Poems about the Poet, and about poetry, are frequently associated with Baudelaire, and find parallels in China.

Baudelaire's Poet is elite. Just as the dog in his prose poem *"Le Chien et le flacon"* ["The Dog and the Flask"] prefers excrement to exquisite perfume, the public is unable to understand exquisite poetry. Wang Duqing had cried in the 1920s: "A poet who seeks people's comprehension is a seller of songs, not a pure poet!" Yet from the Yan'an years and through the Cultural Revolution, poets in the People's Republic were required to be "sellers of songs," and write for "peasants, workers, and soldiers," that is, for the "masses." Yet many intellectuals continued to read Western writers in secret.[14] When the "Misty" poets arose after the Cultural Revolution, many of them had read Baudelaire in secret in the years before. Turning away from the radical egalitarianism of the Cultural Revolution, students and scholars have been drawn back to elite poetry. Duoduo's rejection of the teaching that Mao Zedong was the sun enhanced his delight in finding Baudelaire's image of the poet as the sun.

Baudelaire is also connected with the figure of the *flâneur*, or stroller, in literature. His volume of prose poems presents scenes of Parisian life as observed and narrated by the poet as *flâneur*, who is sometimes sympathetic with what he sees, but is more often ironic, dispassionate and disengaged. Baudelaire's *flâneur* is also known to many readers through his verse poem *"À une passante"* ["To a Passerby"]. In a recent article Wang Yiyan again associates this poem with Dai Wangshu's *"Yuxiang"* ["Rainy Alley"].[15] In my own reading, as presented in chapter 8, Dai Wangshu's poem remains more pastoral than urban. The main subject of Wang's article is neither Baudelaire nor Dai Wangshu, but the fiction writer Shi Zhecun, and how Shi's characters move through Shanghai's urban landscape. By associating Shi Zhecun with the *flâneur* through his friend Dai Wangshu, Wang also lays a claim of Modernism for her subjects.

Baudelaire as *flâneur* moves through the Paris of the Second Empire, through both humble streets and great arcades. But the old familiar city is being torn down for the grand buildings and plans of Baron von Haussmann that we know today. It is hard not to see a parallel with China in the present century, when in China's great cities, Beijing and Shanghai,

whole neighborhoods are being torn down to make way for broad boulevards and enormous buildings.

"Urban literature in China needs Charles Baudelaire," Professor Li
Fengliang of Jinan University declared at the Ninth Guangdong Art Festi-
val in 2005. By this he meant writers who would "devotedly investigate
urban subjects and at the same time be critical of them." He found that
"older writers, though living in cities, could not shake off the psychological influence of their rural upbringings, while young writers tended to
write superficially about the material aspect of urban life without much
critical thought."[16] These comments underline the difficulties of comparison as they call up historical, cultural, generational, and other differences.
But they also spotlight Baudelaire's image and prestige in China. Professor Li could have gone further, to cite from Baudelaire's *"Le Cygne"* ["The
Swan"], *"La forme d'une ville / Change plus vite, hélas! que le coeur d'un
mortel"* [The form of a city / Changes quicker, alas, than a mortal's
heart].[17] In China's headlong rush toward modernization and globaliza-
tion, there also must be writers who speak for the human heart.

Baudelaire also figures in studies on Modernism. Although some
French literary historians point out the absence of *"le modernisme"* as a
French literary movement or school, Chinese critics generally do not
make such a careful distinction between *"le modernisme"* and *"la modernité."* Nor do they make such fine distinctions in associating French poetry
with Chinese Modernists, as mentioned in chapters 8 and 9. Baudelaire's
connection with Modernism comes largely through his art criticism,
which is receiving increasing attention in China. A full examination of
the meanings of Modernism lies beyond the present literary study.

The nineteenth-century French poet even finds a place in critical writings on postmodernism. In an article entitled "Baudelaire as Modernist
and Postmodernist," Fredric Jameson points out that there are "many
Baudelaires," as "each successive period or moment—each successive
new *present*—some new ghostly emanation or afterimage of the poet
peels off the inexhaustible text"[18] While Jameson's focus is elsewhere, his
remarks could not be more apropos of Baudelaire's reception in China.
From the social rebel who dyed his hair green to the aesthetic rebel who
found "beauty in ugliness," from the Decadent obsessed with sex, decay,
and death, to the Symbolist whose allusive language summed up all
poetry, from the Romantic who sought beauty and truth to the Modernist
who turned an ironic eye on his surroundings, Baudelaire was "present"
in each "present." His use of the sonnet form linked him to tradition,
while his use of the prose poem form was new and modern; both inspired poets and critics in China. The Chinese discovery of Baudelaire
and the role he played in the development of Chinese poetics are a not-
able part of twentieth-century literary history.

Baudelaire's protean quality and the inexhaustibility of his writings
assure him a place in the literary world of the twenty-first century. Now

that the meanings of difference and distance have been completely changed by air travel and electronic communication, finding Baudelaire in China no longer comes as a surprise. While the growth of electronic resources has facilitated study across national and language boundaries, however, the sheer amplitude of information has made studying reception across national and linguistic boundaries a more daunting task.

NOTES

1. *OC*, 6. Those who might be disturbed by the gender bias implicit in "mon frère" will be pleased by Chen Jingrong's rendering it as "wode gurou" 我的骨肉 [lit. 'my bone and flesh,' but equivalent to 'my flesh and blood'], in *Tuxiang*, 11.
2. Cowley, "The Golden House," see chapter 2.
3. Graham, trans., *Poems of the Late T'ang*, 91–92.
4. Xu Zhimo, "Bo-te-lai de sanwen shi," 407.
5. Lu Xun 魯迅, *Nahan* 吶喊 (1923).
6. Adolphe van Bever and Paul Léautaud, *Poètes d'aujourd'hui, morceaux choisis accompagnés de notices biographiques et d'un essai de bibliographie* (Paris: Mercure de France, 1900). The anthology had reached its fortieth edition by 1922.
7. Mu Mutian, *Faguo wenxue shi*, 2–3.
8. Tu Kuo-ch'ing, "The Introduction of French Symbolism . . ." *Tamkang Review* 10 (1980), 361.
9. Cheng Ch'ing-mao (Zheng Qingmao 鄭清茂), "Wang Cihui yanjiu 王次回研究: A Preliminary Study of Wang Tz'u-hui," *Guoli Taiwan daxue wen shi zhe xuebao* 國立臺灣大學文史哲學報, 14 (Nov. 1965): 241–99.
10. Recent examples include Jin Siyan's studies, and Lu Wenqian 陸文綪 *Faguo xiangzhengpai dui Zhongguo xiangzheng shi yingxiang yanjiu* 法國象徵派對中國象徵詩影響研究 [*Study of the Influences of French Symbolist Poetry on Chinese Symbolist Poetry*] (Chengdu: Sichuan daxue chubanshe, 1996). Lu gives Yu Gengyu and Shao Xunmei similar treatment.
11. Tu Kuo-ch'ing, "Introduction of French Symbolism," 355.
12. Zhou Liangpei 周良沛, "Juanshou" 卷首 ["Foreword"], in *Feng Naichao juan* 馮乃超卷 (Wuhan: Changjiang chubanshe, 1988), 6–7. Hu Shi rightly called his crude and prosaic poems "Experiments."
13. An anonymous reader made this suggestion.
14. An example from French literature is Dai Sijie's *Balzac et la petite tailleuse chinoise* (Paris: Gallimard, 2000), which has been translated into English by Ina Rilke as *Balzac and the Little Chinese Seamstress* (New York: Knopf, 2001), and made into a movie (New York: Empire Pictures, 2002). In a 2009 television series, "Beifeng nage chui" 北風那個吹 ["The North Wind Doth Blow"], by Gao Mantang et al., the hero gets in trouble by reading Stendhal's *The Red and the Black* to his fellow "sent-down" youths during the Cultural Revolution.
15. Wang, Yiyan. "Venturing into Shanghai: The Flâneur in Two of Shi Zhecun's Short Stories," *Modern Chinese Literature and Culture* 19, no. 2 (Fall 2007): 51–55.
16. Wing, ed., "The Absence of Urban Literature," *Szdaily*, web edition, www.newsgd.com/culture/culturenews/200506300036.htm (accessed 24 Jan. 2010).
17. *OC*, 85.
18. Fredric Jameson, "Baudelaire as Modernist and Postmodernist: The Dissolution of the Referent and the Artificial 'Sublime,'" in *Lyric Poetry: Beyond New Criticism*, ed. Chaviva Hošek and Patricia Parker (Ithaca, NY: Cornell University Press, 1985), 247.

Appendix 1
Baudelaire's Name in Chinese

BAUDELAIRE

Alphabetically by Pinyin:	Characters:	Source
bao-de-lai-er	鮑德萊耳	劉西謂
bao-de-lai-er	鮑得萊耳	張大明
bao-de-lai-er	鮑德来尔	張大明
bao-de-lai-er	鮑德萊爾	張大明
bao-duo-lai-er	鮑多萊耳	新文藝評論
bao-duo-lai-er	鮑多萊爾	張大明
bao-tao-lai- er	鮑桃萊爾	張大明
bao-tai-lai-er	鮑台萊爾	愉之
bao-te-lai	鮑特來	劉簽
bao-te-lai-er	鮑特萊爾	鄭振鐸, 戴望舒
bao-te-lai-er	鮑特來兒	郁達夫
bao-te-lei	鮑特雷	邵洵美
bao-te-lian-er	鮑特連爾	孫俍工
bei-du-li-er	被杜黎爾	邵洵美
bo-de-lai	波得萊	袁昌英
bo-de-lai	波德萊	文錚
bo-de-lai-er	波得萊爾	聞家駟
bo-de-lai-er	波德萊爾	徐霞村
bo-de-lai-er	波德莱尔	郭宏安, 程抱一, 胡品青, 趙聰, 陳敬容
bo-de-lai-ya	波德莱亞	錢鐘書

bo-de-lei-lu	波得雷路	穆木天
bo-de-lie-er	博德列爾	張大明
bo-de-nai-er	波得乃爾	李璜. 周無
bo-de-nai-er	波德奈尒	續楓林
bo-du-li-er	波杜黎爾	石克
bo-duo-lai	波多賴	張大明
bo-duo-lai-er	波多萊爾	邢鵬舉, 穆木天
bo-luo-lai-er	波羅萊耳	張大明
bo-te-lai	波特萊	周作人, 徐志摩, 卞之琳
bo-te-lai-er	波特萊爾	王維克, 杜國清, 覃子豪, 紀弦, 馬斯
bo-te-lai-er	波特萊尒	金志平
bo-te-lai-er	波特萊耳	周作人
bo-te-lai-er	波特來耳	君彥, 聞天, 趙景深, 劉延凌
bo-tuo-lei-er	波陀雷爾	田漢
po-tai-lai-er	婆台來兒	厨川白村
po-te-lai	婆特來	廬月化
po-te-lai-er	婆特來尔	張大明
pu-te-lai-er	菩特萊爾	徐志摩
pu-te-lai-er	浦特萊爾	徐仲年
pu-te-lei	浦特雷	辭海

CHARLES

cha-li	查理
cha-li-si	查理斯
sha-er	沙兒
sha-le	沙勒
xia-er	夏尒
xia-er	夏爾
zhali	乍力
xiao-yu	尚聿

Appendix 2
"Correspondances"

Correspondances

Charles Baudelaire

La Nature est un temple où de vivants piliers
Laissent parfois sortir de confuses paroles;
L'homme y passe à travers des forêts de symboles
Qui l'observent avec des regards familiers.

Comme de longs échos qui de loin se confondent
Dans une ténébreuse et profonde unité,
Vaste comme la nuit et comme la clarté,
Les parfums，les couleurs et les sons se répondent.

Il est des parfums frais comme des chairs d'enfants,
Doux comme les hautbois，verts comme les prairies,
—Et d'autres，corrompus，riches et triomphants,

Ayant l'expansion des choses infinies,
Comme l'ambre，le musc，le benjoin et l'encens,
Qui chantent les transports de l'esprit et des sens.

田漢 (1921)

『自然』是一個大寺院，那裡的話柱
　　時時吐矇矓的語。
人遙逍于象徵之森林，
　　而內觀以親熱的眼，
好像遠處來的悠長的反響
　　混合着陰森深遠的太極。
夜一樣，光明一樣的廣大，
　　香色，和音與他相答。
那種香像小兒的肉一樣的鮮麗，
像木笛一般的優婉，牧場一般的油碧

ーー其他則為腐敗的豐富而凱旋的香氣
備一切事物的膨脹：
　　像琥珀，乳香，安息香，和麝香似的，
對靈魂與官能的法悅。

[少年中國 3， no. 5 (1920): 20 (original typographical disposition)]

卞之琳 (1933)

應和

自然是一個神殿，有許多活柱
不時地講出話來，總模糊不清；
行人穿過一重重象徵底森林，
一路接受着它們親密的注目。

有如漫長的回聲在遠方混合，
變成了一致，又深又暗的一片，
浩渺，無邊如黑夜，光明如白天，
芳香，顏色與聲音在互相應和。

有些芳香新鮮如小孩底肌膚，
悠傷宛轉如清笛，青翠如草地，
還有些芳香，富貴，淫蕩與威武，

展得開，比得上，無界限的東西，
像麝香，琥珀香，安息香與馨香
歌唱心靈上與感覺上的神往。

梁宗岱 (1934)

契合

自然是座大神殿，在那裡
活柱有時發出模糊的話；
行人經過象徵底森林下，
接受着它們親密的注視。

有如遠方的漫長的回聲
混成幽暗和深沉的一片，
渺茫如黑夜，浩蕩如白天，
顏色，芳香與聲音相呼應。

有些芳香如新鮮的孩肌，
宛轉如清笛，青綠如草地，
ーー更有些呢，朽腐，濃郁，雄壯。

具有無限底曠邈與開敞，
像琥珀，麝香，安息香，馨香，
歌唱心靈與官能底熱狂。

穆木天 (1935)

交響

自然是一座聖殿，那裡邊，活的柱子
時時地泄散出漠然不可捉摸的話語；
人在那裡經過，穿過了象徵的森林，
森林在注視着他，用着熟識的眼睛。

如同漫長的回響在遠處融和着，
在一種幽暗的深沉的統一之下，
廣漠地如暗夜又如光明，
各種的薰香、彩色和音響互相呼應，

是有些薰香，如嬰兒的肉肌般新鮮，
如草地般青翠，如木笛般清囀，
——而又有些，是腐朽的、濃郁的、雄壯的、
具有着無限的事物的擴散，
如琥珀、麝香、安息香和檀香，
在歌唱着心靈和官感的狂醉。

穆木天 (1940)

交響

「自然」是一座聖殿，在那裡，活的柱子
時時發出來漠然不清楚的話語。
人穿過象徵的森林，在那裡經過，
森林瞅着他以一副熟視的眼睛。

如深長的回響在遠處互相融和着，
在一種冥暗的幽深的統一之中，
廣漠地如暗夜又如光明似地，
薰香，彩色和聲音在交響着。

穆木天，法國文學史 (Quatrains only)

王了一 (1940)

交感

宇宙一蘭若，
楹柱皆有情。
偶然相攀談，

隱約笑語生。
行人此經過，
森然見群形。
逢人如相識，
凝視不轉睛。

六合祇一體，
深邃而幽冥。
其闊如夜色，
其遠如光明。
色香與音響，
千里相感並。
有如空谷音，
迢迢寄回聲。

世有極品香，
鮮如初生嬰。
其和如燻篪，
其綠如郊坰。
又有腐朽香，
濃郁迷性靈。
琥珀、檀、乳、麝，
粉然難指名。
精神通感覺，
互遞芝蘭馨。

(Preface dated 1940; republished 1980 in simplified characters)

戴望舒 **(1947)**

應和

自然是一廟堂，那裡活的柱石
不時地傳出模糊隱約的語音：
人穿過象徵的林從那裡經行
樹林望着他，投以熟稔的凝視。

正如悠長的回聲遙遙地合併，
歸入一個幽黑而淵深的和協--
廣大有如光明，浩漫有如黑夜--
香味，顏色和聲響都互相呼應。

有的香味新鮮如兒童的肌膚，
柔和有如洞簫，翠綠有如牧場，
--別的香味呢，腐爛，軒昂而豐富。

具有着無極限的品物底擴張，
如琥珀香，麝香，安息香，篆煙香，
那樣歌唱性靈和官感的歡狂。

覃子豪 **(1956)**

交感

自然是住有醉者的宮殿 （一個有着活柱的 for 住有醉者的）
時時發出朦朧的語言； （語音 for 語言）
人們經過象徵之森林
用熟悉的眼光察看。 （熟習 for 熟悉）

如從遠方混合的悠長的回聲 （像 for 如）
出自深沉的單純與黑暗，
廣闊如光明和夜晚，
香氣，色彩，音調的反應。 （是 added to head of line）

新鮮的氣息和兒童的身體，
柔和如笛音，綠色似牧場， （如 for 似）
還有敗壞，財富與勝利，

無限的萬物滋長，
如琥珀，麝香，安息香與阿拉伯香熏，
它歌唱官能與精神的熱情。 （它 omitted）

(The first version formed part of a lecture dated 1956; in the second version the first line was corrected， and minor changes were made for an anthology of translations).

杜國清 **(1977)**

萬物照應

「自然」是一座神殿，在那兒活柱
不時地發出曖昧朦朧的語言；
人經過那兒穿越象徵的林間，
森林望着他，以熟識的凝視。

像那悠長的回聲在遠方混合
於幽暗深奧的一種冥合之中，
廣漠和光明且如黑夜之無窮，
芳香色彩和聲音互相呼應着。

有的芳香涼爽如幼兒的肌膚，
碧綠如牧場而且柔和如木笛，
－－別的芳香，腐爛、得意、豐富，

具有無限物那種無窮擴張力，
像龍涎香麝香安息香與焚香，
在高唱着精神與官感的歡狂。

楊昌年 **(1978)**

交感

「自然」是一座廟宇，那裡有活的柱
不時放出許多迷離紛雜的言語；
人們徘徊着走過象徵的林子
它用熟悉的眼光不斷地審視。

如起自那遠方的回聲，
悠長，深邃，單純，而暗澹，
廣闊如月色柔柔的夜晚，
香氣，色彩，音調，和實體相感應。

X 種新鮮的香味，似嬰孩的肌膚，
長笛似的溫柔，而又草原一般的綠，
還有財富，敗壞，和勝利。

在此，無限的萬物滋長，
如琥珀，麝香，安息香與阿拉伯的香燻，
它們在歌唱着官能與精神的熱情。

程抱一 **(1970， 1980)**

對應

自然是座廟堂，其間萬千活柱
不時吐露出混淆朦朧的話語； (80：綜合 for 混淆)
人穿過這象徵的森林時，它們
以熟識親密的眼光注視着他。

宛如迴蕩不息的回聲，在遠方
混凝成深不可測的渾然一體，
色、香以及音響也互相呼應啊，
比夜影和日光顯得更為廣闊。

有那樣的芳香，鮮潤有如童膚，
柔和有如管樂，青翠有如綠笛。
另外一些則是：腐爛，豐麗，輝煌。

含孕着無盡事物的無邊擴張—— (80：無限 for 無邊)
琥珀啊、麝香啊、色染啊、香末啊，
歌詠着靈魂和肉體的大歡娛！ (80：交歡 for 歡娛)

陳敬容 **(1980)**

通感

大自然是一座神殿，活生生的柱子
時時從那裡吐出嘈雜的語言，
人們穿越過象徵的森林打殿前走過，
柱子朝他們注視，慇懃又親切。

仿彿是長長的回聲從遠方
溶合為神秘而深沉的一體，
浩潮如黑暗又好像光明，
芳香，色彩，聲音在互相感應。

有一些香氣鮮嫩如嬰兒的肌膚，
雙簧管一樣柔和，草原般青綠，
還有一些呢，腐朽、濃郁而神氣。

具有着無限事物的擴展、伸張，
猶如琥珀、麝香、安息香和乳香，
歌唱着精神與感覺的運行來往。

郭宏安 **(1981)**

應和

自然是座廟宇，那裡活的柱子
不時地傳出模糊隱約的話音，
打那經過的人穿過象徵之林，
樹林望着他投以熟悉的凝視。

如同悠長的回聲遙遙地匯合
在一個混沌而深邃的整體中
廣大浩漫，好像黑夜連着光明——
香味、顏色和聲音都互相應和。

有些香味新鮮如兒童的肌膚，
柔和如雙簧管，青翠如綠草場，
——別的則陳腐、濃郁，涵蓋了萬物。

像無機無限的東西四散飛揚，
如同龍涎香、麝香、安息香、乳香
那樣歌唱心靈和感官的熱狂。

（Guo's 1992 version differs enough to be given separately）

莫渝 **(1985)**

冥合

「大自然」是座神殿，那兒的活柱
有時傳出朦朧的語言；
人們從那兒穿過像徵之林
樹林會以親切得眼光注視。

正如遙遠的悠悠回音
混入黝黑深邃的和諧中，
廣漠如黑夜，浩瀚似光明，
馨香色澤和音響互為呼應。

有些馨香清新似孩童肌膚，
溫柔似木笛，碧綠似牧場，
--別的馨香，腐爛、繁富且軒昂，

具有無限事物的擴張力，
宛若龍涎香、麝香、安息香和薰香，
歌唱着性靈與官能的激情。

錢春綺 (1987)

感應

自然是一座神殿，那裡有活的柱子
不時發出一些含糊不清的語音；
行人經過該處，穿過象徵的森林，
森木露出親切的眼光對人注視。

仿彿遠遠傳來一些悠長的回音，
互相混成幽昧而深邃的統一體
像黑夜又像光明一樣茫無邊際，
芳香、色彩、音響全在互相感應。

有些芳香新鮮得像兒童肌膚一樣，
柔和得像雙簧管，綠油油像牧場，
——另外一些，腐朽、豐富、得意揚揚，

具有一種無限物的擴展力量，
仿彿琥珀、麝香、安息香和乳香，
在歌唱着精神和感官的熱狂。

鄭克魯 (1990)

通感

自然是座廟宇，有生命的柱子
有時候發出含含糊糊的話語：

人從這象徵的森林穿越過去，
森林觀察人，投以親切的注視。

仿彿從遠處傳來的悠長回音，
混合成幽暗而深邃的統一體，
如同黑夜又像光明，廣袤無際
香味，顏色和聲音在交相呼應。

有的香味嫩如孩子肌膚那樣，
柔和像雙簧管，翠綠好似草原，
——其餘的腐蝕，豐富和得意洋洋

具有無限事物那種擴張力量，
龍涎香，麝香，安息香，乳香一般，
在歌唱着頭腦和感官的熱狂。

郭宏安 (1992)

應和

自然是座廟宇，那裡活的柱子
有時說出了模模糊糊的話音
人從那裡過，穿越象徵的森林，
森林用熟悉的目光將他注視。

如同悠長的回聲遙遙地匯合
在一個混沌深邃的統一體中
廣大浩漫好像黑夜連着光明——
芳香、顏色和聲音都互相應和。

有的芳香新鮮若兒童的肌膚，
柔和如雙簧管，青翠如綠草場，
——別的則朽腐、濃郁、涵蓋了萬物，

像無極無限的東西四散飛揚，
如同龍涎香、麝香、安息香、乳香
那樣歌唱精神與感覺的激昂。

蘇鳳哲 (1992)

應和

自然是座廟宇，那裡活的柱石，
不時說出模模糊糊的語音。
人們穿過象徵的森林，
森林投以親切的目光注視着行人。

遠方傳來的悠久的回聲匯合
為一個混沌而深邃的統一體，
像茫茫黑夜連着無際的光明，
芳香、色彩、聲音在互相應和。

有的清爽芳香如兒童的肌膚，
柔聲如雙簧管，翠綠如草場，
——還有的腐敗、濃郁、涵養了萬物，

像無極限的東西飄散着飛揚，
如琥珀、麝香、安息香和乳香，
在歌唱精神與感覺的歡狂。

張秋紅 **(1996)**

契合

大自然正是一座神殿，那充滿活力的柱石
往往發出朦朦朧朧的喃喃的聲音：
人漫步穿越這一片象徵的森林，
森林投出親切的目光，注視着人的舉止。

宛如來自遠處的一陣陣悠長的回聲，
融入深邃而不可思議的統一體中，
像光明一樣無邊無際，又像黑暗一樣無窮無盡，
香味、色彩、聲音紛紛互相呼應。

有的香味鮮嫩如兒童的肌膚，
輕柔如雙簧管的音調，翠綠如草地，
-- 有的香味卻異化、絢麗而眉飛色舞，

流露出無限的天地萬物的心跡，
仿佛龍涎香、麝香、安息香和乳香，
歌唱着精神的振奮與感覺的激昂。

尹康莊 **(1998)**

交感

自然是座廟宇，那裡的活柱
不時吐出朦朧的話語：
逍遙於象徵森林的游子，
樹木都親切地把他注視。

恰似融合於遠方的悠長回聲，
在一個黑黨而深邃的整體中，
浩瀚無限，像黑暗和光明不可窮極，

芳香和顏色與它應答不已。

那馨香，似孩童的肌膚沁人心脾，
像笛聲一樣優柔，牧場般油碧，
——其它則為腐敗、濃重、彌漫萬物的氣息。

有如無窮無盡的事物繁衍擴張，
就像麝、琥珀、乳香和安息香，
齊聲歌唱心靈與感官的交歡。

文愛藝 (2007)

契合

大自然是座神殿，那充滿活力的柱石，
時常發出神奇的聲音；
人們從此穿越象徵的森林，
森林一熟識的目光將他注視。

正如悠悠的回聲搖搖地回應，
融入幽遠深邃的和諧之中，
像光明無邊無際，有似黑暗無窮無盡，
芳香、色澤、音響互為感知。

有的馨香清麗如幼兒的肌膚，
柔和如雙簧管的輕音，青翠如綠色，
另外一些，則已腐朽，涵蓋了萬物。

像無限無極的事物四散飛揚，
彷彿龍涎香、麝香、安息香和熏香，
渾然一體抒吐著性靈的振奮與觀感的激昂。

Appendix 3
Poems in Chinese

Xu Zhimo (徐志摩 1897–1931)

這是一個懦怯的世界

這是一個懦怯的世界：
    容不得戀愛，容不得戀愛！
披散你的滿頭髮，
赤露你的一雙腳；
    跟著我來，我的戀愛，
拋棄這個世界
殉我們的戀愛！

我拉著你的手，
愛，你跟著我走；
    聽憑荊棘把我們的腳心刺透，
    聽憑冰雹劈破我們的頭，
你跟著我走，
我拉著你的手，
    逃出了牢籠，恢復我們的自由！

    跟著我來，
    我的戀愛！
人間已經掉落在我們的後背，——
看呀，這不是白茫茫的大海？
白茫茫的大海，
白茫茫的大海，
    無邊的自由，我與你與戀愛！

順著我的指頭看，
那天邊一小星的藍——
    那是一座島，島上有青草，
    鮮花，美麗的走獸與飛鳥；
快上這輕快的小艇，

去到那理想的天庭——
　　戀愛，歡欣，自由——
　　辭別了人間，永遠！

志摩的詩1925, 徐志摩全集II (1969), 40–43.

　　叫化活該

『行善的大姑，修好的爺，』
西北風尖刀似的猛刺着他的臉，
『賞給我一點你們吃賸的油水吧！』
一團模糊的黑影，捱緊在大門邊。

『可憐我快餓死了，發財的爺，』
大門內有歡笑，有紅爐，有玉杯；
『可憐我快凍死了，有福的爺，』
大門外西北風笑說，『叫化活該！』

我也是戰栗的黑影一堆，
蠕伏在人道的前街；
我也只要一些同情的溫暖，
遮掩我的剮殘的餘骸——

但這沉沉的緊閉的大門：誰來理睬；
街道上只冷風的嘲諷，『叫化活該！』

志摩的詩1925, 徐志摩全集 II (1969), 112–13.

　　古怪的世界

從松江的石湖塘
上車來老婦一雙，
顫巍巍的承住弓形的老人身，
多謝（我猜是）普渡山的盤龍藤：

青布棉襖，黑布棉套，
頭毛半禿，齒牙半耗：
肩捱肩的坐落在陽光暖暖的窗前，
畏蒽的，呢喃的，像一對寒天的老燕；

震震的乾枯的手背，
震震的皺縮的下頦：
這二老！是妯娌，是姑嫂，是姐妹？——
緊捱著，老眼中有傷悲的眼淚！

憐憫！貧苦不是卑賤，
老衰中有無限莊嚴；——
老年人有什麼悲哀，為什麼悽傷？

為什麼在這快樂的新年，拋卻家鄉？

同車裡雜選的人聲，
軌道上疾轉著車輪；
我獨自的，獨自的沉思這世界古怪——
是誰吹弄著那不調諧的人道的音籟？

志摩的詩 1925, 徐志摩全集 II (1969), 81–83.

生活

陰沉，黑暗，毒蛇似的蜿蜒，
生活逼成了一條通道：
一度陷入，你祇可以向前，
手捫索着冷壁的黏潮，

在妖魔的臟腑內掙扎，
頭頂不見一線的天光，
這魂魄，在恐怖的壓迫下，
除了消滅更有什麼願望？
五月二十九日

猛虎集 (1931), 90–91. 徐志摩全集 II (1969), 448–49.

Yu Gengyu (于賡虞1902–1963)

山頭凝思

春去了，希望尚深眠於零落的落花之中，
為了生命之慾願終日輾轉於骷髏之塚；
今凝思山頭之林下，痛哭於夕陽之殘紅，
將不老的悲哀投寄於蒼空征途的孤鴻。

海鳥去了，三兩游艇裡謳着幽婉之歌聲，
在夜神統治的天下諧和於葬禮的墓鐘；
此時我以神與魔鬼之樂獨自歌吟新生，
為滿足敵人之歡笑我痛飲於此黑夜中！

『狂夫，將幻想展開，歌着，鞭打天上之群星！』
世紀死了疲憊的靈魂在荒誕之夢未醒；
無人了，野林顫慄之韻為我慘笑於寂靜，
聽鴻鳴，似往日飛逝的夢影哀吟於古井！

悲哉！慘黑之山道上只我個人酩酊，獨行，
挽不回的青春如一屍體正沉默於夜瑩；
從此我嗟嘆着去了，無論走入地獄，天宮，
將一切貽於人間之廢墟，輾轉骷髏之塚。

骷髏上的薔薇, 1927, in Fung, et al. (1974), 370–71.

魔鬼的舞蹈

這正是偉大的夜之世界！

飲宴散了，濃烈的紅酒給我不可捉摸的力量，因而，我尚能在生命的國土的刦餘的殘燼中悲哀，迴憶，痛哭。

不堪言，生命於往日，現在，只是一個飄渺的夢，在魔鬼的舞蹈與歌吟中無痕的逝了！我不能，不堪想像歌舞的慘影；聲韻，步態，只是一片模糊的慘紅與蒼黑的結題。微笑與溫柔變為不忍一視的慘紅，憤怒與慘暴變為刺心慘動的蒼黑：遠了，靈動的生之希望！這一切在今宵的迷醉中，踉蹌中都是毒烈的火箭，射中了已死之心靈。

星月冷明，萬有沉於夢境，只我孤零一人臥於海濱之草茵，任自然無忌的摧殘，傷害；任魔鬼無忌的在心頭舞蹈，歌吟。在它踉蹌的步態，朦朧的歌聲裡，泳化紅酒，紙煙，毒藥於一切希望之宮。呵--昔日金色的蓬髮業已蒼白，蘋果的面顏業已蒼灰，一切，一切如一龍腫的老人－青春死了，其顏色如枯萎的薔薇上之霧水。

毀滅！將生命拋於奇醜的蒼黑的污池，毒斃於死水，無須戀戀於痛苦足下之生命，作魔鬼舞蹈與歌吟之場！嗟呼，孤零，沉醉罷，沉醉於微笑，沉醉於死亡，沉醉於輝煌的宮殿，沉醉於長流的青堤，因是，縱魔鬼歌舞於心峰，髮上，亦能暫時淪於不能記憶的爛醉－有如死滅，將一切遺忘。

噫，如斯進行着生命之韻調，永遠，永遠沉於不可捉摸的夢境。飲宴散了，從毒醉中我窺見了這平靜的生命……

這正是偉大的夜之世界！

魔鬼的舞蹈 (1928), 24–26.

Shao Xunmei (邵洵美 1905–1968)

愛的叮囑

你是知道了的，我怎愿
我底玉石之書去走進那金銀之寶庫！
進去了時你是知道的，
我底有歸宿的心又入了無目的的路。

為什麼呢，好端端的魚
要獨自在泛濫洶湧的浪濤中去游泳？
為什麼呢，小小的羊兒
要獨自在獅洞虎穴狼窩狐窟前游行？

啊使若你心愛的人兒
徘徊在比牢獄更可怕的陷阱之周圍，
你要是是有魂靈的人，
可仍像袒腹的荷葉臨着秋風般安泰？

啊已將疲憊而厭煩了。
從生之戶帶着快樂憂愁到死之門前。
啊關開的門戶太多了，
請勿再問來去的道路而對仇讎乞憐。

花一般的罪惡 (1918), 35–36.

昨日的園子

靜了靜了黑夜又來了；
她披著灰色的尼裳，
懷抱著憂鬱與悲傷，
啊她是殺光明的屠刀。

她隱瞞了上帝的住處；
牛馬雞犬烏龜與人，
于是便迷茫地搜尋，
末後找到了魔鬼之居。

這裡有個昨日的園子，
青的葉兒是黃了的；
鮮的花兒是謝了的；
活潑的鳥兒是死了的。

還有一對有情的人兒，
相相地擁抱了親吻；
沒有氣吓也沒有聲，
啊他們是上帝的愛兒。

花一般的罪惡 (1918), 15.

日昇樓下

車聲笛聲吐痰聲，
倏忽的烟形，
女人的衣裙。

似風動雲地人湧，
有肉腥血腥
汗腥的陣陣。

屋頂塔尖時辰鐘，
十點零十分；
星中雜電燈。

我在十字的路口，
戰顫着欲情；
偷想着一吻。

花一般的罪惡 (1918), 45–46.

Li Jinfa (李金髮 1900–1976)

生之炎火

"La sottise, l'erreur, le péché, la lésive, [*sic*]
Occupent nos ésprit [*sic*] et travaillent nos corps."
—Ch. Baudelaire

我看見魔鬼
在黃金年歲的頭上跳躍,
張牙欲囓,
於是我遨遊着
接收當頭的一棒。

我遨遊着,
鍛鍊這孱弱的心,
如雪花在岩壑裡嗟嘆,
將拉手同訪此神奇:
海浪呻吟着,
洶湧地到崖石之斷落處。
喁喁了一會,
產生無數青白的沫,
如"河之干兮"的揮淚,
頹委地去了。
但有多少徘徊!
他帶了什麼去?

我欲與聞生的滋味,
遂欺騙一切傀儡我的壞人;
來日方長,
心頭的幾片紅英,
就如此飛散麼?
遠處的天鵝,
流血在呼喚裡,
可惜 Diane 深睡了,
我願摸撫其悠長之頸,
縱疏懶的游戲, (呵自然之愛媳。)
阻礙我的前程。
當然可愛,
一片赤銅似的陽光;
河流流出反照,
古松頹臥如女神,
但這等詩意的結局。
將停止心房的音韻,
眼兒失亮,
口角流涎。

我欲與聞生的滋味
遂欺騙一切傀儡我的壞人。
我僅需要一張空地,

油膩處產生多數色螺哥,
在葉之陰處修養,
蟻螞是太擠擁的,
蚯蚓無味!
幾根草兒足矣。

為幸福而歌 (1926), 201–4.

我愛這殘照的無力

"On dit [*sic*] ton regard d'une vapeur couvert;
Ton oeil mystérieux (est-il bleu, gris, or vert?)
Alternativement tender, rêveur, cruel,
Réfléchit l'indolence et la pâleur du ciel"
— Ch. Baudelaire

I

吁,我愛這殘照的無力,
無論其深睡在古牆下,或輕率地點染在叢林之葉上,吁,我愛這殘照的
無力,海兒既入靜寂之境,即細微的不平之氣息,亦不能聽到,惟信託
風兒趕着黑雲去聚會,組成若干不相識之外形。陽光——從其額上穿
過,並給茅蘆幾片反照,但在長林後的成為碎片,在草地上呻吟,沒勇
氣到天涯去退守。(吁我愛殘照的無力。) 銅色的天空,金色的雲,鉛色
的山巔,漆色的洋海,赭色的湖光,橙色的松幹,深青的菜園,都馴服
在殘照的無力裡。

II

東角變成暗赤,他該逃了,夜色一步步地向前,他更無力使雲兒透明,
只待片刻內,黃昏老死在故丘上,吁我愛殘照的無力,烟突裡吹出一片
微白,向天際直奔,似欲向若何人告急,但這城圈倦了,在我目前欲
睡,口裡咿哦其疲乏的聲息,--像遠海波浪衝打和群衆擁擠之沉音,
吁,我愛殘照的無力,以是他抱頭睡了。
我們再留片刻,呵,片刻!最後的陽光將使我們倒影錯亂,或能在這生
疏之地,留下不可忘記之痕跡,然而我恐怖了,何處的矮林,能遮蔽我
四體,吁我愛殘照的無力,何處得霧兒能朦朧我尖銳之眼.

為幸福而歌 (1926), 264–66.

X

我的靈魂是荒野的鐘聲:
明白春之踪跡,
和金秋痛哭的緣故,
草地上少女的私語;
行星反照在殘波上,
他們商量各自的美麗,
更有靈兒傲慢地走過。

惟年歲遷移了,
海潮的鬧聲
震聾了她的耳;

遠方的霧氣
迷離她的兩眼；
他遂休止了這監察。

呵，我們離這苦痛之鄉，
去救殘廢的靈魂，
安放她到錢塘之江畔－
多麼舟楫來往－
夜亦得照着平靜下去。

食客與凶年 (1927), 3–4.

Wang Duqing (王獨清 1898–1940)

我從Café中出來

我從Café中出來，
身上添了
中酒的
疲乏，
我不知道
向那一處走去，纔是我底
暫時的住家……
啊，冷靜的街衢，
黃昏，細雨！

我從Café中出來，
在帶着醉
無言地
獨走，
我底心內
感着一種，要失了故園的
浪人底哀愁……
啊，冷靜的街衢，
黃昏，細雨。

王獨清選集 (1947), 68–69.

賽因河之冬夜

冷酷的冬夜蒙罩了巴黎全城，
繁華都市漸漸地變成寂靜；
埋在灰色下的這近代文明之區，
風在繞着嚎啕悲鳴。
這時那行人稀少的塞因河邊，
有幾個貧民睡在敗葉之中。

天上的月色朦朧，
隱約地可看見這幾個人底形影：

他們都是容顏瘠瘦，
他們都是亂髮蓬蓬，
都是裹着件襤褸的短衣，
像死了一樣的臥着不動。

啊啊，兄弟們，你們冷麼？
你們可是今日給人作了一天的苦工，
纔買了一瓶紅酒，就坐在這地上痛飲不停，
發狂了一般的亂叫雜唱以後，
倒下去便爛醉不醒？
啊，可憐的兄弟們喲，
ABSINTHE 是被他們禁了！
再沒有那樣強烈的好酒，
使你們得安然作長時間的甜夢！

你們可還記得那過去的戰爭？
你們是曾怎樣為了祖國去犧牲！
血泊塗污了你們底兩手，
炮烟熏黑了你們底雙鬢……
到現在他們都吼起了"馬賽歌"歡祝得勝，
又有誰來管你們這些退了伍的苦兵？

啊,兄弟們,醒些兒罷！
你們且傾耳細聽,
是那裡淫蕩的笑聲？
夜珈琲店內的電火正晞,
他們正在那兒逞性亂行:
妖女在猥抱緊擁,
短髮半裸的黑奴做着引起肉感的Chica之樂器動興……
啊,可憐的兄弟們喲,
你們聽！你們聽！

風就不停地這樣悲鳴！
我查這文明都市不過是罪惡的深坑！
兄弟們，醒來罷，醒來罷，
唉！我看你們只是沉睡不醒！
我恨不得學一個羅馬底Nero，
把這繁華的巴黎城用火來一烘！

獨清詩選 (1931), 46–49.

Mu Mutian (穆木天 1900–1971)

蒼白的鐘聲

蒼白的　鐘聲　衰腐的　朦朧
疏散　玲瓏　荒涼的　濛濛的　谷中
---衰草　千重　萬重---
聽　永遠　的荒唐的　古鐘

聽　千聲　萬聲

古鐘　　飄散在水波之皎皎
古鐘　　飄散在灰綠的白楊之梢
古鐘　　飄散在風聲之蕭蕭
---月影　逍遙　逍遙---
古鐘　飄散　在白雲之飄飄

一縷　一縷的腥香
水濱　枯草　荒徑的　近旁
---先年的悲哀永久的　憧憬　新觴---
聽　一聲　一聲　的荒涼
從古鐘　飄蕩　飄蕩　不知哪裡　朦朧之鄉
古鐘　消散　入　絲動的　游烟

古鐘　寂蟄　入　睡水的　微波　潺潺
古鐘　寂蟄　入　淡淡的　遠遠的　雲山
古鐘　飄流　入　茫茫　四海　之　間
---暝暝的　先年　永遠的歡樂　辛酸

軟軟的　古鐘　飛蕩隨　月光之波
軟軟的　古鐘　緒緒的　入　帶帶之銀河
---呀　遠遠的　古鐘　反響　古鄉之歌---
渺渺的　古鐘　反映出　故鄉之歌
遠遠的　古鐘　入　蒼茫之鄉鎮　無何

聽　殘朽的　古鐘　在　灰黃的　谷中
入　無限之　茫茫　散淡　玲瓏
枯葉　衰草　隨呆呆之　北風
聽　千聲　萬聲---朦朧朦朧---
荒唐　茫茫　敗廢的　永遠的　故鄉　之　鐘聲聽　黃昏之深谷
中

(二六，一，二，東海道上)
Fung et al. (1974), 305–7, *Daxi* (1935), 268–69.

雞鳴聲

─與獨清─

雞鳴聲
喚不起
　　真的
　　哀悲
我不知
哪裡是家
　　哪裡是國
　　哪裡是愛人

應向哪裡歸
啊　殘燈　敗頹

雞鳴聲
引不起
　　新的
　　酸情
我不知
　　哪裡是明
　　哪裡是暗
　　哪裡是朦朧
　　應奔哪裡行
　　啊　敗頹　殘燈

二六，四，二四，夜三時半，中野
創造月刊1, no. 5 (1927): 4–5.

Feng Naichao (馮乃超 1901–1983)

消沉的古加籃

樹林的幽語	沉潛的殘照
嗡嗡---	暗紅---
幕靄的氛氳	飄零的游心
朦朧---	哀痛---
遠寺的古塔	片片的鄉愁
峙空---	晚鏑---
消沉的情緒	黃昏的氣息
蒼蒼---	頹唐---
天空的美麗	萬籟的律動
悽愴---	衰亡---
禱堂的幽寂	消沉的古寺
渺茫---	深藏---
萬古的飛翔	蒼茫的懷古
沉淪---	無盡---
夜靜的信仰	傳奇的情熱
身殉---	灰燼---
無言的緘默	墓坟的紀念
逡巡---	青春---

創造月刊, 1, no. 1 (1926) 78.

默

輕煙　籠罩着池塘底安眠
沉默　枯朽着夢裡的睡蓮

冬天來到疲乏的草根頭
靜悄悄地殺着蒼白的微笑
陽光隱在輕盈的煙消
不照樹陰影裡的哀愁

怠倦的枯枝愁訴
黃金的新秋也衰老
銀白的長髮浸池中
輕輕拂掃浪紋的懊惱

我聽得幾句嘎聲的譏嘲
老醜的烏鴉飛鳴在樹梢
沉紅的落葉積滿了空寂的心
怎的感謝那無情的胡鬧

隆冬的嚴肅遠過於祈禱
沒有殉教者的苦惱
憂愁的聖母默現在空間
守護着靈魂的日暮

紅紗燈，1928. Fung et al. (1974), 513–14

紅紗燈

森嚴的黑暗的深奧的深奧的殿堂之中央
紅紗的古燈微明地玲瓏地點在午夜之心

苦惱的沉默呻吟在夜影的睡眠之中
我聽得鬼魅魑魅的跫聲舞蹈在半空

烏雲叢簇地叢簇地蓋着蛋白色的月亮
白練滿河流若伏在野邊的裸體的屍殭

紅紗的古燈緩慢地漸漸地放大了光暈
森嚴的黑暗的殿堂撒了滿地莊重的黃金

愁寂地靜悄地黑衣的尼姑踱過了長廊
一步一聲怎的悠久又怎的消滅無踪

我看見在森嚴的黑暗的殿堂的神龕

明滅地惝晃地一盞紅紗的燈光顫動

創造月刊 1, no. 1 (1927): 19.

Xu Yunuo (徐玉諾 1894–1958)

詩

輕輕的捧着那些奇怪的小時，
慢慢的走入林去；
小鳥們默默的向我點頭，
小蟲兒向我瞥眼。
我走入更陰森更深密的林中，
暗把那些奇怪東西放在溼漉漉的草上。

看呵，這個林中！
一個個小蟲都張出他的面孔來，
一個個小葉都睜開他的眼睛來，
音樂是雜亂的美妙，
樹林中，這裡，那裡，
滿滿都是奇異的，神秘的詩絲織着。

將來之花園 (1922), 91–92.

Liang Zongdai (梁宗岱 1903–1983)

晚禱

--呈汎，捷二兄
不彈也罷，
雖然這清婉潺湲
微颸蕩着的
蘭香一般縹緲的琴兒。
一切憂傷與煩悶
都消融在這安靜的曠野，
無邊的黑暗，
與雍穆的愛慕下了。
讓心靈怡謐的微跳
深深的頌讚
造物主溫嚴的慈愛。

-二三，六。一三
1924, 晚禱 (1933), 49.

Qin Zihao (覃子豪 1912–1963)

髮

(This is the third and final section of original poem, following sections of five and seven lines).

投在牆壁上的是我破碎的影子
我看出是一個流浪於二十世紀的
荷蘭飛行人現代的憂鬱的面像
他將焚去舟楫
葬於你密髮的靜謐之中
同快樂的精靈們
聽你心跳的聲音預示一個死亡的吉兆

華僑文藝第一卷第一期. 覃子豪全集I (1965), 426.

過黑髮橋

佩腰刀的山地人走過黑髮橋
海風吹亂他長長的黑髮
黑色的閃爍
如蝙蝠竄入黃昏

黑髮的山地人歸去
白頭的鷺鷥，滿天飛翔
一片純白的羽毛落下
我的一莖白髮
溶入古銅色的鏡中
而黃昏是橋上的理髮匠
以火焰燒我的青絲

我的一莖白髮
溶入古銅色的鏡中
而我獨行
於山與海之間的無人之境

港在山外
春天繫在黑髮的林裡
當蝙蝠目盲的時刻
黎明的海就飄動着
載滿愛情的船舶
〔註〕黑髮橋為臺東去新港途中之一橋名

覃子豪全集I (1965), 434–35.

Dai Wangshu (戴望舒 1905–1950)

雨巷

撐著油紙傘，獨自
彷徨在悠長、悠長,
又寂寥的雨巷,
我希望逢着
一個丁香一樣地
結着愁怨的姑娘。

她是有
丁香一樣的顏色，
丁香一樣的芬芳，
丁香一樣的憂愁，
在雨中哀怨，
哀怨又彷徨；

她彷徨在這寂寥的雨巷，
撐著油紙傘
像我一樣，
像我一樣地
默默彳亍着，
冷漠、凄清，又惆悵。

她静默地走近，
走近，又投出
太息一般的眼光，
她飄過
像夢一般地，
像夢一般地凄婉迷茫。

像夢中飄過
一枝丁香花，
我身旁飄過這女郎；
她静默地遠了，遠了，
到了頹圯的籬牆，
走盡這雨巷。

在雨的哀曲裡，
消了她的顏色，
散了她的芬芳，
消散了，甚至她的
太息般的眼光,
她丁香般的惆悵。

撐着油紙傘，獨自
彷徨在悠長，悠長
又寂寥的雨巷，
我希望飄過
一個丁香一樣地
結着愁怨的姑娘。

我底記憶, 1929, in Fung et al. (1974) 243–46.

十四行

微雨飄落在你披散的鬢邊，

像小珠碎落在青色的海帶草間
或是死魚飄翻在波浪上,
閃出神秘又凄切的幽光,

誘著又帶著我青色的靈魂,
到愛和死底夢的王國中睡眠,
那裡有金色的空氣和紫色的太陽,
那裡可憐的生物將歡樂的眼淚流到胸膛;

就像一隻黑色的衰老的瘦貓,
在幽光中我憔悴又伸著懶腰,
流出我一切虛偽和真誠的驕傲;

然後,又跟著牠跟蹌在輕霧朦朧,
像淡紅的酒沫飄在琥珀鍾,
我將有情的眼藏在幽暗的記憶中。

我底記憶, 1929, in戴望舒卷 (1977) 28–29.

憂鬱

我如今已厭看薔薇色,
一任她驕紅披滿枝。

心頭的春花已不更開,
幽黑的煩憂已到我歡樂之夢中來。

我的唇已枯,我的眼已枯,
我呼吸着火焰,我聽見幽靈低訴。

去吧,欺人的美夢,欺人的幻象,
天上的花枝,世人安能癡想!

我頹唐地在挨度這遲遲的朝夕,
我是個疲倦的人兒,我等待著安息。

我底記憶, 1929, 戴望舒詩集 (1981), 24.

一個和尚

一天的鐘兒撞過了又一天,
    一個和尚做着蒼白的深夢:
        過去多少年留下來的影蹤
在記憶裡看來就只是一片
在破殿裡到處迷漫的香煙,
    悲哀的殘骸依舊在香爐中

伴着一些善男信女的苦衷，
厭倦也永遠在佛經中蜿蜒。

昏沉沉的，夢話沸湧出了嘴，
　　他的頭兒又和木魚兒應對，
　　頭兒木魚兒一樣空一樣重；
一聲一聲的，催眠了山和水，
山水在暮靄裡懶洋洋的睡，
　　他又算撞過了白天的喪鐘。

漢園集 (1936), 124–25.

幾個人

叫賣的喊一聲'冰糖葫蘆'，
吃了一口灰像滿不在乎；
提鳥籠的望着天上的白鴿，
自在的腳步踩過了沙河，
當一個年輕人在荒街上沉思。
賣蘿蔔的空揮着摸亮的小刀，
一擔紅蘿蔔在夕陽裡傻笑，
當一個年輕人在荒街上沉思。
矮叫化子癡看自己的長影子，
當一個年輕人在荒街上沉思；
有些人捧著一碗飯歎氣，
有些人半夜裡聽別人的夢話，
有些人白髮上戴一朵紅花，
像雪野的邊緣上托一輪落日……
十月十五日

1930–1935 十年詩草 (1942), 9–10.

He Qifang (何其芳 1912–1977)

醉罷

給輕飄飄地歌唱着的人們

醉罷。醉罷。
真正的醉者有福了，
因為天國是他們的。

如其酒精和書籍
和滴蜜的嘴唇
都掩不住人間的苦辛，
如其由沉醉而半解
而終於全醒，
是否還斜戴着帽子，
半閉着眼皮，

扮演一生的微醺？

震儡在寒風裡的蒼蠅
撲翅於紙窗前，
夢着死屍，
夢着盛夏的西瓜皮，
夢着無夢的空虛。

我在我嘲笑的尾聲上
聽見了自己的羞恥：
「你也不過嗡嗡嗡
像一隻蒼蠅！」

如其我是蒼蠅，
我期待着鐵絲的手掌
擊到我頭上的聲音。

1936–1937 預言 (1957) 75–77.

預言

這一個心跳的日子終於來臨。
你夜的歎息似的漸近的足音
我聽得清不是林葉和夜風的私語，麋鹿馳過苔徑的細碎的蹄聲。告訴
我，用你銀鈴的歌聲告訴我
你是不是預言中的年輕的神？

你一定來自溫郁的南方，告訴我那兒的月色，那兒的日光，告訴我春風
是怎樣吹開百花，燕子是怎樣癡戀着綠楊，我將合眼睡在你如夢的歌聲
裡，那溫馨我似乎記得又似乎遺忘。

請停下，停下你長途的奔波，進來，這兒有虎皮的褥你坐，讓我燒起每
一秋天拾來的落葉，聽我低低唱起我自己的歌，那歌聲將火光樣沉鬱又
高揚，火光樣將落葉的一生訴說。

不要前行，前面是無邊的森林，古老的樹現着野獸身上的斑文，半生半
死的藤蟒蛇樣交纏著，密葉裡漏不下一顆星，你將怯怯地不敢放下第二
步，當你聽見了第一步空寥的回聲。

一定要走嗎，等我和你同行，我的足知道每條平安的路徑，我將不停地
唱着忘倦的歌，再給你，再給你手的溫存，當夜的濃黑遮斷了我們，你
可不轉眼地望着我的眼睛。

我激動的歌聲你竟不聽，你的足竟不為我的顫抖暫停，像靜穆的微風飄
過這黃昏裡，消失了，消失了你驕傲的足音…
啊，你終於如預言所說的無語而來
無語而去了嗎，年輕的神？
一九三一年秋

漢園集 (1936), 4–7.

生活是多麼廣闊

給輕飄飄地歌唱着的人們

生活是多麼廣闊,
生活是海洋。
凡是有生活的地方就有快樂和寶藏。

去參加歌詠隊,去演戲,
去建設鐵路,去作飛行師,
去坐在實驗室裡,去寫詩,
去高山上滑雪,去駕一隻船顛簸在波濤上,
去北極探險,去熱帶搜集植物,
去帶一個帳篷在星光下露宿。
去過極尋常的日子,
去在平凡的事物中睜大你的眼睛,
去以自己的火點燃旁人的火,
去以心發現心。

生活是多麼廣闊。
生活又是多麼芬芳。
凡是有生活的地方就有快樂和寶藏。

何其芳文集 (1941) 174.

Chen Jingrong (陳敬容 1917–1989)

夜行

被霓虹燈染紅的夜空下
城市在迸發它罪惡的花
我們如原始的巡遊者
漫步過喧嚷的大街
講着這世界拒絕聆聽的話

呵,世界,我們的莊嚴
一如你固執的癡呆
我們的心徒然為你流血
我們有我們的廣闊
而你有你的狹

1948. 陳敬容詩文集 (2008), 342.

過程

大地腐爛了,
蛆蟲爬出來

吸取從垃圾堆裡蒸發的氣息，
蒼蠅們貪饞地
望着戰場上的死屍
舐舐嘴唇。

大地腐爛了，
血流出來，
流成河，流成海，
淹沒了城市和村莊。
把坦白與無辜一齊沖走，
"大減價－世界的良心！"
孤舟上有人高聲叫賣。

腐爛。
痛苦的過程。
時代喘息着在等候，
等大地爛一個透熟：
那時罪惡的血液凝凍，
新肉在瘡痂下面長成，
當創痕終於平復，
來，還你一個新面目！

                                  1946. 陳敬容詩文集 (1984), 168–69.

Duoduo (多多 1951–)

從死亡的方向看

從死亡的方向看總會看到
一生不應見到的人
總會隨便地埋到一個地點
隨便嗅嗅，就把自己埋在那裡
埋在讓他們恨的地點
他們把鏟中的土倒在你臉上
要謝謝他們。再謝一次
你的眼睛就再也看不到敵人
就會從死亡的方向傳來
他們陷入敵意時的叫喊
你卻再也聽不見
那完全是痛苦的叫喊

http://www.chinapoesy.com/XianDaiD0F589BC-D3CD-4CE6-B923-2E0CDB5F99F6.html

Note: The date of composition, where known, precedes the collection title. The date of the collection follows its title.

Works Cited—English and French

Acton, Harold. "Contemporary Chinese Poetry." *Poetry: A Magazine of Verse* 46 (Apr.–Sept. 1935): 39–46.

Acton, Harold, and Ch'en Shih-hsiang. *Modern Chinese Poetry*. London: Duckworth, 1936.

Aggeler, William F. *Baudelaire Judged by Spanish Critics 1857–1957*. Athens: University of Georgia Press, 1971.

Ai Qing. "Sixty Years of New Poetry in China." *Chinese Literature* Mar. 1981: 92–119.

Alber, Charles J. "Wild Grass: Symmetry and Parallelism in Lu Hsün's Prose Poems" In *Critical Essays on Chinese Literature*, ed. William H. Nienhauser Jr., 1–29. Hong Kong: Chinese University of Hong Kong Press, 1976.

Almberg, Shiu-pang. "The Poetry of Chen Jingrong." Diss., Akademitryic AB Edsbruk, University of Stockholm, 1988.

Almberg, Shiu-pang. *The Poetry of Chen Jingrong: A modern Chinese Woman Poet*. Stockholm: Förenlingen för Orientaliska Studier 21, 1988.

Allen, Joseph R. Review of *A Splintered Mirror: Chinese Poetry from the Democracy Movement*, by Donald Finkel. *World Literature Today* 65, no. 3 (Summer 1991): 547

Bader, Arno L., and Lucien Mao. "Three Modern Chinese Poems." *Tien Hsia Monthly* 10, no. 1 (Jan. 1940): 162–63.

Baudelaire, Charles Pierre. *Oeuvres Complètes*. Edited by Claude Pichois. Paris: Gallimard, 1975–1976.

Baudelaire, Charles Pierre. *The Flowers of Evil*. Edited and compiled by Marthiel Mathews and Jackson Mathews. Norfolk, CT: New Directions, 1955.

Baudelaire, Charles Pierre. *Baudelaire: Prose and Poetry*. Edited and translated by Arthur Symons. New York: Albert and Charles Boni, 1926.

Baudelaire, Charles Pierre. *Les Fleurs du mal: The Complete Text of The Flowers of Evil*. Translated by Richard Howard. Boston: D. R. Godine, 1982.

Baudelaire, Charles Pierre. *66 Translations from Charles Baudelaire's Les Fleurs du mal*. James McGowan. Peoria, IL: Spoon River Poetry, 1985.

Bauer, Wolfgang. *Western Literature and Translation Work in Communist China*. Frankfurt/Main: A. Metzner Verlag, 1964.

Benjamin, Walter. *Charles Baudelaire: A Lyric Poet in the Era of High Capitalism*. Translated by Harry Zohn. 1955; London: Verso Publishers, 1983.

Benjamin, Walter. *Illuminations*. Translated by Harry Zohn. New York: Schocken, 1968.

Bernard, Suzanne. "Dai Wangshu ou la vie rêvée." In *Dai Wangshu Poèmes*, by Suzanne Bernard and Yan Hansheng, 21–29. Beijing: Littérature chinoise, 1982.

Bian Zhilin. "About My Poems: Seven Poems." *Chinese Literature* (Aug. 1981): 87–95.

Bian Zhilin. "The Development of China's 'New Poetry' and the Influence from the West." *Chinese Literature: Essays, Articles and Reviews* 4 (Jan. 1982): 152–57.

Birch, Cyril. *Anthology of Chinese Literature I*. New York: Grove, 1965.

Birch, Cyril. "English and Chinese Metres in Hsu Chih-Mo." *Asia Major* n.s. 8 (1961): 258–93.

Birch, Cyril. "Hsü Chi-mo's Debt to Thomas Hardy (Abstract)." *Transactions, International Conference of Orientalists in Japan*. 9 (1964): 73–77

Bloom, Harold. *The Anxiety of Influence: A Theory of Poetry*. New York: Oxford University Press, 1973.

Boorman, Howard L. *Biographical Dictionary of Republican China*. New York: Columbia University Press, 1967–1979.

Bourdieu, Pierre. *The Rules of Art: Genesis and Structure of the Literary Field.* Translated by Susan Emmanuel. Stanford, CA: Stanford University Press, 1995.

Brown, Caroline T. "Lu Xun's Interpretation of Dreams." In *Psycho-Sinology: The Universe of Dreams in Chinese Culture.* Edited by Carolyn T. Brown, 67–79.Washington, DC: Woodrow Wilson Center for Scholars, and Lanham, MD: University Press of America, 1988.

Bynner, Witter, and Kiang Kang-hu. *The Jade Mountain: A Chinese Anthology, Being Three Hundred Poems of the T'ang Dynasty 618–906.* New York: Vintage Books, 1972. Originally published by Alfred A. Knopf, 1929.

Chao, Yuen-ren. *The Mandarin Primer.* Cambridge, MA: Harvard University Press, 1964.

Chen, David Ying. "Li Ho and Keats: Poverty, Illness, Frustration and a Poetic Career." *Tsing Hua Journal of Chinese Studies* n.s. 5, no. 1 (1965): 67–84.

Chen, Jerome. *China and the West: Society and Culture 1815–1937.* Bloomington: Indiana University Press, 1979.

Cheng Ch'ing-mao. "The Impact of Japanese Literary Trends on Modern Chinese Writers." In *Modern Chinese Literature in the May Fourth Era,* ed. Merle Goldman, 63–88. Cambridge, MA: Harvard University Press, 1977.

Cheng, François. *Chinese Poetic Writing.* Translated by Donald A. Riggs and Jerome P. Seaton. Bloomington: Indiana University Press, 1982.

Cheng, François. *L'Écriture Poétique Chinoise.* Paris: Editions du Seuil, 1977.

Cherkassky, Leonid. "Dai Wangshu: *Wode Jiyi* (My Memory), 1929." In *A Selective Guide to Chinese Literature 1900–1949.* Vol. 3: *The Poem,* ed. Lloyd Haft (Leiden: Brill, 1989), 81–84.

Chi Pang-yuan et al. *An Anthology of Contemporary Chinese Literature: Taiwan: 1949–1974.* Taipei: National Institute for Compilation and Translation, 1975. 2 vols.

Chow, Tse-tsung. *The May Fourth Movement: Intellectual Revolution in Modern China.* Cambridge, MA: Harvard University Press, 1960.

Chung Ling and Kenneth Rexroth. *The Orchid Boat: Women Poets of China.* New York: McGraw-Hill, 1973.

Clements, Patricia. *Baudelaire and the English Tradition.* Princeton, NJ: Princeton University Press, 1985.

Cowley, Malcolm. "The Golden House." *Dial* (Oct. 1927): 339–42.

Dai Sijie. *Balzac et la petite tailleuse chinoise.*Paris: Gallimard, 2000. English translation by Ina Rilke. *Balzac and the Little Chinese Seamstress.* New York: Knopf, 2001.

Davis, A. R. "China's Entry into World Literature." *Journal of the Oriental Society of Australia* 1–2 (Dec 1956): 43–50.

Demiéville, Paul. *Anthologie de la poésie chinoise classique.* Paris: Gallimard, 1962.

Demiéville, Paul. "Aperçu historique des études sinologiques en France." *Acta Asiatica* 11 (1966): 76.

Denton, Kirk. *Modern Chinese Literary Thought: Writings on Literature, 1893–1945.* Stanford, CA: Stanford University Press, 1996.

Denton, Kirkand, Michel Hockx. *Literary Societies of Republican China.* Lanham, MD: Lexington Books, 2008.

Dolezalová, Anna. *Yü Ta-fu: Specific Traits of His Literary Creation.* Bratislava: Publishing House of the Slovak Academy of Sciences. New York: Paragon Reprint Corporation, 1971.

Eberhard, Wolfram. *Guilt and Sin in Traditional China.* Berkeley: University of California Press, 1967.

Eoyang, Eugene Chen, ed. *Selected Poems of Ai Qing.* Translations by Peng Wenlan, Marilyn Chin, and Eugene Chen Eoyang. Bloomington: Indiana University Press, 1982.

Etiemble, René. "Le Sonnet des Voyelles." *Revue de littérature comparée* 19 (1939): 239.

Etkind, Efrem. "Baudelaire en langue russe." *Europe* 456–57 (1967): 252–61.

Fang, Achilles. "From Imagism to Whitmanism in Recent Chinese Poetry: A Search for Poetics That Failed." In *Indiana University Conference on Oriental-Western Literary*

Relations, ed. Horst Frenz and G. L Anderson, 177–92. Chapel Hill: University of North Carolina Press, 1955.

Feuer, Alan, and Allen Salkin. "Terrible End for an Enfant Terrible." New York Times, 26 July 2009, Metro section, 1.

Finkel, Donald, ed. and trans. *A Splintered Mirror: Chinese Poetry from the Democracy Movement*. San Francisco: North Point Press, 1991.

Fowlie, Wallace, ed. and trans. *Flowers of Evil and Other Works*. 1964. Reprint, New York: Dover, 1992.

French, Joseph Lewis. *Lotus and Chrysanthemum: An Anthology of Chinese and Japanese Poetry*. New York: Liveright, 1928.

Frodsham, J. D. *The Poems of Li Ho (791–817)*. Oxford: Clarendon, 1970.

Fung, Mary M.Y., and David Lunde. *The Carving of Insects: Bian Zhilin*. Hong Kong: The Chinese University of Hong Kong Research Centre for Translation, 2006.

Gadoffre, Gilbert. *Claudel et l'univers chinois*. Cahiers Paul Claudel. Paris: Gallimard, 1968.

Gálik, Marián. "Early Poems and Essays of Ho Ch'i-Fang." *Asian and African Studies* (Bratislava) 15 (1979): 31–64.

Gálik, Marián. *Milestones in Sino-Western Literary Confrontation (1898–1979)*. Asiatische Forschungen Band 98. Wiesbaden: Otto Harrassowitz, 1986.

Gálik, Marián. "The Red Gauze Lantern of Feng Nai-ch'ao." *Asian and African Studies* (Bratislava), 10 (1974): 69–98.

Gálik, Marián. "Ten Venetian Poems by Wang Duqing: Chinese Entry into Literary Decadence." *Asiatica Venetiana* 1 (1996): 43–62.

Gautier, Judith. *Le Livre de Jade*. Paris: Plon, 1933. Originally published Paris : A. Lemerre, 1867.

Gautier, Théophile. *Charles Baudelaire: His Life*. Translated by Guy Thorne. New York: Brentano's, 1915.

Giles, Herbert A. *Gems of Chinese Literature*. 1884; New York: Paragon Books Reprint, 1965.

Gilman, Richard. *Decadence: The Strange Life of an Epithet*. New York: Farrar, Straus and Giroux, 1971, 1979.

"Ginffa Lee, a Sculptor, Diplomat, and Poet, Dies in Long Island City." *New York Times*, 31 Dec. 1976, B8.

Godfrey, Sima. "Baudelaire's Windows." *L'Esprit Créateur* 22, no. 4 (Winter 1982): 83–100.

Graham, A. C. *Poems of the Late T'ang*. London: Penguin, 1965.

Grasselli, Fabio. "Interviewing Duo Duo, the Poet of the Clouds, Haikou, 11 Oct. 2004." www.cinaoggi.it/english/culture/duo-duo-interview.htm (accessed 18 Jan. 2008).

Guillermaz, Patricia. *La Poésie chinoise contemporaine*. Paris: Seghers, 1962.

Guillermaz, Patricia. *La Poésie chinoise des origines à la révolution*. 1957. Verviers: Gérard et cie., 1966.

Gunn, Edward. *Rewriting Chinese: Style and Innovation in Twentieth-Century Chinese Prose*. Stanford, CA: Stanford University Press, 1991.

Guy, Basil. *The French Image of China Before and After Voltaire*. Geneva: Droz, 1963.

Haft, Lloyd. *Pien Chih-lin: A Study in Modern Chinese Poetry*. Dordrecht: Foris Publications, 1983.

Haft, Lloyd, ed. *A Selective Guide to Chinese Literature 1900–1949: The Poem*. Leiden: Brill, 1989.

Haft, Lloyd, ed. *Words from the West: Western Texts in Chinese Literary Context: Essays to Honor Erich Zürcher on His Sixty-Fifth Birthday*. Leiden: Centre of Non-Western Studies, 1993.

Hahn, Emily. *China to Me*. Garden City, NY: Doubleday, Doran, 1944.

Hahn, Emily. *Mr. Pan*. Garden City, NY: Doubleday, Doran, 1942.

Hawkes, David. *Ch'u Tz'u: The Songs of the South: An Ancient Chinese Anthology*. Boston: Beacon Press, 1959.

Hightower, James R. *Topics in Chinese Literature*. 1950. Cambridge, MA: Harvard University Press, 1966.

Hockx, Michel, ed. *The Literary Field of Twentieth-Century China*. Honolulu: University of Hawaii Press, 1999.

Hockx, Michel. *A Snowy Morning: Eight Chinese Poets on the Road to Modernity*. Leiden: Centre of Non-Western Studies, 1994.

Hong Zicheng. *A History of Contemporary Chinese Literature*. Translated by Michael Day. Leiden: Brill, 2009.

Hsia, C. T. *A History of Modern Chinese Fiction*. New Haven, CT: Yale University Press, 1962.

Hsia, C. T., and Joseph S. M. Lau, trans. "Sinking," by Yu Dafu, 1921. In *Twentieth-Century Chinese Stories*, ed. C.T. Hsia and Joseph Lau, 1–33. New York: Columbia University Press, 1971.

Hsu, Kai-yu. *Twentieth-Century Chinese Poetry: An Anthology*. New York: Doubleday, 1963.

Hsu, Kai-yu. *Wen I-To*. Twayne's World Author Series. Boston: G. K. Hall, 1980.

Hu Pinqing. *Les Fleurs du mal: Une autobiographie en vers*. Taipei: Zhongguo wenhua daxue chubanbu, 1981.

Huang Yibing. *Contemporary Chinese Literature: From the Cultural Revolution to the Future*. New York: Palgrave Macmillan, 2007.

Hung, Chengfu. *Un Siècle d'influence chinoise sur la littérature française 1815–1930*. Thèse pour le doctorat d'université, Université de Paris. Paris: Domat-Montchrestien, 1934.

Hung, William. *Notes for Tu Fu: China's Greatest Poet*. Cambridge, MA: Harvard University Press, 1952.

Hung, William. *Tu Fu: China's Greatest Poet*. Cambridge, MA: Harvard University Press, 1952.

Hutt, Jonathan. "The Sumptuous World of Shao Xunmei." *East Asian History* 21 (June 2001): 111–42.

Idema, Wilt, and Lloyd Haft. *A Guide to Chinese Literature*. Michigan Monograph in Chinese Studies. Ann Arbor: Center for Chinese Studies: The University of Michigan, 1997.

Jameson, Fredric. "Baudelaire as Modernist and Postmodernist: The Dissolution of the Referent and the Artificial 'Sublime.'" In *Lyric Poetry: Beyond New Criticism*, ed. Chaviva Hošek and Patricia A. Parker, 247–63. Ithaca, NY: Cornell University Press, 1985.

Jauss, Hans Robert. *Toward an Aesthetic of Reception*. Translated by Timothy Bahti. Minneapolis: University of Minnesota Press, 1982.

Jenner, W. J. F., ed. and trans. *Lu Xun: Selected Poems*. Beijing: Foreign Languages Press, 1982.

Jin Siyan. *La métamorphose des images poétiques 1915–1932: Des symbolistes français aux symbolistes chinois*. Dortmund: Project-Verlag, 1997.

Kaplan, Edward K. "Solipsism and Dialogue in Baudelaire's Prose Poems." In *Modernity and Revolution in Late Nineteenth-Century France*, ed. Barbara T. Cooper, 88–98. Newark: University of Delaware Press, 1992.

Kaplan, Harry Allan. "The Symbolist Movement in Modern China." PhD diss., Harvard University, 1983.

King, Richard. Review of *The Red Azalea: Chinese Poetry since the Cultural Revolution*, edited and translated by Edward Morin, Fang Dai, and Dennis Ding. *Pacific Affairs* 64, no. 1 (Spring 1991): 400–401

Kudo, Naotaro. *Chinese Romanticism: The Life and Thoughts of Li Ho Part II*. Tokyo: Waseda University Press, 1972.

Kuhn, Irène, and Claude Pichois. *Baudelaire et l'Allemagne, L'Allemagne et Baudelaire*. Paris: Honoré Champion Éditeur, 2004.

LaFleur, Frances A. "The Evolution of a Symbolist Aesthetic in Classical Chinese Verse: The Role of Li Ho Compared with That of Charles Baudelaire in Nineteenth-Century French Poetry." PhD diss., Princeton University, 1993.

Lappin, Kendall. *Dead French Poets Speak Plain English: An Anthology of Poems*. Paradise, CA: Asylum Arts, 1997.

Lawrence, D. H. *The Escaped Cock*. Paris: Black Sun Press, 1929.

Lee, Gregory. *Dai Wangshu: The Life and Poetry of a Chinese Modernist*. Hong Kong: The Chinese University Press, 1989

Lee, Gregory. "Western Influences in the Poetry of Dai Wangshu." *Modern Chinese Literature* 3, no. 1 (1987): 7–27.

Lee, Gregory B., ed. and trans. *Duoduo: The Boy Who Catches Wasps*. Brookline, MA: Zephyr, 2002.

Lee, Gregory, and John Cayley, ed. and trans. *Duoduo: Looking Out from Death: From the Cultural Revolution to Tiananmen Square: The New Chinese Poetry of Duoduo*. London: Bloomsbury, 1989.

Lee, Gregory, and John Cayley, ed. and trans. *Duoduo: Statements: The New Chinese Poetry of Duoduo*. London: Wellsweep, 1989.

Lee, Leo Oufan, ed. *Lu Xun and His Legacy*. Berkeley: University of California Press, 1985.

Lee, Leo Oufan. *The Romantic Generation of Chinese Writers*. Cambridge, MA: Harvard University Press, 1973.

Lee, Leo Oufan. *Shanghai Modern: The Flowering of a New Urban Culture in China, 1930–1945*. Cambridge, MA: Harvard University Press, 1999.

Lee, Leo Oufan. *Voices from the Iron House: A Study of Lu Xun*. Bloomington: Indiana University Press, 1987.

Lee, Seong-Bok. "L'Itinéraire Baudelairen à la lumière du Yi-King." *Travaux de Littérature* 6 (1993): 263–183.

Leung, Ping-kwan. "Literary Modernity in Chinese Poetry." In *Lyrics from Shelters: Modern Chinese Poetry 1930–1950*, ed. Wai-lim Yip, 43–68. New York: Garland, 1992.

Liang Zongdai. "Two Poems: Souvenir and Vespers." Translated by Liang Zongdai. *T'ien Hsia Monthly* 2 (1936): 85–86

Lin, Julia C. *Modern Chinese Poetry: An Introduction*. Seattle: University of Washington Press, 1972.

Lin, Julia C. *Women of the Red Plain: An Anthology of Contemporary ChineseWomen's Poetry*.New York: Penguin, 1992.

Lin, Yü-sheng. *The Crisis of Chinese Consciousness*. Madison: University of Wisconsin Press, 1979.

Liu, David Jason. "'Chinese 'Symbolist' Verse in the 1920's: Li Chin-Fa and Mu Mu-t'ien." *Tamkang Review* 12, no. 1 (Fall 1981): 27–53.

Liu, James J. Y. *The Interlingual Critic : Interpreting Chinese Poetry*. Bloomington: Indiana University Press, 1982.

Liu, James J. Y. *The Poetry of Li Shang-Yin: Ninth-Century Baroque Chinese Poet*. Chicago: University of Chicago Press, 1969.

Liu, Lydia H. *Translingual Practice: Literature, National Culture, and Translated Modernity—China, 1900–1937*. Stanford, CA: Stanford University Press, 1995.

Liu Wu-chi and Irving Lo, ed. *Sunflower Splendor*. Bloomington: Indiana University Press, 1975.

Loi, Michelle. *Poètes chinois d'écoles françaises*. Paris: Maisonneuve, 1980.

Loi, Michelle. *Roseaux sur le mur: les poètes occidentalistes chinois, 1919–1949*. Paris: Gallimard, 1971.

Louÿs, Pierre. *Les Chansons de Bilitis*. Originally published Paris: Librarie de l'Art indépendent, 1895.

Louÿs, Pierre. "Dialogue au soleil couchant." In *Oeuvres complètes (1929–1931)*, 7:53–63. Genève: Slatkine Reprints, 1973.

Lu Xun. *A Brief History of Chinese Fiction*. Translated by Yang Xianyi and Gladys Yang. Beijing: Foreign Languages Press, 1959.

Lu Hsun. *Wild Grass.* Translated by Yang Xianyi and Gladys Yang. Peking: Foreign Languages Press, 1974.

Ma, Yiu-man. "The Reception of French Symbolism in China, 1919–25." In *The Force of Vision.* Vol. 4, *Translation and Modernisation: Proceedings of the XIIIth Congress of the ICLA*, ed. Theresa Hyun and José Lambert, 46–53. Tokyo: University of Tokyo Press, 1995.

Ma, Yiu-man. "Translating without the Source Text: A Case Study on Liang Tsung-Tai's Baudelaire." *Tamkang Review* 28, no. 1 (Autumn 1997): 91–112.

Ma, Yiu-man. "Translation and Literary Politics: Baudelaire in the New Literature Movement 1921–1925." *Tamkang Review* 28, no. 2 (Winter 1997): 95–124.

Macy, John. *The Story of the World's Literature.* New York: Boni and Liveright, 1925.

Major, John. Review of *Pacing the Void: T'ang Approaches to the Stars*, by Edward Schafer. *Harvard Journal of Asiatic Studies*, 40, no. 1 (June 1980): 280.

Manfredi, Paul. "Quest for the Missing String: On Li Jinfa's 'Symbolist' Poetry." MA thesis, Indiana University, 1998.

Manfredi, Paul. "Writing the Influenced Text: Modern Chinese Symbolist Poetry." *Journal of Modern Literature in Chinese* 5, no. 2 (Jan. 2002): 1–28.

Mathews, Marthiel, and Jackson Mathews, eds. *Charles Baudelaire: The Flowers of Evil.* Norfolk, CT: New Directions, 1955.

McDougall, Bonnie S. "European Influences in the Poetry of Ho Ch'i-Fang." *Journal of the Oriental Society of Australia* 5, nos. 1–2 (Dec. 1967): 133–51.

McDougall, Bonnie S. *The Introduction of Western Literary Theories into Modern China 1919–1925.* Tokyo: The Centre for East Asian Cultural Studies, 1971.

McDougall, Bonnie S. *Mao Zedong's Talks at the Yan'an Forum.* Ann Arbor: University of Michigan Center of Chinese Studies, 1980.

McDougall, Bonnie S. *Paths in Dreams: Selected Prose and Poetry of Ho Ch'i-Fang.* Asian and Pacific Writing. St. Lucia, Queensland: University of Queensland Press, 1976.

McDougall, Bonnie S. "The Search for Synthesis: T'ien Han and Mao Tun in 1920." In *Search for Identity: Modern Literature and the Creative Arts in Asia*, ed. A. R. Davis, 225–54. Sydney: Angus & Robertson, 1974.

McDougall, Bonnie S., and Kam Louie. *The Literature of China in the Twentieth Century.* New York: Columbia University Press, 1997.

Mi, Jiayan. *Self-Fashioning and Reflexive Modernity in Modern Chinese Poetry, 1919–1949.* Lewiston, NY: Edwin Mellen, 2004.

Monsterleet, Jean. *Sommets de la littérature chinoise contemporaine.* Paris: Domat, 1953.

Moréas, Jean. "Un Manifeste littéraire." *Le Figaro* (18 Sept. 1886). www.berlol.net/chrono/chr1886a.htm (accessed 30 Nov. 2011).

Mote, Frederick. *Intellectual Foundations of China.* New York: Knopf, 1971.

Murry, John Middleton. *Countries of the Mind.* London: W. Collins Sons, 1922.

Owen, Stephen. "The Anxiety of Global Influence: What Is World Poetry?" *New Republic* (19 Nov. 1990): 288–32.

Palandri, Angela. *Modern Verse from Taiwan.* Berkeley: University of California Press, 1972.

Pamuk, Orhan. "Turkish Journal: The View and the Dog in the Road." *New Yorker* (5 Mar. 2007): 44–45.

Payne, Robert, ed. *Contemporary Chinese Poetry.* London: Routledge, 1947.

Payne, Robert, ed. *The White Pony: An Anthology of Chinese Poetry from the Earliest Times to the Present Day.* New York: John Day, 1947.

Peyre, Henri. "Baudelaire and English Poets." In *Du romantisme au surnaturalisme: Hommage à Claude Pichois*, ed. James S. Patty, 167–88. Neuchâtel, Switzerland: La Baconnière, 1985.

Peyre, Henri. "Remarques sur le peu d'influence de Baudelaire." *Revue d'histoire littéraire de la France* 67 (1967): 424–36.

Pichois, Claude. "Baudelaire et l'Épouse Chinoise." In *Mélanges de Littérature en Hommage à Albert Kies*, ed. Claudine Gothot-Merscht and Claude Pichois, 87–89. Bruxelles: Publications des Facultés universitaires Saint-Louis, 1985.

Pierrot, Jean. *The Decadent Imagination, 1880–1900.* Translated by Derek Coltman. Chicago: University of Chicago Press, 1981.

Průšek, Jaroslav. *The Lyrical and the Epic: Studies of Modern Chinese Literature.* Edited by Leo Ou-fan Lee. Bloomington: Indiana University Press, 1980.

Rexroth, Kenneth. *Classics Revisited.* Chicago: Quadrangle Books, 1968.

Rodzinski, Witold. *The Walled Kingdom: A History of China from Antiquity to the Present.* New York: Free Press, 1984.

Rousseau, René. "Baudelaire adorateur de la lune." *Synthèses* 19, nos. 217–18 (June–July 1964): 281–94, and no. 219 (Aug. 1964): 87–98.

Rowbotham, Arnold. "Voltaire, Sinophile." *PMLA* 47 (Dec. 1932): 1050–65.

Ruff, Marcel. *Baudelaire.* Translated by Agnes Kertesz. New York: New York University Press, 1966.

Ruprecht, Hans George. "Aspects du baudelairisme méxicain." *Comparative Literature Studies* 11, no. 2 (June 1974): 99–122.

Sanders, Tao Tao, trans. *Red Candle: Selected Poems by Wen I-To.* London: Jonathan Cape, 1972.

Saussy, Haun. "Preface to a Preface—Xu Zhimo, Baudelaire, and the Stakes of Intercultural Reading." *Ex/Change* 5 (Sept. 2002): 5–8.

Schafer, Edward. *Pacing the Void: T'ang Approaches to the Stars.* Berkeley: University of California Press, 1977.

Schwartz, William L. *The Imaginative Interpretation of the Far East in Modern French Literature 1800–1925.* Paris: Honoré Champion, 1977.

Semanov, V. I. *Lu Hsün and His Predecessors.* Translated and edited by Charles J. Alber. White Plains, NY: M.E. Sharpe, 1980.

Shao Xunmei, "Poetry Chronicle." *T'ien Hsia Monthly* 3 (1936): 264–69.

Shen Fu. *Six Records of a Floating Life.* Translated by Leonard Pratt and Chiang Su-hui. Baltimore: Penguin, 1983.

Soulié de Morant, Georges. *Anthologie de l'amour chinois: Poèmes de lascivité parfumée.* Paris: Mercure de France, 1932.

Spence, Jonathan. *The Gate of Heavenly Peace: The Chinese and Their Revolution 1895–1980.* New York: Viking, 1981.

Sturm, Frank Pearce. *The Poems of Charles Baudelaire Selected and Translated from the French, with an Introductory Study.* 1906. In *Frank P. Sturm: His Life, Letters, and Collected Work,* ed. Richard Taylor. Urbana: University of Illinois Press, 1969, 215–34.

Swinburne, Algernon C. *Les Fleurs du Mal and Other Studies.* Edited by Edmund Gosse. London: printed for private circulation, 1913.

Swinburne, Algernon C. *A Choice of Swinburne's Verse.* Edited by Robert Nye. London: Faber and Faber, 1973.

Symons, Arthur. *Baudelaire: A Study.* London: E. Mathews, 1920.

Symons, Arthur, trans. *Baudelaire, Prose and Poetry.* New York: Albert & Charles Boni, 1926.

Tagore, Amitendranath. *Literary Debates in Modern China 1918–1927.* Tokyo: The Centre for East Asian Cultural Studies, 1967.

Tu, Kuo-ch'ing. "Chinese and Japanese Symbolist Poetics." *Comparative Poetics: Proceedings of the Xth Congress of the ICLA* 2 (1985): 665–74.

Tu, Kuo-ch'ing. "The Introduction of French Symbolism into Modern Chinese and Japanese Poetry." *Tamkang Review* 10 (1980): 355, 357, 359.

Tu, Kuo-ch'ing. "Li Chin-Fa and Kambara Ariake: The First Symbolist Poets in China and Japan." In *Essays in Commemoration of the Golden Jubilee of the Fung Ping Shan Library 1932–1982: Studies in Chinese Librarianship, Literature, Language, History, and Arts,* edited by Bingliang Chen, 317–43. Hong Kong: Fung Ping Shan Library of the University of Hong Kong, 1982.

Tu, Kuo-ch'ing. *Li Ho (790–816).* Boston: Twayne, 1979.

Tu, Kuo-ch'ing. "Symbolist Imagery in Li Jinfa's *Weiyu*." *Journal of Oriental Studies* 25, no. 2 (1987): 187–96.

Tung, Constantine. "The Crescent Moon Society: The Minority's Challenge in the Literary Movement of Modern China." Council on International Studies, Special Studies No. 11. Buffalo: State University of New York, 1972

Turnell, Martin. *Baudelaire: A Study of His Poetry*. Norfolk, CT: New Directions, 1954.

Turqet-Milnes, Gladys Rosaleen. *The Influence of Baudelaire in France and England*. London: Constable, 1913.

Valéry, Paul. "Situation de Baudelaire." *Variété II*, 144–45. Paris: Gallimard, 1930.

van Bever, Adolphe, and Paul Léautaud. *Poètes d'aujourd'hui, morceaux choisis accompagnés de notices biographiques et d'un essai de bibliographie*. Paris: Mercure de France, 1900.

van Crevel, Maghiel. *Language Shattered: Contemporary Chinese Poetry and Duoduo*. Leiden: CNWS Research School, 1996.

van Crevel, Maghiel. "Man and Nature, Man and Man: Aspects of Duoduo's Poetry." In *Words from the West: Western Texts in Chinese Literary Context: Essays to Honor Erich Zürcher on His Sixty-Fifth Birthday*, ed. Lloyd Haft, 110–15. Leiden: Centre of Non-Western Studies, 1993.

van Roosbroeck, Gustave L. "The Source of Baudelaire's Prose-Poem *L'Horloge*." *The Romantic Review* 20, no. 4 (Oct.–Dec. 1929): 357.

Verlaine, Paul. *Oeuvres Poétiques Complètes*. Edited by Y.-G. le Dantec. Paris: Gallimard, 1948.

Verlaine, Paul. *Oeuvres Posthumes*. Paris: Albert Messein, 1913.

Waley, Arthur. *Translations from the Chinese*. New York: Knopf, 1919, 1941.

Wang Zuoliang. *Degrees of Affinity: Studies in Comparative Literature*. Beijing: Foreign Language Teaching and Research Press, 1985.

Wanner, Adrian. *Baudelaire in Russia*. Gainesville: University Press of Florida, 1996.

Wang, Yiyan. "Venturing into Shanghai: The Flâneur in Two of Shi Zhecun's Short Stories." *Modern Chinese Literature and Culture* 19, no. 2 (Fall 2007): 51–55.

Weinberg, Terry. *T. S. Eliot and Charles Baudelaire*. The Hague: Mouton, 1969.

Yang, Gladys, trans. *Silent China: Translation of Selected Works by Lu Xun*. London: Oxford University Press, 1973.

Yang, Vincent. "From French Symbolism to Chinese Symbolism: A Literary Influence." *Tamkang Review*, 17, no. 3 (Spring 1987): 221–44.

Yang Xianyi and Gladys Yang. *The Complete Stories of Lu Xun*. Beijing: Foreign Languages Press, 1981.

Yeh, Michelle, ed. and trans. *Anthology of Modern Chinese Poetry*. New Haven, CT: Yale University Press, 1992.

Yeh, Michelle. *Modern Chinese Poetry: Theory and Practice since 1917*. New Haven, CT: Yale University Press, 1991.

Yeh, Michelle. "Nature's Child and the Frustrated Urbanite: Expressions of the Self in Contemporary Chinese Poetry." *World Literature Today* 65, no. 3 (Summer 1991): 405–9.

Yeh, Michelle. "'There Are No Camels in the Koran': What Is Modern about Modern Chinese Poetry?" In *New Perspectives on Contemporary Chinese Poetry*, ed. Christopher Lupke, 9–26. New York: Palgrave Macmillan, 2008.

Yip, Wai-lim, ed. and trans. *Lyrics from Shelters: Modern Chinese Poetry 1930–1950*. New York: Garland, 1992.

Yip, Wai-lim, ed. and trans. *Modern Chinese Poetry: Twenty Poets from the Republic of China, 1955–1965*. Iowa City: University of Iowa Press, 1970.

Yu, Pauline. "The Poetics of Discontinuity: East-West Correspondences in Lyric Poetry." *PMLA* 94, no. 2 (Mar. 1979): 261–74.

Yuan Haoyi, "Survey of Current Developments in the Comparative Literature of China." *Cowrie: a Chinese Journal of Comparative Literature* 1, no. 1 (1983): 90.

Zha, Peide. "Poetic Quality of Prose Poetry: Charles Baudelaire and Lu Xun." *Comparative Literature in Canada* 21–22, no. 2 (1990–91): 77–83.

Works Cited—Chinese

Ai Qing 艾青. 艾青詩全編. Edited by Yang Liu 杨柳 and Mo Wenzheng 莫文征. Beijing: 人民文学出版社, 2003).

Ai Qing 艾青. 新文藝論集. 1950. Shanghai: 新文藝出版社, 1952.

Ai Qing 艾青. 中國新詩六十年 (代序) 現代百家詩. Edited by Bai Chongyi 白崇义 and Yue Qie 乐齐. Beijing: 宝文堂书店, 1984.

Bao Qianyuan, 包乾元, trans. 董丹下地獄: 波特萊爾著. 中央日報詩刊, Sunday March 7, 1937: Section 4, p. 3.

Bian Zhilin 卞之琳. 雕蟲紀歷. Beijing: 人民文學出版社, 1979.

Bian Zhilin 卞之琳. 惡之花零拾. 新月 4, no. 5 (Mar. 1933): 1–8.

Bian Zhilin 卞之琳. 何其芳晚年譯詩 (代序), 何其芳譯詩稿. Beijing: 外國文學出版社, 1984.

Bian Zhilin 卞之琳. 蘆葉船 Beiping: 立達, 1936.

Bian Zhilin 卞之琳. 「魔鬼的Serenade.」詩刊1 (1931): 74–77.

Bian Zhilin 卞之琳. 人與詩: 憶舊說新. Beijing: 生活出版社, 1984.

Bian Zhilin 卞之琳. 三秋草. Shanghai: 新月, 1933.

Bian Zhilin 卞之琳. 十年詩草. 1942. Reprint. Hong Kong: Mee Ming Book Centre 未名書屋, n. d.

Bian Zhilin 卞之琳. 數行集. In He Qifang et al., *Hanyuan ji*.

Bian Zhilin 卞之琳. 西窗集. Shanghai: 商務印書館, 1936.

Bian Zhilin 卞之琳. 序, 戴望舒詩集. Chengdu: 四川人民出版社, 1981.

Bian Zhilin 卞之琳. 魚目集. Shanghai: 文化生活出版社, 1937.

Cai Yizhong 蔡義忠. 從陳獨秀的文學革命到李金髮的象徵派新詩. Taipei: 清流出版社, 1973. See chapter 「中國象徵派詩的創始者—李金髮及其詩的評價,」 199–208.

Cao Baohua 曹葆華. 無題草. Shanghai: 化生活出版社, 1937.

Cao Shunqing 曹順慶, ed. and comp. 中西比較美學文學論文集. Chengdu: 四川文藝出版社, 1985.

Cao Shunqing 曹順慶. 中西比較詩學. Beijing: 北京出版社, 1988.

Chen Bingkun 陳炳坤. 最近三十年中國文學史. Shanghai: 太平洋書店, 1931.

Chen Jingrong 陳敬容. 「惡之花 (選譯),」譯文 7 (1957): 133–43.

Chen Jingrong 陳敬容. 圖像與花朵 Changsha: 湖南人民出版社, 1984.

Chen Jingrong 陳敬容. 「筆會」, 文匯報: 文藝副刊 (上海) 1 (1947): 30.

Chen Jingrong 陳敬容. 「這裡的那裡的.」世界文學 204 (1989): 272–75.

Chen Jingrong 陳敬容. 陳敬榮詩文集, ed. Luo Jiaming 羅佳明 and Chen Li 陳俐 (Shanghai: 復旦大學出版社, 2008).

Chen Shangzhe 陳尚哲. 「何其芳的詩歌創作及其發展.」 中國現代文學研究叢刊 14 (Mar. 1983): 67–69.

Chen Yuankai 陳元愷. 「《野草》與外國文學.」二十世紀中國文學與世界. Xi'an: 陝西人民出版社, 1987.

Cheng Baoyi 程抱一. 和亞丁談法國詩. Taipei: 純文學出版社, 1970.

Cheng Baoyi 程抱一. 「論波德萊爾.」外國文學研究 7 (1980): 58–63.

Cheng Ch'ing-mao (Zheng Qingmao) 鄭清茂. "王次回研究: A Preliminary Study of Wang Tz'u-hui." Taipei: 國立臺灣大學文史哲學報 14 (November 1965): 241–99.

Dai Wangshu 戴望舒. 戴望舒卷. Edited by Ya Xian 瘂弦. Taipei: 洪範書店, 1977.

Dai Wangshu 戴望舒. 戴望舒全集. Edited by Wang Wenbin 王文彬 and Jin Shi 金石 Beijing: 中國青年出版社, 1999.

Dai Wangshu 戴望舒. 戴望舒詩集. Chengdu: 四川人民出版社, 1981.

Dai Wangshu 戴望舒. 戴望舒譯詩集. Changsha: 湖南人民出版社, 1983.

Dai Wangshu 戴望舒. 戴望舒資料集. Hong Kong? s.n. 1976. (University of Washington Library).

Dai Wangshu 戴望舒, trans. 「波特萊爾的位置 梵樂希作」 Paul Valéry, "Situation de Baudelaire," 1915. 笠 48 (Apr. 1972): 94–102.

Du Geling 杜格靈. 「詩問答.」 1935. 詩風1, no. 3 (1978): 14–15.

Du Guoqing (Tu Kuo-ching) 杜國清, ed. and trans. 惡之華. Taipei: 純文學出版社, 1977.

Du Guoqing (Tu Kuo-ching) 杜國清. 「寫在翻譯《惡之華》之前.」 笠 48 (15 Apr. 1972): 75–76.

Du Qinggang 杜青鋼. 「《惡之花》賞析.」外國文學研究 9 (1988): 91–94.

Du Xuezhong 杜學忠, Mu Huaiying 穆懷英, Qiu Wenzhi 邱文治. 「論李金髮的詩歌創作.」中國現代文學研究叢刊 1 (1983): 39–66.

Feng Nai-chao 馮乃超. 馮乃超卷. Edited by Zhou Liangpei 周良沛. Wuhan: 長江文藝出版社, 1988.

Feng Nai-chao 馮乃超.馮乃超文集. Canton: 中山大學出版社, 1986.

Feng Nai-chao 馮乃超. 馮乃超研究資料. Edited by Li Weijiang 李偉江編. Sian: 山西人民出版社, 1992.

Fung, M. M. Y. et al., ed. and comp. 張曼儀，等 現代中國詩選. Hong Kong: Hong Kong University Press, 1974.

Gao Zhun (Paul C. Kao). 中國新詩的風格發展論. Yangmingshan: 華岡出版社, 1973.

Ge Xianning葛賢寧 and Shangguan Yu上官予. 五十年來的中國詩歌. Taipei:正中書局, 1965.

Gong Xianzong 龔顯宗. 廿卅年代新詩論集. Tainan: 鳳凰城圖書公司, 1982.

Guo Hong-an 郭宏安. 「《惡之花》: 按本來面目描繪罪惡.」 外國文學研究 3 (1989): 49–56.

Guo Hong-an 郭宏安. 惡之花: 插图本. Guilin:漓江出版社, 1992. Repr. Taipei:林鬱文化, 1997. Beijing: 北京燕山出版社, 2005; Beijing: 中国书籍出版社, 2006.

Guo Hong-an 郭宏安. 「《惡之花》穿越象徵的森林.」外國文學研究 9 (1989): 103–9.

Guo Hong-an郭宏安. 「論波特萊爾.」外國文學研究集刊3 (1981): 85–102.

Guo Hong-an 郭宏安. 「論《惡之花》.」外國文學研究季刊 8 (Jan. 1984): 51–98, and 9 (July 1984): 355–91.

Guo Hong-an 郭宏安. 「伊甸園中的一枚禁果: 談談波德萊爾的《惡之花》.」 外国文学研究 3 (1982): 89–93.

Guo Hong-an 郭宏安, trans. 1846年的沙龙 : 波德莱尔美学论文选. Guilin: 桂林市 : 广西师范大学出版社, 2002.

Guo Hong-an 郭宏安, trans. 现代生活的畫家. Hangzhou: 浙江文藝出版社, 2007.

Guo Shaohua 郭紹華. 波德萊爾在中國. Master's thesis, Beijing Shifan Daxue Yanjiu-sheng Yuan 北京師範大學研究生院, 2003.

He Qifang 何其芳. 何其芳詩稿. Shanghai: 上海文藝出版社, 1979.

He Qifang 何其芳. 何其芳文集. Beijing: 人民文學出版社, 1982.

He Qifang 何其芳. 何其芳譯詩稿. Beijing: 外國文學出版社, 1984.

He Qifang 何其芳. 刻意集, 1938. Reprint, Hong Kong: 未名書屋, n. d.

He Qifang 何其芳. 燕泥集 in He Qifang et al., *Hanyuan ji.*

He Qifang 何其芳. 預言. Shanghai: 新聞藝出版社, 1957.

He Qifang 何其芳, Li Guangtian 李廣田, and Bian Zhilin 卞之琳. 漢園集. 1936. Hong Kong:未名書屋, 1975?

He Ru 何如. 「波特萊爾和他的《惡之花》(Su: Lie Weike 蘇: 列維克).」 譯文*Yiwen* 7 (1957): 162–66.

Hong Tu 宏徒. 「鮑特萊爾的奇癖—文壇逸話.」 小說月報 18, no. 5 (1927): n. p.

Hu Pinqing 胡品清，巴黎的憂鬱: *Petits poèmes en prose ou le spleen de Paris, 1869*. Taipei: 志文, 1973.

Hu Pinqing 胡品清. 惡之花評析: *Les Fleurs du Mal: Une autobiographie en vers*. Taipei: 中國文化大學出版社, 1981.

Hu Pinqing 胡品清. 「《惡之花》選譯,」 中國一週 632 (4 June 1962): 15, and 633 (11 June 1962): 32.

Hu Pinqing 胡品清. 胡品清譯詩與新詩選. Taipei: 中國文化出版事業社, 1962.

Hu Pinqing 胡品清. 「我所知道的波德萊爾.」中國一週 623 (2 Apr. 1962): 3–32.

Hu Shi 胡適. 嘗試集. 1920. Shanghai: 亞東圖書館, 1926.

Hu Xiaoyue 胡小躍. 巴黎的憂鬱. Shanghai: 上海文艺出版社, 2006.

Hu Xiaoyue 胡小躍. 波德萊爾詩全集. Hangzhou: 浙江文藝出版社, 1996.

Huang Sandao 黃參島. 「《微雨》及其作者.」 美育雜志 2 (Dec. 1928): 211–16.

Ji Xian (Chi Hsien) 紀弦. 新詩論集Kaohsiung: 大業書局, 1956. See chapter 「波特萊爾 及其他,」 62–65.

Jin Dequan 金德全, Shi Kangqiang 施康强, Guo Hongan 郭宏安, 「論繆塞，戈帝埃， 和波特萊爾.」 外國文學研究集刊 3 (1981): 57–102.

Jin Qinjun 金欽俊, ed. 中國新文學大師名作賞析叢書. Taipei: 海風出版社, 1990.

Jin Siyan 金絲燕. 文學接受與文化過濾—中國對法國象徵主義詩歌的接受. Beijing: 中國 人民大學出版社, 1994.

Jun Yan. 君彥. 「法國近代詩概觀.」 小說月報 13 suppl. 號外 (1922): 36–37.

Kang Peichu 康培初. 文學作家時代. Hong Kong: 文學研究社, 1973.

Li Huang 李璜. 「法蘭西詩之格律及其解放.」 少年中國 2, no. 12 (6-1921): 1–9.

Li Jinfa 李金髮. 「巴黎之夜景.」 小說月報 17, no. 2 (10 Feb. 1926): 4.

Li Jinfa 李金髮. 「答痖弦先生二十問.」 創世紀 39 (Jan. 1975): 6.

Li Jinfa 李金髮, trans. 古希腊恋歌, 碧麗蒂著. *Chansons de Bilitis* by Pierre Louÿs. Shang-hai: 開明書店, 1928.

Li Jinfa 李金髮. 李金髮詩集, edited by Zhou Liangpei 周良沛. Chengdu: 四川文藝出版 社, 1987. 「'詩怪' 李金髮,」 1–25.

Li Jinfa 李金髮. 「馬拉美詩抄—附記,」 新文藝月刊 1, no. 2 （Oct. 1929): 249–59.

Li Jinfa 李金髮. 飄零閒筆. Taipei: 僑聯出版社, 1964.

Li Jinfa 李金髮. 食客與凶年. 新潮社文藝叢書. Beijing: 北新書局, 1927.

Li Jinfa 李金髮. 為幸福而歌. 1926. Shanghai: Shangwu yinshuguan 商務印書館, 1931.

Li Jinfa李金髮. 微雨. Beijing: 新潮社, 1925.

Li Jinfa李金髮. 「我的巴黎藝術生活,」 人間世 22 (20 Feb. 1935): 14.

Li Jinfa李金髮. 異國情調. Chongqing: 商務印書館, 1946.

Li Liewen 黎烈文. 「散文詩抄.」 譯文 1, no. 2 (Oct. 1934): 126–33.

Li Liming (Lee, Yip-ming) 李立明. 中國現代六百作家小傳. Hong Kong: 波文書局, 1977.

Li Liming (Lee, Yip-ming) 李立明. 「象徵派詩人李金髮.」 文壇316 (1 July 1971): 333–34.

Li Sichun 李思純. 仙河集. 學衡 47 (Nov. 1925) 6447–6510.

Li Tiejun 李鐵軍. 「慘白與憂鬱：在"廢馳的地獄" 邊沿--《野草》與《巴黎的憂鬱》比 較研究.」 外國文學研究 10 (1991): 46–53.

Li Wanjun 李萬鈞. 歐美文學史和中國文學. Fuzhou: 福建教育出版社, 1989.

Li Yiming 李一鳴.中國新文學史講話. Shanghai: 世界書局, 1943.

Liang Zongdai 梁宗岱. 梁宗岱譯詩集. Changsha: 湖南人民出版社, 1983.

Liang Zongdai 梁宗岱. 詩與真. 1935. Shanghai: 商务印书馆, 1936.

Liang Zongdai 梁宗岱. 晚禱. 1924. Shanghai: 商务印书馆, 1933.

Liang Zongdai 梁宗岱. 「象徵主義.」 文學季刊 2 (Apr. 1934): 15–25.

Liao Xingqiao 廖星橋. 「法蘭西是西方現代派的發源地—法國現代派文學淺探之一.」 外國文學研究 2 (1984) 15–20.

Lin Huanzhang 林煥彰. 「藏起的串兒如何穿着瞧—讀李金髮《為幸福而歌》有感.」 詩風月刊 7, no. 7 (1 Dec. 1978): 40–49.

Lin Qi 林淇. 海上才子:邵洵美傳. Shanghai: 上海人民出版社, 2002.

Lin Xuejin 林學錦. 「評《惡之花》.」 外國文學研究 8 (1992): 92–96.

Lin Yiliang 林以亮 [Song Qi 宋淇]. 「論散文詩.」 林以亮詩話. 1975. Taipei: 洪範書店, 1981, 32–45.

Liu Jixian 劉濟獻, ed. 徐玉諾詩選. Zhengzhou: 河南人民出版社, 1983.

Liu Xianbiao 劉獻彪. 比較文學在中國的興起. Nanning: 廣西人民出版社, 1986.

Liu Xiwei 劉西渭 [Li Jianwu 李健吾]. 咀華集 1936. Shanghai: 文化生活出版社, 1938.

Liu Yanling 劉延陵. 法國詩之象徵主義與自由詩. In Sun Langgong 孫俍工,新文藝評論, 121–34.

Lu Wenqian 陸文緝. 法國象徵派對中國象徵詩影響研究. Chengdu: 四川大學出版社, 1996.

Lu Xun 魯迅. 野草. n.p., n.d.

Lu Xun 魯迅. 野草: *Wild Grass*. Translated by Yang Xianyi and Gladys Yang. Bilingual ed. Hong Kong: The Chinese University Press, 2003.

Lu Yuehua 盧月化. 「簡介法國象徵主義幾其代表詩人.」 東方雜誌 12, no. 12 (6-1979): 39–43.

Lu Yuehua 盧月化. 十九世紀法國文學. Taipei: 中華文化出版事業委員會, 1955.

Luo Dagang 羅大岡. 「關於法國現代派文學的幾點初步認識.」 外國文學研究 1 (Mar. 1924, 1984): 8–12.

Luo Yingchen 羅英辰. 「波特來爾論雨果.」 中法大學月刊 8, no. 2 (Dec. 1935): 67–78.

Ma Chengwu 馬承五. 「《病態的花》的文化心理特徵—中西苦吟詩人比較研究.」 外國文學研究 2 (1990): 24–29.

Ma Si 馬斯. 世界文學史話. Hong Kong: 進修出版社, 1950.

Mo Yu 莫渝 [Lin Liangya 林良雅]. 「波特萊爾—惡魔詩人.」 法國詩人介紹. Taipei: 台灣商務印書館, 1983. 102–13.

Mo Yu 莫渝, ed. and trans. 惡之華. 1985. Taipei: 志文出版社, 1998.

Mo Yu 莫渝. 「覃子豪論.」 笠 89 (Feb. 1979): 50–88.

Mo Yu 莫渝. 「《秋歌》與《異鄉人》中譯次數最多的兩首法國詩.」 幼獅文藝 315 (Mar. 1980): 129–47.

Mou Jueming 牟決鳴. 關于何其芳譯詩稿的一點說明. 何其芳譯詩稿. Beijing: 外國文學出版社, 1984. 149–54.

Mu Mutian 穆木天. 法國文學史. Shanghai: 世界書局, 1935.

Mu Mutian 穆木天. 論徐志摩. 作家論. Edited by Mao Dun 矛盾. Shanghai: 生活書店, 1936.

Mu Mutian 穆木天. 旅心. Shanghai: 創造社出版部, 1927.

Mu Mutian 穆木天. 平凡集. Shanghai: 新鍾書局, [1936?].

Mu Mutian 穆木天. 什么是象征主义. In Zheng Zhenduo 鄭振鐸, 傅東華. 文學百題. 生活書店出版. 1935. Reprinted in 穆木天文學評論選集, edited by Chen Dun 陳惇 and Liu Xiangyu 劉象愚. Beijing: 北京師範大學出版社, 2000.

Mu Mutian 穆木天. 「談詩.」 創造月刊 1, no. 1 (Mar. 1926).

Mu Mutian 穆木天. 「我的詩歌創作的回顧.」 現代 4, no. 4 (Feb. 1934): 717–26.

Pan Shoukang 潘壽康. 「交感.」 世界名著詞典. Taipei: 革新出版社, 1959.

Pan Yihe 潘一禾. 「從波德萊爾看西方現代主義文學.」 外國文學研究 7 (1989): 54–60.

Qian Chunqi, 錢春綺, trans. 惡之花. Beijing: 人民文學出版社, 1986.

Qian Chunqi, 錢春綺, trans. 惡之花; 巴黎的憂鬱. Beijing: 人民文學出版社, 1991. Taipei: 光復網際網路, 2001.

Qian Chunqi, 錢春綺, trans. 惡之花: 波德萊爾詩歌精粹. Beijing: 人民文學出版社, 2008.

Qian Linsen 錢林森. 「法國文學與中國文學的現代化.」 中國比較文學 10 (1990): 32–40.

Qian Zhongshu 錢鍾書. 談藝錄. 1935. Hong Kong: 龍門書店, 1965.

Qian Zhongshu 錢鍾書. 中國詩與中國畫. Hong Kong: 龍門, 1969.

Qin Zihao 覃子豪. 覃子豪全集. 4 vols. Taipei: 覃子豪全集出版委員會, 1965–1974.

Qin Zihao 覃子豪. 世界名詩欣賞. 1956. Taichung: 普天出版社, 1976.

Qiu Wenzhi 邱文治, Du Xuezhong 杜學忠, and Mu Huaiying 穆懷英. 「論中國現代象徵詩派之升沈.」 文學評論 1 (1987): 114–24.

Shao Xunmei 邵洵美. 花一般的罪惡. Shanghai: 金屋書店, 1918.

Shao Xunmei 邵洵美. 火與肉. Shanghai: 金屋書店, 1928.

Shao Xunmei 邵洵美. 詩二十五首. Shanghai: 時代圖書公司, 1936.

Shao Xunmei 邵洵美. 天堂與五月. Shanghai: 光華書局, 1927.

Shao Xunmei 邵洵美. [Hao Wen 浩文, pseud.]. 「書報春秋.」 新月 (1932): 1–4.

Shao Xunmei 邵洵美. 一個人的談話. Shanghai: 第一出版社, 1935.

Shen Baoji 沈寶基. 「鮑特萊爾的愛情生活.」 中法大學月刊 3, nos. 2–3 (Sept. 1933): 159–87, 4, no. 5 (Oct. 1933): 181–98.

Shen Baoji 沈寶基, trans. 「比冰和鐵更刺人心腸的快樂—《惡之花》百週紀念 (法國阿拉貢).」 譯文 7 (1957): 152–61.

Shi Binshi 石彬室. 「李金髮的文藝生活—紀中國象徵主義先驅.」 幼獅文藝 315 (Mar. 1980): 98–112.

Shi Deyi 史德義. 「分析波特萊爾的《靜思》.」 中外文學 2, no. 5 (Oct. 1973): 102–10.

Shi Zhecun 施蟄存. 《戴望舒譯詩集》序. Changsha: 湖南人民出版社, 1983. 1–4.

Shu Lan 舒藍. 北伐前後的新詩作家和作品. Taipei: 成文出版社, 1980.

Shu Lan 舒藍. 五四時代的新詩作家和作品. Taipei: 成文出版社, 1980.

Song Yongyi 宋永毅. 「李金髮: 歷史毀譽中的存在.」 In Zeng Xiaoyi 曾小逸, 走向世界文學, 382–408.

Su Fengzhe 蘇鳳哲. 波德萊爾詩選. Shijiazhuang: 花山文藝出版社, 1992.

Su Xuelin 蘇雪林. 二三十年代作家與作品. Taipei: 廣東出版社, 1980. See chapter 11, 「頹加蕩派的邵洵美,」 and 12, 「新詩壇象徵派創始者李金髮的詩,」 1959.

Su Xuelin 蘇雪林. 「論李金髮的詩.」 現代3, no. 3 (July 1933): 347–52.

Su Xuelin 蘇雪林.文壇話舊. Taichung:文星書店, 1967.

Sun Lang-gong 孫俍工. 文藝辭典. Shanghai: 智民書局, 1928.

Sun Lang-gong 孫俍工 ed.. 新文藝評論. Shanghai: 智民書局, 1923.

Sun Yushi 孫玉石. 戴望舒名作欣賞. Beijing: 中國和平出版社, 1993.

Sun Yushi 孫玉石. 象徵派詩選. Beijing: 人民文學出版社, 1986.

Sun Yushi 孫玉石. 野草研究. Beijing: 中國社會科學出版社, 1982.

Sun Yushi 孫玉石. 中國初期象徵派詩歌研究. Beijing: 京大学出版社, 1983.

Tian Han 田漢. 「惡魔詩人波陀雷爾的百年祭.」 少年中國3, no. 4 (Nov. 1921): 1–6, and 3, no. 5 (Dec. 1921):17–32.

Wang Duqing 王獨清. 獨清創作選. Shanghai: 啟智書局. 1947.

Wang Duqing 王獨清. 獨清詩選. Shanghai: 新宇宙書店, 1931.

Wang Duqing 王獨清. 獨清譯詩集. 1929. Repr. n.p., 1937.

Wang Duqing 王獨清. 王獨清選集. Edited by Ye Wangyou 葉忘憂 and Xu Chensi 徐沉泗. Shanghai: 中央書店, 1947.

Wang Duqing 王獨清. 我在歐洲的生活, 2nd ed. Shanghai: 大光書局, 1936.

Wang Duqing 王獨清. 「再談詩.」 創造月刊 1, no. 1 (Mar. 1926): 95–104.

Wang Fuming 王幅明. 「從腐朽和醜惡中尋找美—淺析波德萊爾的散文詩集《巴黎的憂鬱》.」外國文學研究1 (1987): 114–15.

Wang Guangming 王光明. 「散文詩的孕育和獨立.」 外國文學研究 1 (1987) 48–52.

Wang Li 王力. 漢語詩律學. Shanghai: 新知識出版社, 1958. 上海教育出版社, 1962, 1979.

Wang Liaoyi 王了一 [Wang Li 王力]. 惡之花. Beijing: 外國文學出版社, 1980.

Wang Lin 王林. 「論波德萊爾.」 外國文學研究12 (1987): 41–48.

Wang Nuo 王諾. 「法國象徵主義詩歌的藝術通感.」 外國文學研究 3 (1985): 98–100, 120.

Wang Weike 王維克. 「惡魔詩人波特萊爾 (法蘭西詩話).」 小說月報 22, no. 1 (1931): 84.

Wang Yao 王瑤. 中國新文學史稿. Shanghai: 新文藝出版社, 1954.

Wang Zhijian 王志健. 傳統與現代之間. Taipei: 眾成出版社, 1975.

Wang Zhijian 王志健. 現代中國詩史. Taipei: 臺灣商務印書館, 1975.

Wang Zuoliang 王佐良. 「中國新詩中的現代主義—一個回顧.」 比較文學研究資料. Beijing: 北京師範大學出版社, 1986, 208–29.

Wang Zuoliang 王佐良, ed. and comp. with Cao Shunqing 曹順慶. 中西比較美學論文集. Chengdu: 四川文藝出版社, 1985, 170–93.

Wen Aiyi 文爱艺, trans. 恶之花. Chengdu: 四川人民出版社, 2007.

Wen Jiasi 聞家駟. 「波德萊爾—幾種顏色不同的愛.」 學文 1, no. 3 (1934): 82–90.

Wen Jiasi 聞家駟. 「波德萊爾與女人.」 學文1, no. 4 (1934): 111–22.

Wen Tian 聞天, trans. 「波特來耳研究. 史篤姆著.」 小說月報 13, hao wai (1922): 5–20.

Wen Xing 文星. 「頹廢詩人邵洵美.」 Hong Kong: 明報 (5 Apr. 1974).

Wen Zheng 文錚. 「波德萊之悲劇.」 現代評論 7, no. 159 (Dec. 1924, 1927): 51–55.

Xiao Xiao 蕭蕭. 現代名詩品賞集. Taipei: 普天出版社, 1979.

Xie Kang謝康. 「《惡之花》百年紀年 [sic]—論一部曾被認為不道德而被罰款的詩集.」 文學世界 (Aug. 1957): 47–56.

Xie Liuyi 謝六逸. 「文學上的表象主義是什麼?」 小說月報11, no. 6 (June 1920): 1–7.

Xie Zhixi 解志熙. 美的偏至:中國現代唯美 - 頹廢主義文學思潮研究. Shanghai: 上海文藝出版社, 1998.

Xu Xiacun 徐霞村. 法國文學的故事. Taipei: 商務印书馆, 1947.

Xu Yunuo 徐玉諾. 將來之花園, by Y. N. Sü. Shanghai: 商務印書館, 1922.

Xu Zhimo 徐志摩. 「波特萊的散文詩.」 新月 2, no. 10 (10 Dec. 1929).

Xu Zhimo 徐志摩. 猛虎集. Shanghai: 新月書店, 1931.

Xu Zhimo 徐志摩. 徐志摩全集. Edited by Jiang Fucong 蔣復聰 and Liang Shih-chiu梁實秋. Taipei: 傳記文學出版社, 1969, 2:6.

Xu Zhimo 徐志摩, trans.「死尸.」語絲 3 (1 Dec. 1924): no page.

Xu Zhongnian 徐仲年. 法國文學 ABC. Shanghai: 世界書局, 1933.

Ya Ding 亞丁. 巴黎的憂鬱. Nanning: 漓江出版社, 1982. Beijing: 三联书店, 2004. Taipei: 遠流, 2006.

Ya Xian 瘂弦.「長安才子王獨清.」中國新詩研究. Taipei: 洪範書店1981. 97–111.

Ya Xian 瘂弦. 中國新詩研究 Taipei: 洪範書店, 1981.

Yang Changnian 楊昌年. 現代詩的創作與欣賞. Taipei: 文史哲出版社, 1991.

Yang Changnian 楊昌年. 新詩品賞. Taipei: 牧童, 1978.

Yang Changnian 楊昌年. 新詩賞析. Taipei: 文史哲出版社, 1982.

Yang Li 楊犁 et al., ed.中國現代作家大辭典. Beijing: 新世界出版社, 1992.

Yang Yunda 楊允達.「李金髪的評介之二: 謎一般的生平.」明報18, no. 2 (Feb. 1983): 80–84.

Ye Shengtao 葉聖陶. 葉紹鈞選集. Edited by Xu Chenshe, 徐沉泗, Ye Wangyou 葉忘憂, et al. Shanghai: 萬象書屋, 1936.

Yin Kangzhuang 尹康莊. 象徵主義與中國現代文學. Guangzhou: 暨南大學出版社, 1998.

Yin Zaiqin 尹在勤. 何其芳評傳. Chengdu: 四川人民出版社, 1980.

Yu Dafu 郁達夫. 郁達夫全集. Hong Kong: 生活. 讀書新知三聯書店, 1984. vol. 10.

Yu Gengyu 于庚虞. 魔鬼的舞蹈. Shanghai: 北新書局, 1928.

Yu Zhi 愉之 [Hu Yuzhi 胡愉之]「近代法國文學概觀.」東方雜誌 18, no. 3 (1921): 67–79.

Yuan Changying 袁昌英. 法國文學. 1944. Chongqing: 商務印書館, 1946.

Yuan Kejia 袁可嘉.「象徵主義詩歌.」外國文學研究3 (25 Sept. 1985): 90–97, and 4 (25 Dec. 1985): 3–13.

Yue Daiyun 樂黛雲. 比較文學與中國現代文學. Beijing: 北京大學出版社, 1987,「錢鍾書,管錐篇,」45.

Zeng Xiaoyi 曾小逸, ed. 走向世界文學:中國現代作家與外國文學. Changsha: 湖南人民出版社, 1985.

Zhang Chong-wen 張崇文, trans.「波特來的病理學.」現代 4, no. 6 (1934): 1055–60.

Zhang Daming 張大明. 中國象徵主義百年史. Kaifeng: 河南大學出版社, 2007.

Zhang Dinghuang 張定璜.「散文詩抄.」語絲 (23 Feb. 1925): no page.

Zhang Manyi 張曼儀. 現代中國詩選一九一七-一九四九. See Fung, M. M. Y. et al.

Zhang Mo 張默 and Ya Xian 瘂弦, ed. 六十年代詩選 Kaohsiung: 大業書店, 1961.

Zhang Mosheng 張默生. 異行傳. Shanghai: 東方書店, 1947.

Zhang Taisheng 張太勝. 梁宗岱與中國象徵主義詩學. Beijing: 北京師範大學出版社, 2004.

Zhang Ting 張挺.「波特萊爾及其《惡之花》與魯迅及其《野草》之比較觀.」外國文學研究 4 (1985): 14–30.

Zhao Cong 趙聰. 五四文壇點滴. Hong Kong: 友聯出版社, 1964.

Zhao Jiabi 趙家璧 中國新文學大系. 20 vols. 1935. Hong Kong: 文學研究會, 1962.

Zhao Jingshen 趙景深.「馮乃超與穆木天.」現代文學雜論. Shanghai: 光明書店, 1932, 123–28.

Zhao Jingshen 趙景深. 現代詩選. Shanghai: Beixin 北新書局, 1934.

Zheng Kelu 鄭克魯.「淒苦和頹唐的怪味—《惡之花》中的愛情詩.」外國文學研究 4 (1990): 76–82.

Zheng Zhenduo 鄭振鐸 [Xi Di 西諦 pseud.].「論散文詩.」In Sun Langgong 孫俍工, ed., 新文藝評論, 89–98.

Zheng Zhenduo 鄭振鐸. 文學大綱. 4 vols. Shanghai: 商務印書館, 1927.

Zhou Bonai 周伯乃. 早期新詩的批評. Taipei: 成文出版社, 1980.

Zhou Chengzhen 周誠真. 李賀論. Hong Kong: 文藝書屋, 1971.

Zhou Jin 周錦. 中國新文史. Taipei: 長歌出版社, 1976.

Zhou Songxi 周頌喜.「波德萊爾, 一個轉變的歷史過程 (關於波德萊爾文藝觀的矛盾與他的歷史評價.」外國文學研究8 (1991): 120–27.

Zhou Wu 周無.「法蘭西近世文學的趨勢.」少年中國 2 卷 4 期 (15 Oct. 1920) 14–28.

Zhou Zuoren 周作人 [Zhong Mi 仲密, pseud.], trans. 《窗.》 小說月報 3 (1922): 28. 《游子,》 13, no. 6 (1922): 22.

Zhou Zuoren 周作人, ed. and trans. 歐洲大陸小說集. 1909. Shanghai: 商務印書館, 1924.

Zhou Zuoren 周作人, ed. and trans. 陀螺. Beijing: 新潮出版社, 1925.

Zhou Zuoren 周作人. 「小河序.」 新青年 6 (1919): 2.

Zhu Ziqing 朱自清. 新詩雜話. 1944. Hong Kong, Taiping: 太平書局, 1965.

Zong Lin 宗臨. 「查理波得萊爾.」 中法大學月刊, 4, no. 2 (Dec. 1933): 111–42.

Zhongguo wenxuejia cidian 中國文學家辭典 Beijing: 北京語言學院, 1979, vol. 6.

Index